Arts Therapies and Gender Issues

Arts Therapies and Gender Issues offers international perspectives on gender in arts therapies research and demonstrates understandings of gender and arts therapies in a variety of global contexts. Analysing current innovations and approaches in the arts therapies, it discusses issues of cultural identity, which intersect with sex, gender norms, stereotypes and sexual identity.

The book includes unique and detailed case studies such as the emerging discipline of creative writing for therapeutic purposes, re-enactment phototherapy, performative practice and virtual reality. Bringing together leading researchers, it demonstrates clinical applications and shares ideas about best practice.

Incorporating art, drama, dance and music therapy, this book will be of great interest to academics and researchers in the fields of arts therapies, psychology, medicine, psychotherapy, health and education. It will also appeal to practitioners and teachers of art, dance-movement, drama and music therapy.

Susan Hogan is Professor in Cultural Studies and Art Therapy at the University of Derby.

International Research in the Arts Therapies

Series Editors: Diane Waller and Sarah Scoble

This series consists of high-level monographs identifying areas of importance across all arts therapy modalities and highlighting international developments and concerns. It presents recent research from countries across the world and contributes to the evidence-base of the arts therapies. Papers which discuss and analyse current innovations and approaches in the arts therapies and arts therapy education are also included.

This series is accessible to practitioners of the arts therapies and to colleagues in a broad range of related professions, including those in countries where arts therapies are still emerging. The monographs should also provide a valuable source of reference to government departments and health services.

For more information about the series, please visit www.routledge.com.

Titles in the series

1. Intercultural Arts Therapies Research
Issues and Methodologies
Edited by Ditty Dokter and Margaret Hills De Zárate

2. Art Therapies and New Challenges in Psychiatry
Edited by Karin Dannecker

3. Arts Therapies in the Treatment of Depression
Edited by Ania Zubala and Vicky Karkou

4. Arts Therapies and Gender Issues
International Perspectives on Research
Edited by Susan Hogan

Arts Therapies and Gender Issues

International Perspectives on Research

Edited by Susan Hogan

LONDON AND NEW YORK

First published 2020
by Routledge
2 Park Square, Milton Park, Abingdon, Oxon OX14 4RN

and by Routledge
605 Third Avenue, New York, NY 10017

First issued in paperback 2021

Routledge is an imprint of the Taylor & Francis Group, an informa business

© 2020 selection and editorial matter, Susan Hogan; individual chapters, the contributors

The right of Susan Hogan to be identified as the author of the editorial material, and of the authors for their individual chapters, has been asserted in accordance with Sections 77 and 78 of the Copyright, Designs and Patents Act 1988.

All rights reserved. No part of this book may be reprinted or reproduced or utilised in any form or by any electronic, mechanical or other means, now known or hereafter invented, including photocopying and recording, or in any information storage or retrieval system, without permission in writing from the publishers.

Trademark notice: Product or corporate names may be trademarks or registered trademarks, and are used only for identification and explanation without intent to infringe.

Publisher's Note
The publisher has gone to great lengths to ensure the quality of this reprint but points out that some imperfections in the original copies may be apparent.

British Library Cataloguing-in-Publication Data
A catalogue record for this book is available from the British Library.

Library of Congress Cataloging-in-Publication Data
Names: Hogan, Susan, 1961- editor.
Title: Arts therapies and gender issues: international perspectives on research/edited by Susan Hogan.
Description: Abingdon, Oxon; New York, NY: Routledge, 2019. | Series: International research in the arts therapies | Includes bibliographical references.
Identifiers: LCCN 2019002119 (print) | LCCN 2019002754 (ebook) | ISBN 9781351121958 (eBook) | ISBN 9780815358695 (hbk) | ISBN 9781351121958 (ebk)
Subjects: | MESH: Art Therapy | Gender Identity
Classification: LCC RC489.A7 (ebook) | LCC RC489.A7 (print) | NLM WM 450.5.A8 | DDC 616.89/1656—dc23
LC record available at https://lccn.loc.gov/2019002119

ISBN 13: 978-1-03-209057-3 (pbk)
ISBN 13: 978-0-8153-5869-5 (hbk)

Typeset in Bembo
by Deanta Global Publishing Services, Chennai, India

Contents

About the editor vii
List of contributors ix

PART I
Art therapy, dance movement therapy, drama therapy and music therapy 1

1 Introduction: Arts therapies and gender issues 3

2 Drawing on visions of the future of young women in poverty: Art as a feminist research method 15
MICHAL MAGOS AND EPHRAT HUSS

3 Queering music therapy: Music therapy and LGBTQAI+ Peoples 22
ANNETTE WHITEHEAD-PLEAUX

4 Analysing gender oppression in music therapy research and practice 37
SUE BAINES AND JANE EDWARDS

5 The eye of the beholder: Encountering women's experience of domestic violence and abuse as a male researcher and art therapist 55
JAMIE BIRD

6 Parental gender roles in clay: Perceptions of gender-role issues among Israeli fathers to toddlers as expressed in a clay figure-sculpting task 70
NEHAMA GRENIMANN BAUCH

7 The birth project: Mothers and birth professionals make art 90
SUSAN HOGAN

Contents

8   Queer bodies and queer practices: The implications of queer
    theory for dramatherapy   110
    PATRICK TOMCZYK

9   The therapists' gender identity in dance movement therapy:
    Does it matter?   119
    JOB CORNELISSEN

10 The gendered body in arts therapies research and practice   138
    SUE JENNINGS

PART II
Emergent practices and specialisms   147

11 Multiple gendered abilities: A therapeutic writing approach   149
    MANU RODRÍGUEZ

12 What can a man do with a camera?: Exploring masculinities with
    phototherapy   165
    JOSÉ LOUREIRO

13 Look at me! Representing self: Representing ageing: Older women
    represent their own narratives of ageing, using re-enactment
    phototherapeutic techniques   188
    ROSY MARTIN

14 The treatment of anorexia nervosa and bulimia nervosa among
    female adolescents aged 18–21 using intertwined (integrative)
    arts therapy   210
    ALENKA VIDRIH, ANA HRAM AND VITA POŠTUVAN

15 Complicated gender and problematised bodies: The impact of
    severe illness explored through the lens of portrait therapy   228
    SUSAN M. D. CARR

16 Experimenting with gender roles in virtual reality   247
    NICOLE OTTIGER AND ROSE EHEMANN

    Concluding note   *260*
    Index   *261*

About the editor

Professor Susan Hogan is Professor in Cultural Studies and Art Therapy at the University of Derby, in which role for many years she facilitated experiential workshops and the closed-group component of the art therapy training. She is former Vice-President of the Australian National Art Therapy Association (formerly ANATA, now ANZATA), and has twice served as a regional co-ordinator for the British Association of Art Therapists (BAAT). She has been instrumental in setting up, or helping to set up, several art therapy-training courses in Australia and the UK and also courses in dance-movement and drama therapy. She served for six years as a Health Professions Council (UK) 'visitor' (now HCPC).

Susan qualified as an art therapist in 1985. Her PhD in Cultural History from Aberdeen University, Scotland looked at the history of ideas on madness and the use of the arts, especially within psychiatry. She has a particular interest in group-work and experiential learning, following early employment with Peter Edwards MD, an exceptional psychiatrist who had worked with Maxwell Jones, a psychiatrist who is associated with the 'therapeutic community movement' in Britain.

Susan is a Professorial Fellow of the Institute of Mental Health of the University of Nottingham where she is co-researching health humanities, and has been conducting research with several partner institutions, including co-researching women's experience of ageing with sociologists from the University of Sheffield using visual research methods. She has also published a number of both scholarly and polemical papers on women and theories of insanity. Hogan's work has been innovative in its application of social anthropological and sociological ideas to art therapy; also distinctive is her unwavering challenge to reductive psychological theorising.

Her books are:

- *Feminist Approaches to Art Therapy* (as editor, 1997);
- *Healing Arts: The History of Art Therapy* (2001);
- *Gender Issues in Art Therapy* (as editor, 2003);
- *Conception Diary: Thinking About Pregnancy & Motherhood* (2006);

- *Revisiting Feminist Approaches to Art Therapy* (as editor, 2012);
- *The Introductory Guide to Art Therapy* (with Coulter, 2014);
- *Art Therapy Theories. A Critical Introduction* (2016);
- *The Maternal Tug: Ambivalence, Identity, and Agency* (co-editor, in press for 2020);
- *Gender and Difference in the Arts Therapies: Inscribed on the Body* (concurrent with this book).

Contributors

Sue Baines is an instructor in the Bachelor of Music Therapy programme at Capilano University in North Vancouver, BC, Canada. Her music therapy practice supports persons in long-term care, acute psychiatry, and community mental health. Sue is editor-in-chief for *The Canadian Journal of Music Therapy*. Throughout her career, she has focused on increasing social justice in music therapy practice, research and publication. Her research integrates anti-oppressive practice theory with music therapy.

Jamie Bird is the Deputy Head of Centre for Health and Social Care Research at the University of Derby. He is an art therapist and arts-based researcher who has an interest in the study of experiences of migration and of domestic violence and abuse through the employment of the arts. He is also interested in generating quantitative data that measures the effectiveness of art psychotherapy and the impact of educational approaches to managing risk behaviour. He has been involved in the teaching of undergraduate, postgraduate and doctoral students within the subjects of therapeutic arts and creative expressive therapies for 14 years.

Susan M. D. Carr is an art therapist, artist, and researcher, with 12 years' experience working as an art therapist in palliative care, helping clients resolve issues around illness and self-identity. Since completing her PhD in 2015 Susan has published a book of her thesis entitled *Portrait Therapy*, exploring the theory and practice behind her development of this innovative intervention. In 2017 Susan's work attracted a grant from the Arts Council England, to stage her first major exhibition, including 38 of the portraits generated by the project, at Swindon Museum and Art Gallery. Susan is currently Co-Editor-in-Chief of the *International Journal of Art Therapy* and a member of Council for the British Association of Art Therapists.

Job Cornelissen is a Dutch dance-movement psychotherapist with elderly people with dementia, people with young onset dementia, geriatric psychiatric patients, and multiple sclerosis patients and their partners in multidisciplinary treatment. He also works as a dancer and choreographer in community dance projects with the elderly. He holds a Sandan (3rd dan) degree in the Japanese martial art of Aikido and is a self-taught musician. He is chair of the Dutch Association for Dance Therapy (NVDAT). In 2017 he was a member of the International Panel at the annual conference of the American Dance Therapy Association, presenting on his work with adults suffering from dementia.

Jane Edwards, PhD RMT is a registered music therapist with professional experience in many countries of the world. In Ireland she was the course director for the MA in Music Therapy (1999–2014). She recently sole-edited *The Oxford Handbook of Music Therapy*. She has more than 80 publications. She is Editor-in-Chief for *The Arts in Psychotherapy*. She has served in leadership roles in many associations including as Founding Member and Inaugural President of the International Association for Music & Medicine (2009-2016). She is currently an Associate Dean for Research at the University of New England, New South Wales, Australia.

Rose Ehemann is Director of Ateliers-Living Museum at the Psychiatry St. Gallen North, the Artistic Director of the Atelier-Day Centre in Wil (Switzerland) and President of the Living Museum Association (Switzerland). Her doctorate from Cologne University focused on virtual reality in art therapy.

Nehama Grenimann Bauch holds an MA in Art Therapy from the University of Haifa, Israel, and a BFA from the Academy of Fine Arts, Florence, Italy. She has worked over the years with diverse populations in different settings and countries, such as Ethiopia and Armenia. For the past five years she has been working in Berlin, Germany, with at-risk children from migrant and refugee backgrounds and their parents. Nehama is currently focused on the integration of art therapy in schools and refugee shelters. This chapter is based on her M.A. thesis focused on fathers, clay and mentalization.

Ana Hram is the leader of the Institution Pomoč and Umetnost (helping and art) and is a social worker, specialised in Arts Therapy in the area of prevention and cure working with people with addictive disorders. She has written over 70 professional articles.

Ephrat Huss is a professor at Ben-Gurion University of the Negev in the social work department, where she chairs an MA programme specialising in art therapy for social workers. She has published over 80 articles and three books on arts and social work and social arts therapy and arts-based research within social contexts. She has also received competitive grants in this field, and is currently working on the experiences of Bedouin youth in Israel using arts-based methods. Her books include: *What We See and What We Say. Using the Arts in Social Research and Practice* (2012), and *A Theory-based Textbook for Teaching Art Therapy* (2015). She has also published an edited book in Hebrew about arts-based research in the context of Israeli society called *Researching Creations, Creating Research* (2012).

Sue Jennings is a Visiting Professor in Expressive Therapies, University of Derby, England and a Professor in Play (life time award, European Federation of Dramatherapists). She is President Emeritus of the Romanian Association of Play Therapy and Dramatherapy. Her books include *Creative Play with Children at Risk* (2017); *101 Ideas for Managing Challenging Behaviour* (2013); *The Anger Management Toolkit: Understanding & Transforming Anger in Children & Young People* (2011); *Working with Attachment Difficulties in Teenagers* (2019); *Working with Attachment Difficulties in School Aged Children* (2019).

José Loureiro is a lecturer of psychology at AVM/Cândido Mendes University in Rio de Janeiro, Brazil. His education includes a BA Honours in Psychology; MA in Group and Intercultural Therapy from Goldsmiths College, University of London and a PhD in Sociology. He has also studied photography at London College of Printing. He has conducted research on the prevention of AIDS for the State Health authority of Porto Alegre/RS, Brazil. He works in private with psychotherapy and career counselling. He is currently working on his postdoctoral research on gender issues in Brazil in the historical perspective.

Michal Magos is a practising social worker who works with young at-risk women in the south of Israel. The chapter is based on her MA thesis study.

Rosy Martin is a London-based artist–photographer, psychological therapist, workshop leader, lecturer and writer. She works both as an artist–photographer and as a psychological therapist exploring the relationships between photography, memory, identities and unconscious processes. From 1983, with Jo Spence, she pioneered re-enactment phototherapy. She has run intensive experiential workshops and lectured in international universities and galleries, and worked in community settings in prison and with survivors of sexual abuse. This chapter relates to her work as a consultant researcher in a multi-disciplinary team on 'Representing Self, Representing Ageing' at Sheffield University. She has published extensively in books and in numerous journals.

Nicole Ottiger is the Deputy Head of Ateliers-Living Museum at the Psychiatry St. Gallen North and board member of the Association for Creative Psychotherapy and Art Therapy (GPK), Switzerland. She is currently a doctoral candidate at Planetary Collegium, Plymouth University / Zurich University of the Arts, researching on self-representation in visual arts and neuropsychology.

Vita Poštuvan is an assistant professor involved in the research and prevention of suicidal behaviour and promotion of mental health through the implementation of large-scale public-health projects, as well as through clinical and therapeutic work with individuals and small groups in Slovenia. She has contributed to a large number of professional papers, organised and participated at national and international conferences, and published articles and chapters in prestigious journals (such as the Lancet) in the fields of psychology, medicine and sociology. She was the first psychologist in Slovenia to obtain the EuroPsy – the European Certificate in Psychology.

Manu Rodríguez is a Spanish published author who also writes in English. He has a MSc in Creative Writing for Therapeutic Purposes from Middlesex University and Metanoia Institute in London (2016) and has been researching about writing since 2001, having extensive experience running creative and therapeutic writing workshops. In Spanish he has published *Leyendas Adolescentes* (primeros cuentos de finales de siglo) (1998); *Llorando Palabras* (2005); *Manual de Escritura Curativa* (2010); *La tía que quiero pasa de mí… Y tú riéndote* (2013) *Y Doce historias y un secreto* (2015). In English he has published *Crying Words* (2014) and *Songs Waiting for a Rock Band/Canciones Esperando Banda de Rock* (2016) his most recent published book.

Patrick Tomczyk is a graduate from Concordia University's Drama Therapy Programme. He is working as a counsellor with adolescent youth and as an administrator at a trauma-informed practice school at a therapeutic campus-based care programme. He is a PhD candidate at the University of Alberta. His research is funded through the Social Sciences and Humanities Research Council of Canada and focuses on the intersectionality of queer theory, pedagogy and ethnodrama, in relation to homophobia, bi-phobia and trans-phobia.

Alenka Vidrih is Assistant Professor in Drama/Theatre in Education at the University of Ljubljana, Slovenia. Her main research interest is the correlation between drama and health. In the Faculty of Education she is leading the Study Programme of Arts Therapy. Her interests are also drama across the curriculum and the implementation of the performative drama method AV in teaching and therapy. She has been involved in many international projects and has contributed to international conferences. Her recent published book in 2016 is about using her drama performative *ars vitae* – the art of living (AV) model in teachers' professional development.

Annette Whitehead-Pleaux is Senior Clinical Supervisor at Roman Music Therapy Services, provides clinical supervision, continuing education development, programme development and staff management at a community music therapy centre. Additionally, Annette teaches at Berklee College of Music, St. Mary-of-the-Woods College, Colorado State University and Lesley University, US. Annette is co-editor of *Cultural Intersections in Music Therapy: Music, Health, and the Person* (2017) and a founding member of Team Rainbow. A long-time feminist and social justice advocate, Annette works for equality for all.

Part I

Art therapy, dance movement therapy, drama therapy and music therapy

Chapter 1

Introduction
Arts therapies and gender issues

This edition explores gender theory in relation to arts therapies, highlighting international research. Many of the writers articulate their ideas about gender in their chapters, so this introduction is not definitive. However, assuming that some arts therapists are not conversant with gender theory, this chapter will start with a general introduction to some key concepts and critiques. It then moves on to consider how gender theory may help facilitate a re-conceptualisation of mental distress. A more sophisticated understanding of gender issues has potentially profound implications for both theory and practice in the arts therapies. The chapter then moves on to give a brief summary of the book's contents. As well as offering chapters on art therapy, dance–movement therapy, drama therapy and music therapy, emergent and hybrid practices are also shared, such as re-enactment phototherapy, therapeutic writing, art therapy in virtual reality and therapeutic photography.

Gender

Gender is the social interpretation of sex – well, yes and no. In much academic writing 'gender' is used to refer to **social and cultural aspects of identity**, which manifest as particular ways of being, especially in enactments of masculinity or femininity, rather than referring to biological sex. However, ideas about biological sex are not untainted by notions of gender, as gender stereotypes infuse 'unbiased' scientific explanations. Social and cultural differences result in very different **gender roles** cross-culturally. In our own particular niche, wherever we happen to be, we may think what we experience is 'normal' and 'inevitable', resulting from biology, rather than socially created, but anthropologists have shown cross-cultural variations and sociologists, cultural theorists and cultural historians have pointed towards variations across and within cultures (Hogan 2019). People's concept of themselves is often described as their **gender identity**. There may *be 'gender incongruence'*, the identity not in line with a person's biological sex, or there may be *dissatisfaction about gender roles* (which are constraining for both men and women in different ways and variously across and within cultures). Gender roles, though restricting and oppressive in a multitude of potential ways, are particularly problematic to women because many gender roles reinforce the subordination of women (Hogan 2019). Gender roles have profound consequences; in some cultures, for example, women may not have full access to public domains and therefore be restricted to a limited range of roles and opportunities. In some societies, two men kissing in a public space might result in their deaths.

The contributors to this book acknowledge a plurality of masculinities and femininities, or wish to debunk the idea of this binary altogether, illustrating that gendered identities do not necessarily map perfectly with biological sex. Hogan and Cornish point out that in the art therapeutic imaginary there is some freedom of movement in current thinking (2014). As arts therapists we need to be keenly aware of the oppressive potential of gender norms, otherwise we may unwittingly abuse our clients via the imposition of constraining stereotypical expectations and norms. Terminology varies and language is limiting. The way terms are employed herein may vary also, though writers will explore and explain their particular language use. Language is a potentially sensitive area, as there is a possible *erasure* of experience through an oppressive binary, which is still the dominant paradigm and entrenched in the fabric of grammar. Femininity and masculinity, though 'de-bunked' and investigated as concepts in this book, are still very much to the fore in their despotic force and oppressive potential in the world at large, though their interpretation varies vastly cross-culturally (Hogan 2019). In the arts therapies experimentation with imaginative ways of being is possible.

The body as a symbol

We do not all interpret bodies in the same way – they are open to multiple interpretations from different perspectives: bodies are essentially polysemic. 'Even the human physiology, which we all share in common', (or at least at first glance appear to), 'does not afford symbols which we can all understand' argued anthropologist Mary Douglas (Douglas 1996 p.xxxi). Cross-cultural interpretation of gendered bodies is therefore complex and we are all subject to varying gender-related pressures, constraints and rewards dependent on our particularity and context.

Subjectivities across cultures vary. There is no clear line which can be drawn between self and culture:

> Our bodies (their shape, size, colour, sex) determine our social relations; we experience ourselves differently in varying contexts and we reiterate or 'perform' norms associated with our embodied selves as active agents, as philosopher Judith Butler put it, without necessarily thinking about it too much, with a nearly intuitive sense, … or more simply we *do* sex.
> (Hogan 2016b p.57)

It is potentially useful for arts and health practitioners to think of bodies as symbolic signifiers – '*the medium though which social relations are constructed*'

(Shilling 2016 p.10). Social relations are embodied and our bodies are signifiers of meanings beyond our control (Hogan 2019). The body is not a 'natural thing' beyond culture. As Douglas put it in the 1996 edition of *Natural Symbols* (i):

> There are no such things as natural symbols. Every culture naturalises a certain view of the human body to make it carry social meanings .... Body symbolism is always in service to social intentions, and the body cannot be endowed with universal meanings.

As soon as we begin to think about bodies in this way, we can see that they are subject to a range of, potentially conflicting, meanings and values; nor can they be seen as neutral objects merely subject to interpretations of culture. Our bodies are imbued with the values of our specific culture (and sub-culture) and historical moment. We have an embodied consciousness shaped by context (Hogan 2019).

There is a great deal of diversity concerning how bodies are regarded across different cultures and across different sets of cultural values, so it is not surprising that bodies are subject to different pressures and constraints, to conflicting ideals and expectations. The body as a symbol 'helps people to think, classify, and even engage in discriminatory practices based on physical markers' (Shilling 2016 p.7). The gender theorist Raewyn Connell suggests that certain habits of practice result in a set of hegemonic gender relations, which are oppressive. The hegemony will determine the range of admissible practices, characteristics and responses open to any given group. There are particular conceptual models in different geographical and temporal contexts. Connell gives the example of apparent similarities across cultures in the neo-liberal business class. However, other patterns of masculinity or femininity are available in different milieus; indeed, there are plural configurations of practice (Connell 2017).[1]

I would like to take Connell's theory a step further and suggest that rather than distinctive configurations, or overlapping configurations, actually there are very *conflicting* styles of gender configurations vying for prominence in many contexts, styles which are contained and manifested in many ways, through interactions with others, institutional messages, media and so forth (the system of relations possible that can be established between these elements is what Foucault called the *dispositive apparatus*).[2] These gender styles may be 'overlapping', but can usefully be perceived as possible rival hegemonies, which interact and reverberate, or in more self-conscious ways challenge the other, potentially engulfing and subsuming the other – they are interactive. All this is in a state of flux and the field is dynamic, in movement, in a continual process of contestation (through metaphor, cultural practices and so forth), though this movement is not always evident. This is a complex subject and I have explored in previous work how changes in symbolic practices can result in incremental cultural change (Hogan 2008a). Castoriadis has pointed out that a sense of cultural unity is 'in itself the outcome of the internal cohesion of interwoven meanings, or significations, pervading all of life in society, guiding and directing it: what I call the social imaginary significations' (p.47). Castoriadis goes on to suggest that societies are creations of the social imaginary and that each new state of society is an ontological creation:

> each society contains a system for interpreting the world. But that would be insufficient: each society *is* a system for interpreting the world. Better yet, more strictly speaking, each society is the construing, actually the creation of a world that applies to it, its own world. Its identity is nothing other than that system of interpretation, or better still, of meaning making. For that reason, if you attack that system of interpretation, of meaning giving, you attack it more lethally than if you attack its physical existence, and as a rule it will fight back much more savagely.
>
> (2010 p.50)

Inequality is the result of 'a particular social imaginary positioning of being-man and being-woman' (Castoriadis 2010 p.48). We can think of this social imaginary not as monolithic, but constituted by rival configurations (hegemonies), which contain different styles of gender coming into possible conflict, through all the processes which Foucault describes for how meanings are generated. Castoriadis's quote is helpful for us in understanding that challenging systems of interpretation, of meaning giving, is a fundamental attack upon cultural identity itself. To conclude, meanings ascribed to the body are unstable and we are subject to many conflicting messages about our bodies and what gender means. I have suggested that rival conceptualisations of gender are in flux, creating areas of cultural stress and contestation and personal dis-ease.

Men are from Mars and women are from Venus

Endocrinology suggests that hormones give rise to a 'continuum of sexed bodies', rather than an account of male and female as opposites or fundamentally as different (Shilling 2016 p.35). Masculinity and femininity as binary absolutes are cultural constructs, which 'cannot be reduced to any "logic" of genetic influence' (Shilling 2016 p.36). Or to invoke Castoriadis once more, 'imaginary significations are imaginary because they are neither rational, nor real' (p.48). Regarding increasingly popular genetic explanations for gender differences, 'the significance of genes and groups of genes … is *codetermined* by interactions within the human organism as well as by interactions that people have with the social and material environment in which they live' (Shilling 2016 p.36). Moreover, a major fault in many study designs is an assumption that the 'organising effects' of hormones are permanent (Jordan-Young 2010 p.289). Our hormones are influenced by many factors. S. S. Richardson complains that many research studies lack intragroup analysis. In other words, male and female differences are reported, but not the differences between males (in male only groups), or between females (in female only groups). She explains that this is problematic because in many research results:

> It is almost impossible to know what the differences in gene expression are between women and between men, and what the range of overlap is between women and men. The result is that the differences between sexes may be exaggerated and the differences within a sex may be completely obscured. The danger is that sex differences may be exaggerated at the expense of important similarities between men and women and important differences within each group may be missed, with implications for both women's and men's health.
> (Richardson 2013 p.221)

Assumptions of difference skew seemingly objective research findings resulting in a 'focus on difference in the description, visual representation, and interpretation of study results' (Richardson 2013 p.221) and a neglect of relevant variables in study designs, such as age, weight, nutrition, stress, environmental exposures which 'affect gene expression' (p.222). Richardson also notes that sex and gender are often conflated in genetic sex-difference studies and that the potential interaction between sex and gender is usually overlooked, thus 'the interaction of cultural gender roles and norms with gene expression' is not acknowledged or explored (Richardson 2013 p.220).

Indeed, stereotypes operate at an implicit level in all domains (Nosek & Hansen 2008 p.554). Fine (2010) illustrates, through an analysis of study design, how psychological tests or tasks being perceived as gendered by participants actually results in the performance of those tasks being enhanced or impeded *by both women and men*. In her critique of the application of sex-difference psychological tests (tests which are purposefully looking for differences in performance between men and women), she shows how the interplay of gender in performance is subtle and shifting. Changing the gendered context (physically, or in terms of speech or prompts which manage expectations) changes the performance of participants. Gender is context driven and mobile, and often subtle, in its operation and effects.

This nuanced analysis should hopefully counter banal and reductive pronouncements of the sort that women and men inhabit different planets, or that there are too few senior female engineers at MIT because 'exposure to testosterone during a key phase of foetal development appears to influence spacial ability' (Hausman 2000 p.4). As Fine's analysis shows, such pronouncements mask the multi-dimensional complexity of gender and its operation and obscure barriers to equality, which are both subtle and overt. Jordan-Young (2010) is dismissive of cognitive neuroscience brain organisation theory, dismissing it as 'folk-tales about antagonistic male and female essences' (p.291).

However, the idea of 'sex hormones' as 'chemical messengers of masculinity and femininity' appears entrenched in the popular imagination (Oudshoon 1994 p.17).

Culture imprints itself and moulds gendered bodies through cultural practices. Hence, returning to the question at the outset of this chapter, gender is not merely the social interpretation of sex. As Fausto-Sterling put it, 'our bodies physically imbibe culture' (2005, p.1495). What she means by this is that cultural practices do indeed accentuate and create differences between the sexes. Seemingly innate observed biological sex differences can be created culturally.

Ideas about gender also serve to oppress many people in various contexts in which inequality is a feature. Arts therapists must be critical of gender stereotypes and accompanying restrictive cultural practices that serve to underpin unequal distributions of resources and power, or entrenched sexism within particular domains, such as at MIT in the example above (Hogan 2019). It is important to be critical of such biomedical explanations of difference that offer 'a neat, satisfying explanation, and justification of the gender status quo' – a status quo that arts therapists need to be capable of conceptualising and challenging (Fine 2010 p.xxii). Male and female bodies may be more similar than some authors would have us believe. In conclusion to her work in contemporary genomics, Richardson concludes that 'the body of sex difference research in genetics in fact shows *an overwhelming picture of similarity*' (2013 p.222 my italics).

Challenging the binary

There is, perhaps not surprisingly, a lack of consensus about some aspects of sexuality, sexual identity and sexual expression in relation to gender and how sexuality as 'the realm of erotic desires and practices' intersects with gender (Jordan-Young 2010 p.15). Monro (2005) suggests a plurality of identities, including 'intersex'. Writers use the term 'intersex' differently, but intersex potentially asserts itself as an ambiguous or undefined space, which can disquiet or disrupt binary expectations. It is a difficult space to inhabit, but is a potentially radical space also. Some contributors to this book may assert that 'intersex' should be considered a third sex, rather than a sexual identity, or orientation.

Monro identifies cross-dressers and drag artists as inhabiting a 'fluid space', whilst others point out that drag can accentuate and reinforce gender stereotypes. Monro also suggests that transsexuality is a 'space beyond' the binary, but also acknowledges counter opinion that some transsexual persons only wish to 'assimilate' and 'pass' as male or female – thus reducing transsexuality to 'a patriarchal means of reinforcing stereotypes' rather than a radical assault on hetero-normativity. This is political terrain. On the other hand, that a man can become woman or vice versa may be argued to be fundamentally challenging to reductive notions about essential masculinity or femininity. This is challenged in turn by those who say that it is the *lived experience of inhabiting a gendered body*, which creates gender identity. Ironically, this argument is used both for and against the validity of transsexual identity. Moreover, transsexual experience has also been used by feminists as a means to critique unhelpful disempowering gender norms: 'The more I was treated like a woman, the more woman I became', wrote male to female transsexual, Jan Morris: 'If I was assumed to be incompetent at reversing cars, or opening bottles, oddly incompetent I found myself becoming' (Morris 1987 cited in Fine 2010 p.3). Many authors point out that gendered identities do not necessarily correlate with sex. Monro asserts that gender pluralism, the acknowledgement of gender diversity, is useful as it enables calls for justice and social change, offering a variety of bodily practices, which challenge hetero-patriarchal norms. 'Non-binary' is a term coming to the fore and this can mean any of several things: 'I'm not playing ball with subscribed and limiting conceptualisations of gender' is certainly one of them, though the term is also used by people to describe a sense of fluctuating selfhood.

Intersectional analysis (which shows how gender interacts with other aspects of social identity, such as age, colour, economic position, geographical location, religious affiliation, ethnicity, etc.) has been identified as useful in calling into question the construction of 'monolithic identities' forcing consideration of 'how one is positioned by the intersecting and multiple hegemonies' that structure culture (Lance 2004 p.325). Certainly, an arts therapeutic space offers the opportunity for the imaginative exploration of gender, through performance and art making, and via the therapeutic relationship (Hogan & Cornish 2014). It can provide a 'gender fluid' space. It also offers a compassionate and accepting space for the exploration of self-identity, which is often much needed; as one transsexual author put it:

Many of us have been teased, rejected by our families, threatened with violence, or even physically or sexually abused. We may also spend years uncomfortable in our bodies or our roles in life. There was a time when it was almost impossible to find a mental health provider who could see us as whole people not just as having a mental illness just by being transgender (Tamer et al. 2014. p.305).

Furthermore, arts therapies can be important in promoting agency and, if conducted with awareness, can be congruent with what Hammonds calls 'a politics of articulation' (2004 p.312). Hammonds suggests that black queer female sexualities are not simply identities: 'Rather they represent discursive and material terrains where there exists the possibility for the active production of *speech, desire* and *agency*'.

★★★

This volume contains a very exciting collection of essays, presenting research and research perspectives. Michal Magos and Ephrat Huss point out in their chapter that many art therapy clients are female and suffer from marginalisation in terms of gender, culture and poverty. The chapter challenges the idea that images should be understood in purely individual terms, cut-off from social forms of oppression such as the gender realities that define and construct the subjective experience of identity. They offer techniques for a more socially aware practice. New perspectives on issues, they suggest, may be generated through the compositional elements of the art itself. Whitehead-Pleaux explores working with a diverse range of sexual identities with music therapy. She also offers some useful guidance on terminology. Related to social forms of oppression, Baines and Edwards present the development of feminist theory in music therapy literature and critique problematic gender perspectives in research. Bird's chapter explores being a male researcher and art therapist working with women who have experienced violence, looking especially at notions of home. In particular, this chapter investigates how empathy, reflexivity, feminist standpoint theory and ideas about intersectionality were employed in the research process. The two chapters that follow present research on parenthood: first Bauch shares work undertaken with new fathers who use clay to explore their ideas and ideals about parenting, and reflect on how they themselves had been fathered and how they wish to emulate this, or do things differently. I (Hogan) worked with mothers and birth professionals using the arts to explore their experiences of birth and new motherhood in *The Birth Project*. The research also looks at iatrogenic illness and inhumane hospital protocols. An impassioned plea and argument for the application of queer theory to drama therapy practice follows by Tomczyk. Advocates of queer theory suggest that it 'creates a space for imagining alternatives to the rigid gender binary system' (Monro 2005, p.32). Sue Jennings presents a provocation of sorts: combining clinical reflections and thoughts about anthropological fieldwork, she challenges us to think differently about gender and the body. Cornelissen shares qualitative research that focused on how male and female dance movement therapists experience their gender in the process of a dance movement group therapy with a mixed-sex client group.

One of the distinctive things about this volume is that it features a number of emergent practices. These include creative writing for therapeutic purposes with an intersectional approach to gender (Rodríguez) and re-enactment phototherapy (Loureiro and Martin), a performative practice influenced by drama therapy and co-counselling techniques, pioneered in Britain by Rosy Martin and Jo Spence; Loureiro's work is particularly informed by Raewyn Connell's social theory of gender, where gender is seen as a relation, rather than an identity or discourse. Also included is 'hybrid' work, which mixes types of interventions (Vidrih et al.) or work exploring new techniques (Carr). Carr's work is innovative in developing and assessing distinctive ways of working with terminally ill individuals who are unable to make their own art pieces, but who engage in a creative exchange with her towards extraordinary portraits. Experimentation with virtual reality, as a 'potential space' is also represented. Ehemann and Ottiger explore the use of avatars in creating multiple and modifiable self-representations which create opportunities for self-exploration. They propose that gender is becoming a more fluid concept and increasingly detached from sex. Gender should be seen as a variable that is not constant, but fluid, shifting and changing in different contexts and times. This is evident in virtual reality.

> Produced concurrently with this work is **Gender and Difference in the Arts Therapies: Inscribed on the Body**, which has an emphasis on theory and practice and should form an excellent complement and companion to this work. Readers of my previous edited books will know that I do not have a prescriptive approach; this volume will represent a range of ways of thinking about gender and employ a variety of theories (Hogan 2003, 2008b, 2012, 2013, 2015a, 2015b, 2016a, 2017; Hogan et al. 2015). However, these two news books together should go some way to addressing the 'relative marginalisation of social theories within art therapy' (Huss 2013 p.74).

★★★

Recommended further reading: Hogan, S. 1997. Problems of identity: Deconstructing gender in art therapy in Hogan, S. (ed.) *Feminist Approaches to Art Therapy*. London: Routledge pp. 21–48.
Freely available at:
https://derby.academia.edu/SusanHogan

Acknowledgement

Thanks to Kate Phillips and Phil Douglas for their thoughts on this chapter. I am very grateful, as I find feedback on work in progress invaluable. Thanks also to Caroline Humphrey for sharing her latest paper with me and making me think harder about social processes and oppression.

Appendix of terms

Berkeley (University of California) has put together a glossary of terms, some of which may be useful to share. Included are a few key terms, not the entire list which appears on their website.

- **Androgynous**: 'A person appearing and/or identifying as neither man nor woman'.
- **Ally**: 'Someone who advocates for and supports members of a community other than their own. Reaching across differences to achieve mutual goals'.
- **Asexual**: 'A person who is not sexually attracted to any gender'.

- **Bigender**: 'A person whose gender identity is a combination of man and woman'.
- **Biphobia**: 'The irrational fear and intolerance of people who are bisexual'.
- **Bisexuality**: 'Also bi. A person who is attracted to two sexes ... but not necessarily simultaneously or equally'. (This term is criticised for its binary nature; however, it could include many spaces in-between).
- **Cisgender**: 'A person who by nature or by choice conforms to gender/sex based expectations of society (also referred to as "Gender-straight" or "Gender Normative")'.
- **Cisgenderism**: 'Assuming every person to be cisgender therefore marginalizing those who identify as trans in some form'.
- **FTM/F2M**: 'Abbreviation for a female-to-male transgender or transsexual person'.
- **Gay**: 'Men attracted to men. Colloquially used as an umbrella term to include all LGBTIQ people. A person who either by nature or by choice does not conform to gender-based expectations of society (e.g. transgender, transsexual, intersex, genderqueer, cross-dresser, etc.) preferable to "gender variant" because it does not imply a standard normativity'.
- **Gender Fluid**: 'A person whose gender identification and presentation shifts, whether within or outside of societal, gender-based expectations'.
- **Genderfuck**: 'The idea of playing with "gender cues" to purposely confuse "standard" or stereotypical gender expressions, usually through clothing'. Monro describes 'Gender fuck' as 'a deliberate use of conflicting gender signifiers' (having breasts and a beard, would be one example).
- **Gender Non-Conforming**: 'A person who don't [sic] conform to society's expectations of gender expression based on the gender binary, expectations of masculinity and femininity, or how they should identify their gender'.
- **Genderqueer**: 'A person whose gender identity is neither man nor woman, is between or beyond genders, or is some combination of genders'.
- **Homophobia**: 'The irrational fear and intolerance of people who are homosexual or of homosexual feelings within one's self. This assumes that heterosexuality is superior'.
- **Intersex**: 'Intersex is a set of medical conditions that feature congenital anomaly of the reproductive and sexual system. That is, intersex people are born with "sex chromosomes," external genitalia, or internal reproductive systems that are not considered "standard" for either male or female. The existence of intersexuals shows that there are not just two sexes and that our ways of thinking about sex (trying to force everyone to fit into either the male box or the female box) is [sic] socially constructed'. This term is also used by some writers to indicate a space that is undefined or ambiguous, or it is used as a synonym for 'gender fluidity'.
- **LGBTIQ**: 'Lesbian, Gay, Bisexual, Transgender, Intersex, Queer'. (Sometimes 'questioning', rather than queer).

- **MSM**: 'Men who engage in same-sex behavior, but who may not necessarily self-identify as gay or bisexual'.
- **MTF/M2F**: 'Abbreviation for male-to-female transgender or transsexual person'.
- **Pangender**: 'A person whose gender identity is comprised of all or many gender expressions'.
- **Pansexual**: 'A person who is fluid in sexual orientation and/or gender or sex identity'.

University of California, Berkeley. Definition of Terms: https://campusclimate.berkeley.edu/students/ejce/geneq/resources/lgbtq-resources/definition-terms site visited Dec 2017.

Notes

1 Interview with Raewyn Connell (Colloque Masculinités non-hégémoniques: des configurations ambigües et plurielles, 15-16 mai 2017). Institut Incal, UCL. Published on 14 Jun 2017. https://www.youtube.com/channel/UCynno71fDLHglnZlmbUJ31g/videos
2 Regulatory frameworks have been called *dispositive apparatus*, defined by Foucault as 'a thoroughly heterogeneous ensemble consisting of discourses, institutions, architectural forms, regulatory decisions, laws, administrative measures, scientific statements, philosophical, moral and philanthropic propositions – in short, the said as much as the unsaid. Such are the elements of the apparatus. The apparatus itself is the system of relations that can be established between these elements' (1977 p.194).

References

Castoriadis, C. 2010. *A Society Adrift. Interviews and Debates 1974–1997*. New York: Fordham University Press.
Douglas, M. 1996. *Natural Symbols*. London: Routledge.
Fausto-Sterling, A. 2005. Bare Bones of Sex: Part 1 – Sex and Gender. *Signs*, 30, 2, 1491–1528.
Fine, C. 2010. *Delusions of Gender*. London: Icon.
Foucault, M. 1980. The Confession of the Flesh (1977), interview in Gordon, C (ed.) *Power/Knowledge Selected Interviews and Other Writings*. New York: Harvester Press. New York: Pantheon Books pp. 194–228.
Hammonds, E. 2004. Black (W)holes and the Geometry of Black Female Sexuality in Bobo, J., Hudley, C. & Michel, C. (eds) *The Black Studies Reader*. London & New York: Routledge pp. 301–315.
Hausman, P. 2000. The Tale of Two Hormones. Paper Presented to the National Academy of Engineering. Atlanta. 26 April.
Hogan, S. 1997. Problems of Identity. Deconstructing Gender in Art Therapy in Hogan, S. (ed.) *Feminist Approaches to Art Therapy*. London: Routledge pp. 21–48.
Hogan, S. (ed.) 1997. *Feminist Approaches to Art Therapy*. London: Routledge.
Hogan, S. (ed.) 2003. *Gender Issues in Art Therapy*. London: Routledge.
Hogan, S. 2006. The Tyranny of the Maternal Body: Maternity and Madness. *Women's History Magazine* (Women's History Association), 54, Autumn, 21–30.

Hogan, S. 2008a. The Beestings: Rethinking Breast-Feeding Practices, Maternity Rituals, & Maternal Attachment in Britain & Ireland. *Journal of International Women's Studies (JIWS)*, 10, 2, 141–160.

Hogan, S. 2008b. Angry Mothers in Liebmann, M. (ed.) *Art Therapy & Anger*. London: Jessica Kingsley pp. 197–211.

Hogan, S. 2012. Post-modernist but Not Post-feminist! A Feminist Post-modernist Approach to Working with New Mothers in Burt, H. (ed.) *Creative Healing Through a Prism. Art Therapy and Postmodernism*. London: Jessica Kingsley pp. 70–82.

Hogan, S. 2013. Your Body is a Battleground: Women and Art Therapy. *The Arts in Psychotherapy. Special Issue: Gender & the Creative Arts Therapies*, 40, 4, 415–419.

Hogan, S. 2015a. Mothers Make Art: Using Participatory Art to Explore the Transition to Motherhood. *Journal of Applied Arts & Health*, 6, 1, 23–32.

Hogan, S. 2015b. Lost in Translation. Intercultural Exchange in Art Therapy in Brooke, S. L. & Myers, C. E. (eds) *Therapists Creating a Cultural Tapestry: Using the Creative Therapies Across Cultures*. Springfield: Charles Thomas pp. 11–25.

Hogan, S. 2016a. *Art Therapy Theories. A Critical Introduction*. London: Routledge.

Hogan, S. 2016b. Age is Just a Number, Init?": Interrogating Perceptions of Age and Women within Social Gerontology. *Women's Studies*, 45, 1, 57–77.

Hogan, S. 2017. The Tyranny of Expectations of Post-Natal Delight: Gendering Happiness. *Journal of Gender Studies. Special Issue: Gendering Happiness*, 26, 1, 45–55.

Hogan, S. 2019. Introduction: Inscribed on the Body: Gender and Difference in the Arts Therapies in *Gender and Difference in the Arts Therapies: Inscribed on the Body*. London: Routledge (in press).

Hogan, S. & Cornish, S. 2014. Unpacking Gender in Art Therapy: The Elephant at the Art Therapy Easel. *International Journal of Art Therapy (IJAT, formerly Inscape)*, 19, 3, 122–134.

Hogan, S., Baker, C., Cornish, S., McCloskey, P., Watts, L. 2015. Birth Shock: Exploring Pregnancy, Birth and the Transition to Motherhood Using Participatory Arts in Burton, N. (ed.) *Natal Signs: Representations of Pregnancy, Childbirth and Parenthood*. Canada: Demeter Press pp. 272–269.

Huss, E. 2013. *What We See and What We Say*. Hove & New York: Routledge.

Jordan-Young, R. M. 2010. *Brain Storm. The Flaws in the Science of Sex Differences*. Cambridge: Harvard University Press.

Lance, A. J. 2004. The Politics of Race in the Gay/Military Battle in Bobo, J., Hudley, C. & Michel, C. (eds) *The Black Studies Reader*. London & New York: Routledge pp. 315–329.

Monro, S. 2005. *Gender Politics. Citizenship, Activism, & Sexual Diversity*. London: Pluto Press.

Nosek, B. A. & Hansen, J. 2008. The Associations in our Heads Belong to Us. *Cognition*, 22, 4, 553–594.

Oudshoorn, N. 1994. *Beyond the Natural Body: An Archaeology of Sex Hormones*. London: Routledge.

Richardson, S. S. 2013. *Sex Itself. The Search for Male and Female in the Human Genome*. Chicago & London: University of Chicago Press.

Shilling, C. 2016. *The Body. A Very Short Introduction*. Oxford: Oxford University Press.

Tamer, C., Hopwood, R., Dickey, L. M. 2014. Mental Health Concerns in Erickson-Schroth, L. (ed.) *Trans Bodies, Trans Selves. A Resource for the Transgender Community*. Oxford: Oxford University Press pp. 305–335.

Chapter 2

Drawing on visions of the future of young women in poverty

Art as a feminist research method

Michal Magos and Ephrat Huss

Introduction and literature survey

Overall, the social context for impoverished single women and single mothers points to intense difficulty in finding work alone, let alone in reaching professional self-fulfilment. The statistics in the U.S. on single impoverished women's employment show that firstly, over eighty percent of those living in poverty are women and only a third of these find adequately paid and protected jobs by their late twenties. Additionally, around forty-two percent of at-risk young women return to welfare support within four years of starting work (Bynner & Parsons 2001, 2002; Harris 1996). From this, then the interaction of gender and poverty makes the odds of young impoverished women finding work at all and self-fulfilment in work even smaller (Zucker & Wiener 1993). Within this context, it is not surprising that the focus tends to be on helping these young women find work without stopping to explore how they define self-fulfilment, that is a concept reserved for middle-class women. Indeed, the gap between this dire reality and the prevalent media images of success for young women that magically manage to overcome social disadvantages make the gap between reality and cultural images of self-actualisation even harder to bridge (Harris 1996; Pavetti & Acs 1997; Vincent & Osler 2003). This lack of real chance to 'self-actualise' through employment as compared to middle-class women raises the question of if and how impoverished young women do define success, or future dreams, or self-actualisation for themselves (Brown 2001). Although these young women may not have access to social symbolic and financial capital that enables self-fulfilment through employment, they have the right to self-define goals, or visions of self-fulfilment, that middle-class women take as their natural right: on this level, then images of self-fulfilment can be a base to 'dare to dream', but also a base for critical consciousness raising as to the reality and meaning of these dreams in a shared reality group of other women under poverty.

This paper hopes to provide a better understanding of the women's own definitions and visions of self-fulfilment, as a base for creating contextualised visions of success that are not fantasies that perpetuate their sense of failure, but rather expressions of success or self-fulfilment as defined from within a specific social context – and as a way to change that context. This can help direct the young girls to their goals, and can also enable them to have an overall sense of wellbeing that in turn leads to better functioning, that in turn can buffer the above-described stress symptoms and help to transcend poverty (Norman 1999). Images were used as a trigger to excavate one's inner dreams, before sharing the image in the group. Visions of self-actualisation are by definition visual, and thus using arts-based methods can help capture these 'visions' (Betensky 1995; Eisner 1997; Tutty et al. 1996).

Spivak, a feminist sociologist and historian, describes how 'The place where female and marginalized "speech acts" can be heard is not in historical, academic and political writings that are still male dominated, but in the areas of symbolic self-expression where resistance is removed from reality, and thus does not threaten the central male discourse' (Spivak & Guhah 1988, p.207). Alternative methods of research, such as using images in addition to words, are cited as helpful in revealing marginalised participants' own understandings of the issue as they both draw the image and also explain it, doubling their hermeneutic output (Betensky 1995; Huss 2011; Jones 1997; Tutty et al. 1996).

Additionally, the use of images created by the women themselves, rather than by the media, is considered a form of empowerment and self-definition in itself, as it enabled them to make dreams visible from within, rather than conceding to media-based images (Hogan 2003).

Methods

Two months after the end of a welfare support group for impoverished young women to enter employment, (so as not to confuse with power relations with group leaders) the women were invited to a voluntary activity in which they were asked to draw visions of their dreams, goals, and self-fulfilment and to explain these drawings in a semi-structured interview form. They were notified that the meeting and art work would be used for research but that identifying features would be rubbed out or hidden. All women signed consent. The interviewee (who was trained in an MA specialisation of arts for social workers, and was also their former group leader) asked them to first draw and then to explain their goals and visions of the future. Twelve out of the fifteen women signed forms of consent to have this interview used in research. The other two women came to the interview, but did not agree to have their work used in research.

Data sources: consisted of twelve transcribed interviews, twelve photographed drawings and the field diary of the interviewer.

Field Site: This research utilised a group offering employment support for young women in Israel. These young women were predominantly Sephardic–Israeli, or Russian immigrants in ethnicity. They were mostly born in Israel, but their parents were immigrants or poor, at-risk families that are connected to the welfare facilities. For ethical reasons, more specific information will not be provided (please see the section on Israel and unemployment in my literature survey). The Ministry of Employment in Israel teaches specific professions, and the Ministry of Welfare together with NGOs provide job preparation and support through weekly group meetings (Golan & Lahav-Kastini 1999). The group of this research was led by the Department of Welfare and an NGO, and consisted of fifteen young women between the ages of twenty-one and twenty-four. The group was co-run by a social worker (the second researcher) and an employment director. It focused on skills such as writing CVs and difficulties in finding and maintaining a job. The women received scholarships to study for a profession from the NGO. (In order to maintain the women's anonymity more specific details will not be provided). The twelve research participants of this project were all part of the above group.

Analytical strategy: This included the categorisation according to the women's explanations of their images, and then thematic division of both visual and verbal data by the researcher and additional social workers (Creswell 1998; Tutty et al. 1996; Mason 2002). The data was analysed by the women who drew the pictures and was not interpreted by the researcher using a diagnostic or psychological theory, as is common with images in research (Betensky 1995; Huss 2005).

Validity and trustworthiness: The dual hermeneutic voices of the participants as both drawers and explainers of the art work was replicated in that the participants provided an art work and an explanation of the art work on the subject (Mason 2002). The data was peer analysed three times so as to reach validity first by the researchers, and second by the second group worker who is a vocational social worker. It was analysed thematically with a focus on the theoretical questions of the research – that is with respect to components of visions of self-fulfillment. Third, a peer group of social workers working with similar women who are familiar with the population being interviewed also analysed the findings in a supervisory context (Creswell 1998).

Ethical considerations: One of the two researchers writing this paper first led this group, and then interviewed the women after the group had ended. On the one hand, she was familiar with the group and on the other was not involved in power relationships with them, as the group had ended. All identifying features were removed from the interviews and art work.

The women also signed consent to take part in the research. In order not to endanger the women's privacy, the art work that serves as a trigger for the women's narrative is described and alluded to, but not photographed within the paper (Mason 2002).

Data presentation and discussion

First set of themes: Self-actualisation as inner peace and self-respect:
The first set of themes includes the definition of self-actualisation as passive or reflective self-regulatory characteristics such as self-love, self-care, calmness, and stability.

Stability and calmness: *'I want to be able to work in one job for a long time, so I can start and end things. If I start a new job I want to be there a long time, at least a year or two - so I have stability. I would like my life to be calm, and quiet, without dramas, and messes'.*

Self-care: *'I made the tree large, it symbolises me, so I remember to put myself in the middle of my life - that's what holding down a job means to me, putting myself in the middle ... - and looking after that tree - giving it water and air - it's my responsibility, to look after my own tree'.*

Self-love: *'I drew myself at a desk: When I fulfil my dream and finish my studies so as to work in the job I want, then I know that I will "love myself" and also - I will earn money. I will love myself when I have an education and a set job ... - ...'.*

The second set is formed from assertive characteristics such as the exercise of free choice, independence, and knowledge.

Knowledge: *'I always wanted to study and gain knowledge, I didn't have money so I never thought about the possibility - but now I do think about it'.*

Choice: *'I don't know where I will be or what I will do say in two years' time, the direction isn't clear to me, but it's clear to me that I will choose - I alone will choose - that's why I drew me in the centre of the page'.*

The following themes can be defined as recourses or as tools for reaching the above visions of self-fulfilment and include using diaries for organisation, perseverance, and prayer, as well as support from others.

Focus and organisation: *'I know that it's hard for me to focus and be organised, I saw it in my job interviews, and I tried to work on that, but also, I try to accept who I am, my lack of focus makes me interesting, my vision is to continue being myself - I want to accept and love who I am, as I am'.*

The third set of themes describes the characteristics that the women wish for so as to reach self-love and self-acceptance.

Personal responsibility: *'I know that I am in charge of myself, no one else will do it for me ... I keep reminding myself of this - those clear strong lines represent me'.*
Good choices: *'I know I need to put studies before going out with friends, or hanging out in the neighbourhood - it has to be first place because it's for me, no one else will help me if I don't help myself - so I drew a pile of books'.*
Perseverance: *'Your need to continue, it's not all pink, but you need to continue, although you are angry, you have been hurt, others have hurt you, you need to continue beyond all that - not to give up. I drew me as the colour brown, a realistic, grounded colour'.*
Prayer: *'I pray, every day, I open my prayer book and this gives me strength - so I drew my prayer book in the centre'.*

The fourth set of themes describes the concrete tools that help them reach these characteristics.

The use of a diary: *'I also drew in my diary because it is very important to me: It helps me keep order and most of the pages are empty, so I can see the most important things, and keep order ... but I also write my feelings in my diary, and all my girlfriends have written me blessings in my diary, opening it gives me strength when I'm feeling down'.*

The fourth set of themes describes self-fulfilment in terms of transposing the above self-love and self-respect into relationships.

Choosing good people: *'I need to stand up for myself, I drew a woman with open eyes I hope they will stay open, so I won't be used again by people, parasites who take away my strength - I hope next time I will have open eyes and choose better people to be friends with'.*
Not being alone: *'I learnt that alone - you can't move on, but you have to identify the right people and then you can move on with those people'.*
Independence that is a base for a relationship: *'Once I have a set job, I can find a partner and buy a proper house, and have a child, if you have money you can build a house, plant a garden, and move around inside and outside the house, you can have a child'.*
A supportive relationship that is a base for independence: *'If you have a good partner, you can find a good job, a good partner pushes you in the right direction, he has power, influence, and you can help him also - a partner is very important'.*
Being respected: *'I don't know where I will work in a few years but I want to be in a good place where I am respected, where my wishes are respected, that is important to me ... I drew my head up ... I want to know I am being listened to and people aren't laughing at me - that is most important to me, I am being listened to - I drew myself talking to a group of people and they are all listening to me'.*

Expressing self in relationship: *'I want to say what I really want to say ... I drew the mouth as dominant I can use it to talk, to say what I want, to reach out to others, you know. In the beginning I didn't want to add a mouth, but then I remembered that I do want to let the character express herself, I don't want to be someone who never talks, because then I can't find people to help me, or who could love me'.*

Not taking over-responsibility for others: *'I don't want to worry about other people anymore - maybe a little, for a short time, but then I want to return to my own life'.*

The interdependency between these visions of self-actualisation and having a job is expanded in the following theme, into the concept of 'having it all'– both a good relationship and a good job – but this has to be tempered with the above self-regulatory skills.

'To be a mother, that's most important for me, but also to find love, and to study - and to have a job - I want it all - I want everything. I started using glitter, to signify having it all - all glittery, like an illusion, but afterwards, I changed it into a star shape, a star has many directions and elements, but it's connected at the center, it's not empty glitter'.

Discussion

The women's images on the one hand show the 'end point' of self-fulfilment, and on the other, show the process of reaching self-fulfilment. The images include activities such as fostering self-love next to efforts to find a job. These are cyclical in that qualities of perseverance, hard work, and others that enable finding a job will also bring self-love and calm. Self-love and calm, on the other hand, will help in perseverance. Central skills that will help self-actualisation, but that are in themselves also a definition of self-actualisation, are learning self-regulation and acceptance, but also self-challenge. Thus, the women strive to accept reality, but also to change it. This would make sense in a reality in which one does not have many recourses to change it.

We see that the women describe a search for connection and acceptance, but also independence and power within the relational zone as well as in relation to themselves and in relation to their jobs. This defines self-actualisation as occurring within two separate but interconnected relational zones – self and other. This fits into general humanistic constructions of identity in relation to others, but also more specifically into feminist theories that define women as constructing identity through relationships (Jordan et al. 1991; Saulnier 1996). This can also be developmentally defined as the search for independence and autonomy versus interconnection and acceptance, the latter being more characteristic of our findings.

The use of drawing emerged as an effective feminist methodology in that it enabled the women to 'dare to imagine' how self-actualisation looks for them, and to counteract media images of it (Wiener et al. 2003). We saw that this included elements of relationship, self-regulation, self-acceptance, and elements that enable, but also go beyond financial success.

References

Betensky, M.G. (1995). *What do you See? Phenomenology of Therapeutic Art Experience.* London: Jessica Kingsley.
Brown, L. (2001). Feelings in context: counter-transference and the real world in feminist therapy. *JCLP in Session: Psychotherapy in Practice*, 57 (8), 1005–1012.
Bynner, J., & Parsons, S. (2002). Social exclusion and the transition from school to work: The case of young people not in education, employment, or training (NEET). *Journal of Vocational Behavior*, 60 (2), 289–309.
Creswell, J.W. (1998). *Qualitative Inquiry and Research Design: Choosing Among Five Traditions.* Thousand Oaks: Sage.
Eisner, E. (1997). The promise and perils of alternative forms of data representation. *Educational Researcher*, 26 (6), 4–20.
Golan, M., & Lahav-Kastini, A. (1999). *Group Work with at Risk Young Women.* Publication of the social work department, Tel Aviv University (Hebrew).
Harris, A. (2004). *Future Girl: Young Women in the 21st Century.* New York: Routledge.
Harris, K.(1996). Life after welfare. *American Sociological Review*, 61(3).
Hogan, S. (ed.) (2003). *Gender Issues in Art Therapy.* London: Jessica Kingsley.
Huss, E. (2011). What we see and what we say combining visual information within social work research. *British Journal of Social Work* (Accepted).
Jones, M. (1997). Alice, Doran and Constance from the eve of history. In Hogan, S. (ed.) *Feminist Approaches to Art Therapy.* London: Routledge, pp. 65–79.
Jordan, J., Kaplan, A., Miller, J., Stiver, I., & Surry, J. (1991). *Women's Growth in Connection. Writing from the Stone Center.* New York: Guilford.
Mason, J. (2002). *Qualitative Use of Visual Methods.* London: Sage.
Norman, C.C. (1999). Dispositional tendencies and cognitive processes in future-oriented motivation: A proposed model. *Dissertation-Abstracts-International: Section B: The Science and Engineering*, 59 (8B), 4541.
Pavetti L., & Acs, P. (1997). Moving up, moving out, or going nowhere? A study of the employment patterns of young women and the implications for welfare mothers. Accessed at http://www.urban.org/url.cfm?ID=406697
Saulnier, C. (1996). *Feminist Theories and Social Work.* New York: Haworth.
Spivak, G.C., & Guha, R. (Eds.). (1988). *Selected Subaltern Studies.* New York: Oxford University Press.
Tutty, L., Rothery, M., & Grinnell, R. (1996). *Qualitative Research for Social Workers.* Boston: Allen and Bacon.
Vincent, K., & Osler, A. (2003). *Girls and Exclusion: Rethinking the Agenda.* London: Routledge Palmer.
Wiener, D.J., & Oxford, L.K. (2003). *Action Therapy with Families and Groups: Using Creative Arts Improvisation in Clinical Practice.* Washington: American Psychological Association, pp. 163–196.
Zucker, G.S., & Weiner, B. (1993). Conservatism and perceptions of poverty: an attribution analysis. *Journal of Applied Social Psychology*, 23 (9), 925–943.

Chapter 3

Queering music therapy
Music therapy and LGBTQAI+ Peoples

Annette Whitehead-Pleaux

The populations that music therapists serve are quite heterogeneous. Clients have different intersecting identities of heritage, ability, education, socioeconomic status/class, religion, political affiliation, etc. Within these characteristics are gender identity and sexual orientation. Nearly every music therapist will work with someone who falls under the LGBTQAI+ umbrella whether they are aware of it or not. Recent statistics have shown that these populations are more prevalent than previously thought by many. The research of the William Institute found that the trans★ population in the United States is 0.58% of the total population (Flores et al. 2016). However, Eisenberg et al. (2017) found 2.7% of youth (14–17 years old) identified as transgender or gender nonconforming. The current estimate for people born intersex is 1 in 1500 to 1 in 2000 (Intersex Society of North America [ISNA]). According to the 2017 Gallup Poll, overall, 5.1% of women and 3.9% of men identified as LGBT, with an overall percentage of 4.5% of the United States population identifying as LGBT (Newport 2018).

In their survey of music therapists in the United States, Whitehead-Pleaux et al. (2013) discovered interesting trends within the music therapy community. First, they found that many music therapists anticipated they would encounter LGBTQ clients in mental health settings: (95.4%), neurological care (84.7%), medical/surgical settings (86.8%), settings that serve people with intellectual and developmental disabilities (83.6%), settings that serve at-risk youth (89.5%), older adult care settings (86%), wellness settings (87.6%), substance abuse treatment facilities (87.6%), intimate partner violence (86%), and forensic settings (82.8%). While the numbers are fairly high, it is curious that for many settings, over 15% of music therapists did not anticipate they would encounter LGBTQAI+ individuals in those settings. Second, they found some music therapists who stated they were not trained to work with the LGBTQ community, did not seek supervision when working with LGBTQ clients, or were not prepared to work with these clients, though most "felt they understood the need/challenges/strengths of the population and were comfortable working with them" (Whitehead-Pleaux et al. 2013, p. 413). If some music therapists are not prepared, yet still encountering LGBTQAI+ clients, then education and training about these populations are necessary.

To that end, this chapter explores working with lesbian, gay, bisexual, transgender, queer and questioning, asexual and ally, and intersex (LGBTQAI+) clients as well as the unique experiences of LGBTQAI+ music therapists/students. The chapter has three sections: queer theory framework of sexual orientation and gender identity; music therapy practices with LGBTQAI+ clients; experiences of LGBTQAI+ music therapists and students. The first section focuses on the pedagogic framework of queer theory, describing sexual orientation, gender expression, and gender identity. Fluidity of sexual orientation and gender are explored. Within this theoretical framework, the developmental challenges, including the processes of coming out and transitioning are considered. The following section examines music therapy practices with LGBTQAI+ clients. Next, the author discusses the impact of minority stress on the wellbeing of LGBTQAI+ individuals. Finally, an exploration will follow of the music therapy clinical practice literature, which includes best practices and ways to integrate queer theory into music therapy practice. Best practices for clinical practice, employment, and education are presented along with research about music therapists' attitudes to the LGBTQAI+ communities. This section concludes with a review of innovative practices that integrate queer theory and music therapy.

Queer theory framework of sexual identity and gender identity

In the past, psychologists and psychiatrists have believed that to have sexual orientations other than heterosexual was a disorder. To this day, there are still some who continue to hold that belief despite research showing otherwise. Similarly, psychologists and psychiatrists have in the past and some continue to this day to believe identities outside of the gender binary system are a disorder. Many of us in our music therapy training were taught about the diagnoses of homosexuality or gender dysphoric disorder. I am suggesting the reader suspend the idea that these are disorders and explore sexual orientation and gender identity from a queer theory framework. Queer theory grew out of gender and feminist studies and believes gender identity and sexual orientation are social constructs. Within queer theory, sexual orientation and gender identity are not limited by the societal definitions, which limit us to woman and man, and heterosexual being the only ways to be. Instead, sexual orientation and gender identity are seen as spectrums.

The LGBTQAI+ is a unique grouping of people. It is an umbrella term for many different groups of people. This umbrella group came about when the majority (cisgendered heterosexuals, that is those whose gender corresponds with their birth sex) placed all people whose sexual orientation and gender identity do not conform to societal norms in a category together and labeled them as others. Because it is an artificially created minority group, the LGBTQAI+ communities do not have a singular culture. Similarly, the LGBTQAI+ cultures are not cultures of heritage; many LGBTQAI+ individuals are not born into queer families nor are they raised in queer communities. Because of this non-linear heritage, the cultures are created anew with each generation of LGBTQAI+ people. The cultures of LGBTQAI+ peoples and the members of each subgroup may or may not identify as part of the LGBTQAI+ communities and not all people within the subgroups are welcoming of members of the other subgroups. The acronym LGBTQAI+ developed over time to describe the many different subgroupings of people within this umbrella. Before embarking on the journey through the topics of this chapter, it is important to explore both sexual orientation and gender identity as well as how the letters of LGBTQAI+ (which are Lesbian, Gay, Bi+, Trans*, Queer or Questioning, Asexual or Ally, Intersex, and + for other identities) fit into sexual orientation and gender identity. Within the acronym LGBTQAI+, the identities of LGBQA+ are associated with sexual orientation and QTI+ are associated with gender identity.

Sexual orientation

Sexual orientation describes the attraction a person feels for another person. This can be one or both physical attraction and romantic attraction. Attraction is best conceived as three continuums (male, female, other genders) that range from no attraction to high levels of attraction (see Figure 3.1). The continuum allows for the variability that exists within sexual orientation.

There are different sexual orientation categories within these continuums. Heterosexuals are people who are attracted to the opposite gender (men to women or women to men). A lesbian is a woman who is attracted to women. Gay is a term used for men who are attracted to men. Bi+ is an umbrella term that describes people whose attractions are not bound to the particular gender of the other person. Within bi+ are a variety of terms including bisexual and pansexual. Bisexual means the person is attracted to men and women. Pansexual describes a person who is attracted to all genders. Queer is an umbrella term that describes people whose sexual orientation and/or gender identity do not fit the societal norm of heterosexual and cisgendered. Because queer can be for both gender identity and sexual orientation, some people are confused when someone says they are queer. Asking questions to clarify may be needed. Asexual is someone who "does not experience sexual attraction" (The Asexual Visibility and Education Network [AVEN]).[1] Not all asexual people identify as part of the LGBTAI+ communities. Heterosexual, lesbian, gay, bi+, queer, and asexual are the major categories within sexual orientation. When working with someone who identifies as queer or asexual, it may be useful to explore their sexual orientation and gender identity further to fully understand who they are.

Figure 3.1 Trans Student Educational Resources. The Gender Unicorn www.transstudent.org/gender.

It is important to be aware that there are many additional terms for each sexual orientation. These terms can vary between countries, regions, cultures, and languages. Within the terms, there are some that are acceptable while there are others that are used as hate speech. Some terms, like queer, have been used as hate speech but many within the LGBTQAI+ communities have worked to reclaim the term. Within the reclaimed terms, there are some terms that have been reclaimed that are not acceptable for non-LGBTQAI+ people to use, i.e. dyke. It is important to use the correct term when speaking to someone about their sexual orientation and to understand their comfort with the terms you can use. For example, in the United States, queer is a reclaimed term which many people embrace openly. However, there are some people who reject that word as it was used in a derogatory manner within their lifetime.

Another term associated with sexual orientation is Questioning. People who are questioning are exploring their sexual orientation and/or gender identity. The process of coming to terms with one's sexual orientation and/or gender identity can take time as it is a shift in how one understands themselves and interacts with the world around them as well as how the world around them perceives them. This process can vary from gentle to disruptive and much of it depends upon the individual's internal and external resources.

In their groundbreaking theory of human sexuality, Kinsey and associates studied the sexual behaviors of thousands of men (Kinsey, Pomeroy, and Martin 1948) and women (Kinsey et al. 1953). From the data they collected, they proposed a model of sexual behavior called the Heterosexual–Homosexual Rating Scale (later to be known as the Kinsey Scale). Rather than creating specific categories to place people within, Kinsey et al. created a continuum of sexual behavior. This continuum has seven points that allow for definition which range from 0 – exclusively heterosexual behavior, to 3 – equal amounts of heterosexual and homosexual behavior, to 6 – exclusively homosexual behavior. This allows for the myriad of different levels of attraction and sexual behaviors of human nature. When considering human sexual orientation, it is important to note the majority of humans exist within the realm of experiencing attraction to more than one gender (Kinsey, Pomeroy, and Martin 1948; Kinsey et al. 1953). More recent research has supported the premise that the majority of humans experience attraction to more than one gender. Katz-Wise and Hyde (2015) found 63% of females and 50% of males reported experiencing attraction to both men and women.

Over the past two decades, researchers have proposed that sexual orientation (attractions and identity) can shift over time (Baumeister 2000; Katz-Wise and Hyde 2015; Diamond 2003; Diamond 2015; Peplau 2001; Peplau and Garnets 2000; Savin-Williams 2005; Schwartz, Luyckx, and Vignoles 2011). This has been termed sexual fluidity. At one time, the term bisexual was used to describe sexual fluidity but these two terms are very different (Clarke et al. 2010). Sexual fluidity moves away from the belief that a person's sexual orientation is fixed. Where that fluidity exists and the extent of a person's ability to shift is not fully understood as there is conflicting evidence. Some research has indicated sexual orientation does not change. An example of this is Schwartz et al. who found that aspects of "sexual identity, such as relationships, emotions, behaviors, values, group affiliations, and norms, appear to be relatively fluid" while sexual orientation appears to be stable for many individuals for their lifetime. (Schwartz, S. J., Luyckx, K., and Vignoles 2011, p. 652). However, when Katz-Wise and Hyde (2015) surveyed 188 young adults, they found not only did the subjects report fluidity in attraction (63% of females and 50% of males), subjects with fluidity in attraction reported fluidity in their sexual orientation (48% of females and 34% of males). It is curious that more females than males both reported fluidity both in attraction and sexual orientation and were comfortable with sexual fluidity. Diamond (2008) explored fluidity in attraction and identity in 79 women who identified as non-heterosexual over a period of 10 years. Diamond found at the end of the 10-year period, 67% of the women had changed their sexual orientation identity at least once. 36% of the participants changed their sexual orientation identity two or more times.

When considering sexual orientation and fluidity, the constructs of the categories in which people are placed comes into question. Within queer theory, there is the notion that sexual orientation is a social construct (Foucault 1978).

A social construct is "a social phenomenon or convention originating within and cultivated by society or a particular social group, as opposed to existing inherently or naturally" (*Oxford Dictionary*, 2017). Foucault et al. believed basing identity on sexual behaviors is a phenomenon beginning in the 18th century (Foucault 1978). The ways our societies categorize sexual attractions and actions, categories of heterosexual, gay, lesbian, bi+, and queer are created by humans and these labels often do not encompass the complexity and fluidity of sexual attraction. In younger generations of LGBQA+ people, there is a growing trend of not wanting or not needing to identify one's sexual orientation; often LGBA+ youth and young adults identifying as queer.

Gender identity

For some people, gender identity is a newer concept that is somewhat confusing. Most of us grew up with the experience of having synchronicity between our bodies and our minds. An example is a child is born with a female body, she develops a gender identity of a female, she is seen by the rest of her community as a female, and she wears clothing and adornments of females. We are born, identified as a sex, grow up, and live our lives as that sex, and never think about our gender identity because it is in unison with our bodies. But this is not the experience of many people.

The best starting point to understand gender identity is the body. A child is born and their gender or sex is announced. This is known as sex assigned at birth. Sex assigned at birth is based on a person's anatomy, genetics, and hormones. It can be called sex, gender, or natal gender. Many of the cultures in the world specify there are two genders, male and female; this is known as the gender binary system. This belief that there are two sexes is a fallacy as there are at least three sexes: female, male, and intersex. Sex assigned at birth is a descriptor of the person's body, as depicted in the Gender Unicorn with a DNA icon between its legs.

Intersex is a person whose sex characteristics including chromosomes, gonads, hormone profile, and anatomy do not fit the gender binary system. The Intersex Society of North America defines intersex as "a general term used for a variety of conditions in which a person is born with a reproductive or sexual anatomy that does not seem to fit the typical definitions of female or male" (ISNA). It is estimated that 1 in 1500 to 1 in 2000 births are a child who is intersex (ISNA). Historically, when a child was born intersex, a decision was made by the physicians, with or without the consent of the parents, to alter the child to the gender that the physician determines is the most developed through surgery and/or hormones (ISNA). This practice of assigning a child to a gender has been found to be damaging to the individual, as they grow up constrained by the gender roles of their assigned gender, especially if the child's gender identity differs from their assigned sex. Because of the advocacy of intersex individuals and their allies, these practices are changing and children can grow up intersex and determine for themselves how they wish to identify their gender. Not all intersex people identify themselves as intersex; not all intersex people identify as part of the queer community.

The second term to understand is gender identity. *Gender identity* is the gender which the person identifies as. It is different from sex assigned at birth. Gender identity is how you think about yourself, how a person identifies themselves. In the graphic above, gender identity is within the unicorn's mind. A person's gender identity can be the same as their sex assigned at birth or different. Like sexual orientation, the best way to understand gender identity is through *three continuums* of female, male, and other. To be cisgendered, a person identifies with their sex assigned at birth and accompanying gender attributes. However, there are people whose gender does not align with societal standards, which include trans★ and intersex.

The T in LGBTQAI+ stands for Trans★. Trans★ is an umbrella term that encompasses the many ways a person can transcend gender norms. There are many ways people identify within this umbrella grouping of trans★ which include transgender, bigender, genderqueer, gender nonconforming, gender variant, and agender. In addition, within specific cultures, there exist third genders that lie outside of the gender binary system. Transgender is when one's gender identity does not align with the person's sex assigned at birth and they identify with the opposite sex. Within transgender are terms like MTF (someone whose sex assigned at birth is male and gender identity is female) or FTM (someone whose sex assigned at birth is female and gender identity is male). Not all transgender people transition from one sex to another (via hormones and surgery).

Within the trans★ umbrella there are people who do not identify wholly as either female or male. Some trans★ people experience their identity shifting from male to female, sometimes daily or even more frequently. When a person identifies as both man and woman, they are bi-gender. Genderqueer is an individual who identifies outside of the gender binary system. Gender nonconforming is a person who acts outside of the societal gender norms for their sex assigned at birth. Agender is a person who does not identify with any gender. Gender variant is an umbrella term for those who do not have a cisgendered identity with their sex assigned at birth, nor match the gender norms for male or female. These gender identities are just a few of the many ways to identify gender. New terms are being developed as people explore where they identify upon the continuums of gender.

Like the terms for different sexual orientations, these terms can vary between countries, regions, cultures, and languages. Some terms used as hate speech are not acceptable to use. Some terms have been reclaimed by the trans★ communities and may be acceptable for the music therapist to use. There are some that are acceptable while there are others that are used as hate speech. It is important to use the correct term when speaking to someone about their gender identity.

Transitioning is a term that is associated with being trans★ yet it is important to note not all trans★ individuals transition. To transition is to undergo medical interventions (surgeries and hormone treatments) to modify one's body to bring one's physical gender in line with one's gender identity. Some people transition to ease the dysphoria caused by the misalignment of their natal gender and gender identity. Others are not motivated by dysphoria but a desire to have their physical body match their identity. Some trans★ people choose to have one or many of these treatments while others choose not to. Each person's path to comfort with their gender identity and their body is different. As music therapists, it is our job to support each individual's unique path to their gender identity.

Across the globe exist cultures that acknowledge third genders. In North America, the most prominent is two spirited from Native American/First Nation cultures. Two spirited people have both male and female characteristics and are seen as a third gender with specific privileged roles within their societies. Within Europe, there have existed indigenous cultures that broke from the gender binary system and acknowledged third genders. In ancient Greece, Plato described a third gender in the 4th century, as he describes a creation myth in which there exists three genders, androgynous, male, and female (Scobey-Thal 2014). In Italy, the term femminello is a third gender of a person whose natal gender is male but who assumes the gender roles and dress of women and held privileged places within the society (Independent Lens n.d.). The burrnesha, of Northern Albania, are natal females who vowed chastity, donned male clothing, and were seen as men (Independent Lens n.d.; Scobey-Thal 2014). Burrneshas can be traced to the 1400s and still exist within Albanian culture today. While these cultures are not the majority culture of today, their existence supports that gender is not binary, female or male, but something more complex.

When discussing gender identity, it is important to define gender expression. Gender expression is how people adorn themselves in relation to their gender identity. This can include but is not limited to clothing, accessories, hairstyles, and make-up. If the person is cisgendered, their gender expression usually aligns with their sex assigned at birth. If a person is gender nonconforming, the societal norms for gender expression can be limiting for both men and women.

Lifespan development and coming out

When working with LGBTQAI+ individuals, it is important to understand how their lives and developmental tasks are different from cisgendered heterosexuals. Most of the theories of human development over the lifespan are based on the majority, cisgendered heterosexuals. However, there are some differences in tasks, which include both gender and sexual orientation identity formation which starts in early childhood and can continue through the lifespan. This identity formation can include the process of coming out. Finally, the experiences of a lifetime of oppression and hiding their true selves creates very different needs from the music therapists who work with LGBTQAI+ older adults.

Over the past decade, research into the development of gender identity and sexual orientation has looked to identity formation of gender and sexual orientation. It is believed that children form their gender identity between the ages of 1 and 5 (Stoddard et al. 2011). There is a subgroup of children who are described as gender variant and they begin to experience their gender differences from the ages of 2–10. Gender variance is when one's gender expression does not match their natal gender. A child who is gender variant will engage in play typical of the other gender, express a desire to wear the other gender's clothing, and pretend to be characters of the other gender. Around the time of puberty (10–14), all children form their sexual orientation identity (Stoddard et al. 2011). From this subgroup of gender variant children will emerge heterosexual, sexual minority (gay, lesbian, bi+, and questioning), and trans★ (genderqueer and transgender) youth (Stoddard et al. 2011). Within the queer community, there are some that disagree with aspects of this research as these individuals report experiencing attraction (romantic and/or sexual) prior to puberty.

Children who are gender variant often experience enormous amounts of pressure from parents, family, community, school, and society in general to conform to the static binary gender roles of girl and boy. Within these systems, if the child does not conform, they are alienated and bullied by both adults and children. This alienation and bullying places the child at risk. When working with children, it is vital for music therapists to not only be aware that there are children who are receiving their service who are gender variant, but also to be prepared to work with and support their developmental processes. "Unprepared clinicians risk developing insufficient therapeutic rapport, missing salient information, and inadvertently contributing to risk" (Stoddard et al. 2011, p. 779). To adequately serve these children, music therapists must seek education about gender variance, gender identity, and sexual orientation formation, explore their heterosexual and cisgendered privileges (if applicable), and confront their own biases about LGBTQAI+ populations. Armed with understanding and openness, music therapists can foster healthy therapeutic relationships, understand the subtle cues and communications of children struggling to understand themselves, and become allies and supporters to these children in need. Healthy relationships with adults improve the outcomes of at-risk youth. In addition, music therapists need to be ready to provide referrals to outside organizations that support both gender variant youth and their parents.

Coming out or coming out of the closet is identifying oneself as LGBTQAI+ to other people. It is the process one moves through to come to one's sexual orientation and gender identity (Clarke et al. 2010). Coming out typically occurs in adolescence and young adulthood but can happen throughout the lifespan of an individual. In 1994, D'Augelli proposed a life span model for sexual orientation development. This model allows for a variety of social contexts and represents a broader range of experiences that earlier models did not. D'Augelli's model allows for the fluidity of sexual orientation as well as environmental and biological factors that may influence one's development or a lifetime. Within this model, there are six processes that are not linear and operate as independent processes. The processes are: exiting heterosexuality, developing a personal LGB identity, developing an LGB social identity, becoming an LGB offspring, developing an LGB intimacy status, and entering an LGB community. Within the individual, they may go through all of the processes, or not. A person may have an LGB social identity and have successfully entered the LGB community, but has not engaged in LGB intimacy. Similarly, a person may not exit heterosexuality but still develop an LGB identity, enter an LGB community, and engage in LGB intimacy.

At this time, there is no model that describes the developmental processes of trans* individuals. While it was not created to describe trans* individuals' identity development, many researchers and trans* people use the D'Augelli' model to describe the developmental processes of trans* identity (Bilodeau and Renn 2005; Bilodeau 2005). The six processes, slightly modified, become exiting cisgendered identity, developing a personal trans* identity, developing a trans* social identity, becoming a trans* offspring, developing a trans* intimacy status, and entering a trans* community. At this time, the D'Augelli model is the best model to conceptualize the process of coming out as trans* and the developmental processes of a trans* identity.

Allies

Allies are members of the majority who align themselves with members of a minority, supporting them and often fighting for equality alongside the minority members. Ayvazian (2010) defined ally as part of a dominant group in a society that works to disassemble the systems of oppression which they have power privilege from. Correspondingly, Hardiman, Jackson, and Griffin (2010) describe allies as change agents who have privilege and work in opposition to oppression by the majority. Allies can use the privileges they have to aid the minority they align themselves with. Oswanski and Donnenwerth (2017) explored the role of music therapists as "social justice allies," in essence, music therapist being allies to all minorities. It is important to note that one does not become an ally simply by being a friend of the community. Even though as music therapists, part of our work it to be advocates for our clients, Oswanski and Donnenwerth remind us that "as music therapists, we are not automatically given the title of ally nor do we display ally behaviors and actions unless we have undertaken considerable time working on self-awareness, education/training, and direct action practice" (2017 p. 259).

Allies to the LGBTQAI+ communities can be heterosexual, cisgendered, or other. For example, a heterosexual woman can be an ally to a gay man. A cisgendered man can be an ally to an intersex person. A lesbian can be an ally to a trans★ person. There is essentially a myriad of ways to be an ally. It is important to note that an ally for one of the populations within the LGBTQAI+ umbrella may not be an ally for another population. For example, a heterosexual man who is an ally to bi+ people may not be an ally for trans★ people and may in fact harbor bias or prejudice against trans★ people. Allies are important not only for advocacy for equality, but also for support in everyday experiences.

Music therapy and LGBTQAI+ people

As a profession, music therapy has lagged behind other professions in addressing the needs of LGBTQAI+ individuals, as clients, coworkers, students, and research subjects. In the United States, the first article that delineates best practices was not published until 2012 (Whitehead-Pleaux et al.). At this time, there is minimal research about the care and treatment of LGBTQAI+ individuals in music therapy.

In 2012, a group of music therapists from across the United States unveiled their seminal work, LGBTQ best practices (Whitehead-Pleaux et al. 2012). Within this document, the authors detailed the best practices within music therapy with LGBTQ people. After researching the best practices from related fields, Whitehead-Pleaux et al. (2012) separated the best practices into three sections: clinical, work environment, and education and clinical training. Within these sections, the authors list concrete ways to attain the best practice within music therapy regarding the LGBTQ communities. While to date, this document has not been adopted by a music therapy association as an official best practices guideline, its presence has helped to shape music therapists' approach to treating, working with, and educating LGBTQ individuals.

Within these best practices, Whitehead-Pleaux et al. (2012) discussed ways to modify clinical practice to better serve LGBTQ clients. One suggested practice was modifying assessments/intake forms to include various sexual orientations and gender identity options. Others delineated ways to create open and affirming practices through respect, culturally appropriate language, and creating safe spaces where hate speech is not tolerated. The authors emphasize the importance of becoming educated not just about sexual orientation and gender identities, but also to learn about the cultures, history, music, and LGBTQ friendly organizations in your community. Within the clinical section, the authors describe best practices for research, which include being aware of bias and researching LGBTQ individuals with an understanding of their cultures and histories.

Within the work environment section, the authors describe business practices that are supportive to LGBTQ coworkers and employees. Similar to the clinical best practices, these best practices describe creating open and affirming work environments through respect, culturally appropriate language, and creating safe spaces where hate speech is not tolerated. Equal benefits, salary/wage, and hiring practices are some policies that create equitable environments.

The best practices for education and clinical training cover many aspects of higher education and internship. When recruiting, it is important to have a faculty and student body that reflect the gender identity and sexual orientation diversity that exist in the greater population. Recruitment materials incorporating photos of LGBTQ individuals are key to supporting the building of a diverse student body and faculty. The music therapy curriculum needs to include information about LGBTQ cultures and experiences which includes music, history, developmental processes, bias, and oppression.

This same group of music therapists conducted an international study which explored music therapists' attitudes about the LGBTQ communities. In their preliminary findings, Whitehead-Pleaux et al. (2012) discovered a disturbing trend. First, the majority of music therapists reported they received little to no training on working with LGBTQ individuals and did not understand the needs, challenges, and strengths of these populations. Next, the majority did not feel they were sufficiently prepared to work with this population, nor did they seek supervision about LGBTQ related issues. Third, the majority did not know much about LGBTQ cultures (including music). Fourth, despite 64% reporting they used open and affirming practices, very few could identify three open and affirming practices to use with LGBTQ clients. In addition to not knowing open and affirming practices, the language used by music therapists indicated bias against LGBTQ individuals. Finally, the music therapists reported they felt very comfortable working with LGBTQ clients. If music therapists are not sufficiently prepared, do not have training, do not understand the needs/challenges/strengths, do not seek supervision, do not know about the cultures, and do not know open and affirming practices, but are saying they are very comfortable working with LGBTQ clients, there is a disconnect that is deeply troubling.

In 2016, Bain, Grzanka, and Crow published the first article that proposed several music therapy treatments to address the developmental processes of queer youth. By adapting queer theory to the processes of music therapy, Bain et al. (2016) proposed interventions that embrace sexual orientation fluidity and complexity, allow for expression of oppression, empower through free expression of sexual orientation and gender identity, provide opportunities for positive interpersonal relationships that negate societal pressures, and support unique identities by supporting causes that are common.

Final thoughts

While there is little research about working with LGBTQAI+ individuals, music therapists work with them every day. There are LGBTQAI+ older adults in hospices, teens in residential settings, in hospital for surgery, raising children with developmental and intellectual disabilities, in prisons, with dementia in memory care units, and beyond. Some of the children that music therapists work with are gender variant and have trans★ identities. Within the college and university music therapy programs, music therapy educators are teaching LGBTQAI+ students. Whether we are aware of it or not, it is a fact that we all have and will work with LGBTQAI+ clients and students.

Knowing this fact, the choice is clear. We must seek further education and modify our practices to be inclusive and address the needs of LGBTQAI+ individuals. It is my hope that this chapter has brought further understanding of different sexual orientations and gender identities, some developmental processes, and music therapy practices. This is an area of music therapy research that needs further development for us to better understand how we can support LGBTQAI+ clients better through music therapy.

Note

1 Asexual Visibility and Education Network http://www.asexuality.org.

References

Ayvazian, A. 2010. "Interrupting the Cycle of Oppression: The Role of Allies as Agents of Change." Chapter 135 in *Readings for Diversity and Social Justice*. 2nd ed. New York: Routledge.

Bain, C., Grzanka, P., and Crowe, B. J. 2016. "Toward a Queer Music Therapy: The Implications of Queer Theory for Radically Inclusive Music Therapy." *The Arts in Psychotherapy*, 50, 22–33.

Baumeister, R. F. 2000. "Gender Difference in Erotic Plasticity: The Female Sex Drive as Socially Flexible and Responsive." *Psychological Bulletin*, 126(3), 347–374.

Bilodeau, B. 2005. Beyond the Gender Binary: A Case Study of Two Transgender Students at a Midwestern Research University. *Journal of Gay & Lesbian Issues in Education*, 3(1), 29–44.

Bilodeau, B. L. and Renn, K. A. 2005. "Analysis of LGBT Identity Development Models and Implications for Practice." *Gender Identity and Sexual Orientation: Research, Policy, and Personal*, 2005(111), 25–39.

Clarke, V., Ellis, S. J., Peel, E., and Riggs, D. W. 2010. *Lesbian, Gay, Bisexual, Trans, and Queer Psychology: An Introduction*. Cambridge: University Press.

D'Augelli, A. R. (1994). Identity Development and Sexual Orientation: Toward a Model of Lesbian, Gay, and Bisexual Development. In E. J. Trickett, R. J. Watts, and D. Birman (eds) *Human Diversity: Perspectives on People in Context* (pp. 312–333). San Francisco: Jossey-Bass.

Diamond, L. M. 2003. "Was it a Phase? Young Women's Relinquishment of Lesbian/Bisexual Identities over a 5-year Period." *Journal of Personality and Social Psychology*, 84(2), 352–64.

Diamond, L. M. 2008. "Female Bisexuality from Adolescence to Adulthood: Results from a 10-year Longitudinal Study." *Developmental Psychology*, 44(1), 5–14.

Diamond, L. M. 2015. "Sexual Fluidity." In P. Whelehan and A. Bolin (eds) *The International Encyclopedia of Human Sexuality*. Hoboken: John Wiley & Sons, 1115–1354.

Eisenberg, M. E., Gower, A. L., McMorris, B. J., Rider, G. N., Shea, G., and Coleman, E. 2017. "Risk and Protective Factors in the Lives of Transgender/Gender Nonconforming Adolescents." *Journal of Adolescent Health*, 6(4), 521–526.

Flores, A. R., Herman, J. L., Gates, G. J., and Brown, T. N. T. 2016. *How Many Adults Identify as Transgender in the United States?* Accessed on 09/25/18 at https://williamsinstitute.law.ucla.edu/wp-content/uploads/How-Many-Adults-Identify-as-Transgender-in-the-United-States.pdf

Foucault, Michel. 1978. *The History of Sexuality*. New York: Pantheon Books.

Hardiman, R., Jackson, B. W., and Griffin, P. 2010. "Conceptual Foundations." Chapter 2 in *Readings for Diversity and Social Justice*. 2nd ed. New York: Routledge.

Independent Lens. n.d. *A Map of Gender-Diverse Cultures*. Accessed on 09/07/17 at http://www.pbs.org/independentlens/content/two-spirits_map-html/

Intersex Society of North America. 2008. *What Is Intersex?* Accessed on 06/17/14 at http://www.isna.org/faq/what_is_intersex

Katz-Wise, S. L. and Hyde, J. S. 2015. "Sexual Fluidity and Related Attitudes and Beliefs Among Young Adults with a Same-Gender Orientation." *Archives of Sexual Behaviors*, 44(5), 1459–1470. doi: 10.1007/s10508-014-0420-1

Kinsey, A. C., Pomeroy, W. B., and Martin, C. E. (1948). *Sexual Behavior in the Human Male*. Philadelphia: W. B. Saunders.

Kinsey, A. C., Pomeroy, W. B., Martin, C. E., and Gebhard, P. H. (1953). *Sexual Behavior in the Human Female*. Philadelphia: W. B. Saunders.

Newport, F. 2018. *In U.S., Estimate of LGBT Population Rises to 4.5%*. Accessed on 09/25/18 at https://news.gallup.com/poll/234863/estimate-lgbt-population-rises.aspx

Oswanski, L. and Donnenwerth, A. 2017. "Allies in Social Justice." Chapter 18 in *Cultural Intersections in Music Therapy: Music, Health, and the Person*. Dallas: Barcelona Publishers.

Oxford Dictionary. 2017. Accessed on at https://en.oxforddictionaries.com/definition/social_construct

Peplau, L. A. 2001. "Rethinking Women's Sexual Orientation: An Interdisciplinary, Relationship-Focused Approach." *Personal Relationships*, 8(1), 1–19.

Peplau, L. A. and Garnets, I. D. 2000. A new Paradigm for Understanding Women's Sexuality and Sexual Orientation. *Journal of Social Issues*, 56(2), 329–350.

Savin-Williams, R. C. 2005. *The New Gay Teenager*. Cambridge: Harvard University Press.

Schwartz, S. J., Luyckx, K., and Vignoles, V. L. 2011. *Handbook of Identity Theory and Research*. New York: Springer Science & Business Media.

Scobey-Thal, J. 2014. *Third Gender: A Short History. Foreign Policy*. Accessed on 09/07/17 at http://foreignpolicy.com/2014/06/30/third-gender-a-short-history/

Stoddard, J., Leibowitz, S. F., Ton, H., and Snowdon, S. 2011. "Improving Medical Education about Gender-Variant Youth and Transgender Adolescents." *Child and Adolescent Psychiatric Clinics of North America*, 20(4), 779–791.

The Asexual Visibility and Education Network. 2012. *Definitions and FAQ*. Accessed on 30/06/14 at http://www.asexuality.org/home/general.html#def

Whitehead-Pleaux, A., Donnenwerth, A., Robinson, B., Hardy, S., Oswanski, L., Forinash, M., Hearns, M., Anderson, N., and York, E. 2012. "Lesbian, Gay, Bisexual,

Transgender, and Questioning: Best Practices in Music Therapy." *Music Therapy Perspective*, 2, 158–166.

Whitehead-Pleaux, A., Donnenwerth, A., Robinson, B., Hardy, S., Oswanski, L., Forinash, M., Hearns, M., Anderson, N., and Tan, X. 2013. Serving the LGBTQ Community: Exploring Attitudes and Education within the Music Therapy Profession Preliminary Report. *Arts in Psychotherapy*, 40(4), 409–414.

Chapter 4

Analysing gender oppression in music therapy research and practice

Sue Baines and Jane Edwards

Introduction

Health research approaches and practices have historically developed in a culture of privilege, often described as *white male privilege* (McIntosh 1988). Privilege represents the power and increased status disproportionally afforded to specific groups within culture (Rogers 1984; Pease 2010). White male privilege (McIntosh 1988), hidden within the dominant context of the patriarchy, has profoundly influenced many areas of health research including medical conditions selected for research, research protocols, informed consent and data collection procedures, discussion of results and subsequent conclusions, and real-world application of outcomes (for review see Baines and Edwards 2015).

The primary frame of reference in Western therapeutic and healthcare services is the mainstream allopathic medical model. Alongside medical developments that are ethical, a well-documented history of abuse and discrimination has been reported across medical research (Erickson 1966; Broverman et al. 1970; Chesler 1971; Halleck 1971; Steiner 1974; Wyckoff 1974; Sedgewick 1982; Gilligan 1979; Kaplan, 1983). Current publications continue to report unethical research protocols with a biased interpretation of outcomes and the generation and application of biased psychological theories with unremarked discriminatory gender, race, socioeconomic, and other features (Holm et al. 2017).

Privilege infuses healthcare practice resulting in a focus on individual symptoms and sufferings with minimal or non-existent examination and interrogation of the social structures that produce and compound inequitable distribution of health support and services (Baines 2016). White privilege and male privilege bolster each other, sustained by denial (McIntosh 1998). Access to medical support and care is often determined by privilege. For example, therapeutic drugs can consume up to forty percent of the healthcare budget in developing countries, while a large proportion of the community does not have access to basic medicines (Maiti et al. 2015). Intersectional dimensions of socioeconomic status, gender, race, and age impact the availability of healthcare coverage, the type and accessibility of health insurance or its absence, and where one can access healthcare. For example, whether people attend planned appointments or show up at the Emergency Room with severe symptoms will influence the type and scope of care provided (Martinez-Hume at al. 2017). Cultural factors have a ubiquitous influence on all stages of the disease experience, from first symptoms to medical decisions, duration of illness, and treatment adherence by the patient (Touboul-Lundgren et al. 2015).

Stereotyping, prototyping, and profiling have consequences for treatment choices and medical decisions (Boutin-Foster, Foster, and Konopasek 2008; Freeman et al. 2017). Medical and therapeutic treatments are not culturally neutral. Shared belief systems regarding health can impact every aspect of healthcare service delivery with culture-based norms hidden in patient-doctor interactions (Lorié et al. 2017). Until inclusive research processes incorporating critical methodologies are undertaken across healthcare practices, cultural validity will not be achieved. Studies collaborating with minority population groups in respectful and inclusive ways have yet to be undertaken (Murphy et al. 2015).

Culturally insensitive healthcare contributes to health inequalities (Tucker et al. 2015). Power is ubiquitous; it exists in all practice settings. Even with the best of intentions, healthcare practitioners can cause harm (Prilleltensky 2008). As interpersonal therapies such as music therapy and psychotherapy rely on the therapist's use of the self, it is incumbent on training programs, trainers, and students to first be aware of their own cultural identity, rather than focusing on cultural sensitivity training and awareness that only perceive the "other" (Adams 2015).

There are multiple indications that the practice of medicine is undergoing an international cultural revolution (Baines 2016). The culture of health is being studied (Đorđević et al. 2015) with the development of a range of educational resources to guide culture-change strategies for healthcare workers (Grayson et al. 2015). Teaching cultural competence and accountability is now included in medical and other healthcare trainings (Maiti et al. 2015). The National Initiative on Gender, Culture, and Leadership in Medicine, *C–Change* (for culture change) promotes a change in the culture of academic medicine. *C-Change* aims to foster inclusive, humanistic, relational, and energizing workplace cultures for medical school faculty and trainees while increasing diversity of leadership in academic medicine (Pololi et al. 2013).

Gender is a contested term with multiple meanings and impacts including political, literal, and social. There are not just two genders, female and male; rather gender can be defined more broadly. Personal and collective experiences are relevant to the construction of gender, not just cultural essentialized norms. This has led to the accepted use of more nuanced ideas within gender theory such as gender identity and gender expression (Keuroghlian, Ard, and Makadon 2017). In practice, rather than perceiving a person's gender fluidity as a type of social nonconformity or as a disorder, it is viewed as an expression of self and identity experienced by the person, not imposed by others

(Parker 2016). However, healthcare continues to lag behind the human rights agenda of gender that is beyond the traditional male-female binary identification (Snelgrove et al. 2012).

Music, culture, and gender

Music exists in culture and is shaped by and influences culture (Cross 2001). Music making and consumption is a powerful social-political practice (McClary 1991) that cannot be divorced from its social context (Higgins 1991). Music offers societies a channel for values and underpinning beliefs to become evident to their members (Da Silva, Blasi, and Dees 1984; Guerra and Silva 2015). Music can influence, support, reflect, and guide social, political, economic, linguistic, religious, and other kinds of behavior (Buchanan 2016). From basic physical to elusive abstract, from simple to complex, the experience of music is reliant on the perceiver's consideration and cultural context. Music's role is contextualized by multiple sociocultural and political circumstances (Baines 2016). Music can promote cultural exchange (Gilboa, Yehuda, and Amir 2009) and can be used both as a means of emancipation and a mechanism for domination (Dankoff 2011), with recognition that much of the music produced commercially has progressed within a framework of white male privilege.

Music can transmit oppressive information, including information about gender. There is a gender gap between men and women's legitimization in different genres of music. Studies have revealed gender disparities in popular music (Mduli 2009; Schmutz and Faupel 2010), orchestral music (Davidson and Edgar 2003), jazz (Wehr-Flowers 2006), the fiddle contest circuit in Canada (Johnson 2000), country music (Pruitt 2007), electronic music (Bosma 2016), and traditional Irish Pub music (O'Shea 2008). There is concern that hip-hop ideology reflects the socioeconomic interests of white supremacist, patriarchal, multinational, corporate capitalist interests (Miller-Young 2008). Negative portrayals of women in Zimbabwean male-produced urban grooves have resulted from the integration of Western popular music standards contributing to the erosion of women's equality (Chari 2008; Naidoo 2010). Research exploring men's appropriation of female music in Malawi and Swazi indicated initiatives to further develop female music for female empowerment are required (Lwanda 2003; Mduli 2007; Ashley 2011).

Music therapy is one of the post-war therapies of the 20th century that developed alongside occupational therapy and other newly emerging professions aimed at helping those returning from war (Edwards 2007). Since that time, music therapists writing about practice and research were hesitant to engage feminist perspectives (Curtis 1990; Hadley 2006a) and took even longer to discuss problematic gender perspectives in research and practice (Whitehead-Pleaux et al. 2013). The overall evolution of a feminist consciousness in music therapy has been relatively slow, a tempo that continues. Limited acknowledgment of feminist theory in music therapy has presented possible reasons why the foundational tenet of feminism, gender analysis, particularly with the modern intent of decreasing binary theories of gender, is rarely present in music therapy publications.

Historically, the four major models of practice in music therapy rely on Eurocentric music and therapeutic practices; practices developed adhering to tenets of white male privilege. Musically, they have a common theme of using either improvised music based on European music traditions or pre-composed, mostly pre-1900's European music. These main approaches have provided an historical foundation from which subsequent music therapy theory was developed.

Nordoff-Robbins Music Therapy is based on the philosophical premise that everyone can respond to music (Nordoff and Robbins 1971, 1985). The approach addresses specific therapeutic needs using improvised music based on European music traditions, pre-composed European music from previous centuries, or compositions written by Paul Nordoff in a classical neo-Romantic style (Nordoff and Robbins 1971, 1985). Most of the early clients were children, many of whom were from backgrounds with little connection to these traditions (Baines 2013). Alvin (1978) in her work with autistic children and Priestley (1975) in her Analytic Music Therapy approach also used improvised music based on European music traditions. Guided Imagery and Music (Bonny 1975; Bonny and Savary 1973) continues to primarily employ pre-composed European music from previous centuries although some multi-cultural music is being explored (Grocke and Moe 2015).

Reliance on these European music traditions results in the vast majority of clients not being able to support themselves musically when away from their music therapist. This music requires significant training to play pleasurably and music sales indicate that European historical music is not popular with the wider general public. Instead hip-hop is frequently described as the most listened to music in the world (Speers 2017). Some authors have pointed out the lack of music beyond Eurocentric choices in music therapy (Viega 2016), which echoes the previously reported use of therapeutic models of practice with a similar Eurocentric framework developed with gender, race, socioeconomic, and other unremarked biases.

Music therapy and feminist theory

Music therapists have explored the relevance of feminist theory to the practice of music therapy. Starting with a few key research papers in the 1990s (Baines 1992; Curtis 1990, 1997), it has now grown to an increasingly more active and robust community of researcher and practitioner perspectives shared across different dissemination platforms (for example, Hadley and Hahna 2016). Interspersed with music therapy literature titled feminist are publications that explicitly reference gender in their research encompassing naïve to sophisticated analysis. Bruscia's (1995) reference to the importance of examining gender orientation was described in the conclusion of his chapter in a binary manner, perhaps typical of the times. An appendix to the *Handbook of Music Therapy* (Bunt 2002) mentioned "some gender issues in music therapy" (310) only citing Bruscia's (1995). Bunt was seemingly unaware of the work of Baines (1992) and Curtis (1990, 1997).

Hadley and Edwards (2004) furthered feminist theory in music therapy while Hahna (2004) explored a feminist perspective specifically investigating tropes and norms operating in the Bonny Method of Guided Imagery. Hadley's (2006a) landmark edited text followed soon after, which provided a range of feminist perspectives from multiple authors. The book drew together a group of female writers from different backgrounds, and in various stages of capacity to undertake feminist analysis. Each addressed the role of feminism in the field of music therapy exploring practice, research, theory, and pedagogy. For example, Rolvsjord's (2006) analysis explored post-structuralist feminists' critique of how binary opposition, male/female, perpetuates power and privilege towards maleness in our dominantly patriarchal world while inhibiting celebration of the existing diversity and multiplicity of gender identities.

Curtis and Harrison (2006) linked music therapy with social work to support women survivors of violence, Edwards and Hadley (2007) critiqued the lack of feminist critical analysis in music therapy, Curtis (2007) researched working with childhood survivors of sexual abuse subsequently focusing on working with women survivors (Curtis 2008), and Hadley (2008) debated the role of feminism in music therapy in the *British Journal of Music Therapy* (45–49). Although not identified as feminist analysis, Aigen's (2008) caution for music therapists to acknowledge their aesthetic values and those of their clients consciously addressed how traditional aesthetic standards can be elitist and disempowering for many people, offering a deep critical analysis needed to move the field of music therapy forward politically. Unfortunately, this critique lacked a gender analysis.

O'Grady (2011) offered a depth analysis of the performance of gender in music exploring how dividing gender into binary opposites enables dominant discourses, such as patriarchy, to privilege one false opposite against another. O'Grady shared Judith Butler's (1990) argument that there is no essence underlying the expression of gender and that expressions of gender are not the result of an autonomous source such as biological sex. Gender is an expression of the self that performs fluidly in interaction with the world. O'Grady reviewed gendering music, gendering music-making, gendering the musical object, gendering musical instruments, gendering musical learning and skills, gendering music-listening, gendering musical preferences, gendering reasons for listening, gendering ways of listening, musicking gender, constructing gender through music-making – from Western opera to Madonna – and constructing gender through music listening. Her results indicate the need for a gender analysis in all aspects of music therapy.

Developing a feminist pedagogical approach in music therapy was initiated by Hadley (2006b) and furthered by Hahna (2011) in her doctoral research and subsequent publications (Hahna and Schwantes 2011; Hahna 2013). Concurrently, feminist analysis of music therapy practice and research promoting a social justice approach was flourishing (Curtis 2012, 2013a; Hadley 2013) and more in-depth gender studies appeared (Curtis 2013b, 2013c, 2015a, 2015b; Rolvsjord and Halstead 2013a, 2013b; Halstead and Rolvsjord 2017; Rolvsjord and Stige 2015). A special issue on gender in the creative arts therapies published by *The Arts in Psychotherapy* in 2013 was guest edited by Professor Sandi Curtis. Still other writing reviewed aspects of gender in relationship to specific music therapy practices (Curtis 2013d; Rolvsjord and Stige 2015; Baker 2014; Streeter 2013; Kim 2013; York and Curtis 2015), leading to a proposal for radically inclusive music therapy (Bain, Grzanka, and Crowe 2016).

Ahessy (2011) initiated open dialog in music therapy regarding practice with lesbian, gay, and bisexual persons. His research revealed that a large proportion of music therapy educators and practitioners do not specifically address issues of sexual orientation and/or gender. He proposed this low priority was a response to time constraints and curricular pressure. If one is to presume that there is a similar proportion of LGBTI individuals in every country, it is concerning that almost all of the programs that address issues specific to LGB clients are located in Canada and the United States. This disparity may be because of the prevalence of courses in LGB studies and the longer history of LGB psychology and psychotherapy in universities in these countries.

Hadley (2013) and Whitehead-Pleaux et al. (2013) extended this work broadening gender awareness to LGBTQI. Whitehead-Pleaux et al.'s (2013) survey of music therapists revealed few respondents were familiar with the term heteronormativity, fewer than half integrated gender-neutral language in the workplace, and almost half did not consider the clients' sexual orientation in therapy highlighting the power of the dominant heterosexual culture. Preliminary results reveal that the field of music therapy needs to develop competencies around LGBTQ issues with affirmative approaches in which LGBTQ identities are valued, supported, and affirmed in all aspects of music therapy (Whitehead-Pleaux et al. 2013); results echoed by Bain et al. (2016).

The underlying factors involved in gender disparities continue to confound. There is little empirical research in this area leaving policymakers with few strategies to address the problem. Better ways to assess quality of care across different aspects of managed care are needed, and in particular, designed to be gender specific (Mitchell and Schlesinger 2005). Contemporary critical inquiry must examine ever-present power inequities addressing forces of oppression that systematically block, restrain, and contain members of marginalized groups (Đorđević et al. 2015). Practices must constantly defend and develop strategies to amplify the voice of the voiceless and bring the needs of marginalized clients and communities to the attention of decision makers (Baines 1988). The goal is respectful practice created organically through courteous competence informed by cultural sensitivity and awareness (Baines 2014). This awareness must include a gender analysis. As Edwards and Hadley have proposed,

> The therapist is not a benign helper but rather actively undertakes social and political work. This happens because the helper believes that through belonging to a particular professional occupation and orientation, they are qualified to prompt and support change in others. Believing such interventions are necessary, required, and helpful, the helper takes particular actions. We are not separate from these interactions and experiences in music therapy, but actively engage in their construction, interpretation, and consequently their meaning.
>
> (Edwards and Hadley 2007)

Research is a social action that involves interactions and relationships with ethical, procedural, and political issues (Barton 2005). The minority status of the profession of music therapy within healthcare offers a unique perspective that invites dominant professions to consider power differentials and imbalances in their practices. By ignoring professions such as music therapy in favor of more orthodox traditions of therapy allied with the medical model, oppression of the socially radical and creative occurs. Similarly, within the field of music therapy, more Eurocentric approaches closely allied with the medical model may be privileged as a result of this bias (Baines and Edwards 2015). Highlighting the use of terminology aligned with the medical model creeping into music therapy and other arts therapies has included criticism of the use of the terms such as "intervention" (Kenny 2015).

Employing critical cultural analyses within research and treatment practices can begin to address oppression and inequities. Research reports that respect for service users' experiences and processes that integrate service user preferences can increase healthy responses and in turn a culture of healthier communities. Practitioners in all aspects of healthcare practice can benefit from self-reflective analysis outside conventional ethical terms by profoundly and reliably participating in critical examination of the influence of their worldviews, political perspectives, and privilege on their practice (Baines 2014; Adams 2015). A gender analysis must be a cornerstone of this reflection.

Music therapy practice is embedded in the culture of the music therapist (Ruud 1988, 1998; Stige 2002). As the health workplace is increasingly multicultural in many countries, music therapists must prepare themselves to support the music and cultural practices of service users. A cultural shift is occurring in music and music therapy research as critical methodologies are applied. As music's foundational and significant role in human experience politicizes the role of the music therapist (Aigen 2005), music therapists must continually reflect on their personal culture and the culture of music therapy in their community (Baines 2016).

Reflective feminist practices address disparities and inequities rather than ignoring negative influences, which can insidiously creep into practice in unacknowledged ways. Such reflective practices are required to dismantle social barriers, empowering the voice of marginalized service users to develop co-creative, efficacious, respectful music therapy practice and research processes toward creating a more socially just future (Baines 2013).

Typically, universities and their faculty members conduct research studies. It is widely acknowledged that the higher education context requires further emancipation from its patriarchal roots. There are multiple studies and personal reflections that show the structure and concept of the university is mired in sexist attitudes and behavior (Brabazon 2014; Edwards 2017). As Brabazon has noted, "sometimes in universities, it feels like feminism never happened." (Brabazon 2014: 65). Teelken and Deem (2013) have indicated that universities continue to be rife with sexism, but are much more successful at hiding it. Many authors attest to the impossibility of universities being able to address and dismantle patriarchal structures (Chepp and Andrist 2016).

Who writes and who cites? A gender audit of music therapy journal papers

Citation patterns and authorship are two key areas of gender disparity identified in international scholarship. However, currently these analyses only identify gender by the first name of the authors. Therefore, future studies should seek to find ways to identify author gender more broadly than only the false binary of fe/male.

Citation metrics have offered a way to examine gender dynamics within professions in multiple studies. Within existing review studies it has been shown that male authors tend to be cited more than female authors in large fields such as epidemiology (Schisterman et al. 2017) and biomedical sciences (Larivière et al. 2013). When field leaders' writings normalize the predominance of male citations, problems can occur for the profession body overall. Women researchers can feel overlooked or invisible when their work is never or rarely cited by males, and the profession as a whole experiences limitations when gender normative concepts in thinking and research endeavors remain outside interrogation and reflection. In the university environment, promotion is dependent not just on the number of publications but also citations. Citations are perceived as a marker of quality, with more citations being indicative of successful contribution within the field. If male authors unconsciously but systematically avoid citing female authors, then women will have a smaller pool of citations, and their promotional prospects including attaining tenure may subsequently be impaired. This will then reinforce the heteronormative idea that women's work is not of the same quality as men. For example, there is a frequently cited study that showed women applying for postdoctoral positions needed to be cited 2.5 times more than male academic colleagues to be perceived as having equal status (Wennerås and Wold 1997).

Few published research papers have mapped gender trends in music therapy publications. In 2007 Edwards and Hadley reviewed three journals: *Journal of Music Therapy*, *British Journal of Music Therapy*, and *Nordic Journal of Music Therapy* from 2000–2005. Combined data from the three journals using author first names indicated 280 authors, 168 female (60%), and 112 male (40%). Previously James (1985) found that in papers published in the *Journal of Music Therapy* between 1974 and 1984 women published ten percent more papers than men. He suggested this finding indicated there was parity between men and women in publishing. Curtis (2000) and Hadley and Edwards (2007) subsequently challenged this conclusion since there are so many more women than men in the profession. The exact numbers are difficult to ascertain internationally but estimates include a ratio of ten males to ninety females in the USA (Curtis 2000; Hadley and Edwards 2007).

Citations

Few music therapy papers have examined citation statistics in the field. However, it is easy to find examples of papers in music therapy with far fewer women authors cited, in spite of music therapy frequently described as female dominated (Cameron 2014). For example, one paper with thirty-three references cited only six women authors across the entire paper while seventeen male authors were referenced, some more than once (Aigen 2014). In another paper, when examining the first author citations, only eight female authors were cited across fifty-two references (Stige 2015). To provide a comparison, one of the most recent papers co-authored by one of the authors with a female colleague was also audited (McCaffrey and Edwards 2016). The paper included thirty-eight references. One reference was a citation of a concert performance so was not included in the audit. The paper included eleven references with male first author, and twenty-six references with female first authors. Removing authors included more than once, the reference list reflected twenty female first authors and eleven males. Author gender was not a conscious consideration when the reference list was developed.

In order to examine citation patterns more systematically, a review was undertaken of the reference lists of five papers from each of the leading journal titles in music therapy with oversight by a commercial publishing house. The journals included: *Nordic Journal of Music Therapy* (NJMT), *Journal of Music Therapy* (JMT), *Music Therapy Perspectives* (MTP), *The British Journal of Music Therapy* (BJMT), and *The Arts in Psychotherapy* (AiP).

Selection was based on the following criteria: 1. The paper was the most recently published relevant paper at the time of the search, and 2. The paper reported outcomes of clinical practice. Gender of the authors was not included in the selection criteria. Papers presented at a conference but not published were excluded, as were papers or books authored by a professional association.

There were 236 references cited across the five papers. Where there were more than two authors in a citation, a record was made of the gender of the first author and final author. Where the gender of the author could not be found, the reference was excluded (N=7). References produced by a professional association were excluded, for example DSM 5. Exclusion also occurred in the case a paper was in the form of a professional or conference presentation, or website, rather than a scholarly publication.

Twelve people, five males and seven females, with no duplicated names in the author list, authored the selected papers. Three papers were sole authored by males (Ahessy 2017; Cobbett 2016; Sadovnik 2016), one paper was authored by three females and one male (Aalbers et al. 2017), and the other had five authors, four female, and one male (Baker et al. 2017).

Three of the five papers cited more male than female authors (Aalbers et al. 2017; Cobbett 2016; Sadovnik 2016). The largest discrepancy between male and female authors in the reference list was Cobbett (2016) with fifteen female authors referenced as against forty-two male authors. Across all papers combined there were 156 references that were attributable to female authors, and 167 references that were attributable to male authors.

The reference lists revealed a few slips and errors. However, of most concern, in one of the papers a reference to a book with three authors – a woman and two men – omitted the first female author and only included the two male authors.

This type of audit is challenging due to multiple factors. Many citations did not reference music therapy papers or books so gender dimensions relevant to music therapy may not be easily examined. There were multiple citations to psychology texts from decades ago when most academic fields were predominantly male, leading the authors to recommend that if music therapy wants to be taken seriously, attention to contemporary source materials to inform theoretical perspectives is required.

What needs to change?

Our observations from this brief review should encourage reviewers to scrutinize the reference list carefully. Are there relevant authors who are not cited? Are the references recent and relevant? How does the literature review reflect the state-of-the-art in the field of music therapy? Does the author include a list of publications by the same author? If so, are all of the references discrete? Could they cite only the most recent? Additionally, one strategy that is galling is to refer to a female author's work from many years ago, or to only cite her PhD thesis, when she has published multiple recent papers. The authors perceive this as a silencing and marginalizing strategy. Authors, reviewers, and editors will need to undertake continuing, serious, and focused work to ensure that references are up-to-date and our field is not continually plagued with unconscious bias against female authors.

Auditing author gender in 2016 music therapy journal papers

Examination of authorship across the same five journals in 2016 noted sole author gender and the gender of the first author in multiple authored papers (Table 4.1). Seventy-three papers about music therapy appeared across seventeen journal issues in 2016. Two journals published no male sole authored music therapy papers (JMT and AiP). Fifty-three papers were sole authored or first author led by female authors, and twenty papers were sole authored or first author led by male authors. Two journals published no multiple authored papers in which the first author was male (BJMT and MTP). Female authors appeared in all categories.

Interpretation of these results is challenging. It is not possible to know exactly how many papers these journals received, and/or whether there is any gender discrepancy between being accepted or rejected. However, we find that the high level of collaborative female-led research is a promising trend in this review of papers in 2016.

Previous concerns have included that gender balance in music therapy publications does not reflect the high proportion of women practitioners and researchers, with qualified males estimated to be between only ten to thirteen percent of the total number of music therapists (Curtis 2000; Edwards and Hadley 2007). This audit of published papers from 2016 suggests that female authorial voices are included in the same proportions as the previous gender audit by Edwards and Hadley (2007). As such, male representation in authorship exceeds male representation within the profession. There is more to be done to include and amplify women's voices in music therapy.

Table 4.1 Gender of sole and first authors across five music therapy journals in 2016

	NJMT	AiP		JMT	BJMT	MTP	Total
Gender of the editor	F/M	F		F	F	M	4F/2M
Issues	4	5		4	2	2	17
Papers N=	16	53 total for the journal - 14 music therapy relevant papers		16	8	19	73
Female 1st author	2	4		4	3	7	20
Male 1st author	4	0		0	2	5	11
Multiple author 1st author female	8	5		10	3	7	33
Multiple author 1st author male	2	5		2	0	0	9

Conclusion

Understanding the ways in which the patriarchy is manifest within a profession is the responsibility of all its actors and members. Attempts to interrogate and critique the status quo must be supported by employers, professional associations, colleagues, and professional publications. This review contends that the responsibility belongs to everyone. Examining gender specifically is only one way to investigate power imbalance and to identify areas ripe for much-needed change. Social justice is a process as well as a practice refined through mindfulness and challenging the status quo. It requires commitment to cultural sensitivity and humility, through radically addressing unearned privilege that creates inequity and imbalance in culture. In music therapy, we must be continually mindful of representation as well as balance.

References

Aalbers, S., Spreen, M., Bosveld-van Haandel, L., and Bogaerts, S. 2017. Evaluation of client progress in music therapy: An illustration of an N-of-1 design in individual short-term improvisational music therapy with clients with depression. *Nordic Journal of Music Therapy*, 26(3): 256–271.

Adams, D. M. 2015. The unbearable lightness of being white. *Women & Therapy*, 38(3–4), 327–340.

Ahessy, B. 2011. Lesbian, gay, and bisexual issues in therapy and education: The love that dares not sing its name. *Canadian Journal of Music Therapy*, 17(1): 11–33.

Ahessy, B. 2017. Song writing with clients who have dementia: A case study. *The Arts in Psychotherapy*, 55: 23–31. Retrieved from http://dx.doi.org/10.1016/j.aip.2017.03.002

Aigen, K. 2005. *Music-Centered Music Therapy*. Gilsum: Barcelona Publishers.

Aigen, K. 2008. In defence of beauty: A role for the aesthetic in music therapy theory: Part II: Challenges to aesthetic theory in music therapy: Summary and response. *Nordic Journal of Music Therapy*, 17(1): 3–18.

Aigen, K. 2014. Music-centered dimensions of Nordoff-Robbins music therapy. *Music Therapy Perspectives*, 32(1): 18–29.

Alvin, J. 1978. *Music Therapy for the Autistic Child*. London: Oxford University Press.

Ashley, M. 2011. The perpetuation of hegemonic male power and the loss of boyhood innocence: Case studies from the music industry. *Journal of Youth Studies*, 14(1): 59–76.

Bain, C., Grzanka, P., and Crowe, B. 2016. Toward a queer music therapy: The implications of queer theory for radically inclusive music therapy. *The Arts in Psychotherapy*, 50: 22–33. Retrieved from http://dx.doi.org/10.1016/j.aip.2016.03.004

Baines, D. 1988. A Marxist Feminist Framework for Direct Intervention in Social Work Practice. *Unpublished Paper*. Ottawa: Carleton University.

Baines, S. 1992. The Sociocultural and Political Contexts of Music Therapy: A Question of Ethics. *Unpublished Master's Thesis*. New York: New York University.

Baines, S. 2013. Music therapy as an anti-oppressive practice. *The Arts in Psychotherapy*, 40(1): 1–5.

Baines, S. 2014. Giving Voice to Client Choice: Music Therapy as an Anti-Oppressive Practice. *Unpublished Doctoral Thesis*. Limerick: University of Limerick. Retrieved from https://ulir.ul.ie/handle/10344/4264

Baines, S. 2016. The role of culture in music and medicine: Considerations to enhance health. *Music and Medicine: An Interdisciplinary Journal*, 8(3): 91–95.

Baines, S. and Edwards, J. 2015. Considering the ways in which anti-oppressive practice principles can inform health research. *The Arts in Psychotherapy*, 42: 28–34.

Baker, F. 2014. An investigation of the sociocultural factors impacting on the therapeutic songwriting process. *Nordic Journal of Music Therapy*, 23(2): 123–151.

Baker, F., Tamplin, J., MacDonald, R., Ponsford, J., Roddy, C., Lee, C., and Rickard, N. 2017. Exploring the self through song writing: An analysis of songs composed by people with acquired neurodisability in an inpatient rehabilitation program. *Journal of Music Therapy*, 54(1): 35–54.

Barton, L. 2005. Emancipatory research and disabled people: Some observations and questions. *Educational Review*, 57(3): 317–327.

Bonny, H. 1975. Music and consciousness. *Journal of Music Therapy*, 12(3): 121–135.

Bonny, H. and Savary, L. 1973. *Music and Your Mind: Listening With a New Consciousness*. New York: Harper and Row.

Bosma, H. 2016. Gender in electroacoustic music and other sounding arts. *The Routledge Companion to Sounding Art*: 305. New York: Routledge.

Boutin-Foster, C. C., Foster, J. C., and Konopasek, L. 2008. Physician, know thyself: The professional culture of medicine as a framework for teaching cultural competence. *Academic Medicine*, 83(1): 106–111.

Brabazon, T. 2014. Maybe he's just better than you: Generation X women and higher education. *Journal of Women's Entrepreneurship and Education*, 3–4: 47–70.

Broverman I. K., Broverman, D. M., Clarkson, F. E., Rosencrantz, P. S., and Vogel, S.R. 1970. Sex role stereotypes and clinical judgments of mental health. *Journal of Clinical and Consulting Psychology*, 34(1): 1–7.

Bruscia, K. 1995. Modes of consciousness in guided imagery and music (GIM): A therapist's experience of the guiding process. In C. B. Kenny (ed.) *Listening, Playing, Creating: Essays on the Power of Sound*. Albany: State University of New York Press.

Buchanan, D. 2016. *Soundscapes from the Americas: Ethnomusicological Essays on the Power, Poetics, and Ontology of Performance*. London: Routledge.

Bunt, L. and Hoskyns, S. 2002. *The Handbook of Music Therapy*. Hove: Brunner-Routledge.

Butler, J. 1990. *Gender Trouble: Feminism and the Subversion of Identity*. London: Routledge.

Cameron, C. A. 2014. Does disability studies have anything to say to music therapy? And would music therapy listen if it did?. In *Voices: A World Forum for Music Therapy*, 14(3).

Chari, T. 2008. Representation of women in male-produced 'urban grooves' music in Zimbabwe. *MUZIKI*, 5(1): 92–110.

Chepp, V. and Andrist, L. 2016. Doing critical pedagogy in an ironically sexist world. In *Teaching Gender and Sex in Contemporary America*: 145–154. Basel: Springer International Publishing.

Chesler, P. 1971. *The Myth of Mental Illness*. New York: Avon Books.

Cobbett, S. 2016. Context and relationships: Using the systemic approach with music therapy in work with children, adolescents and their families. *British Journal of Music Therapy*, 30(2): 65–73.

Cross, I. 2001. Music, cognition, culture, and evolution. *Annals of the New York Academy of Sciences*, 930(1): 28–42.

Curtis, S. 1990. Women's issues in music therapy. *Music Therapy Perspectives*, 8(1): 61–66.

Curtis, S. 1997. Singing Subversion, Singing Soul: Women's Voices in Feminist Music Therapy. *Unpublished Doctoral Dissertation*. Montreal: Concordia University Canada.

Curtis, S. 2000. *Singing subversion, singing soul: Women's voices in feminist music therapy*. (Doctoral dissertation, Concordia University, 1997). Dissertation Abstracts International 60 (12-A), 4240.

Curtis, S. 2007. Claiming voice: music therapy for childhood sexual abuse survivors. In S. Brooke (ed.) *The Use of Creative Arts Therapies with Sexual Abuse Survivors*: 196–206. Springfield: C. C. Thomas.

Curtis, S. 2008. Songs of freedom: Music therapy for women survivors of domestic violence. In S. Brooke (ed.) *Creative Arts Therapies and Domestic Violence*: 121–135. Springfield: C. C. Thomas.

Curtis, S. 2012. Music therapy and social justice: A personal journey. *The Arts in Psychotherapy*, 39(3): 209–213. Retrieved from http://dx.doi.org/10/1016/j.aip.2011.12.004

Curtis, S. 2013a. Sorry it has taken so long: Continuing feminist dialogues in music therapy. *Voices: The World Forum for Music Therapy*, 13(1). Retrieved from https://voices.no/index.php/voices/article/view/688/572

Curtis, S. 2013b. On gender and the creative arts therapies. *The Arts in Psychotherapy*, 40 (3): 371–372. doi: 10.1016/j.aip.2013.05.014

Curtis, S. 2013c. Women's issues and music therapists: A look forward. *The Arts in* and Lives, 40(3): 386–393. doi: 10.1016/j.aip.2013.05.016

Curtis, S. 2013d. Women survivors of abuse and developmental trauma. In L. Eyre (ed.) *Guidelines for Music Therapy Practice: Mental Health*: 263–268. Philadelphia: Barcelona Publishers.

Curtis, S. 2015a. Feminist music therapists in North America: Their lives and their practices. In *Voices: A World Forum for Music Therapy*, 15(2). Retrieved from https://voices.no/index.php/voices/article/view/812

Curtis, S. 2015b. Alike and different: Canadian and American music therapists' work and lives. *Canadian Journal of Music Therapy*, 21(1) 12–31.

Curtis, S. and Harrison, G. 2006. Empowering women survivors of violence: A collaborative music therapy-social work approach. In S. L. Brooke (ed.) *Creative Modalities for Therapy with Children and Adults*: 195–204. Springfield: C. C. Thomas.

Dankoff, J. 2011. Toward a development discourse inclusive of music. *Alternatives: Global, Local, Political*, 36(3): 257–269. doi: 10.1177/0304375411418602.

Da Silva, F., Blasi, A., and Dees, D. 1984. *The Sociology of Music*. Notre Dame: University of Notre Dame Press.

Davidson, J. W. and Edgar, R. 2003. Gender and race bias in the judgment of western art music performance. *Music Education Research*, 5(2): 169–181.

Đorđević, V., Braš, M., Kulić, S., and Demarin, V. 2015. The founding of Zagreb's Institute for the Culture of Health: An important step toward a new medical paradigm. *Croatian Medical Journal*, 56(1): 1–3. doi: 10.3325/cmj.2015.56.1

Edwards, J. 2007. Antecedents of contemporary uses for music in healthcare contexts: The 1890s to the 1940s. In J. Edwards (ed.) *Music: Promoting Health and Creating Community in Healthcare Contexts*. Newcastle Upon Tyne: Cambridge Scholars.

Edwards, J. 2017. Narrating experiences of sexism in higher education: A critical feminist autoethnography to make meaning of the past, challenge the status quo and consider the future. *International Journal of Qualitative Studies in Education*, 30(7): 1–14.

Edwards, J. and Hadley, S. 2007. Expanding music therapy practice: Incorporating the feminist frame. *The Arts in Psychotherapy*, 34: 199–207.

Erickson, K. 1966. *Wayward Puritans: A Study in the Sociology of Deviance*. New York: Wiley.

Freeman, R., Gwadz, M. V., Silverman, E., Kutnick, A., Leonard, N. R., Ritchie, A. S., … and Martinez, B. Y. 2017. Critical race theory as a tool for understanding poor engagement along the HIV care continuum among African American/Black and Hispanic persons living with HIV in the United States: A qualitative exploration. *International Journal for Equity in Health*, 16(1): 54.

Gilboa, A., Yehuda, N., and Amir, D. 2009. Let's talk music: A musical-communal project for enhancing communication among students of multi-cultural origin. *Nordic Journal of Music Therapy*, 18(1): 3–31.

Gilligan C. 1979. Woman's place in man's life cycle. *Harvard Educational Review*, 49(4): 431–446.

Grayson, M., Nenad Macesic, L., Khai Huang, G., Bond, K., Fletcher, J., Gilbert, G., Gordon, G. et al. 2015. Use of an innovative personality-mindset profiling tool to guide culture-change strategies among different healthcare worker groups. *PLOS ONE*. Retrieved from http://dx.doi.org/10.1371/journal.pone.0140509

Grocke, D. and Moe, T. (eds). 2015. *Guided Imagery & Music (GIM) and Music and Imagery Methods for Individual and Group Therapy*. London, Philadelphia: Jessica Kingsley Publishers.

Guerra, P. and Silva, A. S. 2015. Music and more than music: The approach to difference and identity in the Portuguese punk. *European Journal of Cultural Studies*, 18(2): 207–223.

Hadley, S (ed.). 2006a. *Feminist Perspectives in Music Therapy*. Gilsum: Barcelona Publishers.

Hadley, S 2006b. Developing a feminist pedagogical approach. In S. Hadley (ed.) *Feminist Perspectives in Music Therapy*: 393–414. Gilsum: Barcelona Publishers.

Hadley, S. 2008. Debate: Feminism and music therapy. A response to "feminist perspectives in music therapy": An essay response by Anthony Meadows. *British Journal of Music Therapy*, 22(1): 45–49.

Hadley, S. 2013. Dominant narratives: complicity and the need for vigilance in the creative arts therapies. *The Arts in Psychotherapy*, 40(4): 373–381. doi: 0.1016/j.aip.2013.05.007

Hadley, S. and Edwards, J. 2004. Sorry for the silence: A contribution from feminist theory to the discourse(s) within music therapy. *Voices: A World Forum for Music Therapy*, 4(2). Retrieved from https://doi.org/10.15845/voices.v4i2.177

Hadley, S. and Hahna, N. 2016. Feminist perspectives in music therapy. In J. Edwards (ed.) *The Oxford Handbook of Music Therapy*: 428–427. Oxford: Oxford University Press.

Hahna, N. 2004. Empowering Women: A Feminist Perspective of the Bonny Method of Mindset Guided Imagery and Music and Intimate Partner Violence. *Unpublished Master's Thesis*. Radford: Radford University.

Hahna, N. 2011. Conversations from the Classroom: Reflections on Feminist Music Therapy Pedagogy in Teaching Music Therapy. *Dissertations Abstractions International: Section A, Humanities and Social Sciences*, ProQuest LLC.

Hahna, N. 2013. Towards an emancipatory practice: Incorporating feminist pedagogy in the creative arts therapies. *The Arts in Psychotherapy*, 40(4): 436–440. doi: 10.1016/j.aip.2013.05.002

Hahna, N. and Schwantes, M. 2011. Feminist music therapy pedagogy: A survey of music therapy educators. *Journal of Music Therapy*, 48(3): 289–316.

Halleck, S. 1971. *The Politics of Therapy*. New York: Science House.

Halstead, J. and Rolvsjord, R. 2017. The gendering of musical instruments: What is it? Why does it matter to music therapy?. *Nordic Journal of Music Therapy*, 26(1): 3–24.

Higgins, K. 1991. *The Music of Our Lives*. Philadelphia: Temple University Press.

Holm, A. L., Gorosh, M. R., Brady, M., and White-Perkins, D. 2017. Recognizing privilege and bias: An interactive exercise to expand health care providers' personal awareness. *Academic Medicine*, 92(3): 360–364.

James, Mark R. 1985. Sources of articles published in the *Journal of Music Therapy*: The first twenty years, 1964–1983. *Journal of Music Therapy*, 22(2): 87–94.

Johnson, S. 2000. Gender consciousness among women fiddlers in Ontario fiddle contests. *Canadian Folk Music Bulletin*, 34(1/2): 3–6.

Kaplan, M. 1983. A woman's view of DSM-III. *American Sociological Review*, 21: 472–479.

Kenny, C. 2015. Performing theory: Playing in the music therapy discourse. *Journal of Music Therapy*, 52(4): 457–486.

Keuroghlian, A. S., Ard, K. L., and Makadon, H. J. 2017. Advancing health equity for lesbian, gay, bisexual and transgender (LGBT) people through sexual health education and LGBT-affirming health care environments. *Sexual Health*, 14(1): 119–122.

Kim, S-A. 2013. Re-discovering voice: Korean immigrant women in group music therapy. *The Arts in Psychotherapy*, 40(3): 428-435. doi: 10.1016/j.aip.2013.05.005

Larivière, V., Ni, C., Gingras, Y., Cronin, B., and Sugimoto, C. 2013. Gender disparities in science. *Nature: International Weekly Journal of Science*, 504(7479): 211–213. Retrieved from http://www.nature.com/news/bibliometrics-global-gender-disparities-in-science-1.14321

Lorié, Á., Reinero, D. A., Phillips, M., Zhang, L., and Riess, H. 2017. Culture and nonverbal expressions of empathy in clinical settings: A systematic review. *Patient Education and Counseling*, 100(3): 411–424.

Lwanda, J. 2003. Mother's songs: Male appropriation of women's music in Malawi and southern Africa. *Journal of African Cultural Studies*, 16(2): 119–141.

Maiti, R., Bhatia, V., Padhy, B., and Hota, D. 2015. Essential medicines: An Indian perspective. *Indian Journal of Community Medicine*, 40(4): 223–232.

Martinez-Hume, A. C., Baker, A. M., Bell, H. S., Montemayor, I., Elwell, K., and Hunt, L. M. 2017. They treat you a different way: Public insurance, stigma, and the challenge to quality health care. *Culture, Medicine, and Psychiatry*, 41(1): 161–180.

McCaffrey, T. and Edwards, J. 2016. "Music therapy helped me get back doing": Perspectives of music therapy participants in mental health services. *Journal of Music Therapy*, 53(2): 121–148.

McClary, S. 1991. *Feminine Endings: Music, Gender, and Sexuality*. Minneapolis: University of Minnesota Press.

McIntosh, P. 1988. White privilege and male privilege: A personal account of coming to see correspondences through work in women's studies. Wellesley: Center for Research on Women.

Mduli, S. 2007. Voicing their perceptions: Swazi women's folk songs. *MUZIKI*, 4(1): 87–110.

Mduli, S. 2009. Swazi women, song and the constructions of social awareness in Swazi culture. *MUZIKI*, 6(1): 58–78.

Miller-Young, M. 2008. Hip-hop honeys and Da hustlaz: Black sexualities in the new hip-hop pornography. *Meridians: Feminism, Gender, and Transnationalism*, 8(1): 261–292.

Mitchell, S. and Schlesinger, S. 2005. Managed care and gender disparities in problematic health care experiences. *Health Research and Educational Trust, Health Services and Research*, 40(5): 1489–1513.

Murphy, J., Goldner, E., Goldsmith, C., Oanh, P., Zhu, W., Corbett, K., and Nguyen, Vu. 2015. Selection of depression measures for use among Vietnamese populations in primary care settings: A scoping review. *International Journal of Mental Health Systems*, 9(31): 1–15. doi: 10.1186/s13033-015-0024-8

Naidoo, S. 2010. Male perspectives of 'womanhood' in selected songs by Thomas Mapfumo. *MUZIKI*, 7(1): 88–96.

Nordoff, P. and Robbins, C. 1971. *Music Therapy in Special Education*. St. Louis: MMB Music.

Nordoff, P. and Robbins, C. 1985. *Therapy in Music for Handicapped Children.* London: Victor Gollancz Ltd.

O'Grady, L. 2011. Musicking and the performance of gender: A double act. In N. Rickard and T. McFerran (eds) *Lifelong Engagement with Music*: 109–120. Hauppage: Nova Science Publishers.

O'Shea, H. 2008. 'Good man, Mary!' Women musicians and the fraternity of Irish traditional music. *Journal of Gender Studies,* 17(1): 55–70.

Parker, S. 2016. Gender fluidity. In S. Moran (ed.) *Ethical Ripples of Creativity and Innovation*: 165–173. London: Palgrave Macmillan.

Pease, B. 2010. *Undoing Privilege: Unearned Advantage in a Divided World.* London: Zed Books.

Pololi L., Krupat, E., Schnell, E., and Kern, D. 2013. Preparing culture change agents for academic medicine in a multi-institutional consortium: The C – change learning action network. *Journal of Continuing Education in the Health Profession,* 33(4): 244–257.

Priestley, M. 1975. *Music Therapy in Action.* St. Louis: MMB Music.

Prilleltensky, I. 2008. The role of power in wellness, oppression, and liberation: The promise of psychopolitical validity. *Journal of Community Psychology,* 36(2): 116–134.

Pruitt, L. 2007. Real men kill and a lady never talks back: Gender goes to war in country music. *International Journal on World Peace,* 24(4): 85–106.

Rogers, C. 1984. The person. In T. Greening (ed.) *American Politics and Humanistic Psychology,* 4: 3–7. New York: Saybrook.

Rolvsjord, R. 2006. Gender politics in music therapy discourse. In S. Hadley (ed.) *Feminist Perspectives in Music Therapy*: 311–328. Gilsum: Barcelona Publishers.

Rolvsjord, R. and Halstead, J. 2013a. The politics of gender identity in music therapy and everyday life. *The Arts in Psychotherapy,* 40(3): 420–427. doi: 10.1016/j.aip.2013.05.015

Rolvsjord, R. and Halstead, J. 2013b. A woman's voice: The politics of gender identity in music therapy and everyday life. *The Arts in Psychotherapy* 40: 420–427. doi: 10.1016/j.aip.2013.05.015

Rolvsjord, R. and Stige, B. 2015. Concepts of context in music therapy. *Nordic Journal of Music Therapy,* 24(1): 44–66. Retrieved from http://dx.doi.org/10.1080/08098131.2013.861502

Ruud, E. 1988. Music therapy: Health profession or cultural movement? *Music Therapy: The Journal for the American Association for Music Therapy,* 7(1): 34–37.

Ruud, E. 1998. *Music Therapy: Improvisation, Communication, and Culture.* Gilsum: Barcelona Publishing.

Sadovnik, N. 2016. Shira Chadasha: A new song for an old community. *Music Therapy Perspectives,* 34(2): 147–153.

Schisterman, E., Swanson, C., Lu, Y-L., and Mumford, S. 2017. The changing face of epidemiology: Gender disparities in citations?. *Epidemiology,* 28(2): 159–168.

Schmutz, V. and Faupel, A. 2010. Gender and cultural consecration in popular music. *Social Forces,* 89(2): 685–708.

Sedgewick, P. 1982. *Psychopolitics.* London: Pluto Press.

Snelgrove, J. W., Jasudavisius, A. M., Rowe, B. W., Head, E. M., and Bauer, G. R. 2012. Completely out-at-sea with two-gender medicine: A qualitative analysis of physician-side barriers to providing healthcare for transgender patients. *BMC Health Services Research,* 12(1): 110.

Steiner, C. 1974. Manifesto. *Readings in Radical Psychiatry*: 3–6. New York: Grove Press.

Stige, B. 2002. *Culture-Centered Music Therapy.* Gilsum: Barcelona Publishers.

Stige, B. 2015. The practice turn in music therapy theory. *Music Therapy Perspectives*, 33(1): 3–11.
Speers, L. 2017. *Hip-Hop Authenticity and the London Scene: Living Out Authenticity in Popular Music*. New York: Routledge.
Streeter, E. 2013. Taking gender into account: Brief report on a survey of music therapists' attitudes to future use of a proposed computer aided evaluation system: The music therapy logbook. *The Arts in Psychotherapy*, 40: 404–408.
Teelken, C. and Deem, R. 2013. All are equal, but some are more equal than others: Managerialism and gender equality in higher education in comparative perspective. *Comparative Education*, 49(4): 520–535.
Touboul-Lundgren, P., Jensen, S., Johann, D., and Lindbaek, M. 2015. Identification of cultural determinants of antibiotic use cited in primary care in Europe: A mixed research synthesis study of integrated design 'culture is all around us.' *BMC Public Health*, 15(908): 1–9. doi: 10.1186/s12889-015-2254-8
Tucker, C. M., Arthur, T. M., Roncoroni, J., Wall, W., and Sanchez, J. 2015. Patient centered, culturally sensitive health care. *American Journal of Lifestyle Medicine*, 9(1): 63–77.
Viega, M. 2016. Exploring the discourse in hip hop and implications for music therapy practice. *Music Therapy Perspectives*, 34(2): 138–146.
Wehr-Flowers, E. 2006. Differences between male and female students' confidence anxiety, and attitude toward learning jazz improvisation. *Journal of Research in Music Education*, 54(4): 337–348.
Wennerås, C. and Wold, A. 1997. Nepotism and sexism in peer-review. *Nature*, 387: 341–343.
Whitehead-Pleaux, A., Donnenwerth, A., Robinson, B., Hardy, S., Oswanski, L., Forinash, M., Hearns, M., Anderson, M., and Tan, X. 2013. Music therapists' attitudes and actions regarding the LGBTQ community: A preliminary report. *The Arts in Psychotherapy*, 40(4): 409–414.
Wyckoff, H. 1974. Problem-solving groups for women. In C. Steiner (ed.) *Readings in Radical Psychiatry*: 80–105. New York: Grove Press.
York, E. and Curtis, E. 2015. Music therapy with women survivors of domestic violence. In B. Wheeler (ed.) *Music Therapy Handbook*: 379–389. New York: Guilford Press.

Chapter 5

The eye of the beholder

Encountering women's experience of domestic violence and abuse as a male researcher and art therapist

Jamie Bird

Introduction

This chapter addresses issues that arose from being a male researcher and art therapist conducting arts-based research with women who had experienced domestic violence and abuse. Engaging in such research required that I critically engage with issues of gender within the context of conducting research. Through the lens of one particular vignette taken from a larger study, this paper will engage with broader ideas about gender and the conducting of arts-based research and art therapy. Whilst this chapter will have relevance for those men engaged in research or art therapy that involves aspects of domestic violence and abuse, it will also have relevance to those who are interested in wider discussions to be had about the influence of gender upon relationships within therapy and research. This has always been a topic worthy of sustained investigation, but the contemporary emergence within public discourse about abuses of male privilege within various professions makes this an especially important subject to attend to.

Drawing upon the work of Sandra Harding (1998, 2004), Jeff Hearn (1998) and Ann Murphy (2012), I will explore how feminist standpoint theory and reflexivity helped to manage, and make sense of, the concerns and anxieties that arose whilst conducting research into violence against women. Anxieties about research becoming therapy merged with anxieties about being a male researcher working with women who had experienced domestic violence and abuse. Whilst this chapter does not aim to outline in depth what an arts-based research methodology looks like within the context of studying domestic violence and abuse, it begins by describing the methodology in enough detail to provide a context within which the nature of the research process can be appreciated. The findings of the research are presented in sufficient detail to allow the overall findings of the research to be understood. There then follows examples of words and images produced by one woman, who used her participation as a way of ensuring that she was seen clearly by myself and by other research participants. This aspect of wanting to be seen became an embodiment of the need to acknowledge my own standpoint and reflexive position as a male researcher. Evaluative comments about participation made by other women are used to show how vulnerability was a feature of taking part in this research for both participants and for me. The concept of vulnerability is examined with reference made to ideas about imagination and empathy from the perspective of feminist philosophy, which in turn helps to shape a discussion about the place of gender within research, art therapy and the boundary between them.

In keeping with the principles of feminist standpoint theory and strong objectivity, as set forth by Harding (1998), this chapter is written from a first-person perspective.

Definitions of domestic violence and abuse

At the time of writing, the UK Government defines domestic violence and abuse as '*any incident or pattern of incidents of controlling, coercive, threatening behaviour, violence or abuse between those aged 16 or over who are, or have been, intimate partners or family members regardless of gender or sexuality*' (Home Office, 2016). The key difference between this definition and earlier definitions is the acceptance that coercion and control underpin all forms of domestic violence and abuse. Similarly, the US Department of Justice states that '[d]*omestic violence can be physical, sexual, emotional, economic, or psychological actions or threats of actions that influence another person.*' (Department of Justice, 2018).

The term 'domestic violence and abuse' does not fully encompass the spectrum of behaviours that current definitions encompass, but it is the most commonly used and understood term that exists right now. The current definitions are useful in incorporating behaviours that would previously have fallen outside of what was considered unacceptable within intimate relationships, and were thus effectively hidden both from public consciousness and state-sponsored measurements and responses.

Context and methodology

The research project that informs this chapter was conducted between 2009 and 2014. Based upon an earlier research project I had contributed to, which used an arts-based and Participatory Action Research (PAR) approach to better understand the experiences of refugees and asylum seekers (O'Neill, 2010), this later research was focused upon employing an arts-based methodology to explore women's responses to having lived with, and moved away from, domestic violence and abuse. Having previously been commissioned to work as an art therapist with women who had experienced domestic violence and abuse, I was confident that I was able to work safely and effectively within this research context. I was curious to know how an arts-based method, with its emphasis upon participants' imaginations, that had been shown to be of value in understanding experiences of asylum and migration could be of equal value in understanding experiences of domestic violence and abuse.

The research methodology synthesised elements of ethno-mimesis (O'Neill, 2009, 2010), sensory and visual ethnography (Pink, 2007, 2009) and feminist standpoint theory (Leavy, 2007; Harding, 1990, 2004). The primary aim was to enable a way for women to use art materials to express their responses to domestic violence, in a form that allowed access to imaginative and sensory representations and that allowed for the appearance of thoughts about the future as well as the past and the present. Alongside the objective to make women's responses visible was that to make participation safe via an ethics of care (Prosser, Clark & Wiles, 2008). Equally, by being reflexively mindful of my own gender, and its potential impact upon the dynamics of power and women's willingness to engage with the research (Beecham, 2009; Harding, 1998; Hearn, 1998), I aspired to communicate in a way that was attentive and non-judgemental. This issue of reflexivity is expanded upon below.

Recruitment was managed with the support of a service affiliated with Women's Aid (a UK-based federation of support services). Several groups were operated over a one-year period. Each group would meet for one morning a week for twelve weeks, with the time being used to produce images and words whilst considering different aspects of living with and moving away from domestic violence and abuse. An earlier pilot group had identified that the topics of home, family, past, present and future were all useful ways in which to frame experiences and expectations. Although several dozen women engaged with the research at various points, the ethical choice was taken to only include the stories of those women who stayed for the whole duration and who were able to present and summarise a completed narrative. A total of eight complete stories have been included in the subsequent dissemination of the research findings (Bird, 2018). A relatively small number, but given the depth of disclosure within those stories, they can be deemed to be of sufficient quantity to render the data meaningful (Baker & Rosalind, 2012).

Transitional stories of domestic violence and abuse

The outcome of the research was the formulation of a concept that I have termed *transitional stories of domestic violence and abuse*. A transitional story of domestic violence and abuse refers to the representation of physical and emotional movement between places, movement through time and changes in personal relationships. These transitions can contribute to how women think about themselves and engage in tactics of agency and resistance. Transitional stories incorporate the past, the present and the future. How women have survived domestic violence and abuse informs the ways in which they resist it in the present and the future. Resistance emerges in mental processes, such as a determination to have a better life or to regain a sense of harmony. It also appears in acts of daily living such as choices made about internal décor, decisions made about food, gardening and countryside visits. Transitional stories illustrate how internal and external features work together and it is this intertwining of the psychological and the physical, and the joining together of the past, the present and the future that makes transitional stories of domestic violence and abuse unique. Transitional stories of domestic violence make reference to processes that Susan Brison (2002) has identified in the way women attempt to remake themselves following sexual violence. They also contain elements of what Vanessa May (2013) identifies as being important to the concept of the relational self and social belonging: change, motion, and the importance of everyday social actions. Both Brison (2002) and May (2013) identify social relationships as central to notions of identity and belonging, which fits with my own findings that show the crucial role of social relationships within transitional stories.

Feminist standpoint theory and reflexivity

Throughout the process of developing, conducting and evaluating the research, I grappled with a number of interconnected issues. The first issue was how to reconcile the uncertainty I had about my own gender when studying a subject that potentially placed me in the position of association with the perpetration of violence against women, in terms of being part of a patriarchal system of power and a representative of masculine aggression. The second issue was the challenge of accommodating non-linear and physical forms of knowledge within the traditionally text-based practice of social science research. A final and related issue was the concern I had that my participation in the research would have the potential to be unsettling for those women taking part in the research or that the research process would become too much like a therapeutic intervention. In addressing these issues I came to the conclusion that they were linked in terms of how gender was an important component of the relationship between myself and participants and between myself and the expressions of knowledge made by those participants. Feminist epistemologies in general and feminist standpoint theory in particular provided a solution to thinking about those issues. Politically, conducting the research without recourse to feminist principles would have been problematic. Given that the historical developments within social and legal attitudes towards domestic violence have only been possible because of those activists and researchers who have explicitly aligned themselves with feminism (Dobash & Dobash, 1992; Hague & Malos, 2005), to not engage with feminism when researching any aspect of violence against women would be to work in a very limited way, ignorant of the gendered forces that enable that violence, and of the ways of countering those forces. Hearn (1998) for example states that the male researcher, 'if engaged in researching any aspect of men's violence towards women, must ensure that research is not planned and conducted in isolation from feminism, as to do so is likely to 'reproduce some of the "knowledge" of anti-feminism' (p.43). Hearn also identifies an epistemological problem when men study violence against women: a problem that centres on the gendered valuing of objective and subjective knowledge. Hearn claims that there is a complex relationship between experience, knowledge, theory and politics; writing that '[i]n many respects, men's knowledge as researchers ... remains severely limited by virtue of men's power locations as members of an oppressor class ... relative to women's knowledge of the effects of men.' (p.42). As a way of addressing this complexity and the gendered valuing of knowledge, Hearn advocates for the 'linking together of fragments of knowledge' (p.42). Similar issues have been addressed by David Beecham (2009). However, whilst Beecham argues that there is a danger of over-simplifying the relationship between gender and power by creating a polarised view of the oppressors and the oppressed, his suggestion that the researcher 'should acknowledge that all knowledge is situated and that there is value to "insider" and "outsider" perspectives' (p.6) complements the linking together of fragments of knowledge advocated by Hearn. Both Hearn and Beecham employ feminist thought to help manage being a male researcher investigating men's violence towards women; they pay particular attention to the effects of gender upon knowledge production and values, whilst suggesting the adoption of an inclusive attitude towards the emergence of different types and expressions of knowledge. It is just such an acknowledgement and valuing of different types and expressions of knowledge that forms a vital element of feminist standpoint theory.

Feminist standpoint theory argues for starting off thought from the lives of others – and in particular those people marginalised in relation to dominant groups. Harding (2004) for example makes the claim that '[s]tarting off research from women's lives will generate less partial and distorted accounts not only of women's lives but also of men's lives and of the whole social order' (p.128). Furthermore, when providing a critique of a number of feminist epistemologies, Harding suggests that 'different epistemologies offer possibilities for different distributions of political power' (1998, p.175) in terms of how they legitimise different kinds of knowledge. For example when considering the limits of empiricism – including feminist empiricism – Harding claims that it overvalues objective reason whilst undervaluing subjective, emotional and embodied knowledge. Harding goes further in suggesting that the traditional way in which objectivity has been conceived and applied is a weak form of objectivity because it rarely – if ever – acknowledges the historical or situated nature of the object of enquiry or the subjectivity of the researcher. It is only when the researcher acknowledges their own standpoint and situated position, and that of the people whom they are working with, that a stronger form of objectivity emerges. It is through rigorous and strong reflexivity and the accommodation of different perspectives that more value-conscious forms of strong-objectivity are generated.

The importance of reflexivity to the researcher who is working within a feminist standpoint framework was therefore important within the context of conducting research about domestic violence and abuse. This is especially so where there is a difference in gender between participants and researcher.

There are some specific areas that will be presented here that show how that gender difference had an influence upon the research process. The first is how participants responded to their engagement with the process and how this was expressed visually and verbally. The second is how I in turn responded to participants, and my concerns about the blurring of the boundary between art therapy and arts-based research. In both of these cases, vulnerability played an important role. I will use images created by one woman to illustrate the first area of concern.

The eye of the beholder

One theme that appeared within women's stories was their response to encounters with professional services. How they felt about being seen, heard and supported by those services seemed to be carried over into how they felt about being supported within the research process. This is evidenced in several images made by Lorraine (names of participants are pseudonyms). Figure 5.1 illustrates where Lorraine explored her sense of sadness in a way that allowed it to be seen by the rest of us in the group. The eye that she placed very centrally within that image acts as a very literal sign for the act of seeing and being seen, and this use of an eye to connect to the viewer was repeated twice more by Lorraine.

The symbol of the eye appeared again in Figure 5.2. Lorraine spoke about this image being to do with the 'eye of the beholder', stating that it showed how she was thinking about herself now, something that she had been unable to do in the past. She later said that she was calm when making this image and that it helped her to sort out her thinking about problems she was having at the time. She also stated that it showed the outline of a fish that was swimming

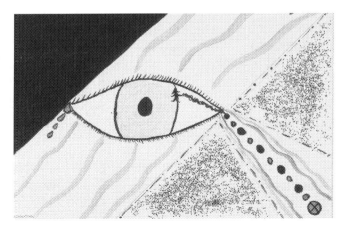

Figure 5.1 Eye with tears by Lorraine. Research conducted with Dr Jamie Bird. 2012.

The eye of the beholder 61

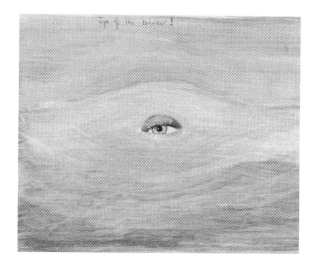

Figure 5.2 Eye of the beholder by Lorraine. Research conducted with Dr Jamie Bird. 2012.

away from it all (the eye is placed centrally within the fish shape). Incidentally, in using the symbol of a fish Lorraine was using the metaphor of nature to represent escape and freedom. Nature motifs were a metaphor used by many of the participants.

My interpretation of Figure 5.2 was firstly to perceive it as calming in its use of pastel blues, greens and pinks. I also found it a particularly emotive image in how the single eye seems to hold the viewer in its gaze. It picks up upon the theme Lorraine had introduced in Figure 5.1 about being seen by the group, but here appears calmer and more serene. As such, this image can be interpreted as an embodiment of Lorraine's growing confidence and sense of self, which meant for her an ability to both perceive her experiences of domestic violence and abuse more clearly and to have those experiences seen and validated by others. In art therapy terms this fits with ideas about witnessing (Leahmonth, 1994). This theme of seeing and being seen carries on into Figure 5.3 that shows a female figure with a crown winking at the viewer.

Lorraine stated that Figure 5.3 was a representation of a queen and that it was about her gaining control and respect. It was representative of new beginnings and about how her participation in groups such as *The Freedom Programme*[1] had helped her to gain new goals and strategies. She did not elaborate upon those goals and strategies, but what is evident is that they had enhanced her confidence in a way that allowed her to engage with others in a more assertive way. In the context of her participation here, this seemed to include the rest of the group and me as the observers or witnesses of the image through the way in which the woman on the page holds the viewer's gaze so forcibly.

Figure 5.3 Winking queen by Lorraine. Research conducted with Dr Jamie Bird. 2012.

There is though an ambiguity within the image. The observation has been made by others who have viewed this image that the winking eye can also be read as a bruised eye and that, despite that possibly violent reference, the queen is still able to hold the viewer's gaze and still wear her crown. This might be a useful visual metaphor of the idea of being simultaneously both a victim in a legal sense, but also a survivor and a resistor of the effects of domestic violence and abuse (Allen, 2012). In that way Figure 5.3 is an image whose meaning is contained within the mind of the viewer – or 'the eye of the beholder' to use Lorraine's metaphor – and that along with all of Lorraine's images and words that allude to being seen clearly, asks questions about the place of witnessing and interpretation within arts-based research and art therapy.

In terms of my own reflexive response to Lorraine's images, as a male researcher I did feel that I was being confronted and challenged, in the sense of becoming the object of her gaze and of being asked to see her clearly. In that sense there is an equalising of the power relationship between Lorraine as a female participant and me as a male researcher in terms of who was the subject and who was the object. There was thus a subversion of what might be considered the ordinary appearance of something like the male gaze (Mulvey, 2009) within arts-based research or art therapy. The consequence of viewing Lorraine's images, and reflecting on the sense of becoming the object of her gaze, was that my sense of uncertainty identified earlier about being a man researching aspects of men's violence against women, was increased.

Vulnerability

In referencing how her participation in *The Freedom Programme* had been of value, Lorraine was echoing observations made by other participants that taking part in the research was useful in terms of contributing to their sense of agency. Whilst there were positive views expressed by women when evaluating their participation, a more ambivalent response emerged where Lisa wrote as part of her assessment of her participation: '*I was reluctant to talk about my issues as I didn't wish to be reminded thank you!*' Although reassured that the methodology was safe, guided as it was by an ethics of care (Prosser, Clark & Wiles, 2008), comments such as those made by Lisa reflected concerns that emerge when employing a methodology that has the potential to leave participants feeling uncertain and vulnerable.

The sense of vulnerability expressed by participants resonates with Ann Murphy's (2012) observations about the place of vulnerability and ambiguity within feminist ontology and political imagination. Building upon Michéle Le Doeuff's (2002) examination of the denial of imagination and imagery within philosophy, Murphy argues that it is vulnerability that makes us open to others, to their corporeal, ontological and ethical otherness, which in turn has the potential to enable empathy. Conversely, Murphy argues that corporeal vulnerability can just as easily provoke a retreat from what is imagined to be the other in fear and repulsion. From this perspective, imagination, and its association to the vulnerable corporal body, can become a potential source of wounding and violence or a prompt for caring and compassion. In Murphy's view, both vulnerability and imagination occupy ambiguous positions within philosophy: something to be drawn back from as well as something to be approached. Murphy talks of an 'emergent feminist ontology of corporeal vulnerability' (2012, p.99) and considers the implications of an ethics based upon vulnerability, where the ambiguous nature of vulnerability is embraced and acknowledged, rather than denied so that the beneficial components of care and compassion do not become 'concealed by [vulnerability's] overwhelming association with violence' (p.98) that so much philosophy espouses. Murphy calls attention to the way in which images of violence permeate continental philosophy's accounts of identity and difference, and argues for a conception of self and otherness that is based upon an interdependence that is both ambiguous and vulnerable. As such, any idea of an emancipatory future (of the sort that feminist politics might imagine and which the research described here came to include) would be required to acknowledge and embrace the ambiguity that is inherent within corporeal vulnerability and its associated influence upon imagination, rather than attempt to transcend it. Murphy's conception of ambiguity and vulnerability is useful in understanding the responses to violence expressed by participants in the way it can assist in appreciating the ways in which women represented their memories and imaginations. It also helps in appreciating their responses to questions about thoughts of participation.

The vulnerability expressed by participants also mirrors the observation made by Abrahams et al. (2004) and Williamson (2000) that narrative and testimony-based research runs the risk of being experienced as traumatically cathartic for women who have experienced domestic violence and abuse. Likewise, Rumbold, Fenner & Brophy-Dixon (2012) identify arts-based research's potential to evoke vulnerability within participants. The research that has been outlined here shows the potential for catharsis and vulnerability to be present when engaging in arts-based research with women who have experienced domestic violence and abuse. Unsettling feelings from the past seeped into thoughts about the present and the future. Uncertainty about the future often generated further anxiety. Such a process may have occurred had the research been purely word-based, but I believe that the image-based nature of the method made this process of emotional catharsis more likely because of the sometimes unexpected and unplanned appearance of unsettling thoughts and feelings that were provoked by images, or emerge in images. However, that participants were able to work slowly, that the groups were contained within the supportive framework offered by the host organisation and that I was able to draw upon my experience as an art therapist meant that where there was the appearance of feelings of vulnerability these were contained and managed in a way that meant participants did not feel out of control.

The relationship between research and therapy

The concerns that Lisa expressed about talking about her past, and that Emma had about being reminded of the past, echoed my own concerns about the methodology moving rather too close to a form of therapeutic intervention. There were times when the process of working with participants felt closer to therapy than it did to research. Above I have spoken about how the expression allowed by the making of images could occasionally be experienced by some women as making them uncomfortably vulnerable. Those women who took part would occasionally refer to the groups as art therapy or state that their participation felt therapeutic. To begin with, this did raise concerns that the participation would in some way be counter-productive. Those concerns dissipated when I observed that participants were able to continue engaging in the process even where it was at points unsettling for them. I also gained reassurance from working closely with the services that I aligned myself with for the purposes of this research: each woman who took part had a named worker within those services and there was a well-established process of ensuring participants well-being and safety. Over time I also came to realise that the subject of enquiry and the methodology I had formed to investigate it was inevitably going to generate the expression of strong thoughts and feelings that had revelatory and cathartic qualities to them, and that the expression of those would be of benefit to the participants. The ethical protocol I had established had taken account of the possibility of a strong effect appearing within the research, and again the support of the host services was a key feature of that protocol. The aspect I was least ready to accept was the therapeutic benefit that the women gained from their participation. What allowed me to become more comfortable with this element was in seeing it as a manifestation of the underpinning philosophy of the methodologies I had chosen to adopt. Participatory arts, PAR and feminist-standpoint methods have an explicit aim of aiding participants as well as future audiences (O'Neill, 2010), but it took some time for this to sit comfortably with my initial assumptions about research needing to be neutral and disinterested and my fears about an overly therapeutic approach to participants' engagement in the research.

There is literature that identifies the complexity of trying to empathise with participants (Rice, 2009) and that acknowledges the potential for participants to be re-traumatised through their participation (Abrahams et al., 2004; Williamson, 2000). Letherby (2003) highlights the tensions that exist between a desire for emancipation and a need for researchers to control the flow of the production of knowledge, a tension that undermines a sense of equality of power within research. This latter point resonates with how certain aspects of therapy have been criticised as exhibiting an unbalanced power relationship between client and therapist, particularly where there are differences of gender between client and therapist (Hogan, 2012). Such observations drive the need to create good ethical frameworks within which to research domestic violence and abuse. What is lacking though is an acknowledgement that participation, whilst running the risk of adding to a sense of trauma, might also have the potential to ease such feelings or to give a renewed sense of hope or to enhance well-being. Had the research I conducted been framed as the trying out of a therapeutic intervention, then such thoughts would not have arisen because the evaluation of therapeutic potential would have been an avowed aim. The research though was not framed in that way and instead was sociological in nature. Where the tension lay was in my sensitivity to women's participation – in the moment-to-moment sequence of events – that was almost indistinguishable to how I have observed people participating in art therapy. What stopped it becoming an explicit expression of art therapy was my careful guidance away from a sustained attention upon the past, and by being more transparent in how I responded to women's images and words than if I was in the role of an art therapist. In hindsight though, guided by how some of the women responded to the question I asked about how my being a male researcher influenced their participation, I wish that I had been even more transparent than I was. For example, my desire to remain neutral and to focus more upon listening than responding was perceived by one woman as being withholding and distant and therefore as an expression of an aspect of power that she associated with me as male; a response that highlights a tension that arises in being a male researcher investigating women's experience of domestic violence and abuse as much as it highlights the tension between emancipation and therapeutic potential.

The tension between emancipation and therapeutic potential fits with a point Alan Radley (2009) makes about the potential conflict between using stories purely as a way of contemplating suffering and using stories as part of an activist agenda for ideological reasons. Radley references Catherine Reismann (2002 cited in Radley, 2009), who when writing about her experience of revisiting a participant's story of domestic violence, realises that in her original desire to find a positive end to the participant's story, failed to confront its full horror. Radley suggests that this example demonstrates 'the need for researchers to face up to difficult moments of witnessing, even where they are powerless to do anything about them at the time' (2009, p.65). This observation chimes with Frank's (1995) advocating for the need to pay attention to those stories about illness that do not have narrative arcs that end with either a cure or a quest fulfilled. It was difficult to be a witness to participants' stories, especially where good endings existed only in the future. The trouble I had reading Figure 5.3 in terms of labelling the eye as winking rather than bruised shows that encountering the tougher story is not easy.

These thoughts about therapeutic potential, emancipation and my own feeling of ambiguity can be viewed as an additional point to be made about the role of vulnerability; only this time they are much more inclusive of my own thoughts and feelings, where I felt a sense of ambiguity and vulnerability about the research process. That I was able to acknowledge such feelings, and that participants were able to express their own similar feelings, suggests that I was able meet the criteria of researcher reflexivity, accountability and openness to being questioned by participants that Richardson (2000) and Finley (2003) put forward as being markers of good quality participatory and arts-based research.

Conclusion

I have referred to how, as a man investigating women's experiences of domestic violence and abuse, I was required to engage with issues of gender. From very early on it became evident that not only would I need to work closely with supporting services, whose ethos was grounded within the principles of feminism, but also on a personal level I would need to acquaint myself, and be comfortable with, those principles. Feminist standpoint theory proved useful in helping me, as a man, appreciate women's perspectives of gender, power and violence. In this chapter I have reflected upon my position as a man investigating women's experience of domestic violence with respect to thoughts about vulnerability and the differences in power within the relationship between participants and researcher. A number of authors have been cited in those discussions (Murphy, 2012; Letherby, 2003; Rice, 2009; Williamson, 2000). The notion of strong objectivity within feminist standpoint epistemology has relevance (Harding, 2004) in terms of embracing reflexivity. Letherby (2003) states that '[feminist standpoint] supporters recognize that the production of knowledge is a political act in that the researcher's own personhood is always part of research' (p.45) and in terms of men being advocates and users of reflexivity within feminist standpoint epistemology. Harding (1998) writes that men can gain from insights provided by a reflexive position in their own 'struggles against androcentrism and male supremacy in family life, in emotional relations, at work, in public agenda politics' (p.185). These thoughts, along with those offered by male researchers who have also adopted a reflexive and feminist approach to research (Beecham, 2009; Brod, 1998; Hearn, 1998), point towards the value and validity of being a male researcher investigating women's responses to domestic violence and abuse. My own encounter with the transitional stories told by women forced me to confront my own memories and desires about home, family and agency and of how those are gendered and become embodied within everyday acts. I was able to reflect upon how my own behaviour within the family home is shaped by my history and culturally situated ideas about the gendered division of labour within the home. Investigating domestic violence and abuse more widely made me acutely aware of how my own communication style and expression of feelings might be perceived as being coercive and controlling. In this way the research was emancipatory for me as well as for the participants. Being in the same room as the women who were sharing their thoughts and feelings about domestic violence meant that the encounter I had with domestic violence was an embodied one. The literature that I accessed throughout the research process did have a profound impact upon my understanding of gender, power and violence, but the encounter with the physicality of women's stories and the face-to-face nature of our communication brought that understanding to life. In this way, the notion of embodied and corporeal vulnerability being an aid to a feminist understanding of empathy (Murphy, 2012), that I associated with the underpinning epistemology of the research, was evident in how participants and I were able to share a physical space and be open to disclosure and the witnessing of stories told.

I have made reference to how one woman found my opaqueness problematic. That same woman also said that my presence as a man meant that she was not able to talk about the violence and abuse she had suffered, in particular sexual abuse, in the way that she would like to have done. This is a real concern and demonstrates that there will be limits to what a male researcher is able to hear and witness when working with women. In contrast, other women were able to say that my presence did not act as a barrier to their participation and even went so far as to say that it allowed them to appreciate that some men are able to listen to what they have to say. That variety of responses to my presence as a male researcher can be read as an example of how the quality of participation within arts-based research will be unique to the individual. To continue the metaphor, the response will be within the 'eye of the beholder'. That unique response will be framed within the context of the gender of both parties. It will also be framed within the context of factors such as ethnicity, economic status or health status. Making sense of the interplay of those various forces requires reference to the notion of intersectionality. This chapter has limited itself to a consideration of gender and has put forward the notion that vulnerability is an important concept to understand and occupy if wanting to be reflexive within the context of arts-based research. The argument that I wish to end on is to propose that vulnerability would be similarly useful when being reflexive about other intersecting factors and just as useful within a more explicitly therapeutic intervention.

Note

1 *The Freedom Programme* is a twelve-week programme that aims to help participants identify patterns of coercion and control that can occur within abusive relationships and to recognise the differences between healthy and unhealthy relationships. It is principally a psycho-educational approach that borrows heavily from the *Duluth Model* of power and control (Shepard & Pence, 1999).

References

Abrahams, H., Hague, G., Malos, E., McCarry, M., Silva, T. & Williamson, E. (2004) Domestic Violence and Research Ethics, In: Smyth, M. & Williamson, E. (eds) *Researchers and their 'Subjects': Ethics, Power, Knowledge and Consent*. Bristol: The Policy Press, pp.195–210.

Allen, M. (2012) *Narrative Therapy for Women Experiencing Domestic Violence: Supporting Women's Transitions from Abuse to Safety*. London: Jessica Kingsley Publishers.

Baker, S. E. & Rosalind, E. (2012) *How Many Qualitative Interviews Is Enough?* National Centre for Research Methods, http://eprints.ncrm.ac.uk/2273/ (last accessed 25/4/14).

Beecham, D. (2009) *What's Your Agenda Mate?* BSA conference paper, unpublished.

Bird, J. (2018) Art Therapy, Arts-based Research and Transitional Stories of Domestic Violence and Abuse. *International Journal of Art Therapy*, 23(1), pp.14–24.

Brison, S. (2002) *Aftermath: Violence and the Remaking of the Self*. Princeton: Princeton University Press.

Brod, H. (1998) To Be a Man, or Not Be a Man – That Is the Feminist Question, In: Digby, T. (ed.) *Men Doing Feminism*. London: Routledge, pp.197–21.

Department of Justice (2018) https://www.justice.gov/ovw/areas-focus (last accessed 2/2/18).

Dobash, R. E. & Dobash, R. P. (1992) *Women, Violence and Social Change*. London: Routledge.

Finley, S. (2003) Arts-Based Inquiry, QI: Seven Years from Crisis to Guerrilla Warfare. *Qualitative Inquiry*, 9(2), pp.281–296.

Frank, A. (1995) *The Wounded Storyteller: Body, Illness, and Ethics*. Chicago: University of Chicago Press.

Hague, G. & Malos, E. (2005) *Domestic Violence: Action for Change*. Cheltenham: New Clarion Press.

Harding, S. (1990) Starting Thought from Women's Lives: Eight Resources for Maximising Objectivity. *Journal of Social Philosophy*, 21(2–3), pp.140–149.

Harding, S. (1998) Can Men Be Subjects of Feminist Thought? In: Digby, T. (ed.) *Men Doing Feminism*. London: Routledge, pp.171–196.

Harding, S. (2004) Rethinking Standpoint Epistemology: What Is "Strong Objectivity"? In: Harding, S. (ed.) *The Feminist Standpoint Theory Reader: Intellectual & Political Controversies*. London: Routledge, pp.127–140.

Hearn, J. (1998) *The Violences of Men*. London: Sage Publications.

Home Office (2016) *Domestic Violence and Abuse*, https://www.gov.uk/guidance/domestic-violence-and-abuse (last accessed).

Hogan, S. (2012) *Feminist Approaches to Art Therapy Revisited*. London: Routledge.
Le Doeuff, M. (2002) *The Philosophical Imaginary*. London: Columbia University Press.
Leahmonth, M. (1994) Witness and Witnessing in Art Therapy. *Inscape. Journal of the British Association of Art Therapists*, 1, pp.19–22.
Leavy, P. (2007) *Merging Feminist Principles and Art-Based Methodologies*, paper presentation at the American Sociological Society Annual Conference, New York City.
Letherby, G. (2003) *Feminist Research in Theory & Practice*. Buckingham: Open University Press.
May, V. (2013) *Connecting Self to Society: Belonging in a Changing World*. Basingstoke: Palgrave Macmillan.
Mulvey, L. (2009) *Visual and Other Pleasures* 2nd ed. London: Palgrave Macmillan.
Murphy, A. V. (2012) *Violence and the Philosophical Imaginary*. New York: State University of New York Press.
O'Neill, M. (2009) Making Connections: Ethno-mimesis, Migration and Diaspora. *Psychoanalysis, Culture & Society*, 14(3), pp.289–302.
O'Neill, M. (2010) *Asylum, Migration & Community*. Bristol: The Policy Press.
Pink, S. (2007) *Doing Visual Ethnography* 2nd ed. London: Sage Publications.
Pink, S. (2009) *Doing Sensory Ethnography*. London: Sage Publications.
Prosser, J., Clark, A. & Wiles, R. (2008) Visual Research Ethics at the Crossroads, *Realities*, http://www.manchester.ac.uk/realties (last accessed 16/3/2009).
Radley, A. (2009) *Works of Illness: Narrative, Picturing and the Social Response to Serious Disease*. Ashby-de-la-Zouch: Inker Men Press.
Rice, C. (2009) Imagining the Other? Ethical Challenges of Researching and Writing Women's Embodied Lives. *Feminism & Psychology*, 19(2), pp.245–266.
Richardson, L. (2000) Evaluating Ethnography. *Qualitative Inquiry*, 6(2), pp.253–255.
Rumbold, J., Fenner, P. & Brophy-Dixon, J. (2012) The Risks of Representation: Dilemmas and Opportunities in Art-Based Research. *Journal of Applied Arts & Health*, 3(1), pp.67–78.
Shepard, F. & Pence, L. (1999) *Coordinating Community Responses to Domestic Violence: Lessons from Duluth and Beyond*. Thousand Oaks: Sage Publications.
Williamson, E. (2000) Caught in Contradictions: Conducting Feminist Action Orientated Research within an Evaluated Research Programme, In: Radford, J., Friedberg, M. & Harne, L. (eds) *Women, Violence and Strategies for Action*. Buckingham: Open University Press, pp.136–148.

Chapter 6

Parental gender roles in clay

Perceptions of gender-role issues among Israeli fathers to toddlers as expressed in a clay figure-sculpting task

Nehama Grenimann Bauch

Introduction

An art therapist's work frequently deals with fathers of all kinds, whether these are fathers of children they work with, adult men in therapy who are parents, or within the context of family and group therapy. This could be, for example, a father of a child experiencing learning or social difficulties in school, or a father spending time in a correctional facility, psychiatric ward, or rehabilitation center – spending time far away from his children. Despite this, the literature and research about men in art therapy (e.g. Vick, 2007; Trombetta, 2007; Liebmann, 2003), and specifically fathers in art therapy settings, is scarce and lacks a deep exploration of the father's subjective experience in this setting. Literature that has touched upon issues regarding fathers or fatherhood in art therapy settings have usually done so in the context of specific clinical populations such as fathers who are drug abusers (Lev-Wiesel and Liraz, 2007), or through case studies discussing the absence of fathers (Havsteen-franklin, 2015; Haesler, 1996). This chapter's aim is to shed light on the experience of fathers of toddlers within an art therapy setting. In doing so, I will also attempt to explore fathers' perceptions of parental gender-role issues in art therapy.

The fathers described and quoted in this chapter took part in qualitative research I conducted in Israel under the supervision of Dr. Michal Bat Or. My study was confined to eleven heterosexual, married, Israeli, Jewish[1] men with a first and only biological child with no known developmental disorders. Discussing the experiences of many other kinds of fathers (divorced, stepfathers, adoptive, estranged, special needs, etc.) is beyond the scope of this study sample. Additional research in this area is much to be desired.

Men, and the interplay of gender, in art therapy

Art therapy, as well as other mental healthcare, social welfare, and child education professions (Adams, 2010; Veras, 2014; OECD, 2012), is currently a predominantly female field. In the United States and Canada, women make up over 80% of art therapists (Greenall, 2014), and about 75% of new psychology doctorates (Michalski et al., 2011). Life experiences of socialization and issues of gender identity inevitably enter the therapy room and influence the therapeutic relationship between therapist and client (Shapiro, 1993). Findings suggest that male art therapists are slightly more willing than female therapists to consider gender at the outset of therapy, as well as during the conduct of therapy (Hogan and Cornish, 2014). In the same study, male art therapists were more inclined towards a process-based, fluid conceptualization of gender, while a significant amount of female art therapists related to the influence of what they, as women, represented to the client and its on-going influence on gender dynamics in the therapeutic relationship. The feminization of the field also affects the minority of male therapists. As a male psychotherapist in Israel, Samana (2016) describes feeling pressured to suppress and change his own behavior and approach – to feminize it – emphasizing the need, in his opinion, for both a feminine and masculine presence in the therapy room. Vick (2007) described experiences unique to male art therapists, such as clients questioning their motives for working with children. As a women art therapist working with men, Liebmann (2003) described an initial resistance to engage, followed by her managing to build a good relationship with men in the criminal justice system. In the mental health system, according to Liebmann, men were less frequently referred to art therapy, less engaged within therapy, and more reluctant to take responsibility for themselves, as opposed to women. She therefore stresses the need for an initial recognition of the extra difficulties men may find in accessing therapy, the importance of focusing on the active 'art part' in sessions, and of creating greater structure, which would help reduce anxieties regarding the (potentially less familiar, due to societal norms) world of expressing feelings. Trombetta (2007) also makes some suggestions of materials that, in his clinical experience, may assist men in containing their anxiety linked to issues of control, emotional expression, and self-disclosure as well as helping to discharge and transform aggression. These materials include comics, graffiti-style art, and three-dimensional media such as clay – the material used for the intervention with fathers which I will describe shortly.

Art therapists working with fathers

Parental representations are a parent's views, emotions, and internal world in relation to their parenting (Mayseless, 2006). These are also called 'introjected objects' in psychoanalytic parlance. Depending on the level of sensitive and responsive caregiving by the parents, a child develops either secure or insecure attachment representations of parenting (Scharf and Mayseless, 2011). These parental representations are internalized implicitly, in an embodied manner – through physical sensations and symbolic representations (Fonagy and Target, 2007), and in turn affect the child's own parenting style when he/she becomes a parent, constituting intergenerational transmission (Shai and Belsky, 2011). Accordingly, an increased interest in developing parent-focused and parent–child (dyadic) interventions (Slade, 2007; Harel et al., 2006) reflects the understanding that parents and their own parental representations play a significant role in the success of their child's therapy (Taylor and Adelman, 2001). The non-verbal and projective nature of art-based parental interventions appear to assist in accessing preverbal, embodied, parental representations (e.g. Bat Or 2012, 2015; Goldner, Gazit, and Scharf, 2017; Gavron and Mayseless, 2015). The specific attributes of clay, such as its plasticity and its multi-dimensional aspect, encourage a therapeutic experience by revealing unconscious materials, concretizing, symbolizing, and facilitating verbal communication (Sholt and Gavron, 2006).

Engaging with fathers, however, is a poorly explored aspect of parental intervention development and research (Panter-Brick et al., 2014; Kaplan, 2010). This is also true for art-based parental interventions and training, which focus primarily on mothers or both parents together (e.g. Shamri-Zeevi, Regev, and Snir, 2015; van Bakel et al., 2013). A few art therapy projects have nonetheless focused on working with fathers. For example, Proulx and Minde ([1995] as quoted in Proulx, 2003) describe working with a group of fathers and their three-year-old children through father–child-dyad art therapy. However, the current situation I've described, in which most art therapists and surrounding staff are female, requires reflection. The predominantly female team, such as the child's teacher, psychologist, and social worker, will frequently be the initiator of an intervention with the parents. Gender bias may therefore affect the relationship (or the possibility of establishing one) between the art therapist and the child's father (Kaplan, 2010) in direct and indirect ways. Indirectly, for example, gender bias towards fathers seeking work flexibility (Vandello et al., 2013) or taking paternity leave (Rege and Solli, 2013) may affect the father's ability to be as accessible to the team as the mother is. On a more direct level, social workers, for example, tend to work according to the notion that interventions should be focused on the mother, thus ignoring the father (Brown et al., 2009). In Israel, specifically, therapists may also be inclined to forget the father, and allow him to be less active in dyadic parent–child interventions (Kaplan, 2010). Such surrounding attitudes may influence the art therapist's approach towards the child's father, resulting in the creation of 'ghost fathers,' who are not contacted or included in the therapeutic process.

Researching fathers in an art therapy context

In the context of medical research, the exclusion of women from research samples has been *criticized*, suggesting that findings and conclusions are skewed, and do not properly reflect or represent over half of the population (Eichler, Reisman, and Borins, 1992). Hogan (2012) describes an age-old western bias in medical and mental health research, in which women, being the object of the male gaze, are viewed as intrinsically pathological and passive objects of male medical power and control. As a women art therapist researching fathers, I find myself in an interesting, almost reverse[2], role: while much parenting-related research, especially in relation to attachment theory, has been conducted and written by men[3] about samples of women (mothers), reflecting a societal and professional norm of assuming the mother to be the primary caregiver (Bornstein, 2002; Palm, 2014), I am a woman who conducted research and has been writing about a sample of men (who are fathers).

Fathers are still rarely included as research participants in pediatric or child health studies (Davison et al., 2017). However, research about fathers is rapidly increasing, due to societal changes in the past three decades (Lamb, 2010), which are partly linked to an increased participation of mothers in the workforce (Weiss, 1999). Such research includes, among many other topics, the study of father–child attachment (Brown et al., 2012; Palm, 2014) and paternal representations (Rouyer et al., 2007; Vreeswijk et al., 2014). Specifically, many contemporary fathers appear to rework their paternal representations, by learning from their fathers what *not* to do in domains such as the expression of affection or the perception of discipline (Bretherton, Lambert, and Golby, 2006). Despite this trend, there appears to be a gap between fathers' representations of themselves as equally involved in childcare and their daily practices in which mothers remain the primary caretakers (Rouyer et al., 2007; Wall and Arnold, 2007). The possible reasons for the existence of such a gap are complex and multifaceted. In part, this may be connected to deeply rooted influences of male socialization, such as a learned tendency to restrict certain kinds of emotion (Levant, 2011), linked to an intergenerational transmission of what Biddulph ([1999] quoted in Liebman, 2013, 110) defines as 'under-fathering'. Socialization and cultural context are not limited, however, to the influence of men's fathers. The mother's beliefs about gender roles and consequent tendency to support the father–child relationship influence the father's level of involvement in domains such as child healthcare (Zvara, Schoppe-Sullivan, and Dush, 2013).

As a therapist who is also a mother, I have no doubt that my personal position and subjective gender-related experiences have influenced my work and research with fathers. It would take a whole additional chapter just to analyze these specific influences. The following quotes and themes rising from my work with fathers are therefore only the tip of the iceberg – a modest and exploratory beginning of what I hope will be a larger body of work to help art therapists deepen their understanding of using art with fathers in therapeutic settings.

The study

The themes and quotes presented in this chapter are based on a sample of eleven Israeli fathers of toddlers (aged two to three years old)[4] who took part in a qualitative study exploring parental representations in the context of a task of sculpting father and child figures in clay. Meetings with the fathers were held individually in their homes (and in two cases in work environments) and included a sculpting task and an interview. The task included a short introduction by the interviewer about working with clay to create three-dimensional sculptures, and a request to 'Please sculpt yourself with your child, or sculpt the relationship between you and your child.' Following the sculpting process, a semi-structured interview (Patton, 2002) was conducted about their experience and the sculptures they had made. The task and study were modeled according to Bat Or's (2010, 2012, 2015) research about mothers of toddlers. Questions sought to elicit a phenomenological and subjective viewing of the sculpture and the process of creating it (asking for example 'What do you see?'; and 'Do you remember whether you had obstacles or frustrations during the sculpting process, and if yes, at what point in the process?'). Some questions were also projective and elicited relational and intergenerational transmission topics (for example: 'If the father figure could talk, what would he say?'). The semi-structured interview was modified to accommodate fathers, and additionally invited them, at the end of the interview, to share their thoughts about the differences between fathers and mothers, fathers' participation in parenting, fathers in therapy, and the effects of the interviewer being a woman and a mother.

The sculpting processes were videotaped from the approximate perspective of the fathers, focusing on their hands. As a result, the data collected was both nonverbal (the sculptures and silent videos of the sculpting process) and verbal (transcripts of the interviews with the fathers together with filled questionnaires). This data was analyzed based on phenomenological and hermeneutic approaches as well as a multiple-case study approach to facilitate methodological triangulation (Janesick, 2000)[5]. Through inductive analysis and deconstruction of the data, categories were consolidated and then meaning was synthesized using the analysis from each of the separate sources. Finally, the most salient common themes were defined and connections between the different channels of information were sought in readiness for theoretical consolidation (LeCompte and Preissle, 1993).

Paternal representations and parenting-related gender roles

In the study, several themes related to paternal representations emerged, including: fathers' encouraging of independence versus protecting; movement and playfulness in the father's experience; using abstraction and metaphor to represent the father–child relationship; and 'leave well enough alone' – being satisfied with imperfections in fatherhood experiences (Bat Or and Grenimann Bauch, 2017). For the purpose of this chapter, I will focus on the themes that relate most closely to perceived parenting-related gender roles. I would like specifically to juxtapose the themes initially raised by the

Table 6.1 Themes of paternal representations – based on the interviews with the fathers

Themes of paternal representations	Number of fathers raising the topic during their interview	Defined by the father as a main topic in the sculpture
Physical closeness and presence; hugging and identification	8	5
• Yearning for more/ feelings of loss/ Wanting to be more present	6	4
• Physical closeness and hugging	5	3
• 'Mini-me'/ Identification/ Only from the father's perspective	5	2
'Leave well enough alone': Themes of dealing with technical and aesthetic challenges	7	–
Distancing/ encouraging independence versus protecting; being passive versus guiding	6	3
Movement and playfulness	6	3
• Bicycle	3	1
• Child on the father's shoulders	2	1
Abstract and metaphorical representations	5	6
• Themes of teaching and nourishing	4	1
Themes based on communication and interaction with the child (focused on the child's unique preference)	4	3

fathers and the topics raised in response to specific gender-related questions posed by the interviewer at the end of the interviews. As seen in Tables 6.1 and 6.2, the responses to these questions were divided into three main categories: 1. Intergenerational transmissions and generational gaps; 2. Themes of social and personal expectations; 3. Perceived gender roles in parenting and therapy. Naturally, these themes were influenced by, and linked to, the topics raised during the process of sculpting and observing. In order to understand the interplay between these topics further, and their implications for working with fathers in art therapy, I chose to relate to them as a timeline: 1. Past – reworking intergenerational transmissions; 2. Present – social and personal expectations of fathers; and 3. Future – relating to perceived parental gender-roles in therapy settings.

Past – reworking paternal intergenerational transmissions

In their sculptures and post sculpting interviews, many fathers (72%) raised topics of physical closeness to their child as well as physical resemblances.

Table 6.2 Themes in response to specific questions by the interviewer

Themes of paternal representations (expressed verbally during the interviews) – in response to explicit topics raised by the interviewer	Number of fathers discussing the topic during their interview
Intergenerational transmissions and generational gaps	11
• Feeling respect/ appreciation towards my father	6
• Analysing vs. not thinking of it	4
• Focused on providing for the family/ functional relationship	4
• Distance vs. physical closeness	4
• Issues of cultural identity and teaching	3
Themes of social and personal expectations – focusing on a perceived 'I should/ will be doing' as a father	8
• Being strong/ making the child proud	4
• Work/ providing/ coming home from work	4
• Dealing with the wife's expectations/ remarks	3
• Self-consciousness of being watched/ tested (by the interviewer)	3
• Expectations and hopes for the future	2
Perceived gender roles in parenting and therapy	8
• Effects of different social perceptions of fathers	4
• Approaching the father as a unique contributor	3
• The child relates differently to father and mother	3
• Effect of the interviewer being a woman and mother	3
• Mothers letting go	2

Interestingly, fathers of boys more frequently represented these topics in the sculptures than fathers of girls (see Table 6.3). While fathers of girls did raise topics related to hugging or holding their daughters, these were presented in much more abstract and metaphorical forms. For example, Itamar, father of Shirley, a two-year-old girl (Figure 10 in Table 6.3), chose to focus on the subjects of *peace* and *connection*, and to do so he decided to sculpt a rainbow, clouds, and an *intertwined knot/ tie* (the word *Kesher* in Hebrew, which also means *relationship*) (see Bat Or and Grenimann Bauch, 2017).

When asked specifically about their relationship with their fathers and generational differences, four of these fathers mentioned their own fathers as being more physically distant than they are, and their wish to be more present and physically close to the child. For example, Shalom, father of Yoel, a two-and-a-half-year-old son (Figure 1 in Table 6.3), emphasized this as the most important part of his sculpture and experience. He related, however, to a general experience rather than one specific to his father:

Parental gender roles in clay 77

Table 6.3 Themes in response to specific questions by the interviewer

Sculptures by fathers of girls	Sculptures by fathers of girls	Sculptures by fathers of boys	Sculptures by fathers of boys
– using non-human objects to symbolize the relationship	– using relatively abstract indications of body parts, with only one sculpture (#2) indicating touching (but non-human) body parts	– The father is holding the child	Higher separation – with signs of movement and/or playfulness
5	11	4	5
10	2 **protecting vs. encouraging independence**	1 **An abstract representation of protecting vs. encouraging independence**	3 *'mini-me' **Reaching for a hug**
	'elephants hugging'	*'mini-me'	*'mini-me'
	6	8	9
		*'mini-me'	
	Reaching for a hug		*'mini-me'

Shalom[6]: I don't have, like, memories {emphasized} of that kind of ... or very few memories of that kind of ... just sort of resting in someone's arms like that. [...] And I want to, like, etch it {emphasized} into his core, so whatever happens he'll remember he had a father that held him.

Among other fathers, when relating to their relationship with their own fathers, words such as *provider* (in the sense of *breadwinner*), *functional*, and *strict* came up. Shmuel, father of Danny, a two-year-old boy (Figure 3 in Table 6.3), spoke specifically about his relationship with his father then describing his wish to provide his son with a different experience:

Shmuel: My father was also stricter than I am. And ... those things were eventually, sort of, encoded in me as an ... unsuccessful experience, that I wouldn't like to repeat with my son. The opposite, I'd like to give him really the full ... respect and autonomy ... and the [his own] choice, and patience towards him, love, attention and softness ... and physical connection. I presume I had this with my father at the beginning, and then it went and faded. So ... In some way I'd like to lead him, and me, through a corrective experience.

However, not all fathers felt such a big gap between themselves and their fathers. More than half of the fathers (54%) emphasized how deeply they respected their fathers and their efforts, identifying with the position they were in.

Physical closeness was one of many topics raised that were linked to intergenerational transmission. An additional topic that appeared in four interviews (36%) was the feeling that their fathers were less verbally preoccupied than they are about their level and style of involvement with the children. As Lior, father of Liel, a two-year-old boy (Figure 8 in Table 6.3), relates: 'If it disturbs me that I come home late from work ... I don't think it's something that preoccupied him.'

In general, the fathers described a feeling of exploring, and learning to master, new turfs – ones they had not necessarily been taught about, and cannot model according to their own fathers. In other words, they were describing (and sculpting) the reworking of their paternal representations.

Present – social and personal expectations of fathers

A topic that came up in many interviews[7] was the societal expectations of fathers, as they had experienced them. Some fathers discussed what they 'should be' doing, or 'fatherly activities' they imagine doing in the future (such as carrying the child on their shoulders or playing sports together), while others discussed their wife's expectations as well as their own. Two comments that repeated themselves in different ways were the Hebrew equivalent of 'leave well enough alone,' *kol hamodif gorea*, lit. 'anyone who adds, subtracts,' and the Arabic word *Mabsut*, meaning 'I am satisfied'[8]. One of the fathers, Oren, expanded on his satisfied reaction to his final sculpture (Figure 6.1), comparing it to his wife's perceived perfectionism. He mentioned that his wife thinks he draws better than her and prefers to send their daughter, Nava, a two-and-a-half-year-old, over to him whenever she wants someone to draw for her. However, he doesn't think he actually draws better than her, he simply says 'I draw badly, but I've accepted it.' When asked further, he reflected on the effect of her work as a nurse, which led her to take long night shifts and leave him on his own with the baby:

Oren: Although it's only drawing with the child ... but there are those mothers, that wouldn't necessarily send [the child over]. I know from my sisters

Figure 6.1 Oren's Sculpture. Photographed by: Nehama Grenimann Bauch. Date: 15.07.2014.

and other women I know, that it was sometimes very hard for them to let go of the child after he was born ... She [his wife] didn't have a choice. She had to go to work or take exams. Every once in a while she had to leave her to work for periods of nine hours at a time, from the age of three months old. [...] It forced me to deal with all the components of raising the child and not just putting her to bed. And it forced her on the one hand to trust me, and on the other hand to believe that I could handle it.

In addition to discussing the mothers' attitudes towards their level of involvement with the child, some of the fathers mentioned receiving praise from their surroundings for merely being present in the child's life, or taking the child for doctor check-ups. Roi, father of Shira, a girl aged three years and three months (Figure 6 in Table 6.3), elaborated on a difference he experienced between a large multicultural city such as Tel Aviv, and peripheral areas, in which his level of involvement as a father evoked a reaction from the local nurses:

Roi: Every time I came to Tipat Chalav [the nurses station for routine newborn check-ups and vaccinations] with Shira, there was a celebration. So many compliments.

These experiences were not necessarily described as positive ones. At times the feelings that were raised involved feeling misunderstood and/ or lonely. As Ariel, father of Yael, a two-year-old girl (Figure 5 in Table 6.3), described: 'I'm still the only guy on the playground. I'm the only guy who picks up from kindergarten.' On the other hand, fathers spoke of expectations they have of themselves, ones that link both to their intergenerational transmissions and to the social expectations and influences they currently feel. Nachshom (Figure 9 in Table 6.3), for example, describes his feelings of not being present or involved enough:

Nachshom: Actually my wife tells me I'm not as terrible as I think ... that I'm harder on myself. So moving forward {referring to moving the sculpted figure of his son forward, closer to the father figure} was a little more for myself, maybe so I will feel better. But ... How does she say? 'there are all kinds of ways to be with him'. And right now I'm with him in more indirect ways. Not playing with him on the rug but I ... I'm busy providing.

The fathers brought up two related aspects of the way they experience their surroundings' social expectations of them as fathers, as well as their own: 1. Enabling and normalizing attitudes towards their level of involvement with their child, versus isolation and being treated as unique; 2. The influence of work-related and financial pressure on the division of parental tasks and roles between mother and father. These aspects were also influenced by their own perceptions of the effects of gender on parenting and their wishes for the future.

Future – relating to perceived parental gender roles in therapy settings

Towards the end of the interviews, questions regarding the topic of gender differences in parenting evoked varied, strong opinions. Three of the fathers emphasized the uniqueness of their contribution as fathers. However, they did not view it as necessarily, or only, gender-based or quantifiable, as Ariel stated:

Ariel: I think every parent plays a different role in her life ... each parent has a different ah ... she perceives us differently, and in that way, each one ... fills up a different need in her life. Sometimes she will need what mommy represents, and sometimes she'll need what daddy represents. Um ... there is no 'more' or 'less' in ... in the way she sees us. At least as far as I understand.

The next topic raised was that of art therapists involving fathers in the child's therapy, and inviting (or not inviting) them to parental intervention sessions. This topic was raised hypothetically, since none of the children were in therapy at the time – however they related it to experiences of being invited to talk to the kindergarten teacher, occupational therapist nurse, or similar examples. For some fathers, this topic raised a lot of emotion and concern. Lior (Figure 8 in Table 6.3), for example, chose to emphasize the importance of feeling included:

Lior: It's a social topic ... and it's very important. [...] Even understanding that the father is a parent, is not always so obvious to a lot of people. And I don't think it's just because ... I think there's a feeling that many times women are very protective of this place of the mother as a parent ... [...] It's important for me as a father to be there. Not because I represent a different aspect {a different parental role}... Maybe also, probably also. [...] But if we put that aside for a moment I just want to know that I'm also a part of it. Just as much as I want to carry him differently on my shoulders {as he sculpted}, I want to know that I can go to his therapy sessions.

Lior concluded his thoughts by highlighting the importance 'for it to be possible to contain and include fathers.' The fact that the interviewer was a woman, as are the majority of art therapists working in schools in Israel today[9], was also explicitly raised by the interviewer at the end of the interview, evoking different reactions. Three fathers stated that the therapist's gender has some sort of influence on them. For example, Tamir, father of a two-year-old son (Figure 5 in Table 6.3), Ram linked this influence to his wife's criticism of him:

Tamir: Somewhere at the end there's some criticism that I raise about myself which is obviously sometimes directed at me from ... my wife. So it could be that in this bit you're wearing the hat of both a woman and a mother ... so maybe I'm also leading the answers to there.

Two of the fathers interviewed were therapists themselves and at the end of the interview, they were welcomed to speak their mind freely and add their professional perspective about the topic of including fathers in a child's therapy and parental intervention. Nachshom (Figure 9 in Table 6.3), who was working in the mental health sector at the time of the interview, elaborated:

Nachshom: Since the profession is mostly feminine ... most of the therapists are female and the mother is at the centre [of the therapy], I feel that we give up on fathers too quickly. [...] I feel that we don't ... In most of the parental education in our clinic, the fathers are peripheral ... if they're present at all. And I feel it's also more comfortable for the therapists. It's easier to release us [from the involvement in therapy] ... [...] And I think it's a mistake. Especially if you look at the family situation, the father is part of it ... an inseparable part of the family. And the other way around ... It perpetuates the prevailing family dance.

Both Nachshom and Shmuel felt that fathers in therapy are less emotionally expressive and more instrumental. Therefore, they felt that the experience of sculpting in clay and answering projective questions 'could connect him [the father] with all kinds of feelings he has towards his childhood, towards the child, towards what ... doesn't always naturally surface,' as Shmuel stated.

To summarize, the fathers expressed a variety of feelings and experiences regarding their unique contributions to their child's upbringing and their wishes to be acknowledged, accepted, and involved in the child's educational and (hypothetical) therapeutic environments. However, they also brought up the complexity of the influence gender may have on the relationship between a female interviewer and/ or therapist and a father. Some of the fathers acknowledged a sensitive approach to encouraging the father's participation in parental interventions, allowing him to gradually explore his experiences and feelings regarding parenthood, through the clay work and the projective and direct questions.

Fathers in art therapy – looking into the future

According to Lollis (2003, 67), time is 'one of the major defining features of a relational perspective.' By arranging the themes and topics that came up in the interviews into past, present, and future categories, I hope to encourage the understanding that the father's experience in the art therapy room is constantly linked to both an inner, personal process and a larger-scale social process. In relation to both processes, time plays a significant role: while the father's present experience as a parent – including his relationships with his child and partner – is important in itself, it is constantly influenced by past experiences and notions, including male socialization and perpetually confusing and complex societal norms regarding parental gender roles. His experience is also influenced by the therapist/ interviewer's expectations of the father and the father's own perception of what is expected of him. Another factor is what they each strive to achieve in the future, be it an acknowledgement of the father's significance to the child or an increased involvement in the child's therapy.

By learning more about his parental representations, through nonverbal art making and verbal reflection, the father has the opportunity to explore his identity as a parent in the framework of today's ever-changing social norms. As Trowell put it:

> The individual man needs to have a good sense of his identity, and also a sense of self – 'this is what I am good at; these are my faults and weaknesses' – so that he feels confident and worthwhile as a person. This sense of a secure base is important if he is to withstand the emotional highs and lows that are an inevitable part of parenthood. It is developed when an individual has had experience of another who is reliably and consistently available, who can contain and process their own and their child's thoughts and feelings. Fathers who have had this then have the capacity to sustain commitment; caring for a child depends more on commitment and containment than having glowing feelings.
>
> (Trowell, 2002, 4)

The act of creating confronts many people with issues of dealing with imperfections – with the fear of making mistakes, or of over-correcting until the original, spontaneous expression is 'lost.' However, it also allows one to experience great satisfaction with the outcome – through a process that requires a certain amount of confrontation with fears. These experiences are not gender specific, but in this context, they can be used as a metaphor for the father's experience of parenting, as one father, Shalom (Figure 2), pointed out: '... trying to shape ... shape yourself, shape someone else.' The use of body expression through physical work with clay, combined with mental processes – through modelling and observing the work – allows the fathers to integrate emotions, memories, and fantasies from different levels of consciousness (Sholt and Gavron, 2006). Thus the father may be able to recognize deeply ingrained ideas he has about gender and parenting roles from new, fresh perspectives.

In this sense, it appears plausible that the themes that arose verbally were influenced by the preceding, nonverbal sculpting experiences – for example the sculpting of a father reaching for a hug, or holding the child's hand may have influenced the way the fathers later described not being held or hugged by their own fathers. The fathers' descriptions of their attempts to rework their paternal representations, consistent with previous findings (Bretherton, Lambert, and Golby, 2006), have the potential of taking on another dimension through the metaphorical enactment of remodelling in clay. The discussion of perfectionism and satisfaction raises many questions about the effects of socialization on parenting roles that go beyond the effects of feeling observed by the interviewer: could the mothers' perceived perfectionism be linked to a social pressure to be the 'perfect' primary caregiver? Could the fathers' worries about not ruining (as expressed by their wishes to 'leave well enough alone'[10]) the sculpture be linked to social pressure regarding the sensitivity required of them as fathers and partners? Or did low social expectations with regard to the level of paternal involvement contribute to their expressions of satisfaction with perceived 'imperfect' sculptures?

Some research has indeed shown that men tend to be slightly more compassionate toward themselves than women (Yarnell et al., 2015), while women tend to be more compassionate toward others than men (Eisenberg and Lennon, 1983). This may be a result of women being socialized to be nurturing and self-sacrificing, as part of their assigned role of caregivers in society (Ruble and Martin, 1998). In the context of parenting, self-compassion signifies having a more forgiving view of one's parenting efforts (Duncan, Coatsworth, and Greenberg, 2009). However, differences in societal expectations regarding motherhood and fatherhood may affect a father's own parenting efficacy expectations (Gross and Marcussen, 2017). A father's apparent acceptance of his paternal imperfections might thus be linked to his parental efficacy expectations, making it harder for an art therapist to detect when he is being self-compassionate, and when there is, in fact, a great need for a paternal intervention. Kaplan (2010) describes a case in which a father was encouraged to get involved in his daughter's therapy through a dyadic father–child intervention.

Being relatively absent from his daughter's childrearing, the father initially treated his daughter's problem as something that would solve itself over time (thus being satisfied with imperfections). The therapist, however, emphasized time and time again his importance to his daughter and to the process. When the father was encouraged to 'meet' his daughter in therapy, Kaplan says, both father and child experienced a new way of being part of a triangular relationship (father–daughter–therapist and subsequently father–daughter–mother), which the child desperately needed at her developmental stage of separation and individuation (Edwards and Liu, 2002).

Curtis (2013) emphasizes the importance of relating to the political aspects of art therapy, and the significance of exploring and discussing issues of social justice and gender. Hogan and Cornish (2014) also recommend that exploration of gender should be a more integral part of art therapy training. I would add to this that trainees would benefit from a specific reflection on the approach to fathers, especially in the context of child therapy, and on the complex interaction between female art therapists and fathers. In that respect, I find that the topic of fathers in art therapy touches on a larger – socially, culturally, and politically influenced – issue regarding father engagement in childrearing and professionals' attitudes towards fathers in different therapeutic or educational settings. Since they are the main providers of therapy for children within school systems, I believe art therapists in Israel (and perhaps around the world) are in a unique position of influence to encourage fathers' participation in their child's therapy.

Conclusions

I tend to agree with Shapiro (1993) that all therapists, male and female, inevitably bring their own social and gendered conceptions into the therapy room. With regard to fathers, for example, this can mean that a female therapist has a preconceived idea of the level of interest the father may have in his child's therapy. Such an approach, even if subconscious and unintentional, may cause the father to feel attacked, uninteresting, or unimportant, resulting in a reluctance to engage in an already uncomfortable situation (Kaplan, 2010). My impression, after interviewing fathers and reading their accounts carefully, was that they may have gotten so used to not being asked about their own experiences, feelings, or intentions – that a mere genuine and curious questioning regarding their point of view has the potential to open up a deep and much-needed discussion that may assist them in their own understanding of themselves as fathers and their relationship with their children. The use of clay and the unveiling of deeply rooted parental representations may allow for a more multidimensional, gradual process to occur. It also allows us, researchers and therapists, to gain a deeper and much-needed understanding of the fathers' experiences and, consequently, a more sensitive, inclusive and encouraging professional approach.

Notes

1 Due to the small study sample, we chose to focus on fathers from one (locally dominant) religion in order to maintain a demographically and culturally homogeneous group, and reduce the potential effects of religious and cultural variables on the study findings. Ten out of the eleven fathers were born in Israel.
2 While the role may be reversed with regards to numbers (small samples of women versus small samples of men) and roles (male researchers studying women versus female researchers studying men), the phenomenon of the male gaze in medical and mental health research is obviously different and not comparable to the phenomenon of the marginalization of fathers from parenting research.
3 Although there have been a respectable amount of world-renowned women researchers and theorists in the field, such as Mary Ainsworth, Melanie Klein, Anna Freud and Mary Target, to name a few.
4 All fathers were Jewish – in order to reduce possible effects of cultural and sociological differences. The children's average age was 2.3. Six of the children were boys and the other five were girls, maintaining a relative child-gender balance. The fathers' ages ranged between 30 and 37, with an average age of 33.8. Most of the fathers (72%) assessed themselves as having an above average income and level of education. All fathers rated themselves as very involved during pregnancy, birth, and the first three days of the baby's life. The father's paternity leave varied greatly, with six fathers who took 2-7 days off, and five fathers who took between 14 to 60 days. Taken together the average paternity leave was 20.36 days.
5 The study has been approved by the Ethics Committee of the University of Haifa. All participants agreed to use the information in the interviews for research purposes and signed consent forms. More details about the research methodology and participant backgrounds can be found in Grenimann Bauch, 2015 and Bat Or and Grenimann Bauch, 2017.
6 All of the fathers' and children's names have been changed to ensure confidentiality.
7 See Table 6.2 for number of fathers mentioning each topic.
8 I have already discussed this phenomenon in a former article (Bat Or and Grenimann Bauch, 2017), however in this chapter I would like to specifically focus on its connection to societal expectations of fathers and their perception of gender differences in parental roles.
9 Haim Bior, *Is Art Therapy a Legitimate Treatment Option? Depends Who You Ask*, Haaretz (English edition), October 7, 2013, accessed May 1, 2017, http://www.haaretz.com/israel-news/.premium-1.551127.
10 For more details about this phenomenon, please refer to Bat Or and Grenimann Bauch, 2017, and Grenimann Bauch, 2017.

References

Adams, T. L. 2010. Gender and feminization in health care professions. *Sociology Compass* 47 (10): 454–65. doi:10.1111/j.1751-9020.2010.00294.x.

Bakel, H. J. A. van, Mass, A. J. B. M., Vreeswijk, C. M. J. M., and Vingerhoets, A. D. J. J. M. 2013. Pictorial representation of attachment: measuring the parent-fetus relationship in expectant mothers and fathers. *BMC Pregnancy and Childbirth* 13 (1): 138. doi:10.1186/1471-2393-13-138.

Bat Or, M. 2010. Clay sculpting of mother and child figures encourages mentalization. *Arts in Psychotherapy* 37 (4): 319–27. doi:10.1016/j.aip.2010.05.007.

Bat Or, M. 2012. Non-verbal representations of maternal holding of preschoolers. *Arts in Psychotherapy* 39 (2): 117–25. doi:10.1016/j.aip.2012.02.005.

Bat Or, M. 2015. Separateness representations in a sculpting task: Revealing maternal subjective experience. *Art Therapy: Journal of the American Art Therapy Association* 32 (2): 70–77. doi:10.1080/07421656.2015.1028005.

Bat Or, M. and Grenimann Bauch, N. 2017. Paternal representations and contemporary fatherhood themes through a clay figure-sculpting task among fathers of toddlers. *Arts in Psychotherapy* 56: 19–29. doi:10.1016/j.aip.2017.07.004.

Bornstein, M. H. 2002. Parenting infants. In *Handbook of Parenting, Vol. 1*. 2nd ed. Edited by M. H. Bornstein. Mahwah: Lawrence Erlbaum Associates.

Bretherton, I., Lambert, J. D., and Golby, B. 2006. Modeling and reworking childhood experiences: Involved fathers' representations of being parented and of parenting a preschool child. In *Parenting Representations – Theory, Research, and Clinical Implications*. Edited by O. Mayseless, 177–207. New York: Cambridge University.

Brown, L., Callahan, M., Strega, S., Walmsley, C., and Dominelli, L. 2009. Manufacturing ghost fathers: The paradox of father presence and absence in child welfare. *Child and Family Social Work* 14 (1): 25–34. doi:10.1111/j.1365-2206.2008.00578.x.

Brown, G. L., Mangelsdorf, S. C., and Neff, C. 2012. Father involvement, paternal sensitivity, and father–child attachment security in the f3 years. *Journal of Family Psychology* 26 (3): 421–30. doi:10.1037/a0027836.

Curtis, S. L. 2013. On gender and the creative arts therapies. *The Arts in Psychotherapy* 40 (3): 371–372. doi:10.1016/j.aip.2013.05.014.

Davison, K. K., Charles, J. N., Khandpur, N., and Nelson, T. J. 2017. Fathers??? Perceived reasons for their underrepresentation in child health research and strategies to increase their involvement. *Maternal and Child Health Journal* 21 (2): 267–74. doi:10.1007/s10995-016-2157-z.

Duncan, L. G., Coatsworth, J. D. and Greenberg, M.T. 2009. Pilot study to gauge acceptability of a mindfulness-based, family-focused preventive intervention. *The Journal of Primary Prevention* 30(5): 605–618. doi: 10.1007/s10935-009-0185-9.

Edwards, C. P. and Liu, W. L. 2002. Parenting toddlers. In *Handbook of Parenting*. 2nd ed. Edited by M. H. Bornstein, 45–71. Mahwah: Lawrence Erlbaum Associates.

Eichler, M., Reisman, A. L., and Borins, E. M. 1992. Gender bias in medical research. *Women and Therapy* 12 (4): 37–41. doi:10.1300/J015v12n04.

Eisenberg, N. and Lennon, R. 1983. Sex differences in empathy and related capacities. *Psychological Bulletin* 94: 100–131. doi:10.1037/0033-2909.94.1.100.

Fonagy, P. and Target, M. 2007. The rooting of the mind in the body: New links between attachment theory and psychoanalytic thought. *Journal of the American Psychoanalytic Association* 55 (2): 411–56. doi:10.1177/00030651070550020501.

Gavron, T. and Mayseless, O. 2015. The joint painting procedure to assess implicit aspects of the mother–child relationship in middle childhood. *Art Therapy* 28(1): 1656. doi:10.1080/07421656.2015.1028007.

Goldner, L., Gazit, O., and Scharf, M. 2017. Separateness and closeness as expressed in bird's nest drawings: Relationships with partners and with the unborn child among expectant parents. *Arts in Psychotherapy* 53: 1–11. doi:10.1016/j.aip.2016.12.002.

Greenall, S. 2014. Gender and career choice in art therapy: A survey (Le genre et le choix d'une carrière en art-thérapie: Un sondage). *Canadian Art Therapy Association Journal* 27 (1): 5–7. doi:10.1080/08322473.2014.11415590.

Grenimann Bauch, N. 2015. Effects of clay figure sculpting of father and child on paternal mentalization. Master's Degree Thesis, The University of Haifa, Faculty of Social Welfare and Health Sciences, Graduate School of Creative Art Therapies.

Gross, C. L. and Marcussen, K. 2017. Postpartum depression in mothers and fathers: The role of parenting efficacy expectations during the transition to parenthood. *Sex Roles* 76(5–6): 290–305. doi: 10.1007/s11199-016-0629-7

Haesler, M. 1996. The absent father: Gender identity considerations for art therapists working with adolescent boys. *Art Therapy: Journal of the American Art Therapy Association* 13: 275–281.

Harel, J., Kaplan, H., Avimeir-Patt, R., and Ben-Aaron, M. 2006. The child's active role in mother-child, father-child psychotherapy: A psychodynamic approach to the treatment of relational disturbances. *Psychology and Psychotherapy* 79: 23–36. doi:10.1348/147608305X52577.

Havsteen-franklin, D. 2015. Mentalization-based art psychotherapy, In *Approaches to Art Therapy: Theory and Technique*. 3rd ed. Edited by J. Rubin, 144–163. New York and London Routledge.

Hogan, S. 2012. Problems of identity. In *Revisiting Feminist Approaches to Art Therapy*. Edited by S. Hogan, 13. New York: Berghahn Books.

Hogan, S. and Cornish, S. 2014. Unpacking gender in art therapy: The elephant at the art therapy easel. *International Journal of Art Therapy* 19 (3): 122–34 . doi:10.1080/17454832.2014.961494.

Janesick, V. J., 2000. The choreography of qualitative research design. In *Handbook of Qualitative Research*. 2nd ed. Edited by N. K. Denzin and Y. S. Lincoln, 379–400. Thousand Oaks: Sage.

Kaplan, H. 2010. The father in dyadic therapy: On the importance of meeting the actual father (Hebrew). In *Dyadic Therapy: Meetings between the Therapeutic Act and Theory*. Edited by H. Kaplan, J. Harel and R. Avimeir-Patt, 199–229. Haifa: The University of Haifa, Department of Psychology.

Lamb, M. E. 2010. How do fathers influence children's development? Let me count the ways. In *The Role of the Father in Child Development*. 5th ed. Edited by M. E. Lamb, 1–26. Hoboken: Wiley.

LeCompte, M. D. and Preissle, J. 1993. *Ethnography and Qualitative Design in Educational Research*. 2nd ed. San Diego: Academic Press.

Lev-Wiesel, R. and Liraz, R. 2007. Drawings vs. narratives: Drawing as a tool to encourage verbalization in children whose fathers are drug abusers. *Clinical Child Psychology and Psychiatry* 12 (1): 65–75.

Levant, R. F. 2011. Research in the psychology of men and masculinity using the gender role strain paradigm as a framework. *American Psychologist*. 66 (8): 765–776.

Liebmann, M. 2003. Working with men. In *Gender Issues in Art Therapy*. Edited by S. Hogan, 108. London: Jessica Kingsley Publishers.

Lollis, S. 2003. Conceptualizing the influence of the past and the future in present parent-child relationships. In *Handbook of Dynamics in Parent-Child Relations*. Edited by L. Kuczynski. Thousand Oaks: Sage.

Mayseless, O. 2006. Studying parenting representations as a window to parents' internal working model of caregiving. In *Parenting Representations: Theory, Research, and Clinical Implications*. Edited by O. Mayseless. New York: Cambridge University.

Michalski, D., Kohout, J., Wicherski, M., and Hart, B. 2011. 2009 Doctorate employment survey. Washington DC: Center for Workforce Studies Science Directorate, American Psychological Association. Accessed at: https://www.apa.org/workforce/publications/09-doc-empl/report.pdf

OECD (Organisation for Economic Co-operation and Development) 2012. *Education at a Glance 2012: OECD Indicators*. Paris: OECD Publishing. Accessed at: http://dx.doi.org/10.1787/eag-2012-en

Palm, G. 2014. Attachment theory and fathers : Moving from 'being there' to 'being with'. *Journal of Family Theory and Review* 6 (4): 282–97. doi:10.1111/jftr.12045.

Panter-Brick, C., Burgess, A., Eggerman, A., McAllister, F., Pruett, K., and Leckman, J. F. 2014. Practitioner review: Engaging fathers – recommendations for a game change in parenting interventions based on a systematic review of the global evidence. *Journal of Child Psychology and Psychiatry and Allied Disciplines* 55 (11): 1187–1212. doi:10.1111/jcpp.12280.

Patton, M. Q. 2002. *Qualitative Research and Evaluation Methods*. Thousand Oaks: Sage Publications.

Proulx, L. 2003. *Strengthening Emotional Ties Through Parent-Child-Dyad Art Therapy: Interventions with Infants and Preschoolers*. London and Philadelphia: Jessica Kingsley Publishers.

Rege, M. and Solli, I. F. 2013. The impact of paternity leave on fathers' future earnings. *Demography* 50 (6): 2255–77. doi:10.1007/s13524-013-0233-1.

Rouyer, V., Frascarolo, F., Zaouche-Gaudron, C., and Lavanchy, C. 2007. Fathers of girls, fathers of boys: Influence of child's gender on fathers' experience of engagement in, and representations of, paternity. *Swiss Journal of Psychology* 66 (4): 225–33. doi:10.1024/1421-0185.66.4.225.

Ruble, D. N. and Martin, C. L. 1998. Gender development. In *Handbook of Child Psychology: Social, Emotional, and Personality Development, Vol. 3*. 5th ed. Edited by W. Damon (Series Ed.) and N. Eisenberg, 933–1016. New York: Wiley.

Samana, R. 2016. Thinking 'outside of the womb' (Hebrew). *Discussions*, 31(1), 7–18.

Scharf, M. and Mayseless, O. 2011. Buds of parenting in emerging adult males: What we learned from our parents. *Journal of Adolescent Research* 26 (4): 479–505. doi:10.1177/0743558411402339.

Shai, D. and Belsky, J. 2011. Parental embodied mentalizing: Let's be explicit about what we mean by implicit. *Child Development Perspectives* 5 (3): 187–88. doi:10.1111/j.1750-8606.2011.00195.x.

Shamri-Zeevi, L., Regev, D., and Snir, S. 2015. The usage of art materials in the framework of parental training. *The Arts in Psychotherapy* 45: 56–63. doi:10.1016/j.aip.2015.07.002.

Shapiro, S. A. 1993. Gender-role stereotypes and clinical process: Commentary on papers by Gruenthal and Hirsch. *Psychoanal. Dial.* 3 (3): 371–387.

Sholt, M. and Gavron, T. 2006. Therapeutic qualities of clay-work in art therapy and psychotherapy: A review. *Art Therapy* 23 (2): 66–72. doi:10.1080/07421656.2006.10129647.

Slade, A. 2007. Reflective parenting programs: Theory and development. *Psychoanalytic Inquiry* 26 (4): 640–57. doi:10.1080/07351690701310698.

Taylor, L. and Adelman, H. S. 2001. Enlisting appropriate parental cooperation and involvement in children's mental health treatment. In *The Mental Health Desk Reference*. Edited by E. R. Welfel and R. E. Ingersoll. New York: Wiley.

Trombetta, R. 2007. Art therapy, men and the expressivity gap. *Art Therapy* 24 (1): 29–32. doi:10.1080/07421656.2007.10129362.

Trowell, J. 2002. Setting the scene. In *The Importance of Fathers: A Psychoanalytic Re-Evaluation*. Edited by S. Budd. New York: Taylor and Francis.

Vandello, J. A., Hettinger, V. E., Bosson, J. K., and Siddiqi, J. 2013. When equal isn't really equal: The masculine dilemma of seeking work flexibility. *Journal of Social Issues* 69 (2): 303–21. doi:10.1111/josi.12016.

Veras, M. 2014. Health professionals in the 21st century: Results from an inter professional and multi-institutional global health competencies survey (A pilot study). *British Journal of Medicine and Medical Research* 4 (10): 2002–13. doi:10.9734/BJMMR/2014/7483.

Vick, R. M. 2007. The boy is father to the man: Introduction to the special issue on men in art therapy. *Art Therapy* 24 (1): 2–3. doi:10.1080/07421656.2007.10129363.

Vreeswijk, C. M. J. M, Maas, A. J. B. M., Rijk, C. H. A. M., Braeken, J., and van Bakel, H. J. A. 2014. Stability of fathers' representations of their infants during the transition to parenthood. *Attachment and Human Development* 16 (3): 292–306. doi:10.1080/14616734.2014.900095.

Wall, G. and Arnold, S. 2007. How involved is involved fathering?: An exploration of the contemporary culture of fatherhood. *Gender & Society* 21 (4): 508–27. doi:10.1177/0891243207304973.

Weiss, J. 1999. 'A drop-in catering job': Middle class women and fatherhood, 1950-1980. *Journal of Family History* 24 (3): 374–90.

Yarnell, L. M., Stafford, R. E., Neff, K. D., Reilly, E. D., Knox, M. C., and Mullarkey, M. 2015. Meta-analysis of gender differences in self-compassion. *Self and Identity* 14 (5): 499–520. doi:10.1080/15298868.2015.1029966.

Zvara, B. J., Schoppe-Sullivan, S. J., and Dush, C. K. 2013. Fathers' involvement in child health care: Associations with prenatal involvement, parents' beliefs, and maternal gatekeeping. *Family Relations* 62 (4): 649–61. doi:10.1111/fare.12023.

Chapter 7

The birth project
Mothers and birth professionals make art

Susan Hogan

The Birth Project is an Arts and Humanities Funding Council (AHRC, UK) supported research project investigating the role that arts engagement could play in ante-natal and post-natal care. Moreover, what an arts-based approach offers in examining birth experiences and the transition to motherhood is a further subject of enquiry. This chapter will discuss the project in depth. It will elucidate the research questions and attempt to answer them. First of all, the rationale for the project will be discussed in more depth.

The Birth Project is particularly interested in exploring women's subjective experience of birth and the transition to motherhood using the arts, within a participatory arts framework (Hogan 2017). Through the project, new mothers have been given the opportunity to explore their experiences of joy, stress, birth suffering and post-natal readjustment via the arts. Three arts-based groups have been run with different groups of new mothers. One group (*Mothers Make Art*) worked with women using contemporary arts practice, particularly the creation of installation art; it was pedagogic as well as participatory in focus, insofar as it sought to teach participants about contemporary art and to give the women the theoretical and practical skills to develop their own enduring arts practice: the skills and confidence to continue with on-going artistic self-expression (Hogan 2015). The second group (*Arts Elicitation: Exploring the Birth Experience*) was more therapeutic in its ambience, using themes in a contained and containing manner to elicit the women's stories and reflections. Participants in this group had experienced a traumatic or troubling birth.

Other aspects of the Birth Project have focused on the birthing professionals involved and their experiences of compassion fatigue and occupational stress. A series of arts-based workshops were organised to explore the experience of birth professionals who may have experienced vicarious trauma and whose traumatising experience of trauma is often overlooked (*Birth Professionals Make Art*). A further group (*At Home*) was constituted by a series of workshops with young mums and dads who had already been meeting in a support group. A focus group and interviews also solicited the stories of fathers and obstetricians to inform a 'verbatim' theatrical production, *Labour Intensive*, devised and performed by *Third Angel*. This was later reworked as *Part-Us*, which was performed in a number of venues during 2016 and 2017 and continued to explore project themes.

The project investigates what is distinctive about an arts-based approach in supporting new mothers (Hogan 2015; 2016b; Hogan et al. 2015). Our overarching research questions, which are listed below, are concerned with the exploration of the role arts and humanities engagement might have to play in antenatal and postnatal provision, as part of routine care, especially where post-birth trauma is being translated into bodily symptoms. The Birth Project is also interested in exploring to what extent clinically related birth practices, which form part of 'routine care', are implicated in post-natal distress.

The different groups of participants joined together in 'mutual recovery' events in which perspectives have been shared, primarily through elucidation of the art works produced. These events were captured using documentary filmmaking. The *raison d'etre* of this project has been to stimulate dialogue between communities with different interests and experiences, to use the arts to interrogate discourses, to challenge embedded assumptions, and in this process, to facilitate a process of recovery – a 'mutual recovery' between all those who experience and are affected by birth. We situate this research endeavour in the context of an emerging practice of health humanities (Crawford et al. 2015). This chapter will synthesise the research results.

Theory underlying the process

During the twentieth and twenty-first centuries, there has been an increase in interest in representations of gender and their significance in generating scripts for us to live by which are potentially constraining, but also of significance in challenging entrenched ways of seeing (Hogan 1997). More recently there has been a burgeoning of interest in the kind of experiential knowledge, which can be conveyed by images and the use of images as routes to ways of knowing, which may not be immediately accessible through conventional text-based research methods (Hogan 2016c; Hogan and Pink 2011). The rich ways of knowing generated by art and art therapy techniques are now being considered and used in arts-based research. Guillemin and Westall (2008) assert that visual methods are a humane way of dealing with sensitive subject matter involving the articulation of painful experiences, as well as offering a novel and powerful means of accessing women's interior worlds.

People often give expression to their experience by using metaphors, which can better conceptualise and articulate their situation. In ideological struggles metaphors are commonly used around a contested site of meaning. This can take the form of pictorial or linguistic strategies to establish one meaning rather than another. When one looks at pictures with these ideas in mind, they can be seen as providing women with a tool for carving out a self-identity which might challenge dominant representations or those representations connected with their particular socio-economic or gender status (Hogan 1997; 2012a). The transition to motherhood, especially the birthing event, is a particularly contested site with regards to male/female power relations and the application of practices; historically every aspect of the management of the event has been potentially highly inflammatory and subject to rival proscriptions (Hogan 2003; 2008; 2012b; 2013; 2016a). The Birth Project is working with a diverse range of new mothers to enable them to explore their experience of childbirth and the transition to motherhood using a variety of art mediums and methods, including art elicitation (structured art making which is then discussed), community participatory arts, photography and theatre. Images produced include those which both represent and defy cultural expectations. This chapter will outline the basis of the project, articulate its research questions, discuss the methodology employed and then articulate some of the discourses that arose in the groups.

Making meaning visually

This study draws on analytical techniques developed within visual anthropology, which often use a collaborative approach to enable individuals or communities to represent themselves or to challenge dominant representations. Drawing on anthropologically informed theories of observation and visual representation (Ruby 2005; Pink 2004; Banks 2001), practical documentary film-making is used in a variety of ways, in conjunction with other art-making techniques, as a part of a case study in its own right, or to elicit further research materials. For instance, in visual elicitation visual data is used in conjunction with interviewing techniques to elicit responses (Newbury 2005 p.2). Marcus Banks, an anthropologist, is keen to emphasise that visual images should be seen in relation to 'the social context that produced the image, and the social relations within which the image is embedded at any moment of viewing' (p.11). These are research techniques, which also acknowledge the possibility of 'displacing' social relations into or 'onto inanimate objects, giving them the semblance of life or agency,' (Banks 2001 p.10).

Taylor and Spencer also emphasise the importance of social relations and the role of images in constructions of self and conceptualise 'identity' as a process of *becoming* rather than as a fixed set of enduring characteristics:

> Identity is a work in progress, a negotiated space between ourselves and others, constantly being re-appraised and very much linked to the circulation of cultural meanings in society. Furthermore, identity is intensely political. There are constant efforts to escape, fix or perpetuate images and meanings of others. These transformations are apparent in every domain and the relationships between these constructions reflect and reinforce power relations.
> (Taylor and Spencer 2004 p.4)

So, returning to my original proposition that individuals and groups often give expression to their experience in metaphorical discourse, which can conceptualise and express their situation, Spencer puts it like this, 'Visual culture can be a powerful dimension for affirming personal as well as collective identity' and our engagement 'with the values of society is frequently mediated through an array of visual signs' (Spencer 2011 p.111). These fields of representation and their conceptual potentials actually constitute and determine the possibilities of self. But these symbolic fields are not stable, but in flux. Contestation, or collision of sense (via pictorial representations), is ongoing and might be articulated in terms of rival hegemonies where different meanings and interpretations rub-up against each other, irritate or sometimes one will engulf another. The meanings embodied in images are open to reinterpretation by different viewers, contexts and epochs and, like the self, are by no means stable.

Attempts to negotiate a sense of self, or the representation of a community, are always located within a broader semiotic environment: what Cowie has called an 'inter-textual space' (a space full of representations which co-construct meaning). Powerful meanings are not generated simply by changed content or 'consciousness', but as the result of a different strategy for production of an image in relation to its inter-textual space (Cowie 1977 p.20). A crucial part of the identity of women is formed by the representations of women that surround us. Our engagement with our inter-textual context may be relatively inchoate or intuitive, or conversely very knowing and deliberate, but it must always be; our sense of knowing and being can never be decontextualised from our particular social context. Stuart Hall suggested that identity is 'a production which is never complete, always in process, and always constituted *within not outside, representation*' (1994 p.222).

Though images may be subject to multiple readings (they are polysemous) and open to distortion or appropriation, they may nevertheless provide women with a tool for carving out a self-identity which might seek to challenge prevailing representations or those representations connected with their particular socio-economic or gender status. In this case, it may be a challenge to the expectations of those organising the birth, or the community's sense of what a mother should be like. It is also possible that the process of using the arts can enhance awareness of representational systems and increase critical awareness, so it has a potential consciousness raising capacity. As I have discussed elsewhere, context is always crucial to both the production and reading of images; the juxtapositions between images are capable of producing unforeseen narratives, which is a complicating factor in using arts-based approaches in research (Hogan 2017).

The 'why'

Postnatal depression, trauma and psychosis are expensive in every sense, with long-term consequences for women and their children's development. Recent figures for perinatal depression, psychosis and anxiety suggest a global figure, with long-term costs, of £8.1 billion per year in the UK (Bauer et al. 2014). Around a quarter of women have symptoms of psychological trauma following birth and some experience post-traumatic stress disorder (PTSD) (Czarnocka and Slade 2000). Moreover, it is estimated that about half of all cases of perinatal depression and anxiety go undetected (Bauer et al. 2014). The quality of life and wellbeing of many women is adversely affected with long-term consequences for them and their children. Unresolved or traumatic birth experiences appear to be one of a number of triggers of post-natal depression (PND). The main cause of maternal death in the UK is suicide (Oates 2013). Effects of poor maternal mental health can have an impact upon foetal, child and adolescent health (NICE 2007). The mother's prenatal anxiety has also been strongly linked to her child's later mental-health problems (O'Donnell et al. 2014).

There is no consensus about the cause of PND and the complexity of contributing factors is a justification for further research (Hogan et al. 2017). Indeed, current classifications *'may not adequately address the range or combination of emotional distress experienced by mothers'* (Coates et al. 2015 p.1). This is a key point. Childbirth is complex and women experience often unprecedented pressures and constraints in their lives during pregnancy and after birth (Hogan 2016). However, effort has been expended in seeking to identify a number of 'psychosocial risk factors'. I'd like to pause to 'unpack' or deconstruct this notion of 'psychosocial risk factors' as problematic, if it is a mode of analysis which seeks to locate the germ or 'seed' of a problem as located within the individual, whose predisposing factors then blossom into illness. Though some women in particular circumstances may be more at risk of psychological distress during pregnancy, or after birth (such as those subject to emotional or psychical violence throughout their pregnancies from their partners, or women who have experienced prior rape, for example), I would like to suggest that the 'psychosocial risk factors' should not be seen as located *within* the individual woman, but rather viewed as a matrix or field of conflicting social forces which act upon women in a destabilising manner; childbirth and all of the practices surrounding it are highly contested and this contestation has effects (Hogan 2016). In particular, a number of hospital practices are illness inducing: iatrogenic. Iatrogenic illness is defined as having been produced by the adverse effects of medical treatments, procedures and practices. This project is interested to look at how hospital practices can result in distress for women. This distress is regarded as understandable rather than 'irrational' or pathological. So whilst is it hard to shake off the rhetoric of post-natal 'illness', there is an underlying interest in institutional *practices* and norms evident as problematic within this research. It is keen to 'de-pathologise' women's experiences, rather than add to a dominant rhetoric of women's instability and inadequacy.

Women who have not been diagnosed as depressed may benefit from support in ways that have significance for their infant's development, *'therefore universal provision of social-support packages should be considered'* (Hogan et al. 2017).

Coates et al. (2015), in a small qualitative study involving in-depth interviews with new mothers, found that women wanted support to be on offer regardless of whether a mental-health diagnosis had been made and that the availability of post-natal support should be 'normalised' and made universal. Coates et al. (2014) note that therapeutic support could explore psychological processes such as 'distancing, guilt and self-blame' associated with different types of emotional difficulties. They noted breastfeeding and birth trauma as key areas with which women felt they needed support that was not readily forthcoming. The 'postcode lottery' leaves women in about half the regions of the UK without access to specialist perinatal services (Bauer et al. 2014).

Our research questions

- What role might arts engagement have to play in ante-natal and post-natal care?
- To what extent are hospital practices, that are iatrogenic in nature, implicated in post-natal distress?
- To what extent is 'mutual recovery' possible through engagement with the arts, and if so, to establish what form this may take?
- What, in particular, does an arts-based approach offer in exploring birth experiences and the transition to motherhood?

The research

A number of arts-based workshops enabled different groups of participants to engage in art making to explore their experience of birth (Hogan et al. 2015). Three of the workshops were filmed (the fourth was audio-recorded). Not all of the participants appear in the footage at their own request and it is important to note that editorial changes to the footage were made at the request of participants, following consultative screenings.

The filming by Sheffield Vision has been used as part of the research method and as a documentation of the research process. The aim of the filming is four-fold.

1 First, as a method to record the research, which will be used to develop new thinking on contemporary birth experience and practice (it is research data).
2 Second, the footage is being edited to produce short films, which address the research questions. These films are a research output.
3 Third, the short films themselves will also function as teaching and training resources and will be made available for this.
4 Fourth, a documentary film of the entire process has been made and shown to a public audience. This aims to highlight some of the issues raised throughout the process.

The short films are rich with narrative sequences, which directly address the research questions. These are an important research output. I would urge readers to view the films which are freely available online (see link below).

Answering the research questions

What role might arts engagement have to play in ante-natal and post-natal care?

Art-based support groups could play an important part in giving women crucial social support at this crucial time. Though it is a fairly short intervention (and therefore relatively inexpensive), women found the intervention to be important (see project reports for narrative statements from participants). Two workshop series: *Arts Elicitation: Exploring the Birth Experience* and the *Mothers Make Art* both ran for twelve weeks and the Warwick–Edinburgh Mental Well-being Scale (WEMWBS) was assessed before and after the experience. This scale allows evaluation of projects which aim to improve mental wellbeing. It explores both feeling and functioning aspects of mental wellbeing with before and after scores generated by the questions. The analysis shows an overall improvement in self-reported measures across most fields and an increase of 37% in the overall WEMWBS scores for both of the arts interventions with the mothers, which is extremely noteworthy. *This is such a substantial improvement that we believe it will have long-term consequences for both the mothers and for their infant's development.* It will be interesting to work with a larger sample-size so that sub-analyses can be undertaken, so as to examine in further detail which aspects of wellbeing are most influenced by the intervention.

Participants' comments indicated increased social support, confidence, motivation and mental wellbeing, in addition to decreased social isolation. Despite small sample sizes, the initial results provide promising evidence of gains in mental wellbeing and social inclusion. The question of longer-term benefits beyond the duration of the workshops remains, but these results add further support to the use of participatory arts in promoting mental health and wellbeing for new mothers.

To what extent are hospital practices, that are iatrogenic in nature, implicated in post-natal distress?

Findings from the groups with mothers would appear to support existing research that indicates *it is the quality of care and the nature of the relationship between the care provider and the women* that is of crucial importance for her birthing experience, no matter where the birth takes place. This is an important finding for healthcare practices, which are increasingly stretched with temporal pressures on professionals, making it hard to form and maintain caring, compassionate relationships with birthing mothers and their partners.

However, institutional practices *did* have negative (iatrogenic) impacts. So-called 'routine induction' was imposed in a way that left one medical-professional mother feeling disempowered and angry; another mother had her baby removed after the birth and taken out of her sight and when the baby was returned to her, she had difficulty believing it was her own; conducting routine checks within the mother's view would be more humane and quite easy to achieve; the discomfort of cannulas (a cannula being a thin tube inserted into a vein to administer medications, which may or may not be part of induction) and feeling unable to remove them was a theme, as well as medical interventions getting in the way of the much-wanted experience of holding the new baby skin-to-skin. The birth professionals also reflected, in interesting ways, upon those aspects of institutional service, which diminish their ability to give mothers the level of care they clearly aspire to, and this is evident in the film footage.

To what extent is 'mutual recovery' possible through engagement with the arts, and if so, how to establish what form this may take?

The supportive nature of the groups and a sense of shared experience was important. Our findings concord with what women say they want: a supportive group experience *with other mothers*. Previously, new mothers had noted a safe space as of crucial importance (one in which medical professionals were not judging them, or potentially reporting on them) and also mentioned valuing having a space in which they could explore feelings not articulated elsewhere, including disturbing or shameful feelings (Hogan 2003; Hogan 2008b; Hogan 2012b). As new motherhood is supposed to be a joyous time, some new mothers find it difficult to find a place in which they can explore those more troubling feelings associated with a difficult birth experience, or the adjustment to motherhood.

One of the distinctive aspects of this project is the way it has been structured to enhance communication between different participatory groups concerned with birth. To recap, first different groups shared with each other in the ongoing group workshops. Participants practiced talking about their art works to each other, their ideas and developmental processes, as well as the end products. Then mothers in the Mothers Make Art group met with the mothers from the Art Elicitation Group in a 'mutual recovery' event, in which women exhibited their work in a gallery space and then reflected upon their art, ostensibly through explaining it to the other group members. This was done with great sensitivity, with an interior room available for art works, for participants who might need to be less 'exposed' (and which remained closed to guests during the set-up period). Some women were self-conscious in front of the camera (as parts of the event were filmed), but generally women who participated were excited and intrigued to see other women's work and pleased to share their own experience. One participant found the event very emotionally challenging and was given extra support, as we had qualified art therapists to hand. A conflict resolution specialist facilitated part of this event, though her particular expertise was not needed, as a tone of mutual tolerance and mutual respect prevailed.

At a further event birth professionals and mothers exhibited their work together. Sharing was less structured but continued informally around the viewing of the art works in the exhibition space. The different groups also got to watch and discuss each other's films at this event (a film having been produced about each of the first three groups). For these screenings we also had discussants, who viewed and then commented on the films from an outsider perspective, followed by the debate between participants: mothers and birthing professionals, enabling and enhancing communication between the different groups concerned with birth. One midwife said the mothers' images had a real impact on her in terms of portraying their distress and thought it might be useful to include such images in midwifery training books.

An art group with young parents also ran and some participants were interviewed. A piece of verbatim theatre captured material from interviews from others who had been marginal to the project at this point, including dads and obstetricians. A play was developed from this material. Participants from the experiential groups were invited to attend a performance in the Derby Theatre. This added a further opportunity for discussion of the birthing experience from multiple perspectives and enriched discourse around the topic. Thus the project explored the topic of 'mutual recovery' through the use of these sharing events, which created layers of analysis and different opportunities for engagement and reflection.

The larger events served to generate a discourse between different groups associated with the birth experience. The final analysis of transcript material may generate further insights here, which will be related to the final project report. Impact activity will be ongoing.

What, in particular, does an arts-based approach offer in exploring birth experiences and the transition to motherhood?

Art groups are a valuable resource for women to make sense of and understand their birthing experiences, as they potentially build self-awareness and self-confidence through the sharing of experience in the process of art making. Talking about and interrogating their experiences allowed women to develop enhanced self-acceptance and self-compassion. Whilst verbal support groups might work well for some women, inchoate emotions can be captured in art in ways, which are fundamentally different to that of a language-based approach (see Hogan 2017 for a detailed analysis of how visual expression is different from verbal expression in general terms with examples from this project).

The use of art materials was important for some of the participants in terms of self-expression, *revealing* their feelings or allowing their feelings to *emerge* and this is captured in the film footage. The transformational quality of art making was emphasised by a number of participants, as well as their increased sense of volition: their capacity to make a creative act happen and to take risks in the process was liberating, exciting and life-enhancing. Making time and space for personal reflection in a moment of transition was also noted as enriching. I will end with the words of one participant from *Mothers Make Art*:

I have absolutely *loved* every session.
They have been the light in my week.
They have been the me time when I have been able to remember who I am and to make contact with myself and my veracity.
After a *very* difficult year, it has been so important to my health to have this space.
I have loved that it hasn't just been about expression, but also taught us about art.

★★★

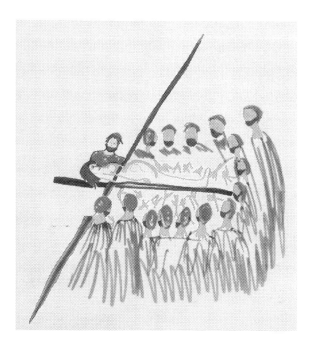

Figure 7.1 The Birth Project. Surrounded by a wall of blue. 2014.

SUMMARY OF PUBLICATIONS THAT EXPLORE THESE QUALITATIVE RESEARCH FINDINGS IN FURTHER DETAIL

Publications about the workshops:

Hogan, S. (2015). Mothers Make Art: Using Participatory Art to Explore the Transition to Motherhood. *Journal of Applied Arts & Health*,6(1):23–32.

This article delves into the methodology employed, producing an in-depth analysis of the innovative workshop techniques used in *Mothers Make Art* and how these were responded to.

Hogan, S., Baker, C., Cornish, S., McCloskey, P., and Watts, L. (2015). Birth Shock: Exploring Pregnancy, Birth and the Transition to Motherhood Using Participatory Arts in N. Burton (ed.) *Natal Signs: Representations of Pregnancy, Childbirth and Parenthood*. Bradford: Demeter Press. pp.272–269.

This chapter gives an overview of *Mothers Make Art* and the *Arts Elicitation Group* workshop series.

Other related publications:

Hogan S. (2017). Working Across Disciplines: Using Visual Methods in Participatory Frameworks in S. Pink, V. Fors, and T. O'Dell (eds) *Theoretical Scholarship and Applied Practice*. London: Berghahn.

Hogan, S., Sheffield, D., and Woodward, A. (2017). The Value of Art Therapy in Antenatal and Postnatal Care: A Brief Literature Review. *International Journal of Art Therapy (IJAT, formerly* Inscape), 22(4): 169–179. DOI: 10.1080/17454832.2017.1299774

Hogan, S. (2016). The Tyranny of Expectations of Post-Natal Delight: Gendering Happiness. *Journal of Gender Studies. Special Issue: Gendering Happiness*. DOI: 10.1080/09589236.2016.1223617

Reports and conference proceedings

Hogan, S. (2016b). *The Birth Project. Interim Report*. October 1–8. Derby: University of Derby. (online at website address).

Hogan, S. (2017). Birth Professionals Make Art. Using Participatory Arts to Think about Being a Birthing Professional in J. Saavedra, A. Espanol, S. Arias-Sanchez, and M. Calderon-Garcia (eds) *Creative Practices for Improving Health & Social Inclusion*. Conference Proceedings of the 5th International Health Humanities Conference. Seville: University of Seville, pp.115–125.

Hogan, S. (2018). *The Birth Project. Final Report*. Derby: University of Derby.

Website

For more information about The Birth Project and links to the films (AHRC grant ref. AH/K003364/1), please visit: http://www.derby.ac.uk/health-and-social-care/research/birth-project/

Acknowledgement

Many thanks to Phil Douglas for reading this through with respect to its legibility; he continues to curb my tendency towards excessive hyperbole and over-use of exclamation marks! Thanks also to Dr Charlie Baker for her feedback. Many people have contributed to this having been an exciting project. I have been particularly pleased to have involvement from the Mental Health Foundation and it has been a real pleasure to work with Professor Paul Crawford and other colleagues in the Creative Practice as Mutual Recovery research consortium. Workshop leaders and mutual recovery event facilitators: Shelagh Cornish, Deborah Gibson, Marian Liebmann and Lisa Watts need acknowledgement, as do current researchers Emma Joyes and Kate Phillips. Last, but not least, Eve Wood of Sheffield Vision has exercised huge amounts of patience in dealing with my editorial requests in my role as executive producer of the film series.

Appendix: Film descriptors

Creative practice as mutual recovery. Visual methodologies

In this film art- and performance-based methods are elucidated and illustrated. As well as giving the context for this project, it is hoped that this film will be a useful resource for research methods training, especially for those practitioners who are thinking of employing visual methods or collaborating with artists as part of social-science research projects; indeed, it is already being used by sociologists.

The film discusses the nature of participatory research. It investigates analytical techniques and collaborative approaches developed within visual anthropology to enable individuals or communities to represent themselves or to challenge dominant representations. The notion of visual elicitation (in which visual data, which have been found or made by respondents, are used in conjunction with interviewing techniques to elicit responses) is explained (Newbury 2005).

Performance-based social-science methods are becoming increasingly employed. These include participatory arts, art elicitation using techniques from art therapy and re-enactment photography, but also include monologues, dance, art installation, poetic and theatrical performance; such work provides new ways of engaging audiences and exploring relevant questions. This project has worked with a theatre company, which is adept at interrogating complex topics theatrically, often producing pieces which straddle the line between theatre and art-installation. An installation space, which invites the viewer to move within it, offers more bodily engagement with the art work and provides a more immersive experience. From a research perspective, we might view the separate strands within this project as complementary and as generating different perspectives, as well as bringing different issues for interrogation to the fore to create a dialogue (Masson 2006). Consequently, the 'findings' from the project's strands form an interchange between different constituencies. This is a discursive approach. Here is what some theorists have said about the benefits of using arts and performance-based methods. The particular quality of the work produced is important, suggests Maggie O'Neill (2008):

> Knowledge is produced forcing us to abandon instrumental rationality and reach towards a more sensuous understanding that incorporates feeling involvement as well as cognitive reflection.
>
> (p.9)

Hallford and Knowles (2005 p.1) assert that:

> working visually involves a significant shift away from the often oddly lifeless and mechanical accounts of everyday life in textual representation towards engagements that are contextual, kinaesthetic and sensual: that live.

Hogan and Pink (2010 p.160) discuss the validity of using the arts in research:

> the act of art making can be a moment of ontological uncertainty, and potentially liberating. Consequently art making can become a route through which interiority might be considered not simply as something that comes to the surface and is recorded as a static event, or crystallized and made static, but rather, and importantly, it offers ways of understanding interiority through an anthropological paradigm that views inner states as being in progress, rather than ever static .... Art in art therapy is of significance not only as a representation of the feelings of the individual at a particular moment in time—an inner 'snapshot', if you like ...The self of art therapy does not become crystallized anywhere.

Running time: 20 minutes.

Keywords: visual research methods; participatory art and motherhood; arts and health; health humanities; transition to motherhood; performance-based methodologies.

Mothers make art

In the Birth Project we are exploring women's experience of childbirth and the transition to motherhood using the arts and then presenting the research findings in films and exhibitions. Our overarching questions are concerned with exploring what role arts engagement might play in antenatal and postnatal provision, especially where post-birth trauma is being expressed as bodily symptoms. The Birth Project is also interested in exploring to what extent routine birth practices are implicated in iatrogenic outcomes and post-natal distress. Furthermore, we are concerned to investigate what is distinctive about an arts-based approach in terms of expressing narratives concerning the transition to motherhood.

A participatory arts group, *'Mothers Make Art'*, was facilitated by the artist Lisa Watts. Watts has a distinctive art practice called Live Art, described by Gorman as 'an art practice that presents the living body to encourage a self-reflective exploration of subjectivity, art and knowledge production' (2014 p.6). One aspect of this way of working is that it 'engages with how the audience experiences the performing body's interaction with objects and materials' (Watts 2010 p.2).

Mothers Make Art asks questions in two ways: what are the effects of participation in workshops for the makers of the art and then what are the effects on others who experience the art that is produced as viewers. The *Mothers Make Art* group comprised eight women who live in a city in the north of England. They chose to participate in a series of twelve workshops. Some of the women were trained in the arts, some not, but all had an interest in visual arts and an openness to learn and to make. The brief was to use a participatory framework to enable exploration of *any* topics related to the birth experience and motherhood.

In *Mothers Make Art* structured techniques were used to enable the participants to explore the nature of meaning making and to construct and deconstruct works (physically and metaphorically). An important method employed was the use of everyday objects (ornaments, clothing, mothering paraphernalia, toys) to help to create stories. There was also an opportunity to be meditative with everyday objects (cling-film, tin-foil, kitchen paper). Rather than making a representation or literal object referring to their birth experience or mothering, the women focused on the formal aesthetic qualities of the materials. This way of working explores objects with a focus on their material capabilities, rather than having a predetermined vision of where the art making might lead. This not only provided a self-reflective space, but functioned to give the women the skills and confidence to manipulate materials so as to create their own original art piece by the end of the series.

The art works were varied; one women pegged up her boy's clothes from the tiny newborn garments to the larger ones representing fads and crazes. She acknowledged the preciousness of each stage with an acute awareness of the fleeting nature of the experience, a heightened awareness of temporality, with poems and a monologue.

Another of the installation pieces explored the maker's sense of stability, with a series of finely balanced and delicately poised fragile mixed-media pieces, comprising living plant bulbs, glass and plastic containers, wire and wood and other materials. Rachel, a medical consultant, spoke of valuing the time and space to make art work. She said that the work was about seeking equilibrium between the domestic, professional and personal realms of her life, as well as exploring notions of what it is to be a good mother. She invited the group to say what her piece evoked: precariousness, balance, complexity, giving the bulbs space to grow, were a few of the reactions.

Running time: 41 minutes.

Keywords: birth and art; participatory art and motherhood; arts and health; transition to motherhood; post-natal distress.

★A short edit has been made of this film called **Mothers Make Contemporary Art** with a running time of 30 minutes. This was shortlisted for the 2017 Innovation Award by Arts and Humanities Research Council (AHRC, UK).

Art elicitation. Exploring the birth experience

In the Birth Project we are investigating women's experience of childbirth and the transition to motherhood using the arts and then sharing the research findings in films and exhibitions. Our overarching research question wishes to explore what role arts engagement might have to play in antenatal and postnatal provision, especially where post-birth trauma is being translated into bodily symptoms. The Birth Project is also interested in investigating to what extent clinically-related birth practices are implicated in iatrogenic outcomes and post-natal distress. Furthermore, we are also concerned to investigate what is distinctive about an arts-based approach in terms of expressing narratives about birth and the transition to motherhood, so we are interested in thinking about different sorts of arts-based methods.

This film is about the art elicitation group which was comprised of mothers who had felt traumatised by their birth experience. The group was facilitated by a Health and Care Professions Council (HCPC, UK) registered art therapist and used a thematic approach, as this was felt necessary to offer containment for the strong feelings being expressed.

The film shows the group making art and talking about it in a supportive setting. Women in the group explored their expectations of childbirth and new motherhood. Their idealism contrasted with the very different reality of their actual birth experiences and their emotional association with these, including feelings of guilt and shame, disillusion and loss. The exploration gave the participants an opportunity to come to terms with those experiences which were not aligned with their hopes. In one session on the myths of childbirth, participants investigated some of the conflicting messages surrounding childbirth and the ways that these put women under pressure to do birth and motherhood in certain ways.

The footage has been edited to highlight discussions and actions that particularly address the project's research questions. For example, there is one section in which the speaker (herself a trained medical doctor) reflects upon the birth of her first baby. She recalls asking to discuss the pros and cons of the proposed induction with the doctor on duty. She was completely overruled and later felt angry with herself for not being more assertive. The disempowering nature of the hospital environment is illustrated. The footage is very powerful because this is someone who understands medical environments and something of the implications of the proposed induction, yet was unable to resist the pressure to conform.

Running time: 24 minutes.

Keywords: birth and art; participatory art and motherhood; arts and health; health humanities; transition to motherhood.

Birth professionals make art

The facilitator, Debra Gibson, used a participatory art approach, drawing on techniques from art therapy. Some of the participants perceived that midwives were not always viewed favourably by the general public and it was felt that this may be because of women having had bad birth experiences. Putting the women at the centre of the birth event and the difficulty of this was articulated. There was a clear acknowledgment and wish expressed that it should be a positive event for women, while recognising the pain and possibilities for complications. One experienced midwife worried that some women left the ward feeling 'assaulted mentally'. She wanted to make women feel she was on their side.

In one of the images, the midwife places a plasticine figure of the birthing women in the centre of the piece and herself unobtrusive, and 'not interfering', at the side, 'hopefully she's at the centre', she says. The mother is depicted 'upright' (though on the bed). The midwife depicts herself as a brick-like shape, 'confident and solid' and 'making it feel safe'. There is also a big pictorial presence of the medical nature of the birthing room. This medical expertise was acknowledged as amazing and life-saving, but not always necessary and that it shouldn't be what 'dominates and guides' the midwife and all the practice. However, an underlying anxiety was also acknowledged. One trainee midwife noted regarding the possibility of emergencies, 'We're trained to recognise every eventuality and you can't un-know that'. It seemed that the possibility for trauma coloured the entire thing. Certainly the medical symbol dominates the art work.

The pace of work was also acknowledged as having risen. The fact that birthing professionals are now managing more births with the same resources was acknowledged. The example of a piece of equipment breaking and then its replacement having to be shared with a larger number of people was given; this could interfere with the flow of work and complicate the midwife's use of her time. One consequence of this greater workload is having to spend more time prioritising where to spend ones time, she said. One hospital midwife put it like this: 'I don't feel I can *be* with women because I'm *doing* midwifery ... being a midwife is about connecting with the person while you are carrying out physical care' and that is what was felt was being lost through having to rush from one person to another. With more than one woman in active labour in a labour suite, the midwife noted that she completed one observation, then wrote it up and then has to 'run' to the next women, as observations should be completed every fifteen minutes. This prevented her from *being with* any of the women in a meaningful way, she felt. This left the midwife feeling guilty and angry.

One area which was highlighted as particularly problematic was breast-feeding support. One midwife described new mothers on an intravenous drip, having had an unwanted Caesarean-section, as exhausted and frightened, while also feeling under pressure to breastfeed and feeling that they'll be a 'bad mum' if they don't. The midwife wanted more time to give emotional support and care.

Another midwife was very explicit about feeling constrained in her practice by hospital policies, with the fear of litigation always at the back of her mind and actually 'doing things as a precautionary measure' when it would be better not to intervene. She described this as a culture of intervention, in which midwives felt that it was better to be doing something rather than nothing, even when not intervening would be better. She felt that hospital environments carried with them the expectation of management and noted concepts such as 'bed blocking' (a woman taking up a bed for longer than the hospital protocol being seen as blocking it for the next person). This added pressure to make unnecessary interventions, such as offering to break the waters, when if progressing normally, there should be no need for this.

She was unequivocal that she could not practice in the way she would like to do because of time pressures and policies. Her art work shows a mask suffocated with a layer of cling-film and with a red cross over the mouth, indicating that it cannot speak. It is an uncomfortable piece to view. The same midwife suggested that home births were preferable because that's where the woman is likely to feel more comfortable, able to eat and drink as she chooses, have visitors 'and hugs' interjected a hypno-birth specialist. There seemed to be a consensus that more homebirths would improve the quality of experience for women experiencing normal labours.

Not articulating 'negative' feelings in the workplace was also discussed and a suggestion that if one saw one's supervisor too often, then one's professional capability might be brought into question. A 'Let's get on with it' culture meant that emotions tended not to be expressed or shared. Furthermore, burn-out and bullying were recognised as reasons why midwives leave the profession. Acknowledging that one is not coping with ones workload can lead to harrying responses, rather than support. Being able to discuss issues and make images to express different layers of experience was articulated as useful.

Complex art work

Some of the artwork produced was very complex. One midwife created a double-faced, mask-like sculptural piece. On one side was a mass of snake-like pipe-cleaners representing a tangle of thoughts, but also the different paths of birth experiences, including one that had ended in a fatality. This was shown with a black blockage or full-stop. On the other side is depicted the midwife who is calm, reassuring and positive. Her demeanour can help to relax the women in labour 'so that everything can happen more naturally'. This midwife persona is surrounded by images of positive or ideal childbirth, such as a man kissing his new-born baby or a woman at home in front of her fire with her cat. These are images of what people hope for. She acknowledged the importance of the event and expressed sadness that sometimes it can be 'a horrible experience' for a couple and that this 'can't be put right'. However, she hoped she might be able to influence how they felt about it.

Another image, made by a hypno-birthing practitioner, was a picture of a party scene with a woman in bed holding her new baby, but this was covered in layers of plastic, so barely visible – 'blurred'. The pieces are entitled 'Celebration of Life' and she articulated how childbirth should be celebrated and how it has become a medical condition fraught with anxiety and fear. She wanted to see it celebrated in the home with friends and family and a party atmosphere and regarded as special, but it is hard to see that because of the pervasive nature of the medical model (represented by the plastic overlaying the entire image).

The film overall illustrates how the arts enabled midwives and other birthing professionals to explore their practice in complex ways.

Running time: 30 minutes.

Keywords: birth and art; participatory art and occupational stress; arts and health; health humanities; birth professionals.

References

Banks, M. (2001). *Visual Methods in Social Research*. London: Sage.
Bauer, A., Parsonage, M., Knapp, M., Lemmi, V., and Adelaja, B. (2014). *The Costs of Perinatal Mental Health Problems Report Summary*. Centre for Mental Health and London School of Economics, PSSRU. 1–4. Accessed at: http://www.centreformentalhealth.org.uk/costs-of-perinatal-mh-problems
Coates, R., Ayres, S., and de Visser, R. (2014). Women's Experience of Postnatal Distress: a Qualitative Study. *BMC Pregnancy & Childbirth*. Open Peer Review Reports, 14: 359.
Coates, R., de Visser, R., and Ayres, S. (2015). Not Identifying with Postnatal Depression: a Qualitative Study of Women's Postnatal Symptoms of Distress and Need for Support. *Journal of Psychosomatic Obstetrics and Gynecology*, 36(3): 114–121.
Cowie, E. (1977). Women Representation and the Image. *Screen Education*, 23: 15–23.
Crawford, P., Brown, B., Baker, C., Tischler, V., and Abrams, B. (2015). *Health Humanities*. London: Palgrave MacMillan.

Czarnocka, J. and Slade, P. (2000). Prevalence and Predictors of Post-Traumatic Stress Symptoms Following Childbirth. *British Journal of Clinical Psychology*, 39: 35–51.

Hall, S. (1994). Cultural Identity and Diaspora in P. Williams, and L. Chrisman (eds) *Colonial Discourse and Post-Colonial Theory: A Reader*. New York: Columbia University Press, pp.392–403.

Hallford, S. and Knowles, C. (2005). More Than Words: Some Reflections on Working Visually. *Sociological Research Online* 10(1). Accessed March 15, 2006 at http://ideas.repec.org/a/sro/srosro/2005-25-1.html

Hogan, S. (ed.) (1997). *Feminist Approaches to Art Therapy*. London: Routledge.

Hogan, S. (2003). A Discussion of the Use of Art Therapy with Women who are Pregnant or have Recently Given Birth in S. Hogan (ed.) *Gender Issues in Art Therapy*. London: Jessica Kingsley Press.

Hogan, S. (2008a). The Beestings: Rethinking Breast-Feeding Practices, Maternity Rituals, & Maternal Attachment in Britain & Ireland. *Journal of International Women's Studies (JIWS)*, 10(2): 141–160.

Hogan, S. (2008b). Angry Mothers in M. Liebmann (ed.) *Art Therapy and Anger*. London: Jessica Kingsley Press.

Hogan, S (ed.) (2012a). *Revisiting Feminist Approaches to Art Therapy*. London: Berghahn.

Hogan, S. (2012b). Post-modernist but Not Post-feminist! A Feminist Post-modernist Approach to Working with New Mothers in H. Burt (ed.) *Creative Healing Through a Prism. Art Therapy and Postmodernism*. London: Jessica Kingsley Press, pp.70–82.

Hogan, S. (2013). Your Body is a Battleground: Women and Art Therapy. *The Arts in Psychotherapy. Special Issue: Gender & the Creative Arts Therapies*, 40(4): 415–419.

Hogan, S. (2015). Mothers Make Art: Using Participatory Art to Explore the Transition to Motherhood. *Journal of Applied Arts & Health*, 6(1): 23–32.

Hogan, S. (2016a). The Tyranny of Expectations of Post-Natal Delight: Gendering Happiness. *Journal of Gender Studies, Special Issue: Gendering Happiness*. DOI: 10.1080/09589236.2016.1223617.

Hogan, S. (2016b). *The Birth Project. Interim Report*. October 1–8. Derby: University of Derby.

Hogan, S. (2016c). *Art Therapy Theories. A Critical Introduction*. London: Routledge.

Hogan S. (2017). Working Across Disciplines: Using Visual Methods in Participatory Frameworks in S. Pink, V. Fors, and T. O'Dell (eds) *Theoretical Scholarship and Applied Practice*. London: Berghahn.

Hogan, S. and Pink, S. (2010). Routes to Interiorities: Art Therapy, Anthropology & Knowing in Anthropology. *Visual Anthropology*, 23(2): 1–16.

Hogan, S. and Pink, S. (2011). Visualising Interior Worlds: Interdisciplinary Routes to Knowing in S. Pink (ed.) *Advances in Visual Methodology*. London: Sage, pp.230–248.

Hogan, S., Baker, C., Cornish, S., McCloskey, P., and Watts, L. (2015). Birth Shock: Exploring Pregnancy, Birth and the Transition to Motherhood Using Participatory Arts in N. Burton (ed.) *Natal Signs: Representations of Pregnancy, Childbirth and Parenthood*. Bradford: Demeter Press, pp.272–269.

Hogan, S., Sheffield, D., and Woodward, A. (2017). The Value of Art Therapy in Antenatal and Postnatal Care: A Brief Literature Review. *International Journal of Art Therapy (IJAT, formerly Inscape)*, 22(4): 169–179.

Gorman, S. (2014). Lisa Watts: Working Inquisitively. In *32 Significant Moments: An Artist's Practice as Research*. London: Roehampton University Press, pp.6–13.

Guillemin, M. and Westall, C. (2008). Gaining Insight into Women's Knowing of Postnatal Depression Using Drawings in P. Pranee Liamputtong and J. Rumbold (eds) *Knowing*

Differently. Arts-Based and Collective Research Methods. Hauppauge: Nova Science Publishers, Inc.

Masson, J. (2006). Mixing Methods in a Qualitatively Driven Way. *Qualitative Research*, 6(1): 9–25.

National Institute for Clinical Excellence (NICE). (2007). Antenatal and Postnatal Mental Health: Clinical Management and Service Guidance. NICE CG 45. Web. Print.

Newbury, D. (2005). Editorial: The Challenge of Visual Studies. *Visual Studies*, 20(1): 1–3.

Oates, M. (2013). Suicide: The Leading Cause of Maternal Death. *British Journal of Psychiatry*, 183(4): 279–281.

O'Donnell, K. J., Glover, V., Barker, E. D., and O'Connor, T. G. (2014). The Persisting Effect of Maternal Mood in Pregnancy on Childhood Psychopathology. *Development and Psychopathology*, 26: 393–403.

O'Neill, M. (2008). Transnational Refugees: The Transformative Role of Art? *Forum: Qualitative Social Research*, 9(2): 1–21.

Pink, S. (2004). Applied Visual Anthropology Social Intervention, Visual Methodologies and Anthropology Theory. *Visual Anthropology Review*, 20(1): 3–16.

Ruby, J. (2005). The Last 20 Years of Visual Anthropology - A Critical Review. *Visual Studies*, 20(2): 159–170.

Spencer, S. (2011). *Visual Research Methods in the Social Sciences*. London: Routledge.

Taylor, G. and Spencer, S. (eds) (2004). *Social Identities: Multidisciplinary Approaches*. London: Routledge.

Chapter 8

Queer bodies and queer practices
The implications of queer theory for dramatherapy

Patrick Tomczyk

Creating a safe, caring and inclusive practice where lesbian, gay, bisexual, trans, queer and intersex (LGBTQI) people feel welcome and safe is a shared responsibility of dramatherapists. It is important to affirm and celebrate our commitment to the principles of diversity and respect of dignity with the ultimate goal of creating positive change, growth, transformation and the promotion of well-being for our clients. Both the North American Drama Therapy Association Code of Ethics (NADTA, 2015) and the British Association of Dramatherapists Code of Practice (BADTh, 2005) indicate that dramatherapists have an ethical responsibility to ensure they practice responsibly and with integrity. Therefore, fostering such spaces creates conditions for clients to thrive and is crucial in fulfilling the purpose of achieving therapeutic goals.

In 2015 I asked if there is a queer dramatherapy. I was seeing quite an alarming number of at-risk LGBTQI youth being victimized by homophobic, biphobic and transphobic harassment and bullying and I had noticed there was little in terms of literature on LGBTQI issues and dramatherapy (Tomczyk, 2015). From there I began to question how we could best serve LGBTQI clients in a manner that moved beyond good intentions and words to a willingness to learn, experience and act in a competent way. Shortly thereafter, in the spring of 2016, the *Drama Therapy Review* published a pioneering study that identified 'the attitudes, strengths and limitations in the field of drama therapy with regard to working with lesbian, gay, bisexual, transgender, queer, intersex (LGBTQI) and gender nonconforming (GNC) communities and to identify implications for training, research and the practice of drama therapy' (Beauregard et al., 2016, 41). The authors conducted a study among 136 active members of the drama therapy community and the 'results indicate that the majority of drama therapists hold an open and affirming attitude towards gender diversity and sexual orientation. Yet, discrepancies remain concerning the training received, overall level of preparedness, and participation in supervision specific to working with LGBTQI and GNC clients. Ongoing training and supervision is needed to bridge the gap between affirming attitudes and actions' (41). The study concludes with recommendations for drama therapists on 'inclusive language practices, inclusive and affirming documentation, heteronormative and gendered assumptions, intersectional realities, and the use of dramatic process to share examples of practice to these communities' (58). Since my initial question 'is there a queer drama therapy?' and the subsequent NADTA study, I have begun to consider how queer theory can complement dramatherapy in a way that promotes competency and sensitivity within practice. This chapter sets out to generate discourse and provocation, in order to move the field forward with respect to inclusive practice with LGBTQI clients.

Sexual orientation, gender identity

Our clients encapsulate a vast multiplicity of subjectivities; together these represent a full range of uniqueness. 'Understanding how these aspects of identity intersect and influence human experience is vital to ethical practice' (NADTA, 2018). A part of these multiple subjectivities includes the expression of their sexual orientation, gender identity and/or gender expression. Developing competencies in dramatherapy practice with LGBTQI clients, their families and the related questions, topics, challenges and issues is more problematic than merely including or incorporating sexual orientation, gender identity and gender expression (SOGI) into already existing disciplinary paradigms – it requires a reconceptualization on the implication of theory and how it impacts practice.

SOGI is impacted by various personal, cultural, political, social and economic influences and considerations. The vocabulary and the respective definitions associated with these concepts are constantly changing and evolving. There are diverse terminologies in use because individuals think about and experience their SOGI in various and diverse ways. Simply stated, everyone has a sex and a gender identity. A person's sex, of either male or female, is assigned primarily by the appearance of their genitals and normally established at birth. Nevertheless, biologically, there exist distinct sex variations in the general population. These variations may comprise chromosomal, hormonal or physiological characteristics that cannot be reduced to just a binary classification of male or female. Consequently, not all people are exclusively categorized as male or female, and so they are often referred to as intersex people. Moreover, a person's gender identity is not always aligned to the sex they were assigned at birth. Gender identity, however, is a personal, profoundly felt sense of being male, female, both, neither or something else. Gender identity may also be fluid and change throughout a person's lifetime. Transgender and gender non-conforming people were assigned one sex at birth, yet later in life they identify with another gender (e.g. assigned female at birth but identify as male). Likewise, there exist people that identify as both genders, neither gender or who experience a fluid and fluctuating gender – often referred to as gender fluid or non-binary identities. All of these identities are no less significant than our historically ensconced male or female gender identities. Furthermore, the various clients who identify as LGBTQI have the right to be open about who they are, and who their families are, in the same way that any of our other clients would. The challenges of dramatherapy practice with LGBTQI populations have been documented in few sources and this chapter proposes a queer theoretical framework to consider these challenges.

What is queer?

In the past the term 'queer' was used as a noun or adjective as jargon for gay men, 'a queer' or 'a queer man', and in some contexts 'queer' was also used as a derogatory and homonegative expression for effeminate and/or gay males, and later to anyone who did not exhibit traditional gender behaviour. With reference to a situation or thing, when used to describe something 'as queer' the implications meant that it was different, bizarre or out of the norm. The term has also been used as a verb 'to query,' to ask a question or to have a 'query.' By the late 20th century, the term 'queer' had been reclaimed by the LGBTQI community and is 'understood as a challenge to traditional understandings of gender and sexual diversity by deconstructing the categories, binaries, and language that support them' (Meyer, 2010, 20). Queer is used in positive ways as an umbrella term to include sexual identity, communities, social movements and even as a post-structuralist 'theoretical model' (Jagose, 1996, 1).

Defining queer theory is particularly problematic because queer theory resists closure and remains in the process of ambiguous (un)becoming; as such, there is 'no critical consensus on the definitional limits of queer' (Jagose, 1996, 3). Jagose further explains that 'it is not simply that queer has yet to solidify and take on a more consistent profile, but rather that its definitional indeterminacy, its elasticity, is one of its constituent characteristics' (1). As there are no definitional limits to queer, and queer theory resists fixing or codifying itself, it can be situated within a 'reworking of the post-structuralist figuring of identity as a constellation of multiple and unstable positions' (3).

What queer theory can do re: critiques of heteronormativity

Stein and Plummer (1994) posit that heterosexuality has become normalized and that queer theorists can interrogate societal understandings and disrupt 'sexual power as embodied in different levels of social life, expressed discursively and enforced through boundaries and binary divides' (181–182). Through queer theory, dramatherapists can interrogate implicit and taken-for-granted assumptions of heteronormativity and homophobia, biphobia and transphobia in their practice and in the greater societal culture. Queer theory responds to the normalizing discourse around heterosexuality. Britzman (1995, 154) writes that:

> Queer theory offers methods of critiques to mark the repetitions of normalcy as a structure as a pedagogy. Whether defining normalcy as an approximation of limits and mastery, or as renunciations, as the refusal of

difference itself, Queer Theory insists on posing the production of normalization as a problem of culture and thought.

Sexuality has been historically constructed as either heterosexual or homosexual and it has been accepted that heterosexuality is the norm. Queer theory attempts to disrupt 'the constructed social nature of these unwritten gender expectations' (Ryan, Patraw, and Bednar, 2013, 92) that have been socially constructed and perpetuated throughout time and are now ensconced within the sociocultural status quo, by contesting imperialist and essentialist notions of self and other. Hesse-Biber and Leavy (2011, 25) write that 'queer theory is an interdisciplinary, social justice-oriented perspective that seeks equality for the sexually marginalized.' Through a queer lens we can begin a discourse that examines heteronormativity and the oppression it may cause. Quinlivan and Town (1999, 511) explain that:

> Queer theory draws on the philosophies of the gay liberation movement and aspects of lesbian feminism in its aims to destabilize and critique heterosexuality, emphasize sexual diversity, draw attention to gender specifics and frame sexuality as institutional rather than personal.

Queer theory has at its origins in an activist approach, in disrupting the status quo to promote social change. Britzman (1995, 152) describes that it 'begins to engage difference as the grounds of politicality and community.' Queer theory is not solely restricted to theorizing about gender and sexual identities, but in addition, it 'offers a critique of reigning ideologies of subjectivity, power, and meaning' (Greene, 1996, 326). Queer theory starts by problematizing our taken-for-granted and (mis)understood notions of identity, followed by queering and disrupting the hegemonic and socionormative application of norms and behaviours onto others, and the practices by which heteronormative normalcy is prescribed (Britzman, 1995; Greene, 1996; Morris, 2000).

Queers must query

Queering practice engenders asking questions that are against the grain, with the aim of creating therapeutic spaces that are safer, more just, nonviolent and at the same time challenge the patriarchal institutions, psychological discourse and politics at play. Having first began my career as a drama educator, and then later a dramatherapist still working with school-aged youth, I situate my thinking within Freire's *Pedagogy of the Oppressed* (1970) and Britzman's *Queer Pedagogy* (1995). Identifying as part of a sexual minority, I believe that the functions of dramatherapy are to build a practice that aims to work toward transformation and emancipation, which can be reinforced by means of 'praxis,' through reflections and actions upon our world in order to transform it (Freire, 1970). The transformation I am referring to, in this case, is a shift in paradigm for dramatherapists to recognize how heteronormativity acts as a hegemonic agent that perpetuates homophobia, biphobia and transphobia in our mainstream culture. Through a queer model we may go beyond our current models of practice to interrogate these categories. The emancipation, I believe, comes through the development of a queer theoretical practice that is able to illuminate how hegemonic, patriarchal and heteronormative forces affect the lives of our clients and then affirm the SOGI dimensions of our clients' identities. Freire (1970) refers to this process as a raising of critical consciousness, conscientization or *conscientização* (in Portuguese). I am proposing not only raising this consciousness with our clients, but within this context; if we are to become more competent practitioners, this conscientization needs to occur within our own practices.

Our social media, mainstream culture, medical models and education systems are major political instruments that can emphasize attitudes of normalcy and submerge open dialogue and reinforce a 'culture of silence' (Freire, 1970). A culture of silence is particularly prevalent for LGBTQI youth developing their understanding of their sexual orientation and gender identity and can result in the continued oppression of sexual and gender minorities and further propagate the heteronormativity upheld by those in privilege and power. Quinlivan and Town (1999) write how *hetero* normalizing practices are upheld by the 'maintenance of silences, the pathologisation of (homo)sexualities, and the policing of gender boundaries' (509). I have witnessed this silence in our culture, as people turn a blind eye to public homonegative remarks such as 'fag' or 'that's gay.' Or, as I have also witnessed, heterosexual therapists often liberally disclosing some information about their husbands or wives, or partners with their clients or colleagues, whereas LGBTQI therapists prefer not to speak about their partners out of discomfort in disclosing their sexuality and perhaps worrying about the implications of transference and countertransference. This silence can also have a consequential negative impact on the clients we serve that are expressing their SOGI in non-normative ways, if they are forced to live on the margins, or even worse, if they need to silence their sexuality or gender expression for fear of what may result if they came out.

Connections with critical theory

Meyer (2007, 28) states that queer theory 'is just another step further down the road initially paved by critical pedagogy, post-structural feminism, and theories of emancipatory education.' As such, queer theory has similarities to a critical approach, as its goals are that of social justice, however, with a focus on problematizing the discourse around traditional, historical and normative notions of sexual and gender identity, by rejecting essentialist practices.

Critical theory and queer theory converge in a place of disrupting the status quo with the aim of questioning and envisioning a potential for change. They both focus on challenging the hegemony of the dominant culture, and within the context of my practice, a heteronormative culture. Edelman (1994, 114) writes that Queer is 'a zone of possibilities;' for me, it is within this zone that I situate my therapeutic work of disrupting, questioning and envisioning. The 'transitional space of the imaginal realm' (Snow, 2000, 220), in conjunction with Edelman's (1994) 'zone of possibilities,' addresses issues of social justice and works with the aim of generating critically queer manifestations, of humanization in these challenging times, by addressing the intersectionality of injustice and polarity within culture and identity, class, gender and sexual identity, sexual orientation, dis/ability, language and religion. If dramatherapists can envision possibilities for change, then we can hope and aim for personal development, change and transformation, which is at the heart of our therapeutic practice. Britzman (2000) proposes queer approaches that address the resistance which is put in place by dominant societal structures. One of these approaches seeks to open up the psychical resistance referred to as the 'conflicts within' (34). Britzman argues for the need to address and raise to consciousness the internal conflicts and ambivalence toward sexuality; this means that dramatherapists ought to recognize and acknowledge their own conflicted experiences, positionalities, subjectivities and understandings of SOGI in order to be able to facilitate therapeutic interventions that support their clients' explorations of these problematic areas.

This is the emancipatory potential that can disrupt a system, so that we can begin to create discourse around how our world functions and through this discourse we can posit new ways of thinking and wellbeing. Such emancipation is not a one time event for dramatherapists to become better practitioners, by reading and understanding definitions or terms for example, but rather, it is a process that creates potential to create SOGI competence and allows practitioners to envision a better world and, as a result of this vision, create agency and action for our clients.

Within my practice, a multiplicity of sexual orientations, gender identities, cultures, ages, ethnicities, languages and expectations converge in the dramatherapy crucible to create zones of therapeutic possibilities. Within this space, my clients can envision personal growth, change, transformation and wellbeing through imaginary role-play, as learning about who they are evolves out of dialogues, narratives, confrontations, accommodations, risk taking and unplanned discoveries.

Meyer (2007), in writing about the similarities between queer and critical approaches explains that 'queer theorists have consciously worked to understand the many intersecting layers of dominance and oppression as possible' (25). Both place equal emphasis on achieving a truly equitable and just society. Critical approaches generally examine, explore and critique historical or current issues through various lenses and from multiple perspectives, uncovering ignored or hidden truths. Hesse-Biber and Leavy (2011, 27) explain that '[critical] approaches seek to reflexively step outside of the dominant ideology (insofar as possible) to create a space for resistive, counter hegemonic knowledge production that destabilizes oppressive material and symbolic relations of dominance.' Freire's (1970) critical framework offers possibilities and opportunities to create social change through critical literacy by being able to read the world critically. As Freire proclaims '[A] critical reading of reality [is] associated above all with the clearly political practices of mobilization and organization, constitutes an instrument of what Antonio Gramsci calls "counterhegemony"' (1987, 36).

I position my dramatherapy practice in a fluid space of magnetic push and pull; a space that intersects creativity and queer theory to act as divergent forces that can become catalysts for transformation and social action by opening up possibilities for queer inclusive practice. I have endeavoured to empower my clients to become active agents in seeking a more just and equal world for themselves, by providing them avenues for their voices to be heard and do this by positioning my work in a space of social change for cultural transformation that recognizes, respects, and accommodates SOGI principles.

Freire (1970) stresses that our ever-changing world is a dynamic problem that continually needs to be worked on and responded to. Through critical and queer lenses, I begin to locate and debunk the incoherencies that exist within our heteronormative world. I believe that continued wellness is a lifelong process and never a once and for all event. By promoting queer understandings, I have raised to consciousness my own 'fear of freedom' as well as that of my clients by queering our privilege, our SOGI and by identifying social, economic and political forces that impede our lives (Freire, 1970).

Implications for a queer dramatherapy

Dilley (2012, 44) writes that queer theory is about 'questioning the presumptions, values, and viewpoints from those positions, especially those that normally go unquestioned;' in so doing dramatherapists can facilitate worthwhile work that promotes change and transformation. I would like to propose a method called Queer Ethnodramatherapy to tie the theoretical framework of queer theory with the ethnodramatherapy (EDT) method that has been developed by Snow (2013). 'Ethnodramaterapy can be seen as a form of drama therapy that deals with a specific cultural group' (Snow, 2013, 2). I propose that a Queer EDT aligns itself quite strongly next to Dilley's (2012) tenets of queer work as it: examines the lives and experience of those considered non-heterosexual, it creates space to explore a juxtaposition of those lives/experiences with lives/experiences considered 'normal' and it offers an examination of how/why those lives/experiences are considered outside the margins (462). Through a queer theoretical framework, EDT can begin to queer, challenge and disrupt traditional ways of knowing and begin to problematize our heteronormative system(s). Britzman (1995) writes that queer theory assumes a positionality outside of the margins of 'normality.' This position offers queer EDT a benefit, in that it creates a sensitivity to exclusionary practices such as naming.

Incorporating some of the themes of queer theory, as highlighted by Plummer (1995) into EDT practice, could include: challenging the heteronormative and homosexual binary, examining the gender and sex split, de-centering identity, exploring SOGI positionalities and questioning normalizing strategies (366). Moreover, it provides dramatherapists opportunities for new ways of seeing, new paradigms of assessing and new methods for working with their clients.

The theoretical ideas that I have proposed here open avenues for further discourse and method development so that dramatherapists may begin to acknowledge and then deconstruct hegemonic systems of power. Recognizing that work remains to be done in order to become SOGI competent is both a personal and professional journey as we come to look within at ourselves and without at the other, for a deeper understanding of the multiple subjectivities that we represent. Considering a queer theoretical framework to current approaches in dramatherapy would benefit not only LGBTQI clients, but would permit dramatherapists to query their practice, beliefs and taken-for-granted attitudes about what they consider normalcy to be and the implications it holds with respect to SOGI and other topics such as the body, race and religion.

References

Beauregard, M., Stone, R., Trytan, N., and Sajnani, N. 2016. Drama therapists' attitudes and actions regarding LGBTQI and gender nonconforming communities. *Drama Therapy Review*, 2 (1): 41–63. doi:10.1386/dtr.2.1.41_1

British Association of Dramatherapists. 2005. *Code of Practice*. Accessed at: http://badth.org.uk/sites/default/files/imported/downloads/information/Code%20of%20Practice%20May%202008.pdf

Britzman, D. 1995. Is there a queer pedagogy? Or, stop reading straight. *Educational Theory*, 45 (2): 151–165.

Britzman, D. 2000. Precocious education. In *Thinking Queer: Sexuality, Culture, and Education*, edited by S. Talburt and S. Steinberg, 33–60. New York: Peter Lang.

Dilley, P. 2012. *Queer Man on Campus: A History of Non-heterosexual College Men, 1945–2000*. New York: Routledge.

Edelman, L. 1994. *Homographesis: Essays in Gay Literary and Cultural Theory*. New York: Routledge.

Freire, P. 1970. *Pedagogy of the Oppressed* (M. B. Ramos, Trans.). New York: Continuum Publishing Corp.

Greene, F. L. 1996. Introducing queer theory into the undergraduate classroom: Abstractions and practical applications. *English Education*, 28 (4): 323–339.

Hesse-Biber, S. and Leavy, P. 2011. *The Practice of Qualitative Research* (2nd ed.). Thousand Oaks: Sage Publications.

Jagose, A. 1996. *Queer Theory: An Introduction*. New York: New York University Press.

Meyer, E. 2007. But I'm not gay: What straight teachers need to know about queer theory. In *Queering Straight Teachers: Discourse and Identity in Education*, edited by N. P. Rodriguez and W. Pinar, 15–32. New York: Peter Lang.

Meyer, E. 2010. *Gender and Sexual Diversity in Schools: An Introduction*. New York: Springer.

Morris, M. 2000. Dante's left foot kicks queer theory into gear. In *Thinking Queer: Sexuality, Culture, and Education*, edited by S. Talburt and S. Steinberg, 15–32. New York: Peter Lang.

North American Drama Therapy Association. 2015. *Code of Ethical Principles*. Accessed at: http://www.nadta.org/assets/documents/2015code-of-ethics.pdf

North American Drama Therapy Association. 2018. *Diversity*. Accessed at: http://www.nadta.org/about- nadta/diversity.html

Plummer, K. 1995. *Telling Sexual Stories: Power, Change and Social Worlds*. London: Routledge.

Quinlivan, K. and Town, S. 1999. Queer pedagogy: Educational practice and lesbian and gay youth. *International Journal of Qualitative Studies in Education*, 12 (5): 509–524. doi: 10.1080/095183999235926

Ryan C, Patraw, J., and Bednar, M. (2013). Discussing princess boys and pregnant men: Teaching about gender diversity and transgender experiences within an elementary school curriculum. *Journal of LGBT Youth*, 10 (1–2): 83–105. doi:10.1080/19361653.2012.718540

Snow, S. 2000. Ritual/theatre/therapy. In *Current Approaches in Drama Therapy*, edited by P. Lewis and D. Johnson, 77–144. Springfield: C. C. Thomas.

Snow, S. 2013. *Empowering Adults with Developmental Disabilities: A Creative Arts Therapies Approach*. Mill Valley: Psychotherapy.net

Stein, A. and Plummer, K. 1994. I can't even think straight: Queer theory and the missing sexual revolution in sociology. *Sociological Theory*, 12 (2): 178–187. doi:10.2307/201863

Tomczyk, P. 2015. Is there a queer drama therapy? *Dramascope*. Accessed at: https://thedramascope.wordpress.com/2015/03/26/is-there-a-queer-drama-therapy/

Chapter 9

The therapists' gender identity in dance movement therapy
Does it matter?

Job Cornelissen

Image from *Gutsman, The Performance*

Foreword

We are living in challenging times when it comes to gender identity and its individual expression in one's life. What to say of the election of Donald Trump as President of the USA, with his overtly sexist opinions about women? Or how LBGTs are being treated in the former Soviet Union, where a patriarchal, heterosexual male stance is still the main perspective? However, due to several feminist emancipation waves, there are also slow changes, resulting in an acknowledgment of homo-bisexual- and trans-gender identities, and with same-sex marriage legal in many countries (see Figure 9.1).

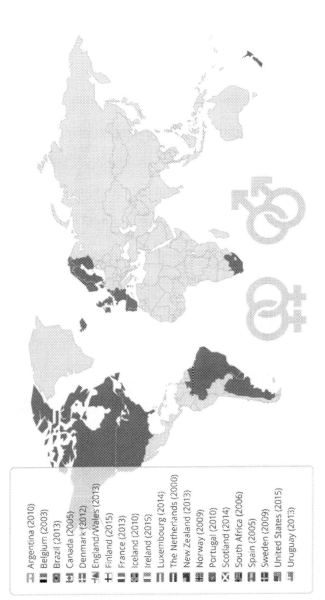

Figure 9.1 Countries where gay marriage is legal. (https://www.statista.com/chart/3594/the-countries-where-gay-marriage-is-legal/, 2018)

As a teenager, even when I realised that my peers were just trying to impress, I still was uncomfortable how they bragged about sexual adventures with girls, like girls were things that could be used. Later, in my professional dance career, I felt sometimes what women, I assume, might feel frequently: objectified (in my case caused by the behaviour of gay men who treated me like a sex object). Later again, during my education as a dance movement psychotherapist, I felt uncomfortable perceiving myself as the representative of the heterosexual and patriarchal perspective on gender identity that still dominates our Western culture. I found myself in an environment I experienced as extremely feminine, and I had to work through some personal issues concerning my masculinity.

In all three situations my gender identity was confronted with the 'norm' of the environment I was operating in at the time, a norm that didn't 'fit'. My perception of my gender identity was questioned. This culminated in the dance piece *Gutsman, The Performance*, an adaptation in movement of a satirical graphic novel, depicting the miscommunication between Gutsman, 'the unyielding defender of male insufficiency' and his girlfriend Tigra, and their touching efforts to balance their gender differences. It was also the personal motive for the research project and thesis for this chapter, and an on-going theme of interest in my life, both professional and private.

From the very beginning, we express ourselves by our movement and bodies, and thus our gender identity. The main tools of dance movement therapists are their own and their clients' bodies. Therefore, I think a dance movement therapist's gender identity, expressed through body language, non-verbal communication, and movement interventions will influence the process of therapy. It is important that all art therapists realise this, not only dance movement therapists, since we all work with experiences that are felt both in our clients' and our own bodies.

Introduction

My research investigated the following questions:

Are there differences in how male and female dance movement therapists experience their gender identity while practising dance movement therapy? *If so, what are they? What do clients experience in relation to the therapist's gender identity and her/his body? Can something be said about the consequences for the process, and outcome of the therapy? Can this all be observed in movement? (Cornelissen, 2012)*

The results are from a small sample, and much more research has to be carried out; but the questions that were raised are worth sharing, especially since there is hardly any research on this topic. And finally what are the implications of the findings for the education of dance movement therapists?

For this chapter I will use the definitions as they can be found on the website of Planned Parenthood.org (2017).

'Sex is biological. It includes our genetic makeup, our hormones, and our body parts, especially our sex and reproductive organs.

Gender refers to society's expectations about how we should think and act as girls and boys, and as women and men. It is our biological, social, and legal status as women and men.

Gender identity is how we feel about, and express, our gender and gender roles—clothing, behaviour, and personal appearance. It is a feeling that we have as early as age two or three.'

Image from *Gutsman, The Performance*

Different perspectives on gender identity in the last 60 years

Within the last 60 years, the theoretical perspective on gender identity has rapidly changed: from a one-dimensional sexual dichotomy of woman–man towards the concept that 'gender identity' consists of factors from a biological, genetic, developmental, demographic, and social origin.

These emancipating developments, starting in the 1960s and '70s, are still going on, providing female clients and therapists with a more equivalent place in psychotherapy and focusing more on what women and men need in therapy. The nowadays well-accepted perspective on the stance of a therapist, whose preferably 'basic posture ... to a client must be one of concern, acceptance, genuineness, empathy' (Yalom and Leszcz, 2005,117), emerged in this era. These therapeutic traits stereotypically are seen as more feminine than masculine, and some researchers generalised this idea even to the hypothesis that women would be better therapists for all client groups (Kirshner et al., 1978; Jones et al., 1987).

Several feminist philosophers proposed solutions to solve the dichotomy, of which I find Luce Irigaray's[1] method particularly interesting. She argued that there is no place for the woman in our society except as a mirror for the man. This implies a mirror of opposition that the man uses to separate himself from the motherly-feminine, thus creating his identity where woman is the negative of man, no innate subjectivity herself *because* of herself; only existing through images man has created of and for her. Irigaray proposes that women should find their own system of values and symbols that fits their femininity to balance the strong patriarchal orientation of society. Instead of adapting or opposing the tools of men, women should take a critical stance within the philosophical and psychoanalytical traditions, *and* using its ways of reasoning at the same time, thus moving and changing the system from inside out. 'Therefore two gestures should be made in the same moment: a gesture of constitution, and a gesture of interpretation' (Irigaray, in Halsema, 1998, 18).

Altogether, a confusing picture is drawn in this era, which is supported by contradicting research, depending on client groups, research designs, and theoretical perspectives: for example, some psychotherapists say the therapists' gender identity doesn't matter (Zlotnick et al., 1998), others say it does (Billingsley, 1977). One thing comes to the surface though: therapeutic traits that are considered more feminine such as 'caring and empathic sharing and self-disclosure' are more emphasised in therapies (Elliot, 1986). Besides that, therapists bring in their personality, including their gender-identity, in contrast to the earlier emphasis on the neutrality of the analyst in the psychoanalytic school of psychotherapy (Seiser and Wastell, 2002,12).

From the 1990s into the 21st century more nuanced views on psychotherapy and gender became more established. Modern feminist theory promotes a stance of multiple perspectives and ambiguity. It eschews a hegemonic femininity and emphasises the heterogeneity of women. Art can be a tool in this stance because 'by its very nature (it) has the deviant potential for ambiguity' (Jones, 2003, 98). According to dance movement psychotherapist and researcher Allegranti (2011), gender and sexuality are both 'performed' through the body. Since dance and movement are ultimate expressions of 'embodied performances', they are the perfect means with which to experiment with multiple perspectives. By creating other embodied performances, gender identity can be freed from stereotypes enforced by society and history.

Another major shift in these 60 years is the concept that *the interplay of several components* shapes one's gender identity. These components have a biological, genetic, developmental, demographical, and social origin. Based on recent research evidence, neuroscientists Schore, Swaab, and Damasio developed different ideas on the fundamental nature of the relation between body, brain, and mind, thus heating up the nature–nurture discussion again.

Schore argues on the neurobiology of attachment: 'attachment experiences (face-to-face transactions between caregiver and infant) directly influence the imprinting or circuit wiring of this system' (2003,15). This suggests a plasticity of mind, rather than a fixed set of characteristics. He furthermore notes that based on evidence by PET scans, 'women display significantly greater activity in this affect regulating structure (= orbifrontal cortex) than do men'(23). Therefore, males and females become 'wired' differently through interactions.

Swaab's perspective (2010), in contrast, is almost completely genetically deterministic: he argues that the base of biological sex, sexual orientation, and through this the basis of one's gender identity, is fixed by genes and thus *before* the development of the foetus in the womb of the mother. There is little solid research evidence for this perspective (Richardson, 2013), but it is often reiterated as a popular view.

Damasio contributes by arguing, 'Sadness and anxiety can notably alter the regulation of sexual hormones, causing not only changes in sexual drive but also variations in menstrual cycle' (1994,120). This implies neurobiology plays an important part in how one's gender identity is experienced and how it interacts with someone to whom one is attracted. So emotions and biological makeup are intertwined in his way of thinking. Hormones *interact* with environmental factors. It is helpful to think here of a continuum of sexed bodies, some of which may be male and others female.

Psychologist Brody focuses on a *social* and *demographic* perspective on gender differences. He argues that people parent their children differently in speech *and* in non-verbal behaviour; that is, for each sex what is appropriate according to the prevailing gender norms of the culture. For example, with young infants, mothers show more expressivity and affect to girls than to boys, and fathers use more emotion-oriented words to their pre-school daughters than to their sons (1993, 98). Do they try to prepare them for the accepted and appreciated gender roles of the prevailing culture they live in?

Moreover, Brody (1993) suggests that females express more emotions regarding stereotypic feminine traits, like vulnerability, bonding, low status, and power. They express more and better verbally and through facial expression. Men express more through action and behaviour, except feelings that are related to stereotypic male gender roles, including differentiation and competition (e.g. anger and pride). Of course, here the author is conflating social status with traits, which is poor theorising, but many psychologists do this. It is important that one's gender identity is partly expressed by the engendered roles taken. Maybe these gender roles exist more through socialisation than through biological factors. For example, men who have a more primary caregiver role display more 'feminine' affects like empathy, warmth, and fearfulness, while women who are in a more masculine role display more 'masculine' affects (114).

Engaging with the ideas of Swaab, Damasio, Schore, and Brody points to the fact that the bodily and non-verbal basis for gender identity is established very early in a human life and socialisation plays its role from the very beginning. The onset of awareness about one's gender and gender identity is embodied and unconscious – and I believe that more knowledge on this topic is needed. Maguire (1995) argues that 'we need to understand more about how *physiological* sensation is mediated through culture, and becomes inscribed on the psyche, so that we can read and interpret it in new ways. Only then will girls and boys come to see women as full objects with their own needs and desires' (68).

Certainly, many institutions seem to represent sexual stereotypical views on gender identity. If psychiatric institutions would be more open, and if practitioners could disclose more of their gender identity, clients could identify with other role models, especially for those that view themselves as homo, bisexual, and transgender. 'As sexuality and gender are constructed politically, socially, locally, and historically (and biologically – my addition), this is fundamental for any major change to clinical practice' (Batista, 2003, 145).

Image from *Gutsman, The Performance*

Gender identity and the therapeutic relationship

Unfortunately, there is not much research on the influence of gender identity in the therapeutic process in DMT or in other body-oriented therapy. The summary below comes therefore mostly from research on verbal and cognitive therapies, and is somewhat confusing.

Research by Ogrodniczuk et al. suggests that standardised therapies are not specific enough to provide the best possible outcome, and that more components, among which gender identity is one, should be taken into account in the treatment plan and goals. 'findings suggest that male and female patients may not benefit equally well from the same types of short-term therapy' (2001, 69). Should we design more specific treatment plans, thus validating how different components, including gender identity, interact with each other?

In the same research, male clients experienced better outcomes in interpretive therapy, working on internal themes and expressing them to create more affective awareness, which were considered more feminine traits. Female clients experienced better outcomes with supportive therapy, which involves greater focus on external problem-solving, traditionally seen as a more masculine trait. The researchers made a distinction between what subjects *prefer* and from what they *benefit*. Apparently, clients didn't experience an instant preference for what most benefitted them. Should people be treated to improve their less developed (*and perceived to be* opposite) gender traits? Can the therapist be a role model in this? Is it more beneficial if that role model is a same-gendered therapist or not?

Research by Wintersteen et al. (2005) on therapy with adolescents that were treated for substance abuse suggests this. Boys had better outcomes with male therapists, and male therapists rated a lower therapeutic alliance with girls. Also, results from a rare research on the influence of the sex of the therapist in a body-oriented therapy could be interpreted like this: male clients tend to be less satisfied with female therapists than are female clients (Schreiber-Willnow and Seidler, 2002). Maybe, if the dance movement therapist, 'statistically likely to be female, heterosexual, physically able, and middle class' (Caldwell, 2013, 2), had been a man, the male clients' satisfaction might have been higher. 'As a role model male therapists offer new possibilities for clients in conversation, movement, and empathy' (Unkovich, 2006, 9).

Apparently, role-modelling is of importance for better outcomes of a therapy. Does that mean, that when the therapist can display different 'roles' within the therapeutic relationship, it benefits the therapy process? If so, the expression of 'a 'mobile' understanding of 'gender'' (Hogan and Cornish, 2014, 133) is an interesting concept: the more a therapist is in tune with both the feminine and masculine aspects of his/her personality, the better the therapy. Petry and Thomas (1986) state: 'The superior relationship with androgynous therapists may be attributed to their uniqueness in dealing with problem-solving and interpersonal situations' (251).

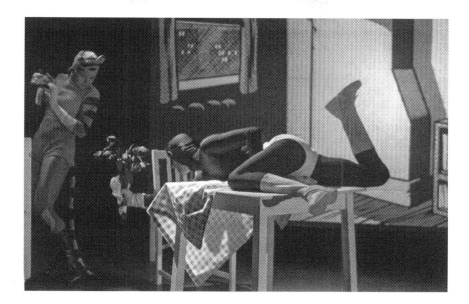

Image from *Gutsman, The Performance*

Gender identity and dance movement therapy (DMT)/body-oriented therapy

'Sex roles are often revealed in non-verbal communication' (Caldwell, 2013, 7), e.g. through the body. Might a body-oriented therapy then bring up more gender-related experiential material that can influence the therapeutic relationship? The scarce research that has been done on gender identity in DMT, or any body-oriented therapy is interesting. In the research of Schreiber-Willnow and Seidler, (2002), there was no worse treatment outcome for men in standard therapy as opposed to those in body-oriented KBT-therapy (KBT= 'Konzentrative Bewegungs Therapie', which means Concentrative Movement Therapy). However, males tended to be less satisfied with a female KBT-therapist than women. Young men benefited least from KBT, while older women benefitted most. This suggests that also in a body-oriented therapy, (young) men and (older) women require differing approaches. And does that imply, when working with the body, differences in gender identity amongst men and women become more apparent in the process and outcome?

Unkovich (2006) states that men show their empathy differently, more in doing than in being. He calls this 'action empathy' as opposed to 'emotional empathy'. Also, Brody states that 'Men express more through action and behaviour' (1993, 114). It is the ability to be aware of behaviour and body language on a body, albeit often on an unconscious level, and anticipation of how the other will show this in action. Emotional empathy is taking another person's perspective in order to be able to help. Action empathy is a daily occurrence for dance movement therapists:

in our work we empathically move with the client by means of methods, amongst others, like mirroring and emphasising certain elements from the clients' movement repertoire, both being ultimate therapeutic expressions of action empathy.

Unkovich (2006) advocates 'recognition of ... action empathy, as a positive response to the plight of self and others. In this way there is a greater possibility for clients, therapists and staff to positively realise the versatility of expression in male gender.' (12). He doesn't ignore the value of emotional empathy: 'it is a challenge for male therapists to model their emotional empathy and pride into masculinity, enabling others to feel confident in their position as a male' (Levant 1995, 248 cited in Unkovich, 2006, 11). However, this presents a question: are male dance movement therapists more familiar perhaps with this typical dance therapeutic tool, since due to their socialisation they are more used to expressing themselves in action? It is an encouraging idea that contrasts with the research arguing that women by nature are better equipped for therapeutic work (Kirshner et al., 1978; Jones et al., 1987).

Röhricht et al. (2011) conducted research on outcomes of body psychotherapy with people experiencing chronic schizophrenia. Here, the outcome was positive for reducing negative symptoms, but more interestingly, the sample – constituting 8 men from mostly non-Western cultures – worked with 3 female dance movement therapists. Should the outcome have been even more profitable had they worked with *male* therapists *not* originating from the dominant culture?

Researching gender identity in movement: Laban movement analysis (LMA)

In the context of DMT, LMA is a well-known and accepted way of describing and analysing movement,[2] also in relation to gender identity: In the research of Nilges (2000), 'Effort qualities' are used to measure differences between men and women performing a gymnastics exercise. This method was also used in this research, as is explained below.

A little explanation about LMA definitions is appropriate at this point:

'*Effort*' describes the dynamics with which a movement is performed: for example, a soccer player that kicks a ball to score will probably do that with a lot of releasing energy (Free Flow) and speed (Sudden Time), with grounded and firm standing at the start (Strong Weight) while being very focused towards the goal (Direct Space).

'*Body*' describes how he holds his body during that action: maybe bend forward with a bent back and keeping one arm to the front of his body while the other arm is stretching backwards.

'*Shape*' describes what his body communicates: probably it will 'feel' closed, since he is focusing on his task to score, and doing so in a way that prevents an opponent from interfering.

'*Space*' describes how his body relates to the space around him; he will probably position himself in such a way that he has room to kick the ball, ensuring that no other players are in the way.

Kaylo (2009) linked movement to the expression of gender identity (building on work by Lamb). She analysed different movement behaviour in social contexts by using the LMA categories of Shape Flow, Directional Movement, and Shaping as modes to communicate different qualities of involvement with the environment and linked them to Jung's Anima/Animus theory. Dance movement therapists can be considered part of the 'environment' for clients in the therapeutic process. She defines Shape Flow and Shaping as Anima/feminine movement qualities, and Directional Movement as Animus/masculine movement quality, in which both women and men can express themselves (e.g. movement is not just attributed to biological sex or to gender, but as different potential that can be part of any individual's movement repertoire).

Action empathy can be considered part of *Interpersonal communication through Physical Behaviour* (Lamb, 1965). He states that, to be effective and trustworthy, behaviour needs to be performed with gesture *and* posture, so the whole body needs to be involved. Performed only with (a) gesture, the behaviour is easily obscured and might communicate inappropriate and unintended messages. Lamb promotes education in the domain of interpersonal communication through physical behaviour, to which a dance movement therapist contributes while working with clients.

Image from *Gutsman, The Performance*

The research

I performed the research in a mental health Institute in The Netherlands during my internship in November 2011 – February 2012. My aim was to obtain data on how the gender identity of the dance movement therapist is perceived by both therapist and client during therapy.

Participants were:

- a female and male therapist on-site, both heterosexual.
- 2 heterosexual female and 3 homosexual male dance movement therapists between 25–65+, whose observations I took into account for triangulation reasons.
- 8 clients from the institute, respectively 5 and 3 high functioning women and men, all heterosexual, between 25–65+, who suffered from adjustment disorders, at that time still in the DSM-4.

The DMT sessions were part of a multidisciplinary treatment of 6–12 weeks, and through them clients experientially researched new 'embodied performances' by recognising (and adapting) their (maladaptive) coping strategies and experiment with new behaviour by embodying these in dance and movement.

In order to know how all participants experienced the therapists' gender identity during therapy, I asked them to fill in a questionnaire in which they rated therapeutic traits that might influence the therapeutic relationship (Table 9.1).

The therapists also filled in an LMA Coding Sheet with the categories Effort, Body, and Shape and Space, thus revealing how they experienced

Table 9.1 Therapeutic traits, deviated in Feminine/ Masculine after Planned Parenthood.org, 2017, and Gehart and Lyle (2001, 449), and as used in the data analysis of the research

Feminine	Masculine
Guidance	Dominant
Passive	Active
In the Background	Initiative
Stimulating	Restraining
Empathic	Critical
Supportive	Clumsy
Sensitive	Powerful
Nurturing	Hard
Soft	Demanding
Emotional	Leading

in body language and movement their own gender identity's influence. To decide whether a therapeutic trait was a reasonably accepted feminine or masculine trait, I used the public website of Planned Parenthood.org (2017)[3] and the research of Gehart and Lyle (2001, 449).

In the clients' questionnaire, the effort qualities were translated into daily movement words as used in the research of Nilges (2000) (Table 9.2). Although not trained in LMA observation, the clients' knowledge about the expressiveness of the body is crucial, and in this way their experiences on the embodied gendered identity and movements of the institutional therapists during therapy could be acknowledged. Besides that, I could also compare the client's perspective with that of the institutional therapists.

The gender reference in Nilges' research of a quality being masculine or feminine was based upon historical conceptions of masculinity and femininity.

(**NB**: In order *not* to unnecessarily trigger stereotypic prejudices, in the questionnaires the traits and LMA effort qualities were offered *without* being labelled 'feminine' or 'masculine'!).

All the therapists rated themselves by filling in the questionnaire; the two on-site therapists also rated each other at the end of the research period. The clients rated the institutional therapists at the end of their treatment or at the end of the research period.

By using the Self Rating instrument, subjective data was inevitably obtained, although I tried to cover these subjectivities by triangulation of the research design: 'the data is a reflection of the lived experience of the participant.' (Caldwell, 2013, 61).

Table 9.2 Effort qualities translated into daily movement words. As explained in the LMA section, I equated the Indulging/ Anima movement repertoire with Feminine and the Fighting/ Animus movement repertoire with Masculine

Lma Effort Quality	Feminine/Indulging/Anima	Masculine/ Fighting/ Animus
Weight	Delicate	Powerful
	Gentle	Strong
	Airy	Solid
Time	Gradual	Quick
	Fleetingly	Leisurely
	Abrupt	Unhurried
Space	Flexible	Straight
	Roundabout	Penetrating
	Meandering	Unswerving *
Flow	On-going	Ready to Stop
	Fluent	Restrained
	Loose	Taut

* This item was inadvertently omitted from the questionnaire.

Image from *Gutsman, The Performance*

Discussion

In this limited research, all therapists experienced that their gender identity plays a role in their practice, which is line with the survey of Hogan and Cornish (2014) amongst 12% of registered British Art therapists.

Two main themes come to the foreground[4]:

- Role-modelling plays an important part in the therapeutic process, is visible in body and movement, and is influenced by the gender identity of the therapist.
- Male therapists seem to struggle with how to balance their Anima/Indulging- and Animus/Fighting movement qualities in the therapeutic process. Stereotypic gender expectations of both therapist and client seem a factor in this.

Concerning the first point:

Therapists seem to be embodied role models for clients. Results from the clients' questionnaire suggest a focus in the group on unexpected gender expressions from the two institutional therapists. The attention of the male clients on stereotypical gender-expected therapeutic traits indicates this too. It stands out for clients whether the female therapist is on the Fighting/Animus or the male therapist is on the Indulging/Anima side, e.g. displaying the opposite of the expected gender behaviour in movement. Since all clients declare that the therapy was beneficial to them, can it be that role modelling, embodied by effort qualities that oppose stereotypical expected gender expectations, has a positive effect on coping mechanisms and provokes healthier behaviour?

Maybe the male clients, by researching stereotypical male traits through unexpected role modelling by and with the therapists, questioned their stereotypic gender behaviour and roles? Did the therapy help them to re-invent their gender identities?

Concerning this re-invention, it is not hard to see that a lot of men struggle these days with the matrix of stereotypic male gender behaviour. What is promising is that dance therapy can apparently serve as a tool to promote this re-invention, *that is,* when more men decide to go into DMT.

Female clients reported more connection with the female institutional therapist due to topics of safety and intimacy. This is confirmed by research that suggests clients benefit more from therapy with a same-gendered therapist. (Ogrodniczuk et al., 2001).

But is embodiment of opposing stereotypical gender expectations by the therapist only appropriate for male clients? If a male therapist were to represent a more androgynous role-model in movement with more Indulging/feminine effort qualities, would that provide more safety for women in therapy? 'Androgyny gives a person (opportunities) to choose from masculine and feminine traits, depending on what is necessary', ([Frosh 1994, 2] cited in Unkovich, 2006, 8). Would the androgyny of a male therapist provide women with opportunities to work through issues with men in a safer way?

Six out of 7 therapists in my research project mentioned that, when working in a group therapy setting, a dyad of a female/male therapist would be ideal. The male clients confirmed this. It would give room for identification, support role modelling with the same-gendered therapist, and provide also possibilities for exploring other gender identities by moving and mirroring with the therapist of the opposite gender.

Concerning the second point:

In my sample, it is not self-evident for the male therapists how to position themselves within the therapeutic relationship. They seem more confused about how to move, both figuratively and literally, than female therapists do, embodied by higher rates of Bound Flow and Strong Weight, masculine movement traits. Male therapists might be *too* conscious and/or critical of themselves, being over-aware of stereotypical expected gender expectations, which are reflected in their ratings. If this is true, then likely it has implications for the process of therapy, since 'therapists may be affirming gender-based expectations, especially in the initial phase of therapy.' (Gerhart and Lyle, 2001, 445). When a (male) therapist is *too* cautious and expressing this unintentionally in a stereotypical gendered movement repertoire, this might confirm gender expectations (about men). Arguably it could affect an open and fresh start of the therapeutic process, especially with women.

On the other hand, this over-anxiousness might be an embodied effort to refute stereotypical ideas about gender identity. The focus of the male therapists on traits that are stereotypically attributed to femininity *or* masculinity suggests this: 'dominant and subculture social rules for relating to males and females (may) play a more central role in therapeutic alliance than we and perhaps many therapists assume' (Gerhart and Lyle, 2001, 450). Even though the male therapists in this research acknowledge, and perhaps even compensate, for this, it probably unconsciously influences their therapeutic relationship with clients on a bodily level. Isn't it ironic that the intention to go *against* stereotypical gender expectations about males might restrict them and *cause* stereotypical gendered male behaviour?

Conclusion

In dance movement therapy (DMT) education and practice, there are more female than male students, teachers, practitioners, and clients. Therefore, I think, in the field there is generally more emphasis on the Indulging/ Anima/ feminine movement repertoire and limited possibilities for (embodied) role-modelling with the Fighting/Animus/masculine movement repertoire for both male *and* female DMT students, clients, and therapists. Since it seems that role-modelling is important in the therapeutic relationship and gender identity plays its part in this, DMT educators should embrace the Fighting/Animus/ masculine movement repertoire, and the merits of 'the versatility of expression in male gender' (Unkovich, 2006, 12), by explicitly implementing it in their curricula. This might bring more male novices to DMT education and more male clients to dance movement therapy.

Once working in the field, these 'androgynous balanced' dance movement therapists will have a 'mobile understanding of gender, and are keen not to foreclose conceptual possibilities because of gender' (Hogan and Cornish, 2014, 133).

I began this chapter by expressing that, to this day, millions of individuals around the globe face serious problems in expressing their gender identity; that is, in being themselves. Since the body is the main agent of this, it is not strange that rulers choose our bodies as one of the 'battlegrounds' for gaining or retaining power (Hogan, 2013). Dance movement therapists that are at ease with their androgynous gender identity can enter this battlefield in the way Irigaray favoured. Being movers, literally and figuratively, we can change the system from within by supporting our clients in embodying their gender identity in a healthy way. By offering differentiated moving role-models we fluidly invite them to explore other gendered performances, and in turn arrive at a position of ease with *their* gender identity.

Image from *Gutsman, The Performance*

Acknowledgements

Thank you Patricia Aarts, Richard Coaten, Chris Fawcett, Susan Hogan, Rosemarie Samaritter, and Sophie Ter Schure for your valuable feedback at different stages of the writing of this chapter. Thank you Ineke Oostveen for the use of the beautiful photographs.

Notes

1 Dutch philosopher Annemie Halsema wrote a book about Luce Irigaray in the Dutch language: *Dialectic of the Sexual Difference: The Philosophy of Luce Irigaray*. This was much easier for me to read then the original literature in French or translations in English. Therefore I used self-translated quotes from this book.
2 For a more extensive but comprehensive explanation of LMA I suggest *Laban for All* by Jean Newlove and John Dalby. New York: Routledge 2008.
3 The definitions on the Planned Parenthood website have not changed since the time the research was conducted.
4 For the complete findings of the research, send an email to job@dansjobs.com

References

Allegranti, B. 2011. Ethics and Body Politics: Interdisciplinary Possibilities for Embodied Psychotherapeutic Practice and Research. *British Journal of Guidance & Counselling*, 39 (5): 487–500, DOI 10.1080/03069885.2011.621712.

Batista Loureiro de Oliveira, J. 2003. A Mediterranean Perspective on the Art Therapist's Sexual Orientation, in Hogan, S. (ed.) *Gender Issues in Art Therapy*. London: Jessica Kingsley Publishers, 126–147.

Billingsley, D. 1977. Sex Bias in Psychotherapy: An Examination of the Effects of Client Sex, Client Pathology, and Therapist Sex on Treatment Planning. *Journal of Consulting and Clinical Psychology*, 45 (2): 250–256.

Brody, L. R. 1993. On Understanding Gender: Differences in the Expression of Emotion. Gender Roles, Socialization and Language, in Ablon, S. L., Brown, D., Khantzian, E. J. and Mack, J. E. (eds) *Human Feelings, Explorations in Affect Development and Meaning*. London: The Analytic Press, 87–121.

Caldwell, C. 2013. Diversity Issues in Movement Observation and Assessment. *American Journal of Dance Therapy*, 35 (2): 183–200, DOI 10.1007/s10465-013-9159-9.

Cornelissen, J. 2012. The Therapist's Gender in Dance Movement Group Therapy: Does it Matter? MA diss., Codarts, Rotterdam.

Damasio, A. 1994, ed. 2006. *Descartes' Error*. London: Vintage.

Elliot, B. 1986. Gender Identity in Group Analytic Psychotherapy. *Group Analysis*, 19: 195–206.

Gehart, D. R. and Lyle, R. R. 2001. Client Experience of Gender in Therapeutic Relationships: An Interpretive Ethnography. *Family Process*, 40 (4): 443–458.

Halsema, A. 1998. *Dialectiek van de seksuele differentie: De filosofie van Luce Irigaray.* (*Dialectic of the Sexual Difference: The Philosophy of Luce Irigaray.*) Amsterdam: Boom.

Hogan, S. 2013. Your Body is a Battleground: Women and Art Therapy. *The Arts in Psychotherapy. Special Issue: Gender & the Creative Arts Therapies*, 40 (4): 415–419.

Hogan, S. and Cornish, S. 2014. Unpacking Gender in Art Therapy: The Elephant at the Art Therapy Easel. *International Journal of Art Therapy*, 19 (3): 122–134, DOI 10.1080/17454832.2014.961494.

Jones, E. E., Krupnick, J. L. and Kernig, P. K. 1987. Some Gender Effects in a Brief Psychotherapy. *Psychotherapy*, 24 (3): 336–352.

Jones, M. 2003. From the Peninsula: The Geography of Gender Issues in Art Therapy, in *Gender Issues in Art Therapy*, edited by S. Hogan. London/Philadelphia: Jessica Kingsley Publishers, 92–107.

Kaylo, J. 2009. Anima and Animus Embodied: Jungian Gender and Laban Movement Analysis. *Body, Movement and Dance in Psychotherapy*, 4 (3): 173–185, DOI 10.1080/17432970902917984.

Kirshner, L. A., Genack, A. and Hauser, S. T. 1978. Effects of Gender on Short-Term Therapy. *Psychotherapy; Theory, Practice and Research*, 15 (2): 158–167.

Lamb, W. 1965. Inter-Personal Communication, Chap. 10 in *Posture and Gesture*. London: Gerald Duckworth & Co.

Maguire, M. 1995. What do Women Want, Chap. 3 in *Men, Women, Passion and Power*. New York: Routledge.

Newlove, J. and Dalby, J. 2008. *Laban for All*. New York: Routledge.

Nilges, L. M. 2000. A Nonverbal Discourse Analysis of Gender in Undergraduate Educational Gymnastics Sequences Using Laban Movement Analysis. *Journal of Teaching in Physical Education*, 19 (3): 287–310.

Ogrodniczuk, J. S., Piper, W. E., Joyce, A. S. and McCallum, M. 2001. Effect of Patient Gender on Outcome in Two Forms of Short-Term Individual Psychotherapy. *Journal of Psychotherapy Practice and Research*, 10 (2): 69–78.

Petry, R. A. and Thomas, R. J. 1986. The Effect of Androgyny on the Quality of Psychotherapeutic Relationships. *Psychotherapy*, 23 (2): 259–251.

Planned Parenthood. org, website, 2017. www.plannedparenthood.org/learn/sexual-orientation-gender/gender-gender-identity#sthash.x3XZHKLD.dpuf.

Planned Parenthood. org, website, 2017. www.plannedparenthood.org/learn/sexual-orientation-gender/gender-gender-identity/what-are-gender-roles-and-stereotypes.

Richardson, S. S. 2013. *Sex Itself. The Search for Male and Female in the Human Genome*. Chicago and London: University of Chicago Press.

Röhricht, F., Papadopoulos, N., Holden, S., Dip, P. G, Clarke, T. and Priebe, S. 2011. Therapeutic Processes and Clinical Outcomes of Body Psychotherapy in Chronic Schizophrenia – An Open Clinical Trial. *The Arts in Psychotherapy*, 38 (3): 196–203.

Schore, A. N. 2003. Interdisciplinary Research as a Source of Clinical Models, Chap.1 in *Affect Regulation and the Repair of the Self*. New York: W.W. Norton & Company.

Schreiber-Willnow, K. and Seidler, K-P. 2002. Is Body Oriented Psychotherapy a Female Matter? A Clinical Process-Outcome-Study of Concentrative Movement Therapy. *Psychotherapie Psychologie Medizin*, 52 (8): 343–347.

Seiser, L. and Wastell, C. 2002. Psychodynamic and Psychoanalytic Psychotherapy, Chap. 2 in *Interventions & Techniques, Core Concepts in Therapy*, edited by M. Jacobs. Buckingham: Open University Press.

Swaab, D. 2010. Seksuele Differentiatie Van De Hersenen In De Baarmoeder (Sexual Differentiation of the Brain in the Womb), Chap. 4 in *Wij Zijn Ons Brein (We Are Our Brain)*. Amsterdam/ Antwerpen: Contact.

Unkovich, G. 2006. MANaging Gender in Dance Movement Therapy. Unpublished article.

Wintersteen, M. B., Mensinger, J. L. and Diamond, G. S. 2005. Do Gender and Racial Differences Between Patient and Therapist Affect Therapeutic Alliance and Treatment Retention in Adolescents? *Professional Psychology: Research and Practice*, 36 (4): 400–408.

Yalom, I. D. and Leszcz, M. 2005. *The Theory and Practice of Group Psychotherapy*. 5th ed. New York: Basic Books.

Zlotnick, C. B., Elkin, I., Brown, S. and Trade, M. 1998. Does the Gender of a Patient or the Gender of a Therapist Affect the Treatment of Patients With Major Depression? *Journal of Consulting and Clinical Psychology*, 66 (4): 655–659.

Chapter 10

The gendered body in arts therapies research and practice

Sue Jennings

Background to this chapter

I have long held an interest in ideas of gender in relation to the human body. I grew up in a family where there were traditional beliefs regarding maleness and femaleness, and therefore there was a built-in control system of what was 'feminine' and what was 'masculine'. However, there were two paradoxes at work within our family: a belief that the male 'head of the household' would be the bread-winner, whose opinions would be paramount, such as 'girls grow up to be wives and mothers'. Therefore, any idea of a career was seen as temporary and transitory: girls being supported to go to university was not on the agenda. The paradox was that my father created a situation of financial precariousness as a GP who would often not send out bills for a year or more. He was the bread-winner in name only as all his five children left home to seek situations that could earn them a living!

The second paradox was in relation to my mother's passion for classical ballet; she herself had been a classical ballet dancer, and hoped that I would follow her. However, her support of male ballet dancers was decried by the 'men' of the family as it went against traditional ideas of male physicality. When I said how I wished I'd be born a boy, her response was that I wouldn't then have had pretty clothes! Additionally, her pressure on me to be a classical ballet dancer when I was entirely the wrong shape, size and without any talent emphasised her wish for me to be this diminutive dainty little girl! It was a fantasy role to be sure, but one that I spent many years trying to fulfil.

My mother's hold on the family was strong in supporting my father in his elevated position and also keeping her five children in their prescribed roles. I did a lot of research on myself through therapy and debate to make sense of these paradoxes, which continued into late teenagerhood, and to some extent even now. It certainly influenced my therapeutic relationships both as client and as therapist. I had to work very hard at not giving way to my traditional perceptions of my own body and also what it was telling me.

Introduction

Until recent years little attention has been paid to bodily reactions in psychotherapy. Essentially bodies remained inert and it was, and still is, the words and silences that have the focus of the therapist. The therapist suggests that the 'blank canvas' stays neutral in order for clients to project their fantasies and relationships,

> the doctor should be opaque to his patient and like a mirror show nothing but what is shown to him (sic).
>
> (Freud 1912 118)

Although therapists from Freud onwards have written and analysed observations of the body, especially the skin, it is at an academic level (Freud) rather than at a lived, experiential level. There are observations of the gestures and movements of the therapist and client, and whether they can be attuned in the therapeutic relationship. This chapter looks at issues around the human body in therapy, both of the client and that of the therapist. It suggests that the therapist's use of body-self enables a deeper understanding of clients and their issues.

The body as knowledge

It is only recently that therapists have been aware of their own bodies as an important means of 'knowing' (Heller and Duclos 2012). The therapist's use of body-self is increasingly used as a means of understanding the people with whom we work as well as giving pointers for the possible direction of therapeutic intervention.

As a therapist I am aware of subtle shifts in my movements, sensations and temperature. However, this is within a body classed as female, and as described above, I was reared with a strong ideology of how a female body should both look and move. Years of therapeutic work have nevertheless not totally neutralised some of my predictable responses.

My real breakthrough came when I eventually did get to university to study social anthropology and was amongst many women who were studying and researching women (MacCormack and Strathern 1980). They were enormously helpful with my total academic naivety as I realised I had to deal with another paradox. Here I was in a context of brains, yet the only world I knew was one of bodies. How could the two possibly come together?

Research example 1

I elected to do some field-work for my final dissertation and chose Malaysia. I had heard about a hobby horse dance, the Kuda Kepang, where men ride on flat-sided woven horses to a strict drum beat. There are assistants wearing masks that look very like 'ex-pat' caricatures. The proceedings start with a short invocation by the local 'bomoh' (healer and religious leader), and then the musicians then begin to play a traditional gong and drum. A circle of mainly women and children are standing to watch.

The 'horses' ride in formation in circles, lines and then wheel around, in a strict military style or chorus-dance formation. The performance is directed by the lead horse-man with a small whip. Some will then go into a trance and become frenzied: charging at the onlookers, tearing up small trees, eating grass – chaos after the orderliness. Some spectators show genuine fear at this loss of control, and we have been warned not to whistle as it will increase the frenzy. The senior horse-man if not entranced, or the shaman or a leading participant observer makes the decision to end the chaos by giving those in a trance a drink from a freshly cut coconut. They come round looking slightly dazed and continue the formation dancing. Thus bringing it to an orderly closure.

I lived in the village where they rehearsed and performed the Kuda Kepang and was able to talk with and observe the participants. The people were all descendants of Javanese migrants to Malaysia, where the dance originates. Women were recently allowed to participate although the men told me they were not strong enough to go into a trance! It is believed to be linked to the spirit world, and the woven horse is thought to contain the horse spirit which needs to be appeased by the drink from the coconut. While in a trance, horse and rider become one, with the rider losing control and becoming like a wild horse stampeding. In the dance, from being very orderly in their formation trotting, bodies upright, similar to dressage posture, bodies went out of control as the spirit of the horse imbued the men. Their movement and sounds were horse-like but also chaotic, showing enormous strength.

There is debate about the origins of the dance in Java, possibly it is linked to the religious wars.

Whatever other function the dance serves, members of the dance company were able to go out of the village to perform at public events and to be paid. None of them had other means of either work or passage from the village. The dance was of particular interest as it involved the recent incorporation of women, although with certain conditions: no trancing (rationalised into a belief they were not strong enough) and dancing as followers, not leaders.

My own reactions to this dance after the initial thrill of doing 'real fieldwork' were in trying to understand the subtle messages being passed between dance members at a non-verbal level. My hunch was they were deciding who would trance and who would guard; always the older man, who led the group, wearing English football socks with his traditional costume and whip, went into a trance. One of the senior men was most perturbed when the same man tranced when they were just having a practice. 'He's not meant to do that now' he said in a fierce whisper to me, as he frantically searched for a fresh coconut and machete!

My gut was picking up subtle bodily messages which I then had to test in reality. And I was developing my experience of using my own body-knowledge in understanding what could be taking place: the dynamic of the performers and the dynamic of the observers.

Clinical example 1

I was working as a dramatherapist in a day-centre for people with mental-health issues. Music therapy and art therapy were also part of the schedule as well as various discussion groups and activities. Most people who attended had been hospitalised in the past and now needed support to maintain their lives outside the hospital. Some people drifted between different activities others followed a clear programme and were members of several groups on a regular basis.

I had been facilitating the dramatherapy group for some months. There was a level of tiredness in the groups, much exacerbated by medication, and the structure of the group depended on people's energy level. The pattern followed the EPR model (Embodiment-Projection-Role) with more time spent on the Embodiment stage including breathing, warm-up and physical stress management. This was needed because many participants followed sedentary lives with little exercise, and their tiredness influenced their low energy levels.

I became aware that I was sitting in an unusual position in my chair and it was uncomfortable. Normally I sat upright with a straight back, the legacy of my classical ballet training! Now I was sitting with my lower back arched, my lower spine was curved and tense. When I reached home, I experimented with this posture, both sitting and standing. What became clear was that the posture of the lower back curvature was the same as that of the boxer, swordsperson or fencer. But why was I sitting like that in the group?

It soon became clear the following week when we met for our usual group. I became aware that my posture had assumed the previous curve so I moved to change to my usual straight back. I was aware of a general level of unease in the group and it was difficult for them to settle. Then one individual suddenly exploded; he was shouting then ranting and waving his arms around. I felt very unsafe and group members looked scared. I decided to fetch a colleague to help me resolve the situation. I said to the group that I was coming back, the angry man followed close behind me and slammed the door with enormous strength. Unfortunately I couldn't remove my fingers quickly enough and they were trapped in the door. Fortunately it was only the tips that were trapped and although my right hand was incapacitated for several weeks, my fingers were not broken.

However, what was the learning here? How might I have known this could happen?

It was necessary for me to do a lot of self-examination and consider other areas of my practice with children and teenagers. And I came back to the original area of my exploration: what can I learn from my own body-self, from possible non-verbal signals?

What became apparent was that my body was acting as a signalling system. The curved back, the posture of the fighter, was telling me there was aggression around, long before I knew it on a conscious level, long before I was able to observe potentially angry situations. This became clearer when I put it to the test in several situations both in therapy as well as in everyday life.

The question was also whether it would generalise to other bodily signals, and could it be a reliable predictor (Ramseyer and Tschacher 2014). It has taken time to understand how it works and how to prepare for it. Dramatherapists will be familiar with the term to 'de-role', which describes the process of coming out of a role after role-play or drama, and returning to one's everyday self. Dramatherapists de-role from their everyday life before entering the therapy space so they do not carry into the session issues from their own lives: sadness, irritability, impatience, fear and plenty more. I was now aware that I needed to de-role from anything that I might be carrying in my body: tension, constriction, sweatiness, panic, nervousness.

It became important to develop a therapeutic body that was neutral from my own issues but nevertheless was sensitive and alert to what was transpiring in the dynamics of the group.

But now it had to be neutral from my own gendered issues!

Clinical example 2

I was working as a dramatherapist at the Royal London Hospital in the Medical College. My brief was to provide what the Professor called 'the human face of obstetrics' in the fertility clinic and he was also interested in the fact that I had had some success through dramatherapy of couples with unexplained infertility becoming pregnant. I was also expected to teach medical students. I was able to recruit a cross-cultural mix, male and female staff including a black art therapist, a Chinese counsellor and a trainee nurse-counsellor. We commissioned murals of fertile imagery and re-named the clinic the Rowan Clinic. The counselling and arts therapies did much to relieve the stress associated with infertility and also seemed to enable a number of pregnancies. We offered one-to-one sessions as well as groups.

I was interested in establishing a group with three facilitators instead of the customary two. This was because one of my theories was that at a deep level some people did not conceive because they did not want the two-person relationship to change to three with a baby. Again this was a hunch from my body-self, that with certain couples the desire for children was stronger in one person than in the other. Since many people relate to a dual led group by projecting parental imagery on to the facilitators, how would they manage with three?

The group was made up of five couples who had experienced long-term infertility and were making decisions whether to continue with medical treatment. The facilitators were me, as a dramatherapist, and two gynaecologists, one white male with no therapeutic experience and one Indian female who had basic counselling skills and some arts therapy experience. I had briefed the two medics that I thought the group should be about being able to obtain advice on the one hand, not personal information but clarification about procedures for example, and on the other should use creative arts techniques to explore stress, decisions and general well-being.

What was remarkable from the very beginning was that one of us was ignored for the whole session and it was not the same person each week. Sometimes it would be me, sometimes the male doctor and sometimes the female doctor. After several weeks the male doctor said he could not deal with being ignored by the group and wished to leave. The two women continued but what was remarkable was that the group did not notice or comment that one facilitator had left until we pointed it out! The significance of the three being reduced to two had relevance for the fertility issues for group members, as they were able to explore the theme of their relationship changing from two to three. And one couple asked to attend for couple's counselling as they felt this was very relevant to them.

My hunch was proving right in this instance and they described how she played very much the little girl role in their partnership and he was like big daddy. Furthermore, he treated her parents as his own parents as he had a disrupted situation in his own family. He realised that he needed to allow his partner to grow up, and he mourned that loss. However, eventually they conceived without intervention as they both became adults!

This situation demonstrated at several levels the importance of understanding gender in therapy and to keep open-minded and neutral. The couple presented like a father and daughter with the woman dressed in 'baby-doll' clothes, very short dresses and frilly knickers, and he came across as the strong, silent and protective person. He admitted that she was like his little girl and how much he enjoyed and encouraged this role. They realised that he needed her to 'grow up' and to allow her to do so, although it was painful. He also realised that he had become very dependent on her parents and perhaps needed some time out from that in order for them both to function as mature adults in their own right.

Research example 2

My doctoral field-work was conducted with the tribal people, known as the Temiar, who live in the Malaysian rainforest (Jennings 2005). They are a marginalised people who continue to be exploited by large companies who are stealing the forest for oil palm plantations. I lived in the rain forest with my three children in a tribal village on the banks of the main river. They were naturally curious about a lone woman with her family coming to live with them. Their main question was whether we were staying short or long term. I was there to look at their child-rearing and dance, since they have the reputation for being one of the most peaceful peoples in the world. We were based in one village but had the opportunity to travel to other villages by log boat when we wished.

The Temiar have a structured view of 'bodies in space' and their spatial world is divided into vertical and horizontal domains: on the ground/off the ground and village/ jungle. The most human and private space is in the house and off the ground which is where healing séances take place, childbirth and where children stay until they can walk independently. Children are not allowed on the ground outside unless they can walk (otherwise they crawl like animals, they told me). Therefore in the house/off the ground is the safest place to be when you are vulnerable. Childbirth is seen as a time of risk once labour has started until the baby is born. Seances for healing mean that the shaman or unwell person will be without their head-souls for a time and that is considered a dangerous state. Therefore, bodies are kept safe by being in the most protected space.

The Temiar healers are various grades of shaman and midwives. They have a defined gendered view of the body for their practice: waist up for shaman, waist down for midwives! The shaman, who is almost always male, dealt with the head-soul which nestles on the crown of the head and is weakened during illness. The head-soul leaves the body during sleep and travels to other terrain and souls, and may bring back important information of a new cure or song or where there is good hunting. This is why you must never wake someone up suddenly as to be soul-less is dangerous. It is very rare for a shaman to be involved in midwifery and the lower body. On the one occasion during our 18-month stay when the midwife asked the opinion of the shaman, he stood behind a screen protecting the woman from view. Not only do midwives deliver babies, they also give information on sexual matters and menstruation.

Whereas the Malay population divide their bodies vertically into right and left, for the Temiar, it is upper body and lower body, (rather like their space).

Temiar children, once walking on the ground, do not cover their bodies (Jennings 2005). Covering up the lower body starts around 5 years old for girls and a little later for boys. There is no modesty regarding the upper body. The only exception I observed was when the girls and women heard a motor boat on the river, which usually meant a visit from Malay officials, then almost instinctively they would undo their sarongs and knot them again above their boobs.

I was recruited as a village midwife quite early on, but sometime after being told by the village midwife that I was her daughter. This fitted the usual practice that midwifery skills are usually passed down in the same family. It was of course ideal for my research as I could be there at the beginning of life. My doctoral thesis was published in 1995 which elaborates on all these themes in detail. However, the core of the research that is relevant to the current topic was basically as follows:

1 *The Temiar differentiate male and female bodies in relation to covering up.*
2 *They also differentiate their bodies in relation to space.*
3 *Healers distinguish their healing practice between the upper and lower body.*

However, they were very uneasy if I visited a village where there was illness, unless it was for a séance. They believed one could carry illness or death back to one's own village, so there was a re-entry ritual where one had to step over burning chili branches at the entrance to the village.

However, they were also willing to vary their attitudes in relation to me and would occasionally allow me into the male domain. For example having said that women, especially me, would not be allowed into the deep jungle because it was too dangerous, they then decided to allow me on a trip to observe marauding animals! If I was wearing jeans then they felt comfortable discussing male matters; when wearing my sarong, then I belonged with the women. They suggested that I might have shamanic skills after some of my dreams; however, I decided that was not a route to go down as it would make everything too complicated.

In the Temiar setting I was able to cross gendered borders in several situations but definitely not in others, it heightened my own awareness of addressing neutrality in the therapist's use of self. There is also the issue of cross-cultural variation in the beliefs about bodies and space, male and female.

Reflections

In this chapter I have given examples of 'gut reaction' and how therapists need to be aware of their own body signalling in relation to clients.

This requires that the therapist de-roles physically in order to create a state of body neutrality.

In the two examples from my research and two from my clinical practice I have illustrated the variation in attitude and belief towards male and female bodies and bodies in space. In the fertility clinic there were beliefs towards male and female roles in relationships. But also in regard to function: doctors, usually male, dealt with the waist downwards, whereas therapists, usually female, addressed the waist upwards, 'the human face of obstetrics'. This was mirrored by the Temiar practice of the reverse principles of the male shaman dealing with the waist upwards and the midwives from the waist downwards.

There is also a clear example of gendered, generational roles that appear to impede conception. The maintenance of the status quo overrode the desire to become pregnant until the dynamic was owned and worked through.

It is important that therapists and counsellors are able to address their own assumptions regarding male and female as well as the cross-cultural variations that exist, no matter how we are re-defining maleness and femaleness.

References and bibliography

Freud, S. (1912) *A Case of Hysteria (Dora)*. Trans A. Bell. Oxford World Classic. Oxford: OUP.

Heller, M. C. and Duclos, M. (2012) *Body Psychotherapy: History, Concepts and Methods*. London: WW Norton.

Jennings, S. (2005) *Theatre, Ritual and Transformation*. London: Routledge.

MacCormack, C. and Strathern, M. (1980) *Nature, Culture and Gender*. Cambridge: CUP.

Ramseyer, F. and Tschacher, W. (2014) Nonverbal synchrony of head-and body- movement in psychotherapy: different signals have different associations with outcome. *Frontiers in Psychology*, 5: 1–37.

Part II

Emergent practices and specialisms

Chapter 11

Multiple gendered abilities
A therapeutic writing approach

Manu Rodríguez

Introduction

In this article I explore the concept of gendered ability and disability through my own experiences, giving the reader a summary of my research within the auto-ethnographical and therapeutic writing field. Auto-ethnography is a research approach, which acknowledges that the researcher's identity is important, and attempts to use this as a strength in the research process, by writing oneself into the picture, rather than pretending to produce 'un-biased' accounts (arguably impossible in qualitative work). It is a sophisticated field, with many useful research tools, such as interviewing oneself about one's research motivation to produce transparency, for example, and a greater depth of self-reflexivity. The work overall is situated within an intersectional approach to gender. The idea of intersectionality comes from the work of Crenshaw (1989), who pointed out that cultural patterns of oppression are interrelated and bound together and intersect, so that sex is bound to gender which is in turn bound to disability, so that although the focus of this chapter is primarily on myself as a disabled person, I am equally a man, and a Spanish man, and a Spanish disabled man, and Spain is a culture, which promotes a strong masculinity, which is at odds with disability in ways different from that of other cultures. So my experience is specific to all these intersectional aspects. These things are not indivisible, as Brah points out: 'structures of class, racism, gender and sexuality cannot be treated as "independent variables"' (1996, p.12).

Firstly, I will briefly outline the methodology and method I used for my research, I will then briefly explore and link the concepts of intelligence and ability. I will explore how the concept of intelligence has evolved since Aristotle's time, and how creativity may be applied to therapeutic writing, so that clients can recognise their physical and psychological abilities and disabilities, weaknesses and strengths for a better understanding of themselves towards a better personal wellbeing and a more productive functioning in society. I will also be bringing a new perspective of what the concepts of 'gendered ability' and 'gendered disability' might mean, introducing the idea that disability can be 'enabling', that 'disabled' might be just a label. I suggest that everyone has abilities and disabilities, strengths and weaknesses and that disability might be just one view of multiple abilities. These multiple abilities in turn intersect with gender and other important features of people's lives and are mediated.

I will also introduce the concept of Positive-Reflective Post-Cathartic Writing (PRPCW), which I have been researching for some time now. This is the idea that focusing on negative thoughts, with the use of negative words and expressions, is the result of distress and other emotional and behavioural disorders that may affect physical health. Awareness of the construction of disempowering patterns of thinking and knowing how to change them positively are the keys to empowering individuals to have a better intrapersonal and interpersonal life. This chapter acknowledges that there are other models of therapeutic writing being employed, which are no-doubt also transformative, but hopes to make a particular case for this model as compatible with an awareness of gender oppression.

This essay suggests that the theory of multiple intelligence, which will be outlined, is highly compatible with an intersectional understanding of gender. When I discuss society moulding persons, or producing an ideal person, it must be remembered that 'gender stands as an omnipresent and epistemically relevant source of background norms and beliefs in the theories, models and descriptive language' of research, even in areas such as 'sex chromosome research' as well as in the daily expressions of selfhood which are delineated by gendered expectations (Richardson 2013, p.226). Though I discuss ability and disability, it is with an implicit awareness that gender mediates disability, and that discrimination intersects in subtle ways with other elements, such as ethnicity, geo-political position and so forth.

Methodology and method

I used an auto-ethnographical methodology for my research. It took me some reading of the literature to arrive at a clearer understanding of what auto-ethnography means, and of what and how I was going to tackle my research within this field. At the beginning, it was difficult for me to find clear distinctions between the autobiographical books and writings I have read in my past and the auto-ethnographical texts I was reading as part of my literature review for my research.

'As a writer I have perhaps myself written some kind of auto-ethnographical pieces of writing without even knowing it', I wrote in my journal. Further evidence to support this premise came from Muncey's interpretation of auto-ethnography as including 'an artistically constructed piece of prose, poetry, music or piece of art work that attempts to portray an individual experience in a way that evokes the imagination of the reader, viewer or listener' (Muncey 2010, p.152). Nevertheless, I decided I should be as analytical and objective as possible, in spite of the subjectivity involved within self-exploration (Chang 2008). Have I ever been 'analytical' and critical with myself in a scientific way?

Probably not. Have I ever tried to see another perspective about my life and my social background like interviewing my family members and/or friends? Absolutely not. Regarding my research method, I wanted to interview some of my family members (and possibly some friends), asking them questions about how my life and gendered disabilities have affected and influenced their lives, to listen to them in an open and non-judgemental way, knowing that I had to be cautious, and reflect on ethical considerations for what I was going to say in my research. To reiterate, this research recognises that gender, though important, is part of multiple identities for those with different abilities and disabilities, and that ethnicity, sexuality and geopolitical position intersect. The aim of my interviews would be to focus on my family's views, emotions and experiences. This would help me to see another perspective of myself, my social background and how my gender and health condition and disability have affected their lives. As a qualitative, rather than quantitative research method, auto-ethnography is closer to my job as a writer, and in addition to a literary review (briefly covering the areas of auto-ethnography, disability studies, therapeutic writing, intelligence and creativity), reflexivity and self-exploration, I chose interviews with family members as they would provide me with a deeper understanding of my personal and social phenomena than I would obtain from structured quantitative methods such as surveys and systematic observations. Interviews would be the main resource data and therefore an ideal technique for my research; they would give me the opportunity to explore views, insights and emotions from both my own and others' experiences. A semi-structured interview plan, which meant that I would use some of the same questions with all of my interviewees, would allow me to uncover their views on the same basic question: what has it meant for you to live with me as a male 'disabled' person? It could also open a dialogue with new questions so that they can tell me their thoughts, experiences and stories in an open and free way. These new questions/answers would emerge during the private conversations to help me in my research process. I decided to do fieldwork in Seville, as it is the place where I was born and where my family lives. This would enable my auto-ethnography to be 'revolving around an interest in biographical particulars as narrated by the one who lives them' (Chase 2005, p.651).

Looking back

I was born in Seville in 1967, in a modest and traditional family. My mum was a primary school teacher and my dad a policeman. I was the first of four brothers and a sister. This might sound like a regular story, but the peculiarity is that my father's father, and my mother's father, were brothers. According to my grandma (my maternal grandmother, who is still alive) they didn't see anything wrong at all with the relationship or the later marriage of her daughter and the son of her brother-in-law. Then, my mum and dad got married very young and I was born about nine months later. Probably their first love... first son. When I was two years old I got really sick. The doctors said I was not going to last very long. I'm in my fifties now and I guess those doctors are probably dead by now. Sometimes fate plays such unpredictable games... I was born before disability rights (such as the 1982 Social Integration for Disabled People Act). I've had to learn how to live and accept my life with health problems, physical limitations and the word society has labelled people like me: 'disabled'. I can't say it's easy because I've got used to it. In fact, some moments in late childhood and adolescence were the most difficult times regarding my relationship with this word, other people and the world that surrounded me. But looking back over the years, I also can say that I've tried to live my life like a 'non-disabled' person, learning how to deal with others and myself, regulating my feelings and emotions, tolerating many sorts of frustrations and, maybe more importantly, accepting myself as a man with my disabilities and abilities, weaknesses and strengths.

And so, some years ago, after observing people whom society apparently considered as non-disabled, but who appeared to me, paradoxically, to have more disempowering emotional and behavioural problems than many so-called disabled, and which caused them to have an unsatisfactory life, I started asking myself: 'What is disability? Who is disabled and who is non-disabled? Who is more disabled, someone who is unable to function properly in life, in his job, with his family and/or friends, or someone who, for example, is deaf, blind or in a wheelchair? Are people like the late Stephen Hawking disabled?'

'If Stephen Hawking was disabled, in which way was he?' Some of Hawking's physical disabilities were obvious, as he has a disease called Amyotrophic Lateral Sclerosis. And yet, how able and productive to society was he? He is a renowned contemporary physicist and cosmologist, he is the former Director of Research at the Centre for Theoretical Cosmology within the University of Cambridge and published numerous academic articles and several books... he was content with his life and productive to society. On the contrary, we all know about athletes, actors and actresses, models, politicians and celebrities of all kinds who are considered as examples of beauty and success and who are disabled in a lot of ways; emotionally unstable, harming themselves and/ or others. It was after pondering these questions and observing my own disabilities that I decided I had to reformulate the concept of gendered disability, relating it directly to the concept of intelligence as well as connecting it to the concepts of multiple intelligences (Gardner 1999) and creativity (Guildford 1950). This coupled with an intersectional understanding allows for a reconceptionalisation of gendered disability.

The concept of intelligence

'Every society features its ideal human being', says Howard Gardner at the beginning of his book *Intelligence Reframed: Multiple Intelligences for the 21st Century* (Gardner 1999, p.1). In fact, it seems to me that it is not the individual who determines whether he/she is more or less intelligent, able or disabled, for certain kinds of activities; rather, it is determined by society. Although there are many cultures in the world, increasingly Western society is creating global values, which in turn has a role in how a culture views abilities and disabilities. Within a particular society, I think individuals should explore and figure out their own unique capacities and potentials, as well as accept and work on their weaknesses, constraints imposed by prevailing gender norms, dealing with them so that the experience of doing so can be of productive use in the society in which they live. In this way, they may self-determine their own lives in the healthiest and most rational way, as much for the good of their society as for themselves. I venture to say that an 'intelligent' person is the one who is able to do this in order to live an 'intelligent life'. It is important to stress the radical nature of multiple intelligence as differentiating different modes of intelligence, rather than seeing intelligence as necessarily governed by a single general ability. This immediately helps to confront the generalised reductive sexual-stereotyping associated with place and time specific gender ideals, which can be so constraining and damaging.

At this point, I think we should review some of the concepts of intelligence that scientists and psychologists have advanced through history. Aristotle, who is often regarded as the father of psychology, gave major importance to the way we perceive and understand the world through our senses. He described the psyche as an entity able to receive knowledge through the five senses. He believed that mental activities themselves were primarily biological, but that the psyche was the 'form' part of the intellectual process, as distinct from the biological processing of the body and brain. For him, the body and the psyche formed a unity. Aristotle's idea may sound naive for some of us today, and this is not just because we now know much more about the different regions of the brain, their specialisation and their flexibility to adapt to new conditions and circumstances. We don't just have to bear in mind that the Ancient Greeks didn't have MRI brain scan technology and all the scientific advancements we have today, but also the particular value that the human 'body – mind balanced' factor had in their society. Nevertheless, actual Western society inherits and still retains this idea, which relates to the productive value system upon which capitalism rests, and that creates situations of many kinds of gendered abilities and disabilities for individuals. It is then again obvious to me that the society in which an individual lives produces certain kinds of impairments and disabilities, as well as abilities and strengths.

At the end of the nineteenth century the British naturalist Charles Darwin came up with the theory of Natural Selection, or Evolution, which has had an enormous influence in psychology and intelligence theories. In fact, analytical, functional and genetic movements in psychology have been strongly influenced by Darwin's achievements. According to Darwin, the human intellectual faculties are variable 'and we have every reason to believe that the variations tend to be inherited. Therefore, if they were formerly of high importance to primeval humans and to their ape-like progenitors, they would have been perfected or advanced through natural selection' (Darwin 1871, 1896, p.128). In his autobiography, talking about his brother Erasmus, he says 'I do not think that I owe much to him intellectually nor to my four sisters I am inclined to agree with Francis Galton in believing that education and environment produce only a small effect on the mind of anyone, and that most of our qualities are innate' (Darwin 1887, quoted in Barlow 1958, p.43).

Since Darwin was the first to formulate the idea of natural selection, the so-called 'survival of the fittest', perhaps it is to be expected that his thoughts on genetic inheritance may seem incomplete today. Now we know a lot more about the brain's ability to change neural structure through experience (plasticity) and the important role that learning and education play in the healthy functioning of the brain, and the formation of gendered behaviours, it would be unlikely that Darwin would claim that education had 'only a small effect' if he were alive today.

At the very beginning of the twentieth century, the French psychologist Alfred Binet and his colleague Theodore Simon, who were specifically interested in children and education, developed what is considered the first intelligence test. They worked empirically, administering hundreds of test questions to children who were having learning difficulties at school, first measuring sensory-based items then verbal memory, verbal reasoning, numerical reasoning, appreciation of logical sequences and the ability to solve some problems of daily living. We could say that the IQ test was born at that time, although it was the German psychologist Wilhelm Stern who gave the name and measure of the 'intelligence quotient' (Stern 1912). By the twenties, the intelligence test was regularly used in educational practice in Western Europe and the United States.

But what is wrong with the IQ test apart from the fact that the results might be ignored? It is useful for measuring the so-called 'general intelligence'; cognitive abilities such as memory, reasoning and verbal components, but it didn't take into account the complex nature of the human intellect and its different components as well as how a person, within their own cultural background, deals with feelings, emotions and with others. It was the Columbia University psychologist Edward L. Thorndike (1874–1949) who first realised the importance of what Harvard University Professor Howard Gardner later called 'interpersonal intelligence'. Observing that an IQ test measured only 'abstract intelligence', he distinguished two more types of intellectual functioning. 'Mechanical Intelligence': the ability to visualise relationships among objects and understand how the physical world worked and 'Social Intelligence': the ability to function successfully in interpersonal situations.

In 1983, Harvard Professor Howard Gardner published the book *Frames of Mind* (Gardner 2011 [1983]) and came up with the Multiple Intelligence theory. In a later book, he explained:

> I was not simply summarising the work of others in a relatively traditional manner. Instead, I was putting forth a rather bold new theory—namely,

that intellect was distinctly pluralistic—and arguing that the singular word 'intelligence' and the term 'IQ' were fundamentally limited and misleading ... I now conceptualise an intelligence as a biopsychological potential to process information in certain kinds of ways, in order to solve problems or create products that are valued in one or more cultural settings ... it suggests that intelligences are not things that can be seen or counted. Instead, they are potentials—presumably, neural ones—that will or will not be activated, depending upon the values of a particular culture, the opportunities available in that culture, and the personal decisions made by individuals and/or their families, schoolteachers, and others.

(Gardner 1999, p.34)

Gardner also puts forward the idea that 'the mind is far from unencumbered at birth; and that it is unexpectedly difficult to teach things that go against early "naïve" theories that challenge the natural lines of force within an intelligence and its matching domains' (Gardner 2011 [1983], p.xxiii). So, neural plasticity can only allow an intelligence to develop to the extent that their environment continues to allow it and this is where gender stereotypes can particularly come into play. That is to say that once something has been learned, and this process begins before even birth, it is difficult to replace that paradigm with a revised version, so long as the environment continues to support the original paradigm.

Howard Gardner's Intelligences (or factors of intelligence, we could say) are:

- Linguistic: is the sensitivity to spoken and written language, the ability to learn languages and the capacity to use languages to accomplish certain goals (speakers, writers, poets...);
- Logical–Mathematical: is the capacity to analyse problems logically, carry out mathematical operations and investigate issues scientifically (mathematicians and scientists);
- Musical: entails skill in the performance, composition and appreciation of musical patterns (musicians, singers...);
- Spatial: the potential of recognising and manipulating the patterns of wide space (navigators and pilots) as well as the patterns of more confined areas (sculptors, chess players, architects...);
- Bodily–Kinaesthetic: the capacity of using one's whole body or parts of the body to solve problems or to fashion items (dancers, actors, athletes, craftspersons, surgeons, mechanics...);
- Interpersonal: a person's capacity to understand the intentions, motivations and desires of other people and, consequently, to work effectively with others (salespeople, teachers, religious leaders...).
- Intrapersonal: involves the capacity to understand oneself, to have an effective working model of oneself – including one's own desires, fears and capacities – and to use such information effectively in regulating one's own life.

These were the seven intelligences, or intelligence factors, which Gardner worked out at the beginning of the eighties and explained in his well-known book *Frames of Mind* (1983). At the end of the nineties, he 'reframed' his theory adding three more intelligences. They are:

- Naturalist: sensitivity, recognition and classification of the numerous species – the flora and fauna – of a person's environment (biologists, geologists, farmers, gardeners...);
- Spiritual: any discussion of the spirit – whether cast as spiritual life, spiritual capacity, spiritual feeling or a gift for religion, mysticism or the transcendent – is controversial within the sciences as well as through the academic world;
- Existentialist: again in Garner's own words is 'the capacity to locate oneself with respect to the furthest reaches of the cosmos – the infinite and the infinitesimal – and the related capacity to locate oneself with respect to such existential features of the human condition as the significance of life, the meaning of death, the ultimate fate of the physical and the psychological worlds and such profound experiences as love of another person or total immersion in a work of art'.

(Gardner 1999, p.60)

Language, music, space, nature and even an understanding of other people all seem comparatively straightforward. Many of us do not recognise the spirit as we recognise the mind and the body, and many of us do not grant the same ontological status to the transcendent or the spiritual as we do to, say, the mathematical or the musical (Gardner 1999, p.53).

Psychometricians, those responsible for measuring intelligence in a traditional and empirical way, were the first ones who strongly criticised Gardner's theory. They were looking for a reliable way to measure accurately these various intelligences. To this, Gardner argued that he had no way of knowing whether the intelligences were independent of one another and that they basically depend on biological, cultural, motivational and resources. At the same time, for him it would be expensive, wrong and definitely not flexible to develop tests which create a straitjacket scenario, for example: 'Johnny is musically smart but spatially dumb'. 'For instance, how do you measure someone's understanding of himself, or of other people, using a short answer instrument? What would be an appropriate short answer measure of an individual's bodily-kinaesthetic intelligence? (Gardner 1999, p.136). Furthermore, these ideas further complicate reductive notions about gendered characteristics and traits.

Nevertheless, Multiple Intelligence (MI) theory caught the immediate attention of educators who were suggesting many different approaches, and many of these techniques are still being explored today. The flexibility of the MI theory helps educators in such a way that students themselves have the possibility of understanding and appreciating their own strengths, as well as identifying and addressing their weaknesses, exploring and learning in multiple and creative ways.

As a result, and having read Gardner's concept of intelligence and the MI theory, I decided to formulate my own concept of disability, which states:

> *Disability is the non-ability to use one's personal physical and psychological capacities and potentials to solve certain problems and to function well in his/her cultural environment.*

Multiple abilities within a therapeutic writing approach

Taking Gardner's MI theory from the perspective of therapeutic writing, as a first approach I think it would be good for the facilitator to start with a rough picture of personal intelligences, and realising their own weaknesses and strengths, by suggesting that clients reflect by writing and answering some initial questions such as the ones I propose here:

How good and concerned do you think you are at:

- Communicating ideas to others by writing and/or talking?
- Analysing problems and investigating issues scientifically?
- Appreciating music?
- Using your body (for acting, dancing, doing exercise... Or even with crafts and manipulating tools)?
- With maps, orientating yourself in new locations, remembering places...?
- Understanding yourself, capabilities and disabilities, and regulating your feelings and emotions?
- Understanding the intentions, motivations and desires of others?
- Appreciating and sensing nature: flora, fauna and the environment?
- Having any kind of spiritual/religious beliefs?
- Thinking about the meaning of life and death, chance and fate, and other existential matters?

And then, maybe in the next session, ask them to reflect by answering these two simple questions:

- In which way do you think your skills, abilities and strengths help you to solve your problems so you are living a healthier and more satisfactory life?
- How do you think you can address your weaknesses to better adapt to the society in which you live and so to have a more empowering present and future?

Even answering all these questions in the most honest way, a person may live in denial, having a wrong and distorted image of himself/herself and the world that surrounds him/her. Or he/she just simply wants to avoid emotions and memories from the past in what acceptance and commitment therapy (ACT) calls 'experiential avoidance'. Then, maybe his intrapersonal intelligence is not well developed and the reflective writing exercises need to be tutored and guided in a less direct and, we can even say, gentler way. We can let our clients know that according to Gardner's definition of intelligence, an intelligence is used when it serves to solve a problem or create a product valued in the society in which an individual lives. If not, then that intelligence would be worthless at that point.

Many of us may be able to answer in a realistic, honest and positive way some of those questions I proposed above, and we might potentially have some of these intelligences, but I think we really should try to think and reflect not just in an intrapersonal way, but as much as possible from 'an outside perspective', in an interpersonal way. One of the writing exercises I propose for this in my book *Manual de Escritura Curativa/Escribir Para Sanar* (Rodríguez 2011) is for the client to reflect on their situation by writing in the third person, and looking at their problem dispassionately, as though belonging to another person.

Other alternative questions we may ask would be something like:

- Which abilities do you think really help you to solve certain problems that affect you, and how do these abilities help you with these problems?
- Do you clearly and honestly know yourself, and your intelligences, to the extent that you can use these various skill levels appropriately to solve certain problems?
- Are you creatively flexible and open minded enough to abandon stereotypes and narrow thinking so that you can find at least one solution for the problem that affects you, that could also be productive for the society, environment or situation in which you live?

To address the answers to these questions, I think we should give our clients some background information looking back again at the history of psychology, briefly analysing the important role that creativity plays in solving problems and in the concept of intelligence.

It was the American psychologist Paul Guilford who is considered as the first to introduce the main importance of the concept of creativity into psychology. Guilford described creativity as sensitivity to problems, as divergent thinking and as the ability to generate multiple ideas to solve problems. He, as well as others, proposed that intelligence is not a unitary concept as it was measured by the traditional IQ test, and he introduced a three-dimensional theoretical model: the so-called Structure of the Intellect (Guilford 1950).

According to him, the intellect may be represented by three aspects:

- Operations: cognition, memory, divergent production, convergent production and evaluation.
- Products: units, classes, relations, systems, transformations and implications.
- Content: visual, auditory, symbolic, semantic and behavioural.

Multiple gendered abilities 159

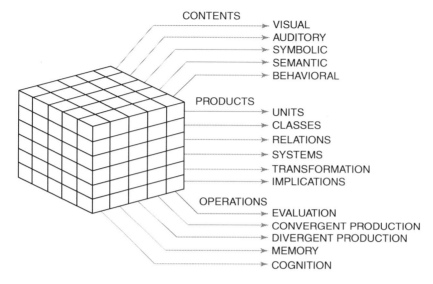

Figure 11.1 Structure of the Intellect. 1988.

The final version of the model (1988) resembled a cube with 6×5×6 dimensions. By then Guilford had introduced some new operations, making the cube able to yield 180 possible unique abilities, which are correlated with each other (see Figure 11.1).

But for Guilford the main ingredient of creativity, which is a fundamental characteristic of any creative person, and so is therefore essential for solving problems, was the concept of divergent thinking. This concept has four characteristics:

1 Fluency: the ability to produce a great number of ideas in order to find a solution to the problem.
2 Flexibility: the ability to simultaneously propose a variety of approaches to the problem.
3 Originality: the ability to produce new, original ideas.
4 Elaboration: the ability to systematise and organise the details of an idea and carry it out.

Having said that, from my personal experience and in my modest opinion as a researcher and facilitator, and applying Guilford's theory, therapeutic writing techniques should propose:

• To recognise and understand the problem, writing about it from different perspectives and points of view, looking always for a fluency and flexibility

of thinking. Stereotypical thinking tends to stop the generation of new ideas that might solve the problem.
- To get a personal vision of the problem, understanding and situating it under one's own unique experience, in particular circumstances and environment.
- To originate one's own personal (and perhaps original) solution/s for the problem, as well as looking always for self-motivation and self-determination.

Another problem that we as practitioners or facilitators may face is that clients may not initially have a very developed sense of what Gardner called 'Linguistic intelligence' in which case we should try to find other activities (oral and craft) to trigger, little by little, the ability to reflect through creative writing. Over time the client can react and communicate in a way that opens them up to further, and more in-depth, engagement with the experience of reflective writing.

Multiple abilities and positive reflective post-cathartic writing (PRPCW)

Gardner's concept of intelligence and his 'Theory of Multiple Intelligences' (Gardner 1999), have influenced my idea of 'Multiple Abilities' as a way to understand that we all have 'Multiple Intelligences' and 'Multiple Abilities'. The breadth of my experience has led me to believe that all of us have weaknesses and strengths, abilities and gendered disabilities. I personally believe that anyone who does not have intellectual disabilities in reading or writing can discover their abilities/strengths and disabilities/weaknesses through reflective and reflexive writing. This can then lead to action being taken to address and develop them for an improved quality of life. Furthermore, any generalisations about gender difference should be tempered by these ideas. Though gender norms can hamper this, an ideal outcome would be to empower so-called 'disabled people' to realise the need to accept their disabilities, start thinking about how to work towards addressing them and discover their potentials and strengths. Furthermore, so-called 'non-disabled people' could also start seeing their gendered disabilities and weaknesses, addressing them and realising how well or badly they are using their abilities and potentials. This should involve thinking critically about gender stereotypes as potentially delimiting and constraining. We could say that a potential ability is not a strength until it is discovered. Consequently, the concepts of disabled and non-disabled would be definitely more flexible; a person may be disabled in one sense and able in another.

Finally, I want to briefly bring to this article my concept of Positive-Reflective Post-Cathartic Writing (PRPCW) (Rodríguez 2011), which I have been researching for some time now. This is based on the idea that focusing on negative thoughts, through the use of negative words and expressions, is the result of distress and many other emotional and behavioural disorders that may affect physical health (Ellis and Harper 1975). Awareness of the construction of disempowering patterns of thinking, and knowing how to change them positively, are the keys to empowering individuals to achieve a better intrapersonal and interpersonal life. Creative writing and the realisation of how we use words to express ourselves is a powerful tool to achieve that. I believe that patterns of negative thinking can be broken and changed with re-thinking, re-reflecting and re-writing negative thoughts, feelings and emotions in a more positive way.

I also took my PRPCW concept from studies on positive thinking and positive writing, such as 'writing about positive futures' (Harrist, Carlozzi, McGovern and Harrist 2007; Layous, Nelson and Lyubomirsky 2012), positive experiences (Burton and King 2004; Burton and King 2009), writing counterfactually (Koo, Algoe, Wilson and Gilbert 2008; Heintzelman, Trent and King 2013), using self-affirmation (Steele, 1988; Creswell, Dutcher, Klein, Harris and Levine 2013), looking for learning opportunities (Watkins, Cruz, Holben and Kolts 2008), practising gratitude (Sergeant and Mongrain 2011; Toepfer, Cichy and Peters 2012), physically disposing of written thoughts (Briñol, Gascó, Petty and Horcajo 2012), reminding oneself about important relationships (Slatcher and Pennebaker 2006) and self-transcendence and values-affirmation (Crocker, Niiya and Mischkowski 2008; Burson, Crocker and Mischkowski 2012).

As an example to illustrate this idea, one exercise I sometimes propose in my workshops after participants have completed a reflexive writing exercise is to take apart what they consider are positive and negative words and/or expressions, dividing them into positive and negative categories. By doing this, they have the possibility of re-thinking their writing, their thoughts and emotions, extracting the positive parts of their stories and rewriting them using more constructive language. In my opinion, this activity integrates a traumatic experience by learning the positive from it. And this could definitely be therapeutic.

Conclusion

The concept and value of abilities and disabilities don't just depend on the potential strengths and weaknesses an individual has, but also on the values and priorities which society presents to this gendered individual. These values and priorities are embedded in gender expectations, but as I suggest at the outset, intersectional analysis calls into question the construction of monolithic gender identities and is potentially very compatible with an approach acknowledging multiple intelligence; we are positioned by the intersection of multiple hegemonies. Everyone has abilities and disabilities, weaknesses and strengths, and they need to be recognised, accepted and addressed as soon as possible to help us live our lives well. Most certainly, being labelled as 'disabled' might sometimes be just a matter of misjudging personal potential strengths and weaknesses, whether coming from a medical or social perspective. This is true too of gender-related expectations. The label itself could intimidate the disabled person and inhibit their growth.

Finally, it is imperative to acknowledge, as Judith Butler (1993) suggests, that gender is performatively constituted by the 'very expressions' that are said to be its results. Butler refutes the idea that there is a 'gender identity' behind these iterations (gender is enacted in subtle and obvious social terrain with regard to how gender may be expressed). We 'do' gender implicitly, whether drawing on gender performance opportunities in enabling or disabling ways. How a person uses his/her potential strengths to address his/her weaknesses in a determined society is going to affect the wellbeing of the individual as much as the society itself. The sooner a person is able to discover his/her abilities and gendered disabilities, recognising and understanding them, beginning to use and address them as 'intelligently' as possible, the sooner he/she can have a healthier and more satisfactory life. In my opinion, it might not be just luck, chance or fate that determines someone's life, but rather a good balance between 'intelligence', creativity, positive thinking and self-determination, which means challenging predominant ideas about gender stereotypes and disability.

The development of creativity from childhood, so individuals are able to freely and openly generate ideas, alternatives or possibilities that might be useful in solving problems on their own behalf and also of the society in which they live, should be considered the most important role in learning and education. From a therapeutic writing perspective, the use of creative and expressive writing in its various forms gives the possibility of exploring deepest thoughts and emotions, of expressing and organising ideas, of understanding oneself and the world that surrounds us and of seeing our weaknesses and strengths so that we can have a better quality of living.

References

Brah, A. 1996. Difference, diversity and differentiation. In Bhavani, K. (ed.) 2001 *Feminism and 'Race'*. Oxford: Oxford University Press.

Briñol, P., Gascó, M., Petty, R. and Horcajo, J. 2012. Treating thoughts as material objects can increase or decrease their impact on evaluation. *Psychological Science*, 24(1): 41–47.

Burson, A., Crocker, J. and Mischkowski, D. 2012. Two types of value affirmation: Implications for self-control following social exclusion. *Social Psychological and Personality Science*, 3: 510–516.

Burton, C. M. and King, L. A. 2004. The health benefits of writing about intensely positive experiences. *Journal of Research in Personality*, 38(2): 150–163.

Burton, C. M. and King, L. A. 2009. The health benefits of writing about positive experiences: The role of broadened cognition. *Psychology and Health*, 24(8): 867–879.

Butler, J. 1993. *Bodies that Matter: On the Discursive Limits of "Sex"*. London and New York: Routledge.

Chang, H. 2008. *Autoethnography as Method: Raising Cultural Consciousness of Self and Others*. Walnut Creek: Left Coast Press.

Chase, S. 2005. Chapter 25: Narrative inquiry. In Denzin, N. K. and Lincoln, Y. S. (eds) *The Sage Handbook of Qualitative Research (3rd edition)*. Thousand Oaks: Sage, pp.651–679.

Crenshaw, K. 1989. Demarginalizing the intersection of race and sex: A black feminist critique of antidiscrimination doctrine, feminist theory and antiracist politics. *University of Chicago Legal Forum, special issue: Feminism in the Law: Theory, Practice and Criticism*. University of Chicago Law School, Chicago.

Creswell, J. D., Dutcher, J. M., Klein, W. M. P., Harris, P. R. and Levine, J. M. 2013. Self-affirmation improves problem-solving under stress. 8(5): e62593.

Crocker, J., Niiya, Y. and Mischkowski, D. 2008. Why does writing about important values reduce defensiveness? Self-affirmation and the role of positive other-directed feelings. *Psychological Science*, 19(7): 740–747.

Darwin, C. 1871, 1896. *The Descent of Man and Selection in Relation to Sex*. New York: D. Appleton and Company.

Darwin, C. 1887, 1958. *The Autobiography of Charles Darwin*. In Barlow, N. (ed.) London: Collins.

Ellis, A. and Harper, R. A. 1975. *A New Guide to Rational Living*. Chatsworth, CA: Wilshire.

Gardner H. 1999. *Intelligence Reframed: Multiple Intelligences for the 21st Century*. New York: Basic Books.

Gardner, H. 2011 [1983]. *Frames of Mind: The Theory of Multiple Intelligences*. New York: Basic Books.

Guilford, J. P. 1950. Creativity. *American Psychologist*, 5(9): 444–454.

Guilford, J. P. 1988. Some changes in the Structure of Intellect model. *Educ. Psychol. Meas.*, 48:1–4.

Harrist, S., Carlozzi, B. L., McGovern, A. R. and Harrist, A. W. 2007. Benefits of expressive writing and expressive talking about life goals. *Journal of Research in Personality*, 41(4): 923–930.

Heintzelman, S. J., Trent, J. and King, L. A. 2013. Encounters with objective coherence and the experience of meaning in life. *Psychological Science*, 24(6): 991–998.

Koo, M., Algoe, S. B., Wilson, T. D. and Gilbert, D. T. 2008. It's a wonderful life: Mentally subtracting positive events improves people's affective states, contrary to their affective forecasts. *Journal of Personality and Social Psychology*, 95(5): 1217–1224.

Layous, K., Nelson, S. K. and Lyubomirsky, S. 2012. What is the optimal way to deliver a positive activity intervention? The case of writing about one's best possible selves. *Journal of Happiness Studies*. Advance online publication. doi:10.1007/ s10902- 012-9346-2.

Muncey, T. 2010. *Creating Autoethnographies*. London: Sage, p.152.

Richardson, S. S. 2013. *Sex Itself. The Search for Male and Female in the Human Genome*. Chicago and London: University of Chicago Press.

Rodríguez M. 2011. *Manual de Escritura Curativa/Manual of Healing Writing: Escribir para Sanar/Writing to Heal*. Spain: Almazara.

Sergeant, S. and Mongrain, M. 2011. Are positive psychology exercises helpful for people with depressive personality styles? *Journal of Positive Psychology*, 6(4): 260–272.

Slatcher, R. B. and Pennebaker, J. W. 2006. How do I love thee? Let me count the words. *Psychological Science*, 17(8): 660–665.

Steele, CM. 1988. The psychology of self-affirmation: Sustaining the integrity of the self. In Berkowitz, L. (ed.) *Advances in Experimental Social Psychology, Vol. 21*. New York: Academic, pp.261–302.

Stern, William (1914) [1912 (Leipzig: J. A. Barth, original German edition)]. Die psychologischen Methoden der Intelligenzprüfung: und deren Anwendung an Schulkindern [The Psychological Methods of Testing Intelligence]. Educational psychology monographs, no. 13. Guy Montrose Whipple (English translation). Baltimore: Warwick & York. https://en.wikipedia.org/wiki/Library_of_Congress_Control_Number"LCCN 14010447. OCLC 4521857. Retrieved 15 June 2010.

Toepfer, S. M., Cichy, K. and Peters, P. 2012. Letters of gratitude: Further evidence for author benefits. *Journal of Happiness Studies*, 13(1): 187–201.

Watkins, P. C., Cruz, L., Holben, H. and Kolts, R. L. 2008. Taking care of business? Grateful processing of unpleasant memories. *The Journal of Positive Psychology*, 3(2): 87–99.

Chapter 12

What can a man do with a camera?
Exploring masculinities with phototherapy

José Loureiro

Introduction

This chapter explores the possibilities of practical applications of the concept of hegemonic masculinity in phototherapy sessions with men. The concept of hegemonic masculinity was introduced by Raewyn Connell in the field of the sociology of gender (1987, 2005). This concept has been applied in several research studies and professional practices with respect to education, health, violence, fathering and counselling. According to Connell (2005), understanding "the construction of masculinity is important for *effective counselling and psychotherapy of men, both individual and group*, in ways that pay attention to gender relations and gender specificity" (Connell 2005, xvi – emphasis added). The social construction of masculinity and hegemonic masculinity will be presented in-depth in the chapter.

What is phototherapy? Phototherapy and its techniques are applied by several mental health specialists; for example, by art therapists, psychoanalysts, family therapists, counsellors and ergo-therapists, amongst others (Kopytin 2013). I will explore dialogues between phototherapy and art therapy to substantiate my research and work with men. Loewenthal and Clark offer a simple definition: "Phototherapy can be seen as the use of photographs to enable clients' expression of their concerns" (2014, 4). It can be used in psychotherapy and counseling and as a tool in art therapy. "Therapeutic photography" on the other hand, often involves the client actually taking photographs as a way of working through an "emotional constriction" (2014, 4). Examples of this approach include the work of Martin and Spence, 1987, 1988; Spence, 1986; Hogan and Warren 2012. However, "the distinctions between phototherapy and therapeutic photography are not always clear, and some practitioners use the methods interchangeably within their practice" so this chapter will not work with this distinction (Clark and Loewenthal 2014, 5).

According to Clark and Loewenthal (2014), Diamond (1856) was the first to use photography as a therapeutic technique using portraiture with patients with mental illness. It is unclear how "therapeutic" Diamond's work was, as he was primarily interested in recording what he believed were physical traits of insanity, as part of a project exploring and documenting insane physiognomy in that

166 José Loureiro

period (Hogan 2001, 45). In the 70s in the USA and Canada, we can mention the work of Spire (1973), Nelson-Gee (1975), Wolf (1976), Zwick (1978), Krauss (1979), Krauss and Fryrear (1983), Stewart (1979a, 1979b), Weiser (1975) among others. In England, phototherapy was established in the years 1980/90 and we can highlight the work of Martin and Spence (1985, 1987, 1988, 2003), Spence (1986, 1991) and Wheeler (2004, 2009) among others.

Phototherapy has been developed and expanded greatly in recent years. In section one, Gender issues in phototherapy, I present a brief discussion of phototherapy and present some projects that work on gender and phototherapy. Section two, What has phototherapy to do with masculinities?, introduces Raewyn Connell's (1987, 2005) theory of hegemonic masculinity, which grounds my research on masculinities. Section three, Dismantling hegemonic masculinity in phototherapy, tackles my psychological practice in phototherapy. Finally, Practical implications in working with men in phototherapy, discusses practical issues followed by a short conclusion.

The photographs in this chapter come from my own photographic work on the male body. At this time, I choose to present my own photographic work instead of presenting the work of phototherapy with my male clients. For this reason, this chapter remains a theoretical discussion.

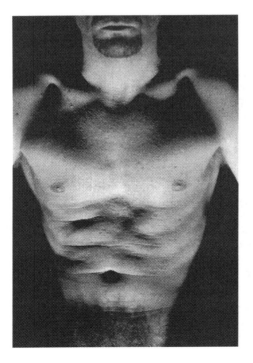

Figure 12.1 Male Body Series by José Loureiro 2001.

Gender issues in phototherapy

In this section, I present the concept of gender and phototherapy, and illustrate the section with some empirical research that works with gender issues in phototherapy.

Gender is very complex. Here is Connell's definition of gender:

> Gender, like other social structures, is multi-dimensional; it is not just about identity, or just about work, or just about power, or just about sexuality, but all of these things at once. Gender patterns may differ strikingly from one cultural context to another, but are still "gender". *Gender arrangements are reproduced socially (not biologically) by the power of structure to shape individual action, so they often appear unchanging.* Yet gender arrangements are in fact always changing, as human practice creates new situations and as structures develop crisis tendencies. Finally, gender had a beginning and may have an end.
>
> (Connell 2008, 11– emphasis added)

Connell's multi-dimensional definition of gender comprehends all gender dimensions, and still tries to deconstruct the binary and polarised vision of the masculine/feminine – which is a source of great oppression for men and women. The masculine/feminine binary vision as a construction of opposites can create a sexist, separatist vision; this makes it very difficult for practices of gender of many men and women who do not fit perfectly in the sexual opposites.

There are a number of researchers worthy of mention. Ellen Fisher-Turk (2018) works on phototherapy with women: "I photograph women who suffer from negative body image brought on by rape, incest, eating disorders, cancer or just plain life. Over the past six years I have seen this use of photography open a way for women to change how they see themselves and how they feel about their bodies" (Fisher-Turk 2018). Turk's work presents the great potential that phototherapy has to work on gender, body and sexual issues. Working with the concept of gender in phototherapy does not mean *only* working on sexual and gender identity, but implies studying and working with all that relates to the person who lives in a gendered society (Kimmel 2011).

David Blackbeard and Graham Lindegger (2014) work with the concept of hegemonic masculinity and autopathography with HIV positive young men in KwaZulu-Natal. They investigate the social construction of young masculinity of those living with HIV and in relation to hegemonic masculinity. In order to explore this gender relation they use photograph techniques (anthropography) and interviews.

Del Loewenthal (2014) has brought the use of phototherapy to a huge project called *Phototherapy Europe in Prisons* which "aims to address the emotional learning of prisoners through the use of phototherapy" (Clark and Loewenthal

168 José Loureiro

2018, 8). This project has used different phototherapy techniques such as photographic genograms, photo-novels, photo-dialogue pictures and storytelling among others. The project has brought phototherapy to many countries in Europe such as Italy, Finland, Malta, Romania and Greece, among others.

Rosy Martin and Kay Goodridge (2003) worked on representations of ageing women: "my response to these issues was to embark upon a process-based art project, using photography, video and phototherapeutic methods, resulting in a body of work which seeks to challenge and subvert simplistic and stereotypical representations of the ageing women" (Martin 2003, 195). The work looks predominately at the women ageing in Western society, which is capitalist, liberal, feminist and consumerist. Similarly, Hogan and Warren (2012) collaborating with Martin explore representations of ageing women through art and photography in their research *Representing Self – Representing Ageing*.

Michael Barbee (2011) worked with a small group of transsexuals using photography to explore the construction of transsexual gender identity; in his work he elicits the visual and verbal "gender stories" from transsexuals. According to Barbee (2011) photography was very helpful because transsexuals normally use photographs to register the process of their sexual transition. According to Barbee, a visual-narrative approach to transsexual experience and

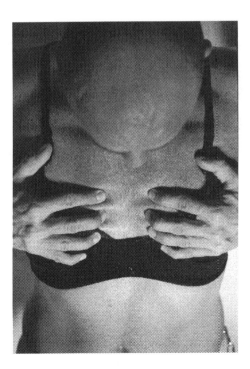

Figure 12.2 From the Male Body Series by José Loureiro 2001.

to clinical treatment is suggested, in the hope of providing a framework for working with transsexual clients that does not pathologise their experience (Barbee 2011, 53).

The research presented here shows the many possibilities of working with gender issues ranging from gender and sexual identity, eating disorders, prisons, ageing, construction of male identity, cancer and sexual abuse, among others. These projects are important because "representations of gender position and limit the individual, playing a vital role in determining our subjective reality. *"That is why as therapists we must be concerned with gender"* (Hogan 2003 12 – emphasis added), and the effectiveness of phototherapy techniques has proven capabilities because it offers us a range of opportunities from creating personal icons to carry with us at a time of crisis, to photographs which enable us to have a better dialogue with ourselves within the world (Spence 1995, 165).

Now I move to the theme of hegemonic masculinity and its possibilities of application in phototherapy techniques.

What has phototherapy to do with masculinities?

Hegemonic masculinities

Connell (2005) defines hegemonic masculinity as:

> Hegemonic masculinity can be defined as the configuration of gender practice which embodies the currently accepted answer to the problem of the legitimacy of patriarchy, which guarantees (or is taken to guarantee) the dominant position of men and the subordination of women. This is not to say that the most visible bearers of hegemonic masculinity are always the most powerful people.
>
> (Connell 2005, 77)

Connell (2005) adapted the concept of hegemony from Gramsci's work.[1] Hegemony is the domination and subordination of the other, mainly of women and gay men. Connell (2005) affirms that the concept of hegemonic man is valid if studied, approached within a *relational situation*, otherwise we fall into the reification of masculinities.

Gender issues studies have penetrated the field of phototherapy. This solid base has been built through research over years as we can see through the work of Hogan (1997, 2003, 2013; 2019); Martin and Spence (1995, 1998); Campbell (1999). Gender is a social structure that changes constantly and therefore it is important to follow its changes, regressions and advances. Gender issues are fundamental to phototherapy because:

> we are very well placed to enable a multi-faceted exploration of self. *This is not merely a theoretical exploration.* Representations of gender position and

limit the individual, playing a vital role in determining our subjective reality. *That is why as therapists we must be concerned with gender.*
(Hogan 2003 12 – emphasis added)

I agree with Hogan (2003) that gender is not only a theoretical exploration. Gender matters. We cannot live outside gender social configurations. Hogan's conception of gender is in line with Connell's work which very much sees gender as practices through the body and social institutions. The concept of hegemonic masculinity is not an abstract concept, neither is it a reification of masculinities. Rather, it has shown that gender as a concept is expanding, standing outside of academic ghettos and has penetrated fields of professional practice. It is important to bring the concept of hegemonic masculinity into the practices of phototherapy because we have to update our professional practices with new research, new paradigms. Phototherapy is a good and efficient technique which can help with masculinity therapy (to be discussed further). Connell (2005) agrees that counselling can help us in understanding the construction of masculinity when we work with men in groups and individually (Connell 2005, xvi).

Connell (2005) suggests that gender-applied research, policy work and professional practice can really be of profit to masculinities studies. Phototherapy offers a good means and technique for the exploration of masculinities and hegemonies in gender relations since phototherapy can:

> be used with many clients or with an individual, throughout the treatment process or in selected parts. As noted earlier, it can be used either actively or passively. It can be used as an adjunct to a verbal process or it can be used as a nonverbal aid to elicit feelings and reflection. *The field is new so there is still limited data regarding differential use with different kinds of client populations.* Photographic materials have the additional advantage of being portable so they can be used in many diverse settings. The permanency of photographs also assures an ongoing record that can be arranged in any sequence.
> (Turner Hogan 1981, 194)

Turner Hogan (1981) notes that phototherapy is still new and has limited data regarding various types of client populations.

Does "the real man" come to phototherapy sessions?

If we were to deepen this question, we would need to go further into class and ethnicity within gender studies, which this section does not permit. According to Kimmel, the answer is yes; men are very eager to discuss feminism, their problems and break the chain of supposition that they are not concerned with their masculinities and sexuality (2017). According to the author, men need to feel safe in order to approach gender issues. Kimmel (2005) suggests that if we ask men what they think the "real man" is, they will certainly reply that to be a man is to: "*never show your feelings, never cry, never asks for help or direction*" (Kimmel 2005). Kimmel (2018) also challenges the axiom that affirms that men are reluctant to talk about their feelings, based on his own work.

Liebmann (2003, 108) has written about her work with two groups of men with art therapy: men in the criminal justice system (probation) and men in the mental health system (in a community mental health system) where she describes her experience of working as a female therapist with men. She found that "*although it seems difficult for men to engage in any kind of personal therapy, it is clear that art therapy has a particular role in helping them to express feelings. However, there is a further problem for some men – far from leaving too soon, they wish to stay for ever!*" (Liebmann 2003, 119 – emphasis added).

There are many reasons for this phenomenon, which I cannot analyse here. I will, however, claim that one important reason is the embodiment of the ideals of hegemonic masculinity. McAllister, Callaghan and Fellin (2018) in their research on military masculinity have found that men have difficulty in emotional expression; one of their interviewees says the following:

Pat: If you're a little bit upset because you're missing your family *you tend to keep that to yourself because at the end of the day that's perceived as weak or, y'know, "stop being a girl" sort of thing*, or "missing your wife arrrr you're with the lads come on". I suppose if something stressful happened on operation like you're involved in when somebody got hurt, injured or killed or whatever then erh, then I suppose yeah they do look after you quite well.

(McAllister, Callaghan and Fellin 2018, 1 – emphasis added)

We can see through the work of McAllister, Callaghan and Fellin (2018) and Liebmann (2003) and Kimmel (2017, 2018) that men have difficulties in expressing themselves. I also can see this male emotional difficulty in my own clinical work in Brazil. In my case, I attribute this difficulty to the extremism of macho cultural and sexual representation in Brazilian culture (where machismo is not often applied as a gender analytical category in gender studies) and the embodiment of hegemonic masculinity; Connell (2005) also mentions the evident machismo in Latin America:

It is a familiar suggestion that Latin American machismo was a product of the interplay of cultures under colonialism. The conquistadors provided both provocation and model, Spanish Catholicism provided the ideology of female abnegation, and economic oppression blocked other sources of authority for men. As Walter Williams has shown, *Spanish colonialism also involved a violent and sustained assault on the customary homosexuality of native cultures*. This has influenced contemporary expressions of masculinity.

Figure 12.3 Holga by José Loureiro 2018.

> In Mexico, for instance, the public presentation of masculinity is aggressively heterosexual, though the practice is often bisexual.
> (Connell 2005, 198 – emphasis added)

As we can see, machismo ideology in Latin American cultures plays an important part in masculinities' gender practices and it reinforces female subordination and despises gay masculinities in Latin America (De Oliveira 2000, 2017); it also inhibits men from attending therapies.[2] If, however, we go in depth into terms of class and race dimensions, men and "real men" go to art therapy and phototherapy sessions when they feel safe, not when being attacked for not subscribing to feminism.

Dismantling hegemonic masculinity in phototherapy

Phototherapy is an excellent tool to work on masculinities because photography gives us concrete results on our gender practices. Gender is something we live in, which is in our bodies; gender is beyond the sex role, social expectations. So the photographic camera can help us to record gender practices:

> *Photography has certain characteristics which make it useful as a treatment tool. It provides the client and others with a recorded image of the self and this image provides a broad integrated perspective of the self.* Most therapists rely on an elicited subjective and often abstract nonspecific representation of the self as elicited from the client. *Photographs, however, provide a concrete representation of many integrated aspects of the person which are a representation of a reality and not a personalized subjective view- point.* A question raised that needs researching

is: How objective are these images when we are collectively socialized to assume a role stance for the purpose of being photographed? This is a valid and necessary question, but it is the client's reaction to perception of and feelings about the self-image that is the sought-after material.

(Turner Hogan 1981, 193 – emphasis added)

It is important to stress the difference between verbal therapy and phototherapy. Turner Hogan (1981) suggests that phototherapy goes beyond verbal therapy because it presents insights and elicitation from the site of the body; she emphasises the value of a concrete form of representation of the reality of the self, which is not a verbalisation or imagination. Liebmann (2003) also suggests that art therapy can offer treatment to men in a better way than verbal therapy because:

> It would seem that art therapy has much to offer men, but some have difficulties accessing it, because of factors connected with male socialisation. *The norms of therapy – openness about feelings, communication, self-reflection, intimacy – are areas where many men have difficulties. And yet it is for this very reason that therapy has something to offer which they need.* Art therapy has a special role in providing a bridge to these skills, in giving time for an activity (and one with very visible boundaries), which may feel safer and more purposeful (in being active) than a verbal therapy.
>
> (Liebmann 2003, 123 – emphasis added)

Art therapy and phototherapy offer advantages in relation to verbal therapy with men because they have elements that facilitate communication with men, especially those who have problems expressing feelings, inhibitions and fear in therapy. In art therapy and phototherapy, the chances of men expressing themselves are much greater because we offer a greater openness to feelings, communication, self-reflection and self-expression which can reveal itself through the creation process. Intimacy is a very important element because we create a safe environment for the expression of feelings and "confessions of male secrets". Here it is worth remembering Kimmel (2017) again, who states that men are eager to talk about their problems, but need a sympathetic and warm environment where at first they do not feel cornered and not threatened with respect to their hegemonic ideals. Turner Hogan (1981) also exhorts that phototherapy is suitable for working with clients in a less defensive way than verbal parts during a session because:

> *In treatment, learning about the self and others can at times be helped by the use of photography as our visual senses are theoretically less defended than our verbal parts.* Another aspect of photography related to the increase in visual material in our society is what Stewart calls the "seductive" nature of photography. *Most people respond to visual material and are particularly fascinated by visual*

representations of the self. Who can resist the impulse to look at a picture of oneself? This aspect enhances the usefulness of photography in treatment as it aids in establishing rapport and in maintaining interest in the process when it becomes difficult to explore feelings and events.

(Turner Hogan 1981, 194 – emphasis added)

According to Connell (2005), gender is not something predetermined, nor the fruit of biology, the Oedipus complex of Sigmund Freud, gender socialisation, the fruit of the sex-role inculcation or the habitus of Bourdieu. For the author, gender involves *gender practices*, and these practices entail embodiment of the masculine values mainly those hegemonic. Connell (1987, 2000, 2005) manages to bring masculinities into the world of gender practices rather than discourses because:

Practice never occurs in a vacuum. It always responds to a situation, and situations are structured in ways that admit certain possibilities and not others. Practice does not proceed into a vacuum either. Practice makes a world. In acting, we convert initial situations into new situations. Practice constitutes and reconstitutes structures. Human practice is, in the evocative if awkward term of the Czech philosopher Rarel Kosik, *onto-formative*. It makes the reality we live in. *The practices that construct masculinity are onto-formative in this sense.* As body-reflexive practices they constitute a world which has a bodily dimension, but is not biologically determined. Not being fixed by the physical logic of the body, this new-made. world may be hostile to bodies' physical well-being.

(Connell 2005, 65 – emphasis added)

But how to work on masculinities in phototherapy? Are there any instructions? Is there a formula to apply? I am not proposing any specific kind of tool to work with in phototherapy. My main concern here is to discuss how the therapist can apply Connell's concept of masculinities in the therapeutic setting and do research in the field since we do not have much research in phototherapy with men specifically (Turner Hogan 1981, Graf 2002). The concept of masculinities is important also for us therapists; we need a theoretical background to work with clients; it is not sufficient to be trained and do psychotherapy during training; we need theory to help us to develop our work; it does not need to be a radical theory – but we need one. Hogan (2016) has written abundantly about this subject and has given so many examples of how to apply one.

During my psychological training in psychology in 1980, I did not see any dialogue between psychology and feminist theory. We were bogged down in psychoanalytic theories only. Now my clinical practice has changed so much since I have encountered feminist theory, and especially feminist art therapy and phototherapy. It has taken so much time to improve my knowledge, and there is still so much to learn and apply between psychology, phototherapy and feminist theory. It is not easy to open up new approaches in clinical work as we can face many conservative theories and practices. Hogan (2003) gives us a typical example of traces of psychopathological views of homosexuality which are very much active in healing professions:

> Disruption to gender expectations can be extremely disturbing. To take the example of homosexuality, we must remember that homosexual practices carry the death penalty in some regimes. In Britain homosexuality was regarded as a mental illness by some psychiatrists until very recently. Homosexuality was only declassified as a mental illness in the International Classification of Diseases (ICD) in the 1992 edition. As Davies and Neal (1996, p.16) point out, some analytic associations still regard homosexuality as a sickness. The example of homosexuality illustrates how the disruption to gender categories can provoke extreme reactions.
> (Hogan 2003, 19)

Hogan (2003) exemplifies the problems faced by subordinated masculinity. Homosexuality is abhorred by hegemonic masculinity. The patriarchal principles of hegemonic masculinity are against the practice of anal sex present in homosexual practices. Anal sex is a synonym of passivity, femininity and pathology because:

> Popular homophobia, so far as I have been able to trace its themes, says nothing about God but is graphic about sex. *Anal sexuality is a focus of disgust, and receptive anal sex is a mark of feminization.* Homophobic humour among straight men still revolves around the limp wrist, the mincing walk and innuendo about castration.
> (Connell 2005, 219 – emphasis added)

A large part of gender ideologies against homosexuality are based on psychological axioms and Freudian theories from the nineteenth and twentieth century. Connell (2009) has made critiques about psychology in general and also the psychoanalytic axiom that postulates the Oedipus complex as a model for acquiring gender identity:

> *I do not believe there is a standard set of stages in gender formation – though a number of psychologists, from Freud on, have thought there is.* What we know about the diversity of gender orders makes it unlikely that there are universal rules for the way gender is learnt. *Perhaps the nearest thing to a universal rule is the fact of qualitative change. Any particular gender project, for an individual or a group in their distinct historical setting, is likely to involve points of transition, different moments of development.*
> (Connell 2009, 102 – emphasis added)

Connell (2009) deconstructs the universal assumption of the Oedipus complex as the main means to acquire gender. Her principal argument is that there are many different gender orders in different cultures. So we cannot generalise gender identity acquisition. Masculinities and femininities are not always in accordance with Western male and female binary. Furthermore, our sexuality is not practiced in accordance with a universal paradigm but is rather anchored in our personal and cultural practices in multiple gender orders. Connell (2005) presents the case of Don Meredith where he discovers anal sex through onto-formative gender practices after a series of sexual fiascos:

> Don Meredith, a great storyteller, offered a long comic tale of his youthful search for the First Fuck. After a series of fiascos he reached the goal, formed a relationship and then found himself unable to ejaculate. In time, however, he became more sophisticated: I am very anal oriented. And I discovered this in a relationship with a young woman quite accidentally, I really enjoyed it. She was inserting her finger into my anus and I thought "My god this is fantastic." And like even with masturbation I sort of generally touched round that area but never really gone into it. But I guess that was like a trigger for it. When this young woman was doing it, it was just really electrifying me, and I never found it difficult to ejaculate with her. She really touched a spot well and truly. So I thought now what I would really like is to have a relationship with a man where I would be inserted into. And that really excited me, the whole idea of it.
>
> (Connell 2005, 60)

Don Meredith first exemplifies the deconstruction of the stages of the acquisition of gender and sexuality, and second illustrates very well the male sexual practices through the gender practices that are constructed through the body. The discovery of his sexuality has been through onto-formative sexual practices. Don Meredith made several sexual attempts until he found a comfortable and enjoyable sexual life.

Phototherapy is a good place to deconstruct truths about "true" masculinities. The instruments offered by phototherapy can work with the concept of the masculinities of Connell (2005). Working with subordinate masculinity implies working with that which homosexual masculinity suffers in different gender regimes and gender orders. Sexual discrimination occurs within the gender regimes such as the workplace, families, schools, army and political parties. When we work with gay men we can empower them and deconstruct the idea that gay men are effeminate, not real men because:

> Gay theory and feminist theory share a perception of mainstream masculinity as being (in the advanced capitalist countries at least) fundamentally linked to power, organized for domination, and resistant to change because of *power relations. In some formulations, masculinity is virtually equated with the exercise of power in its most naked forms. This critique has been hard for*

many heterosexual men to take. The connection of masculinity with power is the point most persistently denied in the anti-feminist turn in the men's movement, a denial reinforced by pop psychology and neo-Jungian theories of masculinity.

(Connell 2005, 42 – emphasis added)

Power is a strong component in the construction of masculinities. Men fight for hegemonies; according to Connell (2005), the relations among masculinities are alliance, domination and subordination. The hegemonies are in constant construction and deconstruction and consequently men exchange positions in social gender relations, for example sometimes they can be hegemonic, now marginalised, now and then accomplices or subordinates. In phototherapy we can work with the issue of power among men in many ways because in phototherapy we can work in a less competitive environment where power can be represented, shared in many ways because:

> The process of phototherapy is essentially collaborative; it is not something which is either done to you, or for you. Our introduction to therapy was through co-counselling in which when working in pairs we give each other complete attention and an equal amount of non-judgmental listening time. This has been carried through into phototherapy. The easiest way to understand it is as a form of phototheatre of the self; it is basically about the making visible of psychic reality. It is not documentary photography because everything is stage—managed and deliberately placed in images, though it could be called "self- documentation."
>
> (Martin and Spence 1995, 165)

Here we have a yet broader understanding of the scope of phototherapy, which presents a greater flexibility than verbal therapy, and an embodied engagement. I suggest we can work out the issues of broader masculinity in the phototherapy sessions via such photo-theatre.

The work of David and Brannon (1976) aligns with the work of Connell (2005). Kimmel (2005) summarises the four pillars of masculinity presented by David and Brannon (1976):

> This definition of manhood has been summarised cleverly by psychologists Robert Brannon and Deborah David (1976) into four succinct phrases:
>
> 1 "No Sissy Stuff!" One may never do anything that even remotely suggests femininity. Masculinity is the relentless repudiation of the feminine.
> 2 "Be a Big Wheel". Masculinity is measured by power, success, wealth, and status. As the current saying goes, "He who has the most toys when he dies wins".

3 "Be a Sturdy Oak". Masculinity depends on remaining calm and reliable in a crisis, holding emotions in check. In fact, proving you're a man depends on never showing your emotions at all. Boys don't cry.
4 "Give 'Em Hell". Exude an aura of manly daring and aggression. Go for it. Take risks.

(Kimmel 2005, 30–31)

The four pillars of masculinity presented by David and Brannon (1976) represent the elements that constitute the hegemonic masculinity in Connell (2005). In general, all men identify with these hegemonic values. Kimmel (2005) explains how men comply with these prescriptions:

Failure to embody these rules, to affirm the power of the rules and one's achievement of them is a source of men's confusion and pain. Such a model is, of course, unrealizable for any man. But we keep trying, valiantly and vainly, to measure up. The chief test is contained in the first rule. *Whatever the variations by race, class, age, ethnicity, or sexual orientation, being a man means "not being like women". This notion of antifemininity lies at the heart of contemporary and historical conceptions of manhood, so that masculinity is defined more by what one is not rather than who one is.*

(Kimmel 2005, 30 – emphasis added)

Kimmel (2005) affirms that pillar one "No sissy stuff" is the typical test for men to prove their genuine masculinity. Men must prove that they are not a woman. Masculinity is then defined in a sexist way; it is aversive to women. Kimmel (2005) also alerts that these pillars are unrealisable for any man, but they must try as hard as they can. The definition of hegemonic masculinity complements David and Brannon's (1976) definition of masculinity because the values of hegemonic masculinity are not carried on by all kinds of men, but rather remain as an hegemonic ideal.

The pyramid (see Figure 12.4) gives us inspiration to work with men in phototherapy. It shows many possibilities of dismantling hegemonic masculinity. It depends on how the therapist works with phototherapy and their favourite techniques. When we work with the masculinities in phototherapy, we can adopt the four pillars as a theoretical tool to elicit and research male behaviours such as aggression, lack of contact with emotions, power, wealth, femininity and escapism from the feminine world.[3]

McAllister, Callaghan and Fellin (2018) have found in their research that men have serious difficulties in approaching emotional problems in the male workplace and rarely search for psychological help because:

What can a man do with a camera? 179

Figure 12.4 Pyramid Built by the Author Based on the Work of Deborah David and Robert Brannon (1976) on the Four Pillars of Masculinity cited by Kimmel (2008):"No Sissy Stuff!".

Dominant discourses of military servicemen position them as more prone to psychological damage than the general population, but as reluctant to seek psychological assistance, because of the military culture of "toughness", a *military masculinity*, that values stoicism, emotional control and invulnerability and implicitly excludes "feminine" characteristics like emotionality. This is seen as a barrier to military personnel seeking help, by implicitly discouraging emotional disclosure and expression.

(McAllister, Callaghan and Fellin 2018, 1)

Men have emotions and like to feel them, but they do not express them because the "real man" is not supposed to manifest his emotions (Kimmel 2017). In the army this problem is even worse due to the ideals of hegemonic masculinity embodied by soldiers (Connell 2005). Soldiers control their emotions and also police the emotions of male peers as a way to maintain the level of hegemonic masculinity. Men police men to construct hegemonic masculinity. "No sissy stuff" is the most surveilled element among men. It is at the top of the pyramid (see Figure 12.4) because:

> Hegemonic masculinity was distinguished from other masculinities, especially subordinated masculinities. Hegemonic masculinity was not assumed to be normal in the statistical sense; only a minority of men might enact it. But it was certainly normative. *It embodied the currently most honored way of being a man, it required all other men to position themselves in relation to it,* and it ideologically legitimated the global subordination of women to men.
> (Connell and Messerschmidt 2005, 832 – emphasis added)

In this section, I have introduced the concept of hegemonic masculinity as a framework for working in phototherapy. Connell's concept aligns with the work of Kimmel (2005), David and Brannon (1976) and Hogan (2016). This theoretical framework can work well in order to explore more deeply masculinities in male groups or individual sessions in phototherapy. Feminist art therapy has already constructed a firm body of work and it is open for further research on gender issues inclusive of masculinity therapy and theories of masculinity. We have to do more research in the field of masculinity and phototherapy because:

> To understand gender, then, we must constantly go beyond gender. The same applies in reverse. We cannot understand class, race or global inequality without constantly moving towards gender. Gender relations are a major component of social structure as a whole, and gender politics are among the main determinants of our collective fate.
> (Connell 2005, 48)

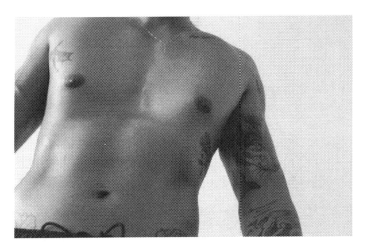

Figure 12.5 The Social Construction of Masculinities by José Loureiro 2018.

Practical implications in working with men in phototherapy

In this section, I present a discussion about some practical points in psychological work with men. The discussion is based on the work of Marian Liebmann in particular (2003) with groups of men in art therapy.

When I have new clients in phototherapy the most common questions that men ask me are: Are you gay? Why do you work with men with psychological problems? Do I have to be photographed in the nude? Is your work completely confidential? I would say that these questions should first be understood with reference to the client's anxiety; often, if in therapy previously, they have met a woman therapist, not a man. A man treating a man can increase anxiety. If it can still be said that all psychological defences may also be a product of hegemonic masculinity where "a core element of the construction of hegemonic masculinity is heterosexuality, and to a greater or lesser extent hegemonic masculinity is constructed as a gender position that is as much 'not gay' as it is 'not female'"(Jewkes et al. 2015, 113), then such anxiety may be inevitable.

Connell (2005) has alerted us to the different types of therapy that work with men. Firstly, Connell (2005) does not believe in the crisis of masculinity because: "different masculinities do not sit side-by-side like dishes on a smorgasbord. There are definite social relations between them. Especially, there are relations of hierarchy, for some masculinities are dominant while others are subordinated or marginalized" (Connell 2000, 10). Masculinities are not a closed system, static or rigid, but they are practical and there is nothing beyond the practices. The author says that we can then talk about transformation and disruptions around the masculinities in such a gender order. I believe that the question of the crisis of manhood is a starting point for us therapists to position ourselves on what we believe. Connell (2005) also suggests a difference between "*popular forms of masculinity therapy and masculinity therapy as a form of masculinity politics*". This distinction is fundamental in order to establish work with men. They are two different forms of conceiving the work on masculinity. One looks beyond emotional wounds, personal conflicts and also engages men in the politics of masculinity: fighting again sexual abuse, homophobia, transphobia, misogyny and the patriarchal dominance of women; whereas popular forms of masculinity try to reconnect men with patriarchal values claiming that men are entitled to recover their "true masculinity" disguised in the form of new masculinities. In other words, popular masculinity tries to heal men in a more functionalist way by keeping patriarchal values such as subordination, heterosexism, homophobia and domination.

I advocate masculinity therapy as a form of masculinity politics because we are there not only to treat emotional problems, but also to raise awareness of gender, class, sexism and power in gender social relations (a point Huss and Hogan have both made in their work with women). Therapy must happen in a social context where transformation and disruption may occur. This implies that we, as therapists, have to deal with power too because "feminism requires an analysis of power; indeed, one of feminism's central tenets is that gender relations are constructed in a field of power" (Kimmel 1995, 10). Power is not something invisible or theoretical conjuncture. Power is sophisticated, embodied and is exerted ubiquitously.

In order to apply masculinity politics, I also subscribe to feminist phototherapy (Hogan 2016). Feminist theory is very complex and has different applications. It is also misused and misunderstood. Hogan (2016) explains the concept of feminism:

> *This is a much maligned and misused term.* Feminism is the principle of advocating the social, political and other rights of women as equal to those of men.
> (Hogan 2016, 144 – emphasis added)

The feminist theory is what connects the work of Connell (2005), Kimmel (1995) and Hogan (2016). Kimmel (1995) believes that "feminism provides both women and men with an extraordinarily powerful analytic prism through which to understand their lives, and a political and moral imperative to transform the unequal conditions of those relationships" (Kimmel, 1995, 6). I consider this link important because they are the authors who inspire and give weight to my academic work and gender issues in phototherapy. Hogan (2016) highlights the three elements which define feminist art therapy:

> *First* is the cultivation of an acute critical awareness of issues of inequality. *Second*, linked to this, is a critical investigation of the construction of knowledge, including an analysis of the power dynamics within institutional practices, use of language and pictorial representation which sustain inequality. There is an interest in tearing down false suppositions (deconstruction) in order to expose and to challenge the theoretical foundations of prejudice and oppressive practices. *Third*, through these engagements is consciousness-raising and empowerment.
> (Hogan 2016, 125)

I consider the three fundamental elements that constitute the practice of the feminist phototherapy. The issue of inequality, the construction of knowledge and empowerment are elements that align with the theory of masculinity. The relationship between masculinities is charged with power and inequalities promoted by hegemonic masculinity that work against subordinate masculinity, complicit and marginalised masculinities. To work with the masculinities in phototherapy we need a good theoretical basis that is not only rooted in the techniques of phototherapy, but which also gives a non-reductive theoretical basis rooted in the social and political context where we work.

Liebmann (2003) affirms that "art therapy provides an active phase which can then lead more easily to reflection" (Liebmann 2003, 124) because we have a client´s product which is concrete bridging feelings, perceptions, fantasies and insights into gender practices. Art therapy brings us inside and outside of ourselves raising awareness of our gender practices which are imbedded in gender subordination, alliance and domination (Connell 2005). Liebman (2003) has suggested six strategic points to work with men in art therapy which are applicable to phototherapy:

1 There needs to be a recognition of the extra difficulties men may find in accessing therapy; perhaps some literature, in which men speak of the benefits, could help the cautious to be reassured about art therapy – in particular the vulnerability (and "un-macho-ness") of being a client. (Liebmann 2003, 124)

   Liebmann (2003) points out a strategic element to bring men into art therapy. We need strategies to work with men as the "real macho does not come to therapy". Information is a key point to overcome male ignorance and stereotype about art therapy and gender issues. We should provide information to our clients about art work with men in order to break the ice, break feelings of shame, constraints such as humiliation and fear of having phototherapy sessions. "Real men" are not supposed to talk about their emotions although they are dying to do so if they feel safe and not exposed to judgmental assumptions (Kimmel 2018); phototherapy can make it happen.

2 The "art part" of an art therapy session is likely to be the more important part for many men, especially at the beginning of therapy. (Liebmann 2003, 124)

   The art work is also important when the client is forming a therapeutic alliance with the therapist. I think that art creation reassures men as being a creator, a powerful man and able to attach to the therapist when his work is welcome. Here it is important to work on the feeling of shame, inhibition and incentive to go on exploring more deeply emotions, fears and representations of masculinity. In phototherapy "photographs of the client are a primary means of providing the client with feedback regarding appearance and presentation of self". (Turner Hogan 1981, 194).

3 Sessions comprising structured exercises may be helpful in containing men's anxiety about the unfamiliar world of feelings. (Liebmann 2003, 124)

   Phototherapy can offer structured exercises in order to contain and help male anxiety during therapy sessions. It has a huge variety of different photographic techniques that can be used in groups or in individual sessions. Weiser (2010) has suggested five phototherapy techniques: (1) Pictures taken or created by the subject; (2) Portrait of the subject taken by another who determines the subject's post, time and place of shooting; (3) Self-portrait taken by the subject; (4) Family albums or other collection of biographical photos; (5) Photo-projections.[4]

4 Work around feelings may need to be divided into smaller, more manageable steps. (Liebmann 2003, 124)

   We have to apply some techniques in order to avoid possible psychological defenses and also withdrawal from therapy sessions. I would also suggest approaching first general gender issues in a group in order to advance to personal issues such as exploring feelings towards representations of hegemonic masculinity. Hogan (2016) suggests some art therapy techniques that can also be applied in phototherapy sessions. Sometimes, when using directive art therapy, it is possible to introduce exercises that can help participants reflect on their sex and sexual orientation (Hogan 2016, 144–5).

5   Some men may find group work easier than individual work, because it is less intimate, and group solidarity compensates for their feelings of being "deficient men" for needing therapy. (Liebmann 2003, 124)

  Graf (2002) also agrees with Liebmann (2003) that phototherapy in groups would be beneficial to men especially to work with issues of isolation, stigma and inadequacy for therapy. Graf (2002) believes that "the advantages of group work include cost-effectiveness; facilitation of new skills, behaviours, and social interactions; and support for members". (Graf 2002, 205)

6   Men's groups may help men to look at their specific needs without instinctively relying on women to "do the emotional bit". (Liebmann 2003, 124)

  Depending on the male group we are working with, it is important to work with them in groups. The mutual identification among men in groups is helpful in order to share not only the pain, hostile feelings, but also they can work together in setting goals and building bonds together. Graf (2002) affirms that male sessions in a group are productive for men in therapy because they can have insight about their own masculinity and can be empowered, especially the ones who feel fragile and powerless. Men in phototherapy sessions may learn a lot about their emotional world without being haunted by hegemonic masculinities.

I agree with Graf (2002) that we still need much research on phototherapy to substantiate the efficacy of phototherapy. We now have many different theoretical backgrounds to apply in phototherapy (see Hogan 2016) and have to choose the one which suits us to work on phototherapy. I would like to close this section with the words of Hogan (2016) who alerts us to the importance of contextualising our work with clients. It is not enough to apply a technical expertise and theoretical background, as we need to contextualise where and with who we are in our sessions because:

> It is acknowledged that any generalisation made about gender differences *must take into account a myriad of factors, including class, culture, age, health issues, sexuality and geographical location*, as important contributory factors in how women are perceived and treated. Many feminist writers adhere to a model of selfhood which sees it in flux in relation to multiple forces.
> (Hogan 2016, 125)

Conclusion

In this chapter I have attempted to bring the concept of hegemonic masculinity into the practice of phototherapy. It remains a work in progress since we need further research in the field. The concept of masculinities gave a fundamental turn to the studies of gender during the second wave of feminism in the 1980s. The concept of hegemonic masculinity is valid and its usefulness is widely recognised worldwide; however, there remain several criticisms about its uses (Connell 2000,

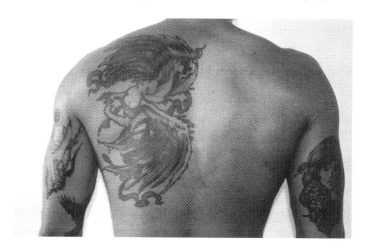

Figure 12.6 Masculinities by José Loureiro 2018.

2005). We need art therapists to do research into this field to construct a body of literature and new ways of working with phototherapy. Liebmann (2003) has shown that art therapy has great potential for working with masculinities, and her experience is pioneering in the field. The combination of the theory of masculinities (Connell 2005; Kimmel 1995) with feminist art therapy (Hogan 2016) is certainly an important area where we can work with women and men individually or in groups considering intersectional dimensions of gender such as class, culture, age, health issues, sexuality and geographical location.

Masculinity therapy with phototherapy is not an easy task. It implies working with feminist theory, which is frequently misunderstood or blocked by antifeminist and misogynistic professional groups. The very concept of feminism is still misconstrued (Hogan 2016), and has caused alarming disagreements not only in academia, but in different places, such as school and religious environments. To help bring an understanding of gender as socially embodied practices of immediate relevance in the real world, discussions are required with other professionals. This work is necessary in order to avoid the perception of gender as a restricted topic for discussion, solely among academics and activists. The contrary must surely be the case.

Notes

1 Connell (2005) uses the Gramsci concept of hegemony to build studies on masculinities. It is important to note that the concept of hegemony is quite elastic, flexible, social and mobile. The concept of hegemony is critical to understanding the criticism of the theory of masculinities. Hogan (2016) defines hegemony as: "hegemony has been used to mean political predominance. In cultural theory, from the work of Gramsci, it is often used to

mean what is taken for granted as "common sense" or it refers to unquestioned assumptions. It is also used to refer to the dominant ideology" (Hogan 2016, 145).
2 This topic requires in depth analysis of dimensions of class, race and ethnicity which I do not discuss in this paper.
3 Pyramid built by the author based on the work of Deborah David and Robert Brannon (1976) on the four pillars of masculinity cited by Kimmel (2008): "No Sissy Stuff!"; "Be a Big Wheel"; "Be a Sturdy Oak"; "Give 'Em Hell".
4 For further phototherapy techniques, see Martin (2009), Loewenthal (2013), Clark and Loewenthal (2014), Barbee (2002).

References

Barbee, Michael. 2002. A Visual-narrative approach to understanding transsexual identity. *Art Therapy*, 19 (2): 53–62. doi: 10.1080/07421656.2002.10129339.
Blackbeard, D. R. and Lindegger, G. 2014. Dialogues through autophotography: Young masculinity and HIV identity in KwaZulu-Natal. *European Journal of Social and Behavioural Sciences*, 10: 1466–1477.
Campbell, Jean. 1999. *Art Therapy, Race, and Culture*. London; Philadelphia: Jessica Kingsley Publishers.
Connell, Raewyn. 1987. *Gender and Power : Society, the Person, and Sexual Politics*. Cambridge: Polity Press in association with B. Blackwell.
Connell, Raewyn. 2000. *The Men and the Boys*. Berkeley: University of California Press.
Connell, Raewyn. 2005. *Masculinities*. 2nd edition. Cambridge: Polity Press.
Connell, Raewyn. 2009. *Gender: In World Perspective. Short Introductions*. 2nd edition. Cambridge: Polity.
Connell, Raewyn W. and Messerschmidt, James W. 2005. Hegemonic masculinity: Rethinking the concept. *Gender & Society*, 19 (6): 829–859. doi: 10.1177/0891243205278639.
David, Deborah S. and Brannon, Robert. 1976. *The Forty-nine Percent Majority: The Male Sex Role*. Reading: Addison-Wesley Pub. Co.
De Oliveira, José B. L. 2000. Deconstructing 'Machismo': Victims of 'Machismo Ideology' Dominating in Brazil. LASA XXII International Congress of the Latin American Studies Association, Miami USA.
De Oliveira, José B. L. 2017. Entre Machos e Maricas: Um estudo sobre masculinidades gays em ambiente corporativo na cidade do Rio de Janeiro/RJ. PhD diss., IUPERJ, Cândido Mendes University.
Graf, Noreen M. 2002. Photography as a therapeutic tool for substance abuse clients who have a history of sexual abuse. *Counselling and Psychotherapy Research*, 2 (3): 201-208. doi: 10.1080/14733140212331384835.
Hogan, Susan. 1997. *Feminist Approaches to Art Therapy*. London: Routledge.
Hogan, Susan. 2003. *Gender Issues in Art Therapy*. London; Philadelphia: Jessica Kingsley Pub.
Hogan, Susan. 2012. *Revisiting Feminist Approaches to Art Therapy*. Oxford: Berghahn Books.
Hogan, Susan. 2016. *Art Therapy Theories : A Critical Introduction*. London; New York: Routledge, Taylor & Francis Group.
Hogan, Susan and Warren, Lorna. 2012. Dealing with complexity in research processes and findings: How do older women negotiate and challenge images of aging? *Journal of Women & Aging*, 24 (4): 329–350. doi: 10.1080/08952841.2012.708589.
Jewkes, R., Morrell, R., Hearn, J., Lundqvist, E., Blackbeard, D., Lindegger, G., Quayle, M., Sikweyiya, Y. and Gottzén, L. 2015. Hegemonic masculinity: Combining theory and practice in gender interventions. *Culture, Health & Sexuality*, 17 (sup2): 96–111.

Kimmel, Michael S. 1995. Fear of Feminism. The Annual Meetings of the American Philosophical Association, New York City.

Kimmel, Michael S. 2005. *The Gender of Desire : Essays on Male Sexuality*. Albany: State University of New York Press.

Kimmel, Michael S. 2011. *The Gendered Society*. 4th edition. New York: Oxford University Press.

Kimmel, Michael S. 2018. *What Drives Men to Violent Extremism*. edited by Korva Coleman. National Public Radio. Accessed at https://www.npr.org/2018/04/01/598630207/what-drives-men-to-violent-extremism.

Krauss, D. A. 1979. The uses of still photography in counseling and therapy: Development of a training model. Unpublished Doctoral Dissertation. Kent: Kent State University.

Krauss, D. A. and Fryrear, J. L. 1983. Phototherapy introduction and overview. In J. L. Fryrear and D. A. Krauss (Eds.) *Phototherapy in Mental Health* (pp. 3–23). Springfield: Charles C. Thomas.

Liebmann, Marian. 2003. Working with men. In *Gender Issues in Art Therapy*, edited by Susan Hogan, 108–125. London: Jessica Kingsley Publishers.

Loewenthal, Del. 2014. http://www.phototherapyeuropeinprisons.eu/. Retrieved on 30 December 2018.

Martin, Rosy. 2009. Inhabiting the image: Photography, therapy and re-enactment phototherapy. *European Journal of Psychotherapy & Counselling*, 11 (1): 35–49. doi: https://doi.org/10.1080/13642530902723074.

Martin, R. and Spence, J. 1985. New portraits for old: The use of the camera in therapy. Feminist Review, 19: 66–92.

McAllister, Lauren, Callaghan, Jane E. M. and Fellin, Lisa. 2018. Masculinities and emotional expression in UK servicemen: Big boys don't cry? *Journal of Gender Studies*, 1–14. doi: 10.1080/09589236.2018.1429898.

Nelson-Gee, Ellen. 1975. Learning to be: A look into the use of therapy with polaroid photography as a means of recreating the development of perception and the ego. *Art Psychotherapy*, 2 (2): 159–164. doi: https://doi.org/10.1016/0090-9092(75)90017-4.

Spence, J. 1986. *Putting Myself in the Picture: A Political, Personal and Photographic Autobiography*. London: Camden Press.

Spence, J. 1991. Family Snaps: The Meanings of Domestic Photography, Edited by: Holland, P. London: Virago.

Spence, Jo. 1995. *Cultural Sniping : the Art of Transgression*. London: Routledge.

Spire, R. H. 1973. Photographic self-image confrontation. *American Journal of Nursing*, 73 (7): 1207–1210.

Turner Hogan, Patricia. 1981. Phototherapy in the educational setting. *The Arts in Psychotherapy*, 8 (3): 193–199. doi: https://doi.org/10.1016/0197-4556(81)90031-9.

Weiser, J. 1975. PhotoTherapy: Photography as a verb. The B.C. *Photographer*, 2: 33–36.

Weiser, J. 2010. When I was your age: PhotoTherapy techniques for families. In Lowenstein, L. (Ed.), *Creative Family Therapy Techniques*. Toronto: Champion Press, 270–277.

Wheeler, M. 2004. Photography, fantasy and fine-print encounters: An exploration of making and viewing. Bath: Unpublished dissertation held by Royal Photographic Society.

Wheeler, Mark. 2009. Photo-psycho-praxis. *European Journal of Psychotherapy & Counselling*, 11 (1): 63–76. doi: 10.1080/13642530902745812.

Wolf, R. I. 1976. The Polaroid technique: Spontaneous dialogues from the unconscious. *Art Psychotherapy*, 3 (3): 197–201.

Zwick, Deborah S. 1978. Photography as a tool toward increased awareness of the aging self. *Art Psychotherapy*, 5 (3): 135–141. doi: https://doi.org/10.1016/0090-9092(78)90003-0.

Chapter 13

Look at me! Representing self: Representing Ageing

Older women represent their own narratives of ageing, using re-enactment phototherapeutic techniques

Rosy Martin

> The overall aim of the project was to use creative arts therapies and community arts to negotiate and challenge images of ageing and explore their potential contribution to participatory approaches to research in social gerontology.[1]

Introduction

It was turning fifty that prompted my personal and intellectual engagement with the issues concerning ageing and gender. Extensive research showed that the dominant representations of older women within popular culture and medical discourse showed predominantly stereotypes of decline and redundancy. If and when more 'positive' images were encountered at all, it was by the rare examples of marathon runners in their eighties, which only served to enhance the sense of exceptionalism.

In the west, emphasis is placed upon a culture of celebrity, advertising and TV make-over shows that focus on appearance and the ideal of a youthful body. When images of middle-aged and older women do appear in popular culture these often highlight a re-touched and botoxed youthfulness. (For example, Cher in *Mamma Mia: Here We Go Again*.)

This emphasis produces a heroine/victim dichotomy in which older women are either well maintained or 'letting themselves go', are either super fit marathon runners or couch potatoes, are either mature polished consumers or abject pensioners shivering in the loneliness of poverty. Rather than the once respected roles of wise-woman and matriarch, the post-menopausal woman is too often characterised as representing notions of decline and decay.

The rhetoric of lack and loss is reiterated in medical discourses on the menopause. The World Health Organisation defines menopause as an estrogen deficiency disease. The vivid imagery of atrophy, withering and decline used to describe 'senile ovaries' (Martin 1992, p.39) reiterates Dr. Reuben (1969) who considered the menopause to be a time of sexual degeneration, which he [sic] characterises as 'tragic', once the reproductive function is lost:

Look at me! Representing self 189

The vagina begins to shrivel, the breasts atrophy, sexual desire disappears ... Increased facial hair, deepening voice, obesity ... coarsened features, enlargement of the clitoris, and gradual baldness complete the tragic picture. Not really a man but no longer a functional woman, these individuals live in the world of intersex.

(Reuben 1969, p.242)

Thus women can feel caught between disavowal and acceptance of their own ageing process and may actively deny or defy their chronological age.

'Outrageous Agers'

I wanted to find ways of representing my ageing self through my photographic practice in a subversive, playful and resistant way to challenge existing simplistic visual narratives.

'Outrageous Agers' is a body of photographic and video works, based upon this extensive research and cultural studies' critiques of how older women are

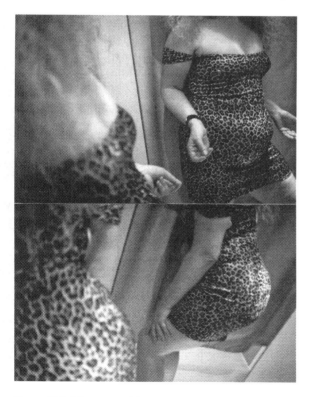

Figure 13.1 'Trying it on' from Outrageous Agers. Rosy Martin in collaboration with Kay Goodridge.

represented and perceived (Martin 2012). It was produced in collaboration with Kay Goodridge. We used phototherapeutic techniques to explore our personal histories and feelings about these mis-representations. We developed a range of strategies to confront these limiting stereotypes of the ageing woman and the discourses of decline and redundancy. The work we produced was about the unruly, carnivalesque even grotesque body, which refuses to be ignored. By using irony, humour and transgression, clichés for example 'mutton dressed as lamb' were subverted (Figure 13.1). This was an exploration of embodied sentient knowledge – not a study of 'the other' – but rather what it meant to occupy and resist cultural stereotypes We used our own bodies as older women, who are artists/photographers, as a medium for exploring social and psychic realities. (Martin 2003, 2012) We chose to confront prescriptive and normative definitions of ageing women by projecting these texts upon our naked bodies, so that the physicality of flesh overpowered the words. We made two exhibitions and showed both photography and video works. For the second show, we added more video performance pieces developed out of the series of workshops we led with Freudian Slips, a theatre group of older women, based in Cambridge (Martin and Goodridge 2001, www.outrageous-agers.co.uk).

'Look at me' – The research context

The United Nations Second World Assembly on Ageing identified as one of its objectives the 'need to facilitate contributions of older women and men to the presentation by the media of their activities and concerns' (2002).

So, having previously immersed myself in research on representations of the ageing woman's body and how one might challenge these internalised self-limiting notions, I was pleased to be invited to become a member of the team for this research project, Representing Self: Representing Ageing, in collaboration with The University of Derby and Eventus. This was part of the New Dynamics of Ageing research programme at Sheffield University.

The research aims were:

1. To enable older women drawn from different community settings to create their own images of ageing using a variety of participatory visual methods.
2. To explore the relationships between cultural and creative activity and later life wellbeing: to reflect upon the contribution of visual methods to participatory processes.
3. To demonstrate the contribution of arts and humanities to critical gerontology.
4. To enhance recognition by policymakers and the wider public of the authority, wisdom and productivity of older women.

I was a member of the planning and coordinating group and took part in all the discussions and debates on formulating, developing, producing and evaluating this research project. Sociologists are becoming very aware of the power of using visual methods within their practice. It's now a burgeoning field, within the social sciences (Rose 2001, 2016; Pink, Hogan and Bird 2011; Hogan 2012; Milne, Mitchell and deLange 2012; Pink 2013; Banks 2015). The International Visual Studies Association (IVSA) and the International Visual Methods Conference bring practitioners together to share and explore their cross-disciplinary research.[2]

This project was a pioneering example in which social gerontologists worked with art therapy, photo-elicitation, phototherapeutic approaches and two photographic artists whose work was coordinated by Eventus, a Sheffield-based community arts project, to generate and use images within their research practices. (Richards, Warren, and Gott 2012; Hogan and Warren 2012; Hogan, 2013; Hogan and Warren 2013; Hogan 2015; Hogan 2016). The participants were directly involved in the production of their images by the use of these different creative arts. It was important that this research was conducted with 'ordinary' older women, to try to gain insights into how attitudes towards ageing were experienced across a full range of 'identities': of class, race, sexualities and different stages of ageing. It was decided that the research group would not set a specific age range for those who took part in the research workshops, but that the participants would self-define as ageing.

The workshops using phototherapeutic techniques

The workshops were advertised widely in the Sheffield area, in libraries, community centres, other social spaces and the local paper. A leaflet was distributed raising key questions about how older women think and feel about ageing and how they are represented in the media. 'What does it mean to be an older woman – both the positive and negative sides of this identity? How do I want to be, and be seen, as an older woman? Can I make images to capture the complexities of my life?' An outline of the workshop processes was described, mapping out how participants would create more complex and alternative images to those found in popular culture, in a supportive and therapeutic setting. No formal background in photography was needed, rather just an openness to trying out new ways of being creative. It was made clear that the workshops required a high level of commitment and openness to challenge from the participants and that attendance at all the workshops in the series was vital to maintain group dynamics. It was acknowledged that difficult and sometimes painful memories can come to light in these group sessions and that a secure setting would be created and maintained. Because of the requirements of the research project it was specified that a selection of the images produced would be shown in an exhibition, but only with the expressed permission of each participant. Each was to receive a DVD of their work, the film of the project and an enlarged framed print.

Potential participants completed forms, to explain why they were interested in taking part, what they felt they could bring to the project and what they thought they might gain from it. It was made clear that any support requirements would be met (e.g. access, hearing loop, special diets, etc.) so as not to exclude any potential members. Commitment to attend all six days of the workshop was a fundamental requirement. The researcher, Naomi Richards, interviewed applicants and twelve participants were selected. We were aiming for diversity of experience and background as well as evidence of commitment to group working and openness to a therapeutic approach. Many did have experience of working creatively, but what mattered most was a willingness to explore one's own creative potential.

Good quality DSLR cameras were provided for the participants, because the planned outcomes included an exhibition and I wanted beautiful large prints to be a possibility (hence the need for large digital files). I wanted participants to enjoy the full range of photographic possibilities offered by manual control as well as a variety of pre-programmed settings and a zoom lens with a range of focal lengths that enabled more individual creativity for those who wished to experiment.

The University of Sheffield Sociological Studies Ethics Committee set very strict guidelines for the whole research project. Because I was using therapeutic methods, I set even tighter criteria, requiring confidentiality regarding everything said in the group and in pair work, which I explained at the beginning of the workshops. I would therefore not permit any filming or recording of the workshops, nor for the researcher to attend.

In my own strivings for an ethical practice – as a therapist, as a maker of images and of cultural interventions – I am very aware of the power of images to communicate, to communicate multiple readings or even to mis-communicate; indeed, images are inherently polysemic. When I started exhibiting work, I did so before I had fully dealt with the issues within myself, and so when I received negative criticism, it was hard to separate the work from the self. So, I learnt that it was necessary to maintain firm boundaries and allow time for the emotional work to take place before any photographic work was shown. My concern regarding ethics was much more that yes, it is necessary to get permissions at the start of the research project, but really the women didn't know what they were giving permission for. 'Consent' is a very contested area.

I wanted to create a playful, experimental place for exploring ageing, but as with any therapy, one does not know what will 'come up' and therefore some participants may need to maintain their own boundaries with regard to what is seen or shown and to what audiences in what contexts. How to record the revelations about ageing and its multiple processes without blocking the very possibility of such openness and freedom to speak one's story? Therefore, the participants had to have the right to veto the showing of any work produced, regardless of previous permission obtained during the ethics process.

As a researcher, group leader and older woman, I am both responsible for initiating and containing the photo-therapeutic work and dealing with my own identifications with the subject of 'ageing'. I am very much embedded, and embodied within the object of the research. Not to mention countertransference (i.e. my emotional histories, reactivated in the presence of the participant's material). I must be aware both of my presence as a fully congruent member of the group and as the initiator/leader/container. I ensured that I had supervision available to support my working practices, which I used to deal with any difficulties which arose during this series of workshops. It was invaluable.

I invited participants to write about what they personally learnt, in reflective diaries, both for themselves and for the research project, if they were willing to share this, as a route to giving back control. And, yes indeed, I kept my own detailed reflective diary on the whole process.

It was part of the research remit to make a film about the work. To maintain participant control, volunteers were identified who were willing to be filmed as they made their alternative photographic diary work and reflected upon their own ageing, during the weeks between the workshops. For those who were willing, a separate day for filming of the processes and sharing the resultant images, through which participants told their stories whilst I facilitated the group, was organised at the end. This acted as a useful summing up and opportunity for reflection for the participants and was a much less intrusive way of 'collecting data'. The final edit was subject to their approval.

The workshops were held in a well-appointed community centre in Sheffield and we were given the complete run of the space, with no disturbances. They took place on consecutive Saturdays, with one full two-day weekend (later feedback said this weekend was too intensive and emotionally tiring). There were twelve women in the group, whose ages ranged from forty-seven to sixty, the majority were in their late fifties. I was surprised to realise that I was the oldest.

My focus in the therapeutic group work was starting from the individual and then approaching the 'issue' of what it meant to be an ageing woman. I used a series of structured exercises, visual examples and carefully planned focused sessions to enable the women to develop ideas. Using a therapeutic group approach the women worked in pairs, and then each was invited to share within the group. The focus was on exploring each woman's individual experiences, feelings and thoughts in the work in pairs. As one woman spoke in the pair, the other offered primarily skilful listening, support and empathetic thoughtful intuitive questions to help her to articulate. Then the roles were exchanged. Each had equal time. When these feelings, thoughts and insights were voiced in the group work, there was a sense of recognition and acknowledgement, so that each could feel 'heard' and understood.

This approach concentrates upon the individual, and from that moves out into the social, to make more 'general' observations. My approach is always to see each individual within her social and cultural contexts. Each woman thus explored, re-considered and gained new perspectives upon herself and her experiences of ageing.

Each workshop day started with an opening circle, in which everyone checked in, and aimed to leave behind day-to-day concerns. Each day ended with a closing circle to ground the energies. I asked each woman to voice and thereby begin the task of thanking her partner(s) and herself and to articulate ways in which she would nurture and take care of herself. Initially this might seem unfamiliar. However, over the weeks the quality and depth of mutual support and validations, both for each other and themselves, increased.

I introduced the ground rules for the workshop first, since it was vital to establish confidentiality as a way of being in the group, so that everyone would feel able to talk about whatever came up safely. I encouraged everyone to take responsibility for themselves, to do a little or as much as they chose, to respect each other, to listen carefully and non-judgementally and to respect boundaries. I emphasised that my aim was to create a sense of safety and trust and as we worked together and got to know each other through sharing our feelings and thoughts, that the group itself would become a safe holding environment. I asked each to think of the support structures they have within their lives. I also distributed a list of local therapy and support groups, both free and fee-paying so they could contact them after the workshop if they needed to.

Figure 13.2 The objects that participants brought to introduce themselves. Rosy Martin.

I had asked everyone to bring in an object to introduce herself with: a delightful opening exercise, which encourages metaphor, association and a certain playfulness (Figure 13.2). I showed a selection of dominant media images of ageing women, which prompted an on-going lively discussion in the group. Most of the women were angered by the predominance of plastic surgery, highly photoshopped images and the unrealistic demands made of celebrities, such as the critiques in the popular press of Madonna's hands, Nicole Kidman's strands of grey hair and Brigitte Bardot looking her real age. I then showed portraits by artists and photographers of older women, which showed more diversity and honesty (e.g. Rembrandt's portrait of his mother, Paula Rego's portrait of Germaine Greer, Madame Bijou by Brassai) and self-portrait images made by older women artists that offered a much more expansive range of possibilities as to how stereotypes and lazy thinking could be challenged (e.g. Alice Neel, Kathe Kollwitz, Anne Noggle). Then they worked in pairs to each talk about one image that brought up some feelings and resonances with their own life.

To prompt the idea of photographs as fictions I provided a selection of old family album photographs, which I had found on market stalls. These were therefore anonymous. I asked each to choose one they were drawn to immediately and then they worked in pairs to tell the stories which they imagined, using this photograph as a starting point, to their partner (Martin 2013). What great stories they were, when shared in the group and indeed for each they subtly touched upon a personal note, even if at the outset that was not recognised or acknowledged. Then we did a group brainstorm, writing on two huge sheets of paper, one on hopes, and the other on fears of ageing. I asked everyone to choose one idea from each, and work in pairs to explore their feelings, which we then shared in the group.

Then I introduced the idea of alternative photographic diaries, with examples and explained how to use the project cameras. The workshop participants were encouraged to experiment and use these cameras to tell the story of their lives to one another in a complex and challenging way that goes far beyond the traditional family album style. The brief I gave was:

> To use the digital camera to make images that 'speak' about yourself and your experiences, feelings and thoughts about yourself as an ageing woman. These images can be images of places, objects, people, your own selection of things, placed as you want, you may choose the everyday or the extraordinary. You may photograph what you find, or actively construct your images. It is important to let your unconscious lead, see what you find, explore. Then edit and select ... chose about twelve to print out. It is important to view this final selection of photographs as a kind of diary, something that speaks for you and about you, the story of your life now.

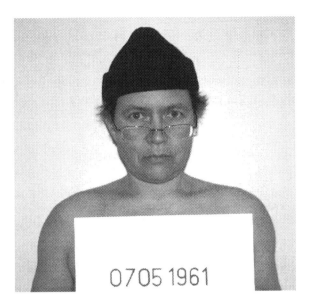

Figure 13.3 Claudia Kuntze.

> '*I feel like a prisoner of the numbers*' *was how Claudia described this image from her diary work – however, by the end of the workshop her feedback was* '*Something which became clear through the phototherapy process was that, for me, ageing now means owning the time I have lived. This is very different from hiding the time I've lived, a huge change*'.
>
> Claudia Kuntze

This photographic and self-reflective work was done during the week between workshop sessions, and for some was also an introduction to using a digital SLR camera. In the next workshop, the women worked in pairs, to articulate these stories of their lives through exploring their chosen images, in an open-ended way, whilst their partner listened, asked key questions and offered support. These personal narratives were then shared within the holding empathy of the group.

This is a wonderfully vivid example of this self-reflective diary work and the process of photographing, as a means of recording:

> *Jen - My diary images:*
> *2 events happened this week connected to my self-image as a 55-year-old, post-menopausal single woman.*
> *The 1st: I went with a friend to have our "style and colours" done. It had taken me a couple of years to reconcile this with my feminist/ex-lesbian politics:*

how superficial, how plastic, but also how honest in acknowledging my need to feel more positive about my changing body and place in the world. I couldn't feel "me" in makeup: it felt like a mask and I don't want to hide my real skin. I haven't worn it again. Finding colours that brought me to life was great and I have bought accordingly since (mostly from charity shops). Wearing shapes that balanced out, but showed off, my body was celebratory. I now only hide in 'baggies' when I feel bad, and recognise that as a tell-tale sign that I need to work on my feelings.

The 2nd: losing my senses. A grey mist suddenly descended over my right eye. I was terrified, especially when the optician sent me for further tests. In the end, all was well: it was just 'jelly' come loose. The shots represent what I could see from my left, and my right, eye, and the joy from visual beauty I feared I might lose. I have to use subtitles to hear some TV. Going deaf as well? Already? More fear. I snapped Holby City at random. Hey presto - a shot reading 'we all have to die alone', featuring an empty wheelchair. Well - I will make sure that's not how it is for me.'

Jen Greenfell

I had asked everyone to bring in images from their family albums. I introduced this session by mapping a context for the family album. I drew upon work by cultural theorists who have critically examined vernacular domestic photography (Martin and Spence 1985, 1988, Martin 1991, Spence 1986, Spence and Holland, 1991, Rose 2016).

A family album contains a mini-history of photography as a medium and a variety of genres, as interpreted by a succession of photographers both amateur and professional. Editorial control is held by the archivist, most often the mother, whose preferences are shaped by an unconscious desire to provide evidence of her own good mothering. The conflicts and power struggles inherent within family life are repressed. Like a public-relations document, the family album mediates between the members of the family, providing a united front to the world, in an affirmation of successes, celebrations, high days and holidays, domestic harmony and togetherness. It is bound within established codes of commemorative convention, so ubiquitous that they are taken for granted, even minutely reconstructed and sold back to us by ad-men. Paraded in ranks on the mantelpiece or safely stowed away, family photographs stand in for the extended family, now dispersed.

Looking at an old family album often prompts nostalgia, a dream of a return 'home' to an idealized golden past, where the sun shone and everyone smiled. In forgetting the directorial role of the photographer, recycled notions of what makes a 'good' photograph, and the technical limitations of Brownie Box or Instamatic cameras, we are often inclined to give these fading fragments the status of evidence. And yet, photographs offer up a slippery surface of meanings to reflect and project upon and contain a myriad of latent narratives. Family albums can provide a starting point for autobiographical storytelling and an exploration of family systems, how it was to be part of a particular family, and how early experiences continue to act upon individuals.

(Martin 1996, p.4–5)

I showed a selection of family album images, mostly my own, and interrogated simplistic assumptions concerning these everyday yet overlooked photographs using these questions. What images do we choose to keep, and why? What can we learn from these? What new readings can we find? What do we see in the family album? What is left out? What can we read off from the elisions? What do the images stimulate? What changes over time e.g. through loss or bereavement? What does only the person in the picture know? What happened before or after?

Working in pairs, with their own photographs, each participant began to open up old, hidden feelings, submerged memories and explored her histories and identities, with the support of her counselling partner. Personal stories and insights thus gained were then shared in the group.

Figure 13.4 Barbara Harriott in collaboration with Jen Greenfield. Re-enacting two important childhood images of myself and my sister. Barbara Harriott.

At the very start of the workshop series I asked them to move around the room and specifically to choose to work with someone they did not know. Throughout the workshops, I had asked participants to choose different partners for different exercises, so they could get to know and trust one another, and thus I built a supportive group. For the re-enactment work, I asked them to choose their partners carefully, emphasising that the unconscious is very wise. I suggested they choose intuitively.

On the next workshop day I introduced the participants to re-enactment phototherapy. I showed many images from my practice, including my collaborative work with Jo Spence, some were when I was in the picture, others where Jo's story was shown. (Martin and Spence 1985, 1988, Martin 1991, 1997, 2003, 2012, 2013) I emphasised the collaborative qualities of this practice. I also showed the video *The Donkey's Tale* from Outrageous Agers (Martin 2003), since this gave a sense of the on-going story of the self as an ageing woman. It is poignant, funny and finally self-affirming. By sharing these images of my own issues and vulnerabilities, I modelled the possibilities of this practice and indicated how insights can be gained. I showed examples of different ways of working, including examples from work I have done with others, for example: finding a key moment or scenario to re-stage, working on stereotypes and archetypes, starting from an existing photograph, re-staging and then exploring different aspects or imagining a future. I took the participants through the stages of how to do this work, so they could find which aspects they wanted to explore and how to make these visible, through re-enactments. The ultimate decision as to what they chose to work on was their own, with the guidance to make a celebratory transformative shift.

Because ageing has negative connotations, I emphasised the necessity of finding transformations and offered up suggestions for transformative goals: 'me as a creative person'; 'living out my dreams'; 'my creative, playful inner child-self'; 'my idea of what an older woman can be'; or 'a stereotype of the older woman that I want to challenge'. I also asked everyone to make images of self-nurturance at the close of the session. It is important to have these self-affirmations to balance more painful material and offer shifts of energy within the photo-therapy session itself.

Since this is a performative practice, it is important to identify key props and clothes to enable the stories to unfold. Finding and collecting these together was the task for the week between workshops, and is itself an emotionally re-stimulating process. A list of all the local charity shops was handed out to help in this search.

I arranged for each pair to have their own discrete room for the photography day, lit by natural light, and provided background paper to create a performative space for each to work in. There was so much energy as everyone arrived, weighed down with such an amazing assortment of props and clothes and a vibrant sense of possibilities. Then one member arrived with the shocking news that due to an extreme medical emergency she could not attend that day. We all offered her loving support. But her partner did feel abandoned.

So, I found a way to cope in this crisis, by volunteering to work with her. Once everyone was set up and working well, I took the time to deal with her disappointment, then listen, support and learn her story, so I could step in and be her photo-therapist. I reminded everyone of the need to de-role after being the 'subject' and suggested they took their lunch break then, when changing roles.

In this approach to image-making, re-enactment phototherapy, the photographer offers a therapeutic gaze, which could be seen as having parallels with that of the 'good enough mother' (Winnicott 1971), who mirrors back the reflection of what is there, within a context of safety, trust and acceptance. The photographer/therapist acts as witness, advocate and nurturer, and offers permission and encouragement to the 'subject'. The woman in front of the camera is the protagonist who 'performs' her narratives, using her chosen clothes and props, having determined how she wanted to be represented. She asks for what she wants, and the photographer is supportive, encouraging and 'there for' her partner. It is an active unfolding process, a staging of the selves and not about set poses. The body expresses the emotions through gesture and movement, whilst its eloquence is recorded. It is like a form of adult play, in which a space for creativity and openness to ideas can emerge. It is important that a transformative shift occurs within the session, to make images of the potential for change, and other ways of being. Then the roles are exchanged, so both have the opportunity to be in the picture, and to be the photographer. It is a truly collaborative process.

I originally developed this work, from 1983, with Jo Spence. We used film, with no possibility of reviewing the work until we got the prints. Using digital has changed all this. We are now used to sharing photos, even instantaneously. Take a photograph; show the result to the one in the image. This is now common practice. With the possibility of reviewing comes the temptation. I emphasised that it was vitally important to trust the process and the photographer, and let the session flow and evolve. The risk of reviewing is that the 'subject' can become self-conscious and mentally block the flow of the process. Everyone always over-shoots; producing so many photographs that editing becomes more challenging. I asked them to delete the ones they did not want after the photo session i.e. those that were redundant, repetitive, or not useable yet to keep examples from each series that they did, the ones that hold the energy, the intention of the work. I asked that they did not just edit out the ones where they may not look great; those are not the criteria at this stage.

For the following workshop day, we needed prints to work with. So each participant was asked to select and print out a maximum of forty to fifty images of themselves. These needed to include an overview of the whole process e.g. creating a stereotype and then shifting, challenging and changing it, and including the transformative and self-nurturing images.

They worked in their pairs with the prints, retaining the intimate confidentiality they had built during the photography session. They took it in turns to lay out all the images, to enjoy the sense of having been really seen by another and to thank their partner. Then they told their story through these images, from which deep emotions surfaced, as their partner supported them and also drew upon the transformative and self-nurturing images to offer up another perspective, if there was any risk of becoming stuck in despair.

I then invited each to share in the group, after editing the work further, if they so wished. This is a roller-coaster of emotions, which I both entered and contained. This group work is about making the feelings visible: being heard, being understood and sharing often painful and traumatic stories. Sharing our thoughts and imaginative responses to ageing. Consciously working on the material we have generated, this is a very important part of the therapeutic process, it is both cathartic and integrative. By speaking and making conscious what we have each learnt, seeing our issues and distresses, out there, as objectified photographs, just bits of paper, helps to shift emotions and enables each to gain some distance from old pains. No longer hidden away, such pains can lose some of the power that secrecy and disavowal creates. The support that we, as a group, give to each individual in this process helps each to articulate her issues and to begin to take up other perspectives. We work together to support one another in this process. It is also about celebrating ourselves, and seeing how we have made ageing visible in new ways.

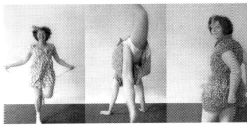

Figure 13.5 Judy Grundy in collaboration with Sue Hale.

'I'm this mischievous little girl, looking off to the side and clearly planning the next exploit. As a child, I was quite a lot in trouble, not, keeping myself clean, making mischief with my cousin.

I wanted to try and recreate those feelings ... All the physical stuff was linked to that notion that you have to lose that because you've got to be ladylike ...

It's coming to terms with the "me" and the "me" I am. I'm trying to find that core 'me' who likes to play and dress up.'

Jude Grundy

Look at me! Representing self 203

On the day after the formal group had finished, filming took place with those participants who chose to take part. The process of sharing the images with the group was fresh, dynamic and of value to the participants, as well as showing the work as a 'live' event. The women also spoke in the group, whilst they were filmed, of their feelings about ageing and the shifts that had happened during the workshop. A re-enactment session was re-staged. Although in some senses this did feel 'false', because of the need to repeat shots, the dynamic of the work itself was strong enough, and since I had had to step in to partner S. I was able to stay focused on enabling the transformational aspects, despite the distractions of being filmed. It is very useful to have this record, as part of the research process, for dissemination and impact (see the website to view the film at http://www.representing-ageing.com/photo_therapy_film.php).

Figure 13.6 Chris Herzberg in collaboration with Laura Richardson.

From gaga to Lady Gaga – *'I'd really wanted to see myself as a performer, yet I found that when I looked at all the photos we produced I was comfortable looking at myself as I really am'*.

Chris Herzberg

I offered a further day to work with the images two months after the workshop series. Since the research project was organising an exhibition, and wanted to use some of these photographs, it needed to be work that the participants were willing to share. In this session we worked to support each in her responses to images being made public, given the sensitivities around the images. There may be aspects that each wanted to work on further, with the support of a partner and/or the group. I know it is not appropriate to show work until one has separated one-self from what is in the image i.e. no longer over-identify with it. Let it be just one of a multiplicity of selves.

Figure 13.7 Laura Richardson in collaboration with Chris Herzberg.

'I chose Madame Bijou as my starting point. Rather than using an image from my own past I wanted to get under the skin on why this photograph was becoming something of an archetype for me. There was something quite mournful about being Bijou. The mournfulness and sense of loss seemed important and insistent. I decided to emphasise it using a fan and a plastic bust form, which became a kind of breastplate. The feeling was one of rigidity and inaccessibility. This began to seem like an image of "Death" to me. Important, in the light of recent health problems and the period of worry I had been through. I became aware of how static I was, and how I really longed to move. So being photographed became a kind of game … I wondered whether dancing might transform this rather static energy … When I uploaded the photos I noticed something that seemed almost uncanny. It is the little fist of someone trying to be born … Then I experienced a real sense of freedom. I found the phototherapy workshops offered a great opportunity to do some deeply reflective work in the company of others who were also making their own journeys. Whilst we started with some very personal material it was also possible to be very playful – which was a joy. I felt inspired by sharing the developing stories of other group members. Because we worked in pairs in photographing each other's re-enactments, it was also a privilege to assist another in capturing the story they wanted to tell.'

Laura Richardson

Images are polysemic, their meanings are not fixed, and the audience makes their own meanings from their perceptions, experiences, histories, prejudices etc. This is both the richness of working with images, since so much meaning is projected onto an image by the viewer, and also at times the frustration, when images are not read as intended by the creator. I call photographs 'slippery surfaces of meanings' (Martin 2001, p.17).

A curator, Alison Morton, was engaged to select work for the final exhibition. Although I was consulted, my preference for showing the works as narrative fragments alongside one powerful image was only partially acknowledged. Given the space available, this was a good compromise for making a strong exhibition from that work, but it did not, probably could not, represent the process. This is a familiar dichotomy – much complexity must be lost in order to produce an exhibition that will be seen as 'art', both visually strong and with the ability to communicate the ideas addressed within it.

Figure 13.8 Jen Greenfell in collaboration with Barbara Harriott.

'The first one was just me dancing as a little girl and the last one was me dancing now. It's like a joy sandwich with some deep, dark, difficult stuff in the middle … I feel more positive about how I can use my life and my time now that I am no longer caught in the carer sandwich that happens to so many women in their 50s.'

Jen Greenfell

The film of the workshop was screened on a large TV, with head-phones for the audio, and a comfortable settee so audience members could relax to view it. The diary work was mounted and displayed in a folio. Key quotes from the participants enlivened the display, giving them a voice. Yes, the work in the exhibition looked stunning, but was only a taste of the depth and wisdom that had been revealed.

A selection of the work from the whole project, including community arts projects coordinated by Eventus, art elicitation workshops run by Susan Hogan, and my phototherapeutic workshops was shown in an exhibition, 'Look At Me!', held at the Showroom, Sheffield March 2011, and in 'The Moor' Shopping Centre and Jessop West Exhibition Space, Sheffield in April 2011.

Look at me! Representing self 207

Figure 13.9 Shirley Simpson in collaboration with Rosy Martin.

'I took all the jewellery off, the mask, the wig. My hair was grey, pinned back but the face was very vibrant and I liked that, I liked me. I don't need the mask and the wig, yes, it's fun but actually it's me underneath ... You start off very dressy and you don't need all that, you're still fun you.'

Shirley Simpson

Here is an example of participant feedback after the prompt '*Has this project impacted on your feelings about ageing at all?*'

'When I reflect on this question what comes in to my mind that sums up the impact that the project had on me is what I now appreciate and accept about myself and what I will not accept in terms of what is often a given in our society.
 I am now more confident/accepting of how I look at this point in my life. That it is not what you look like but how you feel and how you express yourself. It is possible to look, happy, fun, joyful and even beautiful however old you are. This was reflected in the photos I had taken during the project. I now feel that it is ok to have my photograph taken – this is me at fifty-seven wrinkles and all. I no longer need to be camera shy just because I am not as youthful as I once was.

> *However, I will no longer accept how society sometimes treats women of a certain age as though they are invisible and inconsequential and are pushed in to the background. I will strive even more not to be ignored and for other women also.'*
> Shirley Simpson

In conclusion, the women who took part explored their relationships to their visual representations and found ways to take control, transform and define for themselves a myriad of ways of being seen as older women. They created powerful, challenging images and gained confidence and increased self-acceptance through the workshop process. They continued to meet as a group after the workshop ended; a strong bond had been created.

Notes

To read more about the Representing Self – Representing Ageing project visit:
http://www.representing-ageing.com/ index.php
For the phototherapeutic work visit:
Film – http: //www.representing-ageing.com/phototherapy_film.php
Images – http://www.representing-a geing.com/phototherapy.php
Brief description – http://www.representing-ageing.com/workshops.php#photo
Overview of 'Look at me' Project – New Dynamics of Ageing
http://lookatme.group.shef.ac.uk/workshops.php
http://www.newdynamics.group.shef.ac.uk/assets/files/NDA%20Findings_10.pdf
https://www.youtube.com/watch?v=K_PyRYXrSPU
For the research and photographic project Outrageous Agers see:
http://www.outrageousagers.co.uk

1. The Representing Self – Representing Ageing project, based in the Sociological Studies Department at Sheffield University, was funded by the Economic and Social Research Council (ESRC) New Dynamics of Ageing (NDA) programme, award reference number RES-356-25-0040. Principle Investigator - Lorna Warren University of Sheffield
2. International Visual Studies Association for information about current practice, conferences and the journal *Visual Studies* https://visualsociology.org/
    International Visual Methods Conference http://www.visualmethods.info/about/index.php

References

Banks, M. 2015. *Visual Methods in Social Research*. London: Sage Publications.
Hogan, S. 2012. Ways in which photographic and other images are used in research: An introductory overview. *International Journal of Art Therapy*, 17(2): 54–62.
Hogan, S. 2013. Peripheries and borders: Pushing the boundaries of visual research. *International Journal of Art Therapy*, 18(2): 67–74.
Hogan, S. 2013. Your body is a battleground: Women and art therapy. *The Arts in Psychotherapy, Special Issue: Gender & the Creative Arts Therapies*, 40(4): 415–419.
Hogan, S. 2015. Interrogating women's experience of ageing – reinforcing or challenging clichés? *The International Journal of the Arts in Society: Annual Review*, 9(1): 1–18.
Hogan, S. 2016. Age is just a number init? Interrogating perceptions of ageing women within social gerontology. *Women's Studies. An Interdisciplinary Journal*, 45(1): 57–77.
Hogan, S. and Warren, L. 2012. Dealing with complexity in research findings: How do older women negotiate and challenge images of ageing? *Journal of Women & Ageing*, 24(4): 329–350.

Hogan, S. and Warren, L. 2013. Women's inequality: A global problem explored in participatory arts. International perspectives on research-guided practice in community-based arts in health. *UNESCO Observatory, Special Issue*, 3(3): 1–27.

Martin, E. 1992. *The Woman in the Body: A Cultural Analysis of Reproduction*. Boston: Beacon Press.

Martin R. 1991. Dirty linen. *Ten8*, 2(1): Spring.

Martin R. 1991. Unwind the ties that bind in Holland, P. and Spence, J. (eds) *Family Snaps: the meanings of domestic photography*. London: Virago.

Martin, R. 1996. You (never) can tell: Phototherapy, memory and subjectivity. *Blackflash*, 3(6).

Martin, R. 1997. Looking and reflecting: Returning the gaze, re-enacting memories and imagining the future through phototherapy in Hogan, S. (ed.) *Feminist Approaches to Art Therapy*. London and New York: Routledge.

Martin, R. 2001. The performative body: Phototherapy and re-enactment. *Afterimage: The Journal of Media Arts and Cultural Criticism*, 29(3): 17–20.

Martin, R. 2003. Challenging invisibility: Outrageous agers in Hogan, S. (ed.) *Gender Issues in Art Therapy*. London: Jessica Kingsley Publishers.

Martin, R. 2012. Outrageous agers – Performativity and transgressions in Dolan, J. and Tincknell, E. (eds) *Ageing Femininities: Troubling Representations*. Newcastle: Cambridge Scholars Press.

Martin, R. 2013. Inhabiting the image: Photography, therapy and re-enactment phototherapy in Loewenthal, D. (ed.) *Phototherapy and Therapeutic Photography in a Digital Age*. London and New York: Routledge.

Martin, R. and Goodridge, K. 2001. *Outrageous Agers* (mark 2 - including 6 video installations). Focal Point Gallery, Cliffs Pavillion and the Shopping Centre. Southend Essex.

Martin, R. and Spence, J. 1985. New portraits for old: the use of the camera in therapy. *Feminist Review*, 19: 66–92.

Martin, R. and Spence J. 1988. Phototherapy – psychic realism as a healing art? *Ten8, No 30 Spellbound*, October Birmingham.

Milne, E. J., Mitchell, C. and de Lange, N. 2012. *Handbook of Participatory Video: Critical Issues and Challenges*. Lanham: AltaMira Press.

Pink, S. 2013. *Doing Visual Ethnography*. 3rd edition. London: Sage Publications.

Pink, S., Hogan, S. and Bird, J. 2011. Intersections and inroads: Art therapy's contribution to visual methods. *International Journal of Art Therapy*, 16:(1): 14–19.

Richards, N., Warren, L. and Gott, M. 2012. The challenge of creating 'alternative' images of ageing: Lessons from a project with older women. *Journal of Aging Studies*, 26(1): 65–78.

Reuben, D. 1969. *Everything You Always Wanted to Know About Sex but Were Afraid to Ask*. New York: McKay.

Rose, G. 2001. *Visual Methodologies: An Introduction to the Interpretation of Visual Materials*. 4th edition. London: Sage.

Rose, G. 2016. *Doing Family Photography: The Domestic, The Public and The Politics of Sentiment (Re-Materialising Cultural Geography)*. London and New York: Routledge.

Spence, J. 1986. *Putting Myself in the Picture*. London: Camden Press.

Spence, J. and Holland, P. 1991. *Family Snaps: The Meanings of Domestic Photography*. London: Virago.

Winnicott, D. W. 1971. *Playing and Reality*. London: Tavistock Publications.

Chapter 14

The treatment of anorexia nervosa and bulimia nervosa among female adolescents aged 18–21 using intertwined (integrative) arts therapy

Alenka Vidrih, Ana Hram and Vita Poštuvan

Introduction

Eating disorders are not an exclusively female phenomenon as perceived by many. Such a perception can trigger feelings of shame and isolation among males suffering from eating disorders (Robinson et al., 2013). Substantially more males are affected than previously thought (Welch et al., 2015). Studies indicate that males may account for 10–25% of anorexia and bulimia cases (Sabel et al., 2014). One study reported the most common diagnosis among male adolescents was binge eating, while among female adolescents it was anorexia nervosa (Smink et al., 2014). The first known case of anorexia nervosa being documented centuries ago was a description not of a 16-year-old adolescent girl, but a boy (Wooldridge, 2016). The choice of gender selection in this study was not influenced by a stereotype and assumption that eating disorders are gender specific. Deciding for a gender-specific group was a consequence of the fact that in the centre where the research took place, no male as yet has sought treatment for an eating disorder. Therefore, the sample of this study comprised only girls: 11 in total, aged between 18 and 21 years old, out of which two were diagnosed with bulimia nervosa and nine with anorexia nervosa. With this, the study aimed to understand the effectiveness of the treatment of anorexia nervosa and bulimia nervosa among female adolescents using intertwined arts therapy. All 11 girls were provided with group and individual treatment for 15 months. This intertwined arts therapy treatment is provided in The Private Institute for Arts Therapy of Ljubljana, where therapy has a strong background in social work and experience of treating addicts. The findings of this study showed that the physical condition of the participants was improved including normal BMI, stable menstrual cycle and the absence of inappropriate compensatory behaviours. The mental health of the participants was also improved. The domains in which statistically significant improvement was found include self-image, self-esteem and in all dimensions of general well-being (physical, emotional, mental, social and spiritual).

Anorexia nervosa (AN) and bulimia nervosa (BN) as eating disorders

Manifestations of various eating disturbances have been documented throughout the course of history. Medical science has almost always defined the avoidance of food and overeating as symptoms of a physical condition, most often digestive disorders. Preoccupation with weight and body shape and weight control strategies (including extreme dieting and vomiting) attracted the attention of the medical profession and the public in western and westernised countries towards the end of the 20th century (Vandereycken, 2002; Modic, 2003). The International Statistical Classification of Diseases and Related Health Problems (ICD-10, WHO, 1992) and the Diagnostic and Statistical Manual of Mental Disorders (DSM–5, American Psychiatric Association, 2013) classify various eating disorders including among them anorexia nervosa and bulimia nervosa.

Anorexia nervosa is characterised by excessive control over the needs of the body, restrictions in food intake and often includes excessive exercise, resulting in severe weight loss. Anorexia nervosa includes the following two subtypes (Sernec, 2003, 2010):

- *Restrictive subtype*: 25% of people with anorexia nervosa suffer from the restrictive subtype (Sernec, 2003). Weight loss is achieved through various regimes such as starvation, and/or excessive exercise (Pandel Mikuš, 2002; Arzenšek et al., 2005, p. 270). By refusing to eat, the person is symbolically refusing the acceptance of their environment, their family or themselves. Some reject food and eating to the degree that it threatens their lives (Gostečnik, 2002; Arzenšek et al., 2005, p. 270).
- *Purging subtype*: 75% of those with anorexia nervosa exhibit the purging subtype (anorexia nervosa with bulimic characteristics). This is also known as the binge-eating subtype (Sernec, 2003; Arzenšek et al., 2005, p. 270). The subtype is characterised by the engagement in overeating, commonly followed by self-induced vomiting or use of diuretics, laxatives or enemas. In some cases, people do not necessarily overeat, but purge after eating only small quantities of food (Pandel Mikuš, 2003; Arzenšek et al., 2005, p. 270). These people perceive food as a substitute for an emotional deficit. In other words, people with anorexia have a tendency to use their relationship with food and weight to deal with their emotional problems. The inability to digest food can be seen as symbolic or a physical manifestation of an inability to deal with the unpleasant emotional situation in their family (Gostečnik, 2002; Arzenšek et al., 2005).

Bulimia nervosa is characterised by excessive control or loss of control, and recurrent binge eating followed by purging rituals (vomiting and/or taking laxatives).

Both bulimia and anorexia nervosa are characterised by the strong drive for thinness and disturbed eating behaviour. The prime difference is that anorexia nervosa is characterised by self-starvation with a significant loss of weight of 15% or above; however, patients suffering from bulimia nervosa are generally at normal weight or above that (Fairburn, 2001).

Anorexia nervosa and bulimia nervosa are often described as recent diseases because their occurrence in the last several decades has reached epidemic proportions. However, anorexia nervosa was described as early as 1669 by John Reynolds (Reynolds, 1669). In 1689, Richard Morton gave the first medical account of the disease (Morton, 1689, 1694). William Gull first used the term anorexia nervosa in autumn 1868 at a lecture in Oxford when describing the case of a female patient who refused food despite her obvious malnutrition (Gull, 1873). Gull wrongly diagnosed a simple lack of appetite. In 1979, Gerald Russell first described and named bulimia nervosa (Russel, 1979), which of course does not mean that the disease did not exist before then.

Causes of anorexia nervosa and bulimia nervosa

There is no overall agreement as to the causes.

Genetic vulnerability: Research so far has indicated the existence of genetic propensity in the development of anorexia nervosa and bulimia nervosa. Genetic predispositions mostly influence the development of the disorders through the genes that are clustered around governing reward-pleasure responses, mood, metabolism, as well as food intake and appetite (Stice, 1994).

Individual's characteristics and personality traits: Traits such as harm avoidance, obsessive compulsiveness, negative emotions, perfectionism, persistence and sensation seeking are present in those with anorexia nervosa and bulimia nervosa (Ogburn, 1951).

Socio-cultural influences: According to Stice (1994), those exposed to the western beauty ideal of being thin are more likely to experience dissatisfaction with their bodies, causing negative emotions and fasting in excess. Equating beauty with thinness is propagated by media and fashion, and infused into teenagers who are mesmerised into looking and acting like those seen in the media and fashion industries they perceive as their role models.

Family dynamics in anorexia nervosa and bulimia nervosa

To a greater extent, purging anorexia nervosa and classic bulimia nervosa rather than restrictive anorexia nervosa are noticeable in the context of numerous partner disagreements, conflicts, divorce, dependency and neurotic behaviour (Mrevlje, 1995; Modic, 2003).

The conviction that the lack of desire for anything, including food, makes someone powerful can imprint into a person's soul especially in one with anorexia nervosa (Podjavoršek, 2004). One theory is that the child's adjustment to the parental demands or expressed needs often leads to the creation of the development of a 'false self'. Gradually, the child expresses only what is wanted or expected of him or her. In such an atmosphere, an adolescent has difficulty building positive feelings of self-evaluation and performance (Bruch, 1978; Modic, 2003). Depression, loneliness, anxiety and stress are a few reasons behind being withdrawn and eating a large amount of food to release tension (Kastelic, 1995, p. 35).

Family attitudes in cases of anorexia nervosa: Bruch (1978), Mushatt (1992) and Modic (2003) suggest that the traits which are commonly found within the families of children with anorexia nervosa include over-supervision, ambition, restrictions in forming opinions, denying the right of a child's individualisation, infantilisation, suppression of emotions and instilment of guilt.

Family attitudes in cases of bulimia nervosa: Mrevlje, (1995) Modic (2003) and Hromc (2006) suggest that the traits which are found within the families of children with bulimia nervosa include perfectionism, overprotective relations, chaos, emotional, physical and sexual abuse.

Family values in cases of anorexia nervosa and bulimia nervosa: Bruch (1978), Mushatt (1992) and Modic (2003) suggest that the values which are commonly found within the families of children with eating disorders include an emphasis on beauty, physical fitness, ascetic posture, needlessness, perfection, excellence, loyalty, selflessness, sacrifice and concern for material wealth.

Assessing the physical consequences of anorexia nervosa and bulimia nervosa

The physical consequences of anorexia nervosa and bulimia nervosa are, as with other eating disorders, best monitored using the body mass index (BMI), its measurement and statistical distribution throughout a given population. The body mass index is the simplest and most informative indicator of body condition (from being underweight, to normal, to obese). It is calculated using the formula below:

$$\mathbf{BMI} = \left(\text{body weight in kg}\right) / \left(\text{height}^2 \text{ in m}\right)$$

$$\left(\text{Reljič – Prinčič, 2003, p. 24; IVZ RS; /2/}\right)$$

However, body mass index describes only one aspect of anorexia nervosa and bulimia nervosa, namely inappropriate weight, or the physical consequence of eating or not eating, and not the causes of the condition, or motives, dynamics, oscillations, stability and instability, compensatory behaviour (overeating, vomiting, starvation etc.) and accompanying psychological experiences. The body mass index distribution of the UK adult population is not statistically normal when compared to the World Health Organisation's body mass index values. Rather, it is asymmetrical with a longer right end, which indicates a relatively higher body mass index than the average global median (see Table A1 and Table A2 in the Appendix).

Objectives of the study

The main objectives of the study were to determine whether intertwined arts therapy has a positive effect on the psychophysical conditions of female adolescents aged 18–21 with eating disorders, specifically anorexia nervosa (AN) and bulimia nervosa (BN).

Research methodology

Research design

This study used an experimental study design in which participants of the study were tested regarding different psychological, physiological and physical attributes of well-being before and after the mixed arts therapies intervention (intertwined arts therapy). Later these pre and post scores were compared in order to measure the effectiveness of the treatment.

Data collection

The data for this research were collected by using mixed methods, including quantitative methodology, qualitative methodology and mixed research design. Quantitative work includes structured data collection techniques, grading scale of well-being, questionnaires and objective data. Qualitative work includes data on motivation, mood and communication.

Sample

The research described here was undertaken at the Association for Psychosocial Help with Art (Društvo za Psihosocialno pomoč z Umetnostjo, PU) in Slovenia that offers psychosocial support mostly to people with eating disorders. For nearly 20 years the majority of users have been female adolescents. This study was conducted with a group of 11 girls (nine diagnosed with anorexia nervosa and two diagnosed with bulimia nervosa) aged between 18 and 21 years old. The girls had been going through individual and group treatment for a period of 15 months, between January 2015 and 2016. The pre-measure for the study was taken on 15th January 2015, whereas the post measure was taken on 15th January 2016 and the post-treatment observation was made on 17th April 2016.

Therapy

The participants of the study were given quadruply intertwined arts (QUINART) therapy. QUINART therapy is an amalgam of theory and practice of arts therapy, utilising the *Ars Vitae* (AV) model developed by the long-standing actor, singer and arts therapist Alenka Vidrih. *Ars Vitae*, meaning the art of living in Latin, as a model consists of three steps: (i) attunement with oneself, (ii) attunement with others and (iii) attunement with creativity.

The first step encompasses techniques of self-awareness and training of voice, speech and movement. The aim of learning these techniques is to be able to express oneself authentically on the stage, and in the various roles, one has in a family, society and professionally. In the second step, one is applying the acquired techniques in the presence of others. The third step is a creative one, which entails role-playing, extended beyond the stage into everyday life.

One can use the AV model to become more authentic, sensitive and empathic towards oneself and others. The creative process can lead to a wealth of benefits such as a stronger creativity potential, a broader imagination, an instrumented body (the body as a resonator or musical instrument) and harmonious communication with the environment (Vidrih, 2016).

Instruments

A number of psychological tests were used in the study. All the psychological questionnaires were applied by a certified psychologist, along with the analysis of the results. These tests include:

(i) Overall well-being index (OWI), as measured by the evaluating scale ranging from 1 (worst) to 10 (best).
(ii) The self-esteem scale (SESTES), which consists of 4-dimensions (Lamovec, 1988): self-confidence and social, emotional and physical self-image.
(iii) Physical, emotional, mental, social and spiritual consequences of eating disorders assessed with a questionnaire on the extent of eating disorders (QUDED) tailor-made for this research by one of the authors, Ana Hram.
(iv) The core reasons for the development of eating disorders assessed with a questionnaire on core causes for the development of eating disorders (QUCED) tailor-made for this research by one of the authors, Ana Hram.
(v) The indicators of emotional state measured with the emotional state scale (EMOSS) (Lamovec, 1988) of the U1 participant.
(vi) The indicators of emotional state measured by the emotions profile index (EPI) (Plutchik and Kellerman, 1979) of the U1 participant.

Special attention was given to verbal communication and non-verbal communication in general. All group meetings and one-on-one sessions were conducted in such a way that ensured communication was performed effectively by using non-verbal cues (55%), tone of voice (38%) and words (7%) (Mehrabian, 1969; Shapiro & Čertalič, 1999, p. 203). Because the voice is of paramount importance at delivering the message to individuals with eating disorders, the tone and pitch of the voice are of key importance in communicating with these people. Full attention should at the same time be given to non-verbal communication, since those with addiction problems are particularly receptive to every body movement.

Some aspects of these were measured by:

- Laban movement analysis (LMA) (Laban, 1975);
- Emerging body language (EBL) (Rutten-Saris, 1992);
- The Bales interaction process analysis (IPA) (Bales, 1951);
- The questionnaire for the measurement of negative and disruptive aggressiveness[2] (Buss, 1961; Lamovec and Rojnik, 1978, p. 75);
- Scale of socio–emotional skills (Schilling, 2000, p. 1–2).

The physical condition of the participants was assessed by the body mass index (BMI), which was calculated according to the formula: BMI = body weight (in kg) / height (in m). The following symptoms were also noted: inappropriate behaviour and amenorrhoea (loss of menstrual cycle), (before, during and after sessions and meetings of therapy).

Procedure

Group intertwined arts therapy was provided twice a week for 13 months, including a three-month terminating process within the group. Intertwined arts therapy was provided three times a week for one year. A social worker led the group, with a psychologist as a co-leader. All the research participants underwent regular medical check-ups, done with the cooperation (and under the authority) of their GPs.

The research protocol followed the Ethical Standards in the Field of Social Work, Ethical Code of the University of Ljubljana and the Helsinki declaration. The leader and co-leader of the group collected the data and provided qualitative and quantitative research frames for the analysis. Detailed recordings were kept for every session, which were partly recorded within the group meeting and partly just after.

The intervention process was split into 3 parts, each one of them emphasising one of the three aspects of relationships according to Buber (1937). The focus of the first six sessions was on *building a relationship with I (self)* by embodying self-esteem, self-confidence, self-expression, intuition, emotion, sensation and perception. The focus of the second six sessions was on *building a relationship with thou (others)* by thematising communication – verbal and non-verbal, negative emotions, anger, setting boundaries, conflict resolution, friendship and partnership. The focus of the last four sessions was on *building a relationship with it* (the environment) by staging the various roles each one has in the family, at school, at work and in the group (Buber, 1937).

Results

The results of the group as a whole

Significant improvements in the psychophysical condition are shown from the quantitative data. The group achieved progress in their mental and physical health across all variables. The BMI improved by 3.4 and OWI improved by 0.9. The self-esteem scale also showed a positive improvement, especially in the physical and emotional dimensions with an increase in the range of 15.4 and 12.4. A positive assessment was also noted on the dimensions of social self and self-esteem attributes, whereby an increase of 18.8 and 12.7 was observed. The questionnaire on eating disorders also recorded results indicating an improvement with an increase of the averages from 2.7 to 5.6 in the physical, emotional–cognitive, social and spiritual domains (See Table A3 in the Appendix).

Body mass index (BMI): The referential value of BMI for people aged 18 and over is between 18.5 and 25. The participants' BMI at the beginning of the study was between 14.1 and 17.3 and the increase is noticeable among all of them. The mean scores of BMI show an increase from $M = 15.61$ to $M = 19.01$ after therapy.

Overall well-being index (OWI): The mean scores of OWI show an increase from $M = 6.78$ before therapy to $M = 7.70$ after therapy as shown in Table A4. In the columns 5–7 are the results ranking from lowest to highest. On average, the overall well-being of all participants increased between meetings by almost one point (from 6.79 to 7.71, i.e. 0.92). The overall well-being during the course of intervention improved by almost three points: starting at 5.79, before the first meeting, rising to 5.91 after the first meeting, reaching 8.55 prior to the last meeting and ending at 9.04 thereafter. For individual results, please see Table A5.

Results of the individual case study

The individual case study of the U1 participant was one of the most difficult ones in the therapist's (AH) two-decade-long practice, because the participant had a persistent type of eating disorder (anorexia nervosa restrictive), and also the most numerous, unsupportive and harmful roles in the family with minimal cooperation and support of the parents in the process of recovery. The U1 participant's results are shown in Tables A6 and A7 which revealed that the overall well-being increased from 3.2 to 6.5, and along with that, the self-esteem scale also shows an increase in scores.

Seven goals are achieved by using the emerging body language (EBL) method including increased establishment of communication with the self and others, gradually achieving a sense of security, support and acceptance, increased eye contact, increased acceptance of one's own body and movement, increased recognition and expression of feelings, increased relaxation and greater confidence.

Reflections

From numerous observations and notes, the following findings were observed:

A. The correlation

Between an interaction and a personal experience: Samples of normal interactions occur in a prominently positive experience of a meeting; negative samples (with destructive aggression) in a negative one.

The socio-emotional skills and personal experiences: Samples of socio-emotional skills appear in a prominently positive experience of a meeting, otherwise only to a lesser extent in meetings in which the experience was less positive.

B. Expressing the social roles or emotional states through arts:
Different roles or emotional states were expressed through arts, particularly aggressiveness. First, we identified it as a part of the group dynamics and then tried to understand their characteristics better, also by feeling the impact of the aggression on the environment. Then we faced the aggression and tried to understand how the environment was impacting the aggression. At the end, it was ensured that aggression leads to catharsis, as a way of transforming into positive ambitions.

C. Improvement of the communication skills of the participants:
Significant improvements appeared in the communication skills as emotions turned from negative, being imbued with fear, anxiety and anger into positive, being wrapped in expressed interest. Body language was more open and more closely in harmony with the spoken words. Crafting one's own opinion was done in a more confident fashion, and the voice became louder and more expressive.

D. Negative reaction of the social environment of the participants:
Parents participated in the therapy as follows: (i) an 8-hour introductory seminar about the basics of addiction, the dynamics of eating disorders and forms of help, (ii) the possibility of being a part of the one-to-one therapeutic process every week, (iii) a three-hour lecture each three months and (iv) two joint workshops with all the participants.

Findings and conclusions

Improvement of the physical condition: Between the pre- and post measures, the physical condition of all participants improved, evidenced by the normalisation of body mass index, stabilisation of the menstrual cycle and absence of inappropriate compensatory behaviours. During the 15 months, BMI normalised in all participants, increasing 3.4 points for the group as a whole, and individually at least by 2.3 points. Among six participants it reached the referential value; among five participants it was very close. These differences are statistically significant. The menstrual cycle was re-established in all participants, except for the U1 participant.

Compensatory inappropriate behaviour such as self-inflicted vomiting, excessive exercise, use of laxatives and diuretics, fasting and gluttony ceased in most participants in the first three-months of individual therapeutic treatment (for the U1 Participant after six months). Physical activity was reduced to a recommended half an hour per day.

Improvement of the mental condition:
Improvements were noted in the:
QUDED (Questionnaire on the extent of eating disorders), EPI (Emotions profile index), LMA (Laban movement analysis) and EBL (Emerging body language).

Restoring health to a significant extent: While there was no control group, there was no crucial outer event that is thought to have impacted the participants. We feel confident in concluding that this therapy was the key factor, which contributed to the observed improvements detailed above.

Using the World Health Organization's definition of health, a state of 'complete physical, mental and social well-being' (WHO, 2006), it can be concluded with certainty that the health of those participating in the intertwined arts therapy presented here was restored to a significant extent.

Discussion

As Hogan suggested in the introduction, there is a danger of exaggerating sex differences at the expense of similarities between men and women, though women are arguably more under pressure from sexualised social-media influences. Having a fata morgana (distorted) image of your own body is core to eating disorders regardless of being male or female (Mitchison et al., 2017). But dissatisfaction with one's own body has a great impact on males when experienced causing high levels of psychological distress (Griffiths et al., 2016). Those mesmerised by the western beauty ideal of being thin are likelier to have eating disorders. Such a perplexity sucks individuals into dissatisfaction with their bodies contributing to food restriction tendencies and negative emotions, which are likely to cause bulimia (Gumz et al., 2017). Sociocultural idealisation has therefore a great impact on developing an unreal image of one's own body (Culbert et al., 2015) causing many young male youths to engage in over exercising, even up to 70% of them according to a sample study (Coelho et al., 2015).

If a fluctuating self-hood that moves beyond the binary and opts for a transsexual identity contributes to balanced eating habits, then this could not be investigated in this study. Only female adolescents knocked on the door seeking treatment for their eating disorder at the centre where this study took place. In our opinion, anorexia and bulimia are not so commonly reported among male adolescents, because they seek help exceptionally, only when they are close to breaking point. They tend to solve their problems themselves and look around for a helping hand only when they are already extremely exhausted, broken inside and consumed by depression. The rare cases of anorexia and bulimia that do occur in male adolescents are so much harder to resolve than those cases of anorexia and bulimia found in female adolescents.

The sample of the study comprised only of female adolescents aged 18–21: two were diagnosed with bulimia nervosa and nine with anorexia nervosa. While there was no control group to help further back up our results, there was also no crucial outer event that is thought to have impacted on the results. We can discuss the positive impact of the interventions, which are in accordance with the study done by Frisch et al. (2006). They claim that art-based therapies have a generally positive outcome on eating disorders, but there is very limited evidence regarding the use of art therapy for eating disorders. The reason behind these positive outcomes is that people suffering from eating disorders are generally over-reliant on the verbal defence mechanisms like persuasion, intellectualisation and rationalisation (Frisch et al., 2006). Art therapy is the established profession of mental health as it utilises art to enhance and improve the emotional, physical and mental well-being of individuals of all ages. Art therapy is based on the strong belief that artistic expression helps people to resolve problems and conflicts, develop understanding of interpersonal conflicts, develop skills, reduce stress, manage behaviour, increase active insight and self-awareness (Beck, 2009). According to Reindl (2002), they argue obsessively with friends, family about weight and food-related topics. This display of knowledge helps these individuals to feel their control in the relationships (Reindl, 2001). This defence mechanism is used in order to protect the self as well as to provide a sense of control. This reliance on the intellectualisation, arguments or rationalisation could slow down the progress of therapy, and it creates frustration for the therapist as well as the patient. The patients with eating disorders also tend to avoid the intimacies from relationships or psychotherapy by arguing. Use of art in this regard could help them in focusing on the therapeutic work and the relevant issue (Reindl, 2001). Furthermore, arts provide a different method for communication in which the interference of language or arguments is minimum (Rehavia-Hanauer, 2003). The art making process that bypasses defence mechanisms compels an individual to produce new images, which leads to the use of creative processes in solution formation. This could be particularly relevant for the treatment of people with eating disorders as they experience difficulty in verbally expressing themselves (Rehavia-Hanauer, 2003). Moreover, it is important to note that artistic skills and abilities are not essentially required for the self-exploration via art. It has been postulated that skilled artists may find it hard to produce less defensive and spontaneous artistic creations (Wadeson, 1980). Rehavia-Hanauer (2003) also identified a tension between 'the need for complete control and the feeling of lack of control' (p. 142) in artwork production, which perhaps mirrors some aspects of the anorexic experience. Importantly, the use of art allows the active role of the patient in treatment, which is essential to ensure the effectiveness of the treatment (Hinz, 2006).

Appendix

List of tables

Table A1 BMI values according to the World Health Organization (WHO) for persons over 18 (IVZ RS, 2008; /1/)

Category	BMI (kg/m^2)	Body mass
Severely underweight	≤ 16.0	(Reduced body mass)
Moderately underweight	16.0–17.0	
Mildly underweight	17.0–18.5	
Normal weight	18.5–25.0	Normal body mass
Overweight	25.0–30.0	Increased body mass
Class I obesity	30.0–35.0	Obesity
Class II obesity	35.0–40.0	
Class III obesity	≥ 40.0	

Table A2 Body mass index ranges – Girls (UK)

Age	Low weight	Normal weight	Overweight	Obesity
13	15.0 and <	15.1–22.8	22.9–25.8	25.9 and >
14	15.6 and <	15.7–23.3	23.4–26.6	26.7 and >
15	15.8 and <	15.9–23.9	24.0–27.2	27.3 and >
16	16.2 and <	16.3–24.4	24.5–27.7	27.8 and >
17	16.9 and <	17.0–24.7	24.8–28.2	28.3 and >
18	17.2 and <	17.3–24.8	24.9–28.6	28.7 and >
19	17.9 and <	18.0–24.9	25.0–29.3	29.4 and >
20 and over	18.4 and <	18.5–24.9	25.0–29.9	30.0 and >

Table A3 The results of the group as a whole

		Referential norms	Before M(SD)	After M(SD)	Difference (+)
Individual test measurement		18.5-25	15.6	19.0	3.4
Overall well-being index		–	6.8	7.7	0.9
Self-esteem scale	Physical self	45.0	35.1	50.4	15.4
	Emotional self	43.9	37.1	47.7	12.4
	Social self	70.3	58.7	77.5	18.8
	Self-esteem	66.9	60.5	73.2	12.7
Questionnaire on the extent of eating disorders	Physical	–	3.6	7.7	4.1
	Emotional – cognitive	–	3.1	8.7	5.6
	Social	–	4.0	6.7	2.7
	Spiritual	–	3.6	8.9	5.3

Table A4 Body mass index (BMI)

Measures	Before M	SD	After M	SD
BMI	15.61	1.09	19.01	1.40
Overall well-being	6.78	1.40	7.70	1.49

Table A5 Individual test measurement

Participants	Before	After	Difference (+)	Before	After
U1	14.10	16.42	2.32	Severe malnutrition	Moderate malnutrition
U2	17.31	20.88	3.57	Mild malnutrition	Normal body weight
U3	16.87	20.72	3.85	Moderate malnutrition	Normal body weight
U4	14.62	18.03	3.41	Severe malnutrition	Mild malnutrition
U5	16.12	18.45	2.33	Moderate malnutrition	Mild malnutrition
U6	15.78	19.94	4.16	Severe Malnutrition	Normal body weight
U7	16.59	19.53	2.94	Moderate malnutrition	Normal body weight
U8	16.23	20.49	4.26	Moderate malnutrition	Normal body weight
U9	15.11	18.07	2.96	Severe malnutrition	Mild malnutrition
U10	14.33	17.96	3.63	Severe malnutrition	Mild malnutrition
U11	14.70	18.71	4.01	Severe malnutrition	Normal body weight
M	15.62	19.02	3.40		
SD	1.10	1.39			
Wilcoxon's test	$W = 0 / p \leq 0.01$				

Legend: M = Arithmetic mean
SD = Standard deviation

Table A6 U1 participant's results: A higher value indicates a higher evaluation

C	U1	Before	After	Difference
Individual test measurement		14.1	16.4	2.3
Overall well-being index		3.2	6.5	3.3
Self-esteem scale	Physical self	1	3	14
	Emotional self	2	4	14
	Social self	1	5	30
	Self-esteem	1	8	24
Questionnaire on the extent of eating disorders	Physical	3.6	7.7	4.1
	Emotional – cognitive	3.1	8.7	5.6
	Social	4	6.7	2.7
	Spiritual	3.6	8.9	5.3
Emotional states scale	Satisfaction	1.8	2.7	0.9
	Depression	3.2	2.4	−0.8
	Aggression	2.7	1.8	−0.9
	Apathy	3.0	2.0	−1
	Negative	−3.2	2.0	−1.2
	Positive self-evaluation	2.0	2.6	0.6
Emotional profile index	Reproduction	1	3	2
	Incorporation	1	1	0
	Uncontrollability	1	45	44
	Self-protection	45	45	0
	Deprivation	99	79	−20
	Opposition	99	10	−89
	Exploitation	66	99	33
	Aggression	99	49	−50
	Distortion	1	9	8
Questionnaire on core causes for the development of eating disorders	Introversion		Less expressed	
	Perfectionism		Less expressed	
	Harmful role		Less harmful roles	
Observed differences in characteristics	Demands of the mother		Fewer demands	
	Emotional relationship (cold – warm)		Warmer	
	Role of mother		More appropriate role of mother	

Table A7 Laban movement analysis (Laban, 1975) after the 9th and 14th meeting

	Categories	First analysis (9th meeting)	Second analysis (14th meeting)
1	Space	direct (−)	indirect (+)
2	Posture	closed (−)	more opened (+)
3	Weight	heavy (−)	lighter (+)
4	Strength	weak (−)	stronger (+)
5	Rhythm	repeating (−)	more linked (+)
6	Time	lost in time (−)	slow (+)
7	Music	gentle (+)	gentle (+)
8	Flow of movement	on side and controlled (−)	quite freely (+)
9	Level of movement	standing (−)	standing and leaning (+)
10	Direction of movement	left – right (−)	left – right, in front (+)

References

American Psychiatric Association. (2013). Feeding and eating disorders. *Diagnostic and Statistical Manual of Mental Disorders* (5th ed.). Washington: American Psychiatric Association.

Arzenšek, P., Turčin, Z., and Lahe, M. (2005). Anoreksija nervoza s prikazom primera. (Anorexia nervosa with a case report). *Zdravstvena obzorja*, 39, 4, 269–275.

Bales, R. F. (1951). *Interaction process analysis: A method for the study of small groups.* Cambridge: Addison-Wesley Press.

Beck, E. H. (2009). Art Therapy with an Eating Disordered Male Population: A Case Study.

Bruch, H. (1978). *The Golden Cage: The Enigma of Anorexia Nervosa.* Cambridge: Harvard University Press.

Buber, M. (1937). *I and Thou.* Edinburgh: T. & T. Clark.

Buss, A. H. (1961). *The Psychology of Aggression.* New York and London: John Wiley & Sons.

Coelho, J. S., Kumar, A., Kilvert, M., Kunkel, L., and Lam, P. Y. (2015). Male youth with eating disorders: clinical and medical characteristics of a sample of inpatients. *Eating Disorders*, 23, 5, 455–61.

Culbert, K. M., Racine, S. E., and Klump, K. L. (2015). Research review: what we have learned about the causes of eating disorders – a synthesis of sociocultural, psychological, and biological research. *Journal of Child Psychology and Psychiatry, and Allied Disciplines*, 56, 11, 1141–64.

Fairburn, C. G. (2001). *Eating Disorders.* New York: John Wiley & Sons.

Frisch, M. J., Franko, D. L., and Herzog, D. B. (2006). Arts-based therapies in the treatment of eating disorders. *Eating Disorders*, 14, 2, 131–142.

Gostečnik, C. (2002). *Sodobna psihoanaliza (Contemporary Psychoanalysis).* Ljubljana: Brat Frančišek, Frančiškanski družinski center.

Griffiths, S., Mitchison, D., Hay, P., Mond, J. M., Rogers, B., McLean, S., et al. (2016). Sex differences in the relationships between body dissatisfaction, quality of

life and psychological distress. *Aust N Zealand J Public Health*, 40, 6, 518–522. doi: 10.1111/1753-6405.12538.
Gull, W. W. (1873). *Anorexia nervosa (apepsia hysterica, anorexia hysterica)*. In: *Transactions of the Clinical Society of London*. London: Society for Spottiswoode, 22–27.
Gumz, A., Weigel, A., Daubmann, A., Wegscheider, K., Romer, G., and Löwe, B. (2017). Efficacy of a prevention program for eating disorders in schools: a cluster-randomized controlled trial. *BMC Psychiatry*, 17, 1, 1–13.
Hinz, L. D. (2006). *Drawing from Within: Using Art to Treat Eating Disorders*. London and Philadelphia: Jessica Kingsley Publishers.
Hromc, A. (2006). *Družine in zasvojenosti in omame (Families and Addictions and Dazes)*. Otrok in družina: Družine, 36–37.
Kastelic, A. (1995). Celostna obravnava oseb z motnjami hranjenja (Comprehensive treatment of people with eating disorders). In: Tomori, M. (ed.) *Motnje hranjenja: IX. seminar o delu z mladostniki (Eating disorders: IX. seminar on work with adolescents)* (p. 29–37). Ljubljana: Department of Psychiatry, Faculty of Medicine, Ljubljana. Psychiatric clinic.
Laban, R. (1975). *Laban's Principles of Dance and Movement Notation* (2nd ed.). Edited and annotated by R. Lange. London: MacDonald and Evans. (First published 1956.)
Lamovec, T. (1988). *Priročnik za psihologijo motivacije in emocij* (A handbook of motivational and emotional psychology). Ljubljana: Faculty of Philosophy, Department of Psychology.
Lamovec, T. and Rojnik, A. (1978). *Psihologija agresivnosti (Psychology of Aggression)*. Ljubljana: DDU Univerzum.
Mehrabian, A. (1969). Significance of posture and position in the communication of attitude and status relationships. *Psychological Bulletin*, 71, 5, 359–372.
Mitchison, D., Hay, P., Griffiths, S., Murray, S. B., Bentley, C., Gratwick-Sarll, K., Harrison, C., and Mond, J. (2017). Disentangling body image: the relative associations of overvaluation, dissatisfaction, and preoccupation with psychological distress and eating disorder behaviors in male and female adolescents. *The International Journal of Eating Disorders*, 50, 2, 118–126.
Modic, M. (2003). *Točka simptomalnosti: razprava o problematiki motenj hranjenja (The Symptomatic Point: A Discussion of the Problem of Eating Disorders)*. Ljubljana: Univerza v Ljubljani, Pedagoška fakulteta.
Morton, R. (1689). *Phthisiologia, seu exercitationes de phthisi tribus libris comprehensa, totumque opus variis historiis illustratum*. Londini: Impensis Samuelis Smith.
Morton, R. (1694). *Phthisiologia; or, A treatise of consumptions:* ... Translated from the original. London: Sam. Smith and Benj. Walford.
Mrevlje, G. (1995). *Sociološki vidiki motenj hranjenja (Sociological aspects of eating disorders)*. V: Tomori, M. (ur.) Motnje hranjenja: IX. seminar o delu z mladostniki. Ljubljana: Katedra za psihiatrijo medicinske fakultete v Ljubljani. Psihiatrična klinika, 18–27.
Mushatt, C. (1992). *Anorexia Nervosa as an Expression of Ego-Defective Development*. In: C. P. Wilson, C. C. Hogan, and I. L. Mintz, (eds), *Psycho-Dynamic Technique in the Treatment of the Eating Disorders*. New York: Jason Aronson. 301–311.
Ogburn, W. (1951). The biology of human starvation, Vols. I and II. In A. Keys, J. Brazek, A. Henschel, O. Mickelsen, and H. L. Taylor (eds). *American Journal of Sociology*, 57, 3, 294–295.
Pandel Mikuš, R. (2002). Eating disorders in women. Proceedings of 1st International Workshop and Summer School on Nursing Research, 27–29 August, Maribor, Slovenia, 50–52.
Plutchik, R. and Kellerman H. (1979). *Profil index emocij*. Ljubljana: Zavod SR za produktivnost dela.

Podjavoršek, N. (2004). Anoreksija ni le bolezen posameznika, ampak je bolezen celega sistema (Anorexia is not only an individual's disease, but is a disease of the entire system). *Psihološka obzorja*, 13, 4, 119–133.

Rehavia-Hanauer, D. (2003). Identifying conflicts of anorexia nervosa as manifested in the art therapy process. *The Arts in Psychotherapy*, 30, 137–149.

Reindl, S. M. (2002). *Sensing the Self: Women's Recovery from Bulimia*. Cambridge: Harvard University Press.

Reynolds, J. (1669). *A Discourse upon Prodigious Abstinence Occasioned by the Twelve Months Fasting of Martha Taylor, the famed Derbyshire Damosell*. London: Simmons N. and Newman D.

Robinson, K. J., Mountford, V. A., and Sperlinger, D. J. (2013). Being men with eating disorders: perspectives of male eating disorder service-users. *Journal of Health Psychology*, 18, 2, 176–86.

Russell, G. F. M. (1979). Bulimia nervosa: an ominous variant of anorexia nervosa. *Psychological Medicine*, 9, 3, 429–448.

Rutten-Saris, M. (1992). *Porajajoči se jezik telesa (The Emerging Body Language)*. Assen: Van Gorcum & Co.

Sabel, A. L., Rosen, E., and Mehler, P. S. (2014). Severe anorexia nervosa in males: clinical presentations and medical treatment. *Eating Disorders*, 22, 3, 209–20.

Schilling, D. (2000). *50 dejavnosti za razvijanje čustvene inteligence (50 Activities for Developing Emotional Intelligence)*. Ljubljana: Inštitut za razvijanje osebne kakovosti.

Sernec, K. (2003). Motnje hranjenja (Eating disorders). V: Čebašek - Travnik, Z. (ed.), *Preprečimo odvisnosti od kajenja, alkohola, drog, hranjenja, dela, iger na srečo*. Ljubljana: Društvo za zdravje srce in ožilja Slovenije, 259–264.

Sernec, K. (2010). Sodobni vidiki in načini zdravljena motenj hranjenja (Modern aspects and ways of eating disorders). *Farmacevtski vestnik*, 61, 2, 106–109.

Shapiro, L. E., and Čertalič, V. (1999). *Čustvena inteligenca otrok: Kako vzgojimo otroka z visokim čustvenim količnikom (How to raise a child with a high EQ: A parent's guide to emotional intelligence)*. Ljubljana: Mladinska knjiga.

Smink, F. R. E., Hoeken, D., Oldehinkel, A. J., and Hoek, H. W. (2014). Prevalence and severity of DSM-5 eating disorders in a community cohort of adolescents. *International Journal of Eating Disorders*, 47, 6, 610–619.

Stice, E. (1994). Review of the evidence for a sociocultural model of bulimia nervosa and an exploration of mechanisms of action. *Clinical Psychology Review*, 14, 7, 633–661.

Tozzi, F., Thornton, L. M., and Klump, K. L. (2005). Symptom fluctuation in eating disorders: correlates of diagnostic crossover. *American Journal of Psychiatry*, 162, 4, 732–740.

Vandereycken, W. (2002). History of anorexia nervosa and bulimia nervosa. In: C. G. Fairburn and K. D. Brownell (eds), *Eating Disorders and Obesity: A Comprehensive Handbook*. New York: The Guilford Press, 151–154.

Vidrih, A. (2016). *Dramski performativni metod AV – Ars Vitae za razvijanje veština komunikacije (The AV Performative Method of Drama - Ars Vitae for Developing Communication Skills)*. Čačak: Regionalni centar za profesionalni razvoj zaposlenih u obrazovanju.

Wadeson, H. (1980). *Art Psychotherapy*. New York: John Wiley & Sons.

Welch, E., Ghaderi, A., and Swenne, I. (2015). A comparison of clinical characteristics between adolescent males and females with eating disorders. *BMC Psychiatry*, 15, 45.

Wooldridge, T. (2016). *Understanding Anorexia Nervosa in Males: An Integrative Approach*. New York: Routledge, Taylor & Francis Group.

World Health Organization. (2006). *Constitution of the World Health Organization – Basic Documents* (45th ed.). Supplement. Geneva: WHO.

Electronic resources

/1/ UK obesity data for the adult population (accessed 01. 12. 2015). Available at: http://www.slideshare.net/deheij/vid-17667-slides-for-websiteadultdec2013.

/2/ World Health Organisation (accessed 07. 01. 2016). Available at: http://apps.who.int/bmi/in.

/3/ Global Burden of Disease Study (2013) (accessed 01. 12. 2015). Mortality and causes of death collaborators (2014). Global, regional, and national age–sex specific all-cause and cause-specific mortality for 240 causes of death, 1990–2013: a systematic analysis for the Global Burden of Disease Study 2013. *Lancet*, 385 (9963): 117–171. Available at: doi:10.1016/S0140–6736(14)61682–2. PMC 4340604. PMID 25530442

/4/ National Institute of Mental Health, Eating disorders (accessed 01. 12. 2015). Available at: http://www.nimh.nih.gov/health/topics/eating-disorders/index.shtml.

/5/ The Center for Eating Disorders (n.d) (accessed 01. 12. 2015). Available at: http://eatingdisorder.org/eating-disorder-information/anorexia-nervosa/

/6/ Mixed Methods Research (accessed 03. 01. 2016). Available at: http://www.sagepub.com/sites/default/files/upm-binaries/27397_Pages138_141.pdf.

/7/ Johnson, R. B, Onwuegbuzie A. J., and Turner, L. A. (2016) (accessed 06. 03. 2015). Toward a definition of mixed methods research, *Journal of Mixed Methods Research*, 2007, 1, 112. Available at: http://mmr.sagepub.com/cgi/content/abstract/1/2/112 doi: 10.1177/1558689806298224.

/8/ A brief overview of Laban movement analysis (accessed 06. 03. 2015). Available at: (http://www.movementhasmeaning.com/wp-content/uploads/2010/09/LMA-Workshop-Sheet.pdf.

Chapter 15

Complicated gender and problematised bodies

The impact of severe illness explored through the lens of portrait therapy

Susan M. D. Carr

Within this chapter I will discuss two portraits co-designed by patients Paul and Rose, who took part in my PhD study, developing and researching portrait therapy as an intervention for people who experience life threatening and chronic illnesses (LT&CIs) as a disruption to their sense of self-identity (for a full description and protocol, see Carr 2017). A phenomenological approach to data collection and analysis was used within this project, characterised by Edmund Husserl's (1977 [1929]) call for a 'return to the things themselves' which is achieved by bracketing out all preconceived ideas and assumptions about a phenomenon. Utilising a phenomenological approach (Tjasink 2010) was important as it allowed a focus on experiences of illness *as lived* by the patients, and the creation of 'essence statements' for each portrait. I have used Kenneth Wright's (2009) theory of 'mirroring and attunement' to underpin the use of portraiture as a way to *re-vision* self-identities. Wright argues that the surface of the canvas in a painting is 'derivative, or 'analogue' to the (m)other's expressive face in infancy, functioning in a similar way as a responsive and mirroring extension of the 'self' or 'surrogate adaptive mother' (Wright 2009, 13).

The portraits discussed in this chapter illuminate a vision of gender and self-identity complicated by illness, with 'gendered norms' rejected in favour of intentionally distorted gender identities. Illness is stigmatising, meaning that those people who are unable to maintain an appearance of *wholeness* and *coherence*, be it in the body, mind or gender, are seen as ambiguous, problematic, polluting and ultimately dangerous. The PhD analysis, on which this chapter draws, reveals how the exclusions and stigma of illness are *revisioned* (Carr 2014, 2017; Carr and Hancock 2017) through the portraits, offering insights into the self, whilst also managing, through the use of props and 'performance', what is *seen* or *not seen*.

Whilst a person's 'sex' relates to biological differences, gender refers to a range of roles, behaviours, relationships, values, power and influences that are socially constructed and then attributed by society to the two sexes. Engendered roles and behaviours are defined through their relationship to each other and also by their 'social differences' (Vlassoff 2007, 47). Judith Butler claims that there is no 'gender identity' behind these behaviours, rather she suggests that 'identity is performatively constituted by the very "expressions" that are said to be its results' (Butler 1990, 34). The results from my PhD analysis seem to corroborate this, in that both Rose and Paul 'chose' to align the portrayal of their self-identities with genders different to those they were living.

At the day-hospice where I worked as an art therapist for over 12 years, there was a gender divide chosen by the patients in the form of 'tables' to sit at. There was a 'men's' table and a 'lady's' table and no amount of persuasion would induce the genders to mix; there was a resolute preference for a gender divide. There were of course exceptions to the rule, sometimes unlikely friendships developed between the genders, often a younger man might develop a protective or jokey relationship with an older lady and join the 'female' table. There was a third table, known as the 'self-segregation' table, where people who wanted to be alone would sit, and this is invariably where Paul chose to position himself.

When evaluating portrait therapy, issues relating to 'gender' appeared as an underlying tension in some of the portraits and collages, highlighting the covert pressures patients suffer in trying to maintain roles and expectations around gender in the face of LT&CIs. What also became clear was that men and women experience illness differently, and yet until recently, in clinical research a 'male' model of health was used 'almost exclusively' and findings were then 'generalized to women' (Vlassoff 2007, 51). It wasn't until the 1990s that reservations were raised regarding the legitimacy of using a male model for female health issues 'highlighting significant gender differences in the biological determinants of health and illness' (ibid.).

Within the Western world, the idea of *ambiguity* regarding gender is seen as something 'other' than the norm, something that is 'dangerous' and 'deeply problematic' (Latimer 2009, 56). Likewise, people living with LT&CIs who are unable to uphold a 'bounded' body (Lawton 1998, 132; Sibbett 2005b, 69) are also seen as problematic or 'abject' (Kristeva quoted in Latimer 2009, 56). Abject bodies are 'ambiguous, they leak, are penetrable, and their parts keep fragmenting and coming into view as parts: they make visible the space between object and subject' (Latimer 2009, 56). It seems that the very nature of 'difference' threatens and undermines the encultured 'norms' within society, and complicates gender for those living with LT&Cs.

This binary division of gender into 'masculine' and 'feminine' is also a path of inequality, as globally more women than men live in poverty, and more men than women receive a basic education or are appointed to positions of power. There may be significant, yet diverse, obstructions for both genders in accessing services such as healthcare and mental healthcare, or even accessing art therapy, and this deserves recognition, particularly when developing gender specific interventions. For someone being engendered 'female' there may be significant issues around having to choose between being the 'good girl' or the 'powerful women'. As Walkerdine (1991, 12) says:

> I still had difficulty with other's envy of my power. It is still so much easier to see myself as the good girl, who is looking for the good place, the

good Other to save me – so much easier than letting out all that rage and becoming a powerful woman.

The remainder of this chapter draws on two case-studies, created collaboratively with Rose and Paul. All the patients who took part in this study were living with LT&CIs and attending the day-hospice where I worked as an art therapist for over 12 years, and I am grateful to them for the time they dedicated to this and to the inspiring stories of self-identity they freely shared through their portraits.

Rose, a 61-year-old divorced lady, was diagnosed with Motor Neuron Disease (MND), which is a degenerative neurological disorder that can result in patients becoming 'locked' within their paralysed body. Rose described having what she called a 'slow onset' form of MND, which had primarily affected her speech, swallowing and the muscles in her face. Rose also had a facial palsy and her lower lip fell open unless she held it closed. She was unable to smile or make any other facial expression and her speech was severely affected, with communication therefore difficult.

When Rose first began attending the day-hospice, she was very quiet and subdued and didn't really interact with anyone. With communication so difficult for her I used several simple creative tasks to help elicit stories of self-identity, one of which was a Lego elicitation task (Gauntlett 2002). Lego is a familiar, non-threatening and yet expressive material and I invited Rose to use this to construct a model of her self-identity. Rose said that her self-identity was overshadowed by MND and therefore her Lego sculpture represented herself and her disease combined (Figure 15.1).

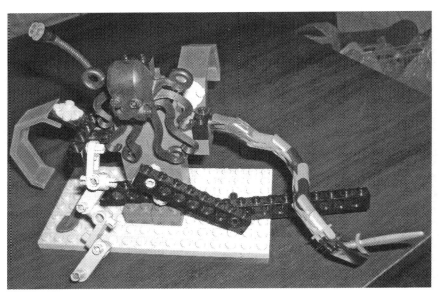

Figure 15.1 Rose's Lego self-identity construction.

I collaborated with Rose to write this prose-poem, reflecting Rose's lived experience of MND as shown through her Lego identity construction:

> Holding my face
> To stop it falling
> Waiting ...
> For the unpredictable disease
> An enigma to most
> Personal to me
> It creeps up
> Takes hold
> And will never let go
> Disabling
> Blocking brain signals to muscles
> It ties me to the chair
> Deep in a dark abyss I cry
> And yet ...
> Even in this dark place
> Music comes to me
> Filling my being
> Giving me the strength I need
> To dig myself out
> Taking up my sword
> To fight and live ...
> Another day.

For the purposes of this chapter, I will discuss one of the three portraits that Rose and I co-designed and I painted, called *Bohemian Rhapsody* (Figure 15.2). When I first visited Rose's home it was immediately obvious that she was a fan of Freddie Mercury, as on almost every surface of her lounge there was a picture or reminder of him. Therefore, Rose's request to be painted as Freddie wasn't a great surprise, although her choice of the iconic Bohemian Rhapsody pose was. Reflecting on it now, it seems that Rose was choosing to align herself with a *masculine* identity – something that is highlighted within her Lego sculpture, where she claims that survival means 'taking up my sword to fight and live another day'.

The following prose-poem grew out of the statement of intention for Rose's portrait, outlining her identification with Freddie Mercury.

Rose said:

> Paint me like Freddie Mercury
> in Bohemian Rhapsody
> Strong and defiant
> I'll wear his rings ... I have copies you know

Figure 15.2 Bohemian Rhapsody by Susan Carr (co-designed by Rose), 2011.

And a rose in my garden named after him
Roses are sparky, like me
Like I've had to become
To survive the uncertainty
I used to visit Freddie's house every year
A kind of pilgrimage
To read the messages on the wall
To light a candle
Now it's all gone ... there is nothing there
People complained it was untidy
But then life is untidy ... and I have learned
Not to complain ... but to live

When practicing portrait therapy, I avoid 'imposing pictorial ideas or preferences' (Kramer 1986, 71) on patients by asking them to choose the style in which they would like their portrait painted. I show patients images of portraits painted in different styles, and Rose chose to be painted in the style of Lucian Freud. I was mindful that by using the Bohemian Rhapsody photograph of Freddie Mercury as a template for this portrait, by default it would bring in connotations about his death from AIDS. I was also aware that by combining this with the 'cold' painting style of Lucian Freud, I may inadvertently create a 'disturbing' image of Rose. However, I have learned to trust the patient's instincts on this and as preparatory work, I arranged with Rose to take reference photographs of her for the portrait. Rose dressed up for the part, wearing a similar outfit to Freddie's and replicas of his rings. I was aware of Rose becoming Freddie in that moment, however, when I saw the photographs, I was taken aback by the 'corpse like' pose, and Rose also had reservations that she did not reveal at the time, but discussed later in her end of project interview (EPI):

S: So, looking at the paintings now, is there anything you would change about them?
R: No. ... No ... I was a bit bothered about that to start with [indicating *Bohemian Rhapsody* portrait] when I saw the [reference] photographs.
S: Bothered about it?
R: Yeah, I thought "oh dear I don't like that", but the painting has changed it completely, *I like it now.*
S: I think it has a real strength to it ...
R: It's got that ...
S: A real strength ... that is in you ...
R: And determination.
S: Yes determination.
R: *That's determined!* [Indicating *Bohemian Rhapsody* portrait]

S= *Susan (ATR) Artist–Therapist–Researcher, R= 'Rose'*
(PR) Patient–Researcher (EPI 27/03/2011).

Freddie Mercury's own self-representation of gender was complicated by illness (AIDS) and also by being homosexual, and as Butler (1990, 179) explained, within the media there is a 'hysterical and homophobic response' to AIDS meaning that the disease becomes 'a specific modality of homosexual pollution'. The fear of severe illness as 'pollution' is still part of the illness experience, with diseases such as MND and cancer often making patient's feel as though they are 'untouchable', even though their disease cannot be transmitted through touch. This was underlined for Rose when her husband left her shortly after being diagnosed with MND.

The idea of 'difference' as 'pollution' is linked to moral values, with certain social beliefs characterised by theories of 'dangerous contagion ... which threaten transgressors' (Douglas 1966, 3). This 'pollution', particularly where the ill and marginalised are concerned, may also carry symbolic meanings, which mirror the hierarchy within a larger social system (ibid., 4).

One of the key findings from the PhD project was the patients' search for a sense of 'belonging', as not only have they themselves been changed by illness, but so has their world, often resulting in feelings of isolation and 'unhomelike-being-in-the-world' (Svenaeus 2011, 337). The sense of belonging that Rose felt through aligning herself with her idol was outlined within the *Statement of Emergent Learning:*

In posing as her musical idol Freddie Mercury, Rose is demonstrating her solidarity and identification with him and his suffering, yet gains personal strength, courage and determination to "keep on fighting to the end".

When individuals experience feelings of existential anxiety and vulnerability, they often wish to 'reaffirm a threatened self-identity, and any collective identity that can provide such security is a potential pole of attraction' (Kinnvall 2004, 742). An increase in Rose's sense of *immortality* is also highlighted where she says that bringing her stories to life through the portraits has meant she has changed from being a 'nobody' to someone who has 'done something' with their life, a clear sense of *achievement* and *self-worth*.

S: But what I am saying is, has it given you a stronger sense of self-identity?
R: Yes, because now, instead of being a nobody, this is as if I have done something with my life, you know [...] instead of "well ... I was born, went to school, gone on holiday, grew up" ... that's *ordinary* ... now you have made it into something ... *extra-ordinary* .... interesting ... so instead of just going through the motions with my life, you made it into *something*.
S: So, creating meaning?
R: Yes that's it, yes.

S = Susan (ATR) Artist–Therapist–Researcher, R = Rose (PR) Patient–Researcher (EPI: 22/03/2011).

The idea of immortality has historically been tied to religious doctrine; however, with the movement away from a belief in organised religion in the West, there has been a growing secular focus on 'fame' and celebrity (Taylor 1989, 43). The implied 'immortality' within that is something that the portraits offer through their potential exhibition and publication, and this becomes part of the patients' *future*, 'immortalised' self-identity, something Rose recognised as an embodied change from being a 'no-body' to a 'some-body'.

When analysing Rose's portraits, I noticed a progression within them from a position of 'invisibility' or 'hiding' herself, to being highly visible in *Bohemian Rhapsody*, where Rose confronts the viewer with a defiant, strong and forthright look. As she said 'Paint me like Freddie Mercury ... strong and defiant!' This sense of confrontation, and determination to be seen on her own terms, was highlighted in the statement of emergent knowing:

Rose takes a risk and steps out of the shadows into the light ... through self-acceptance and strength ... she will be seen and heard.

For Rose the invisibility of being an aging woman (Hogan & Warren 2012, 332) is contrasted with the unwanted visible signs of illness imprinted on her face, and this is further complicated by the 'pervasive cultural condition' within which the lives of women are 'either misrepresented or not represented at all'

(Butler 1990, 2). Art therapy and portrait therapy both listen to and privilege the 'experiences of those who feel disenfranchised or defined as "other" by socially dominant groups' (Eastwood 2012, 100); however, portrait therapy enables patients to be 'seen' as well as 'heard'. While being able to physically *see* their individual portraits fulfilled different needs for Rose and Paul, as this project progressed, it became clear that it was equally important for them to know that their portraits were going to be *seen by others*.

Increasing perceptions of 'control' was another theme identified within the analysis and Rose used the portraits as a way to 'control' her image and how people saw her. Charmaz and Rosenfeld (2006, 37) talk about how 'embodiment complicates self-identity for people with chronic illness' and the tension between visibility and invisibility results in people attempting to control how they are portrayed. For Rose, aligning herself with the 'masculine' Freddie, was perhaps part of a subconscious effort to be seen as 'strong' and 'in control' as this seems to be an important part of what *Bohemian Rhapsody* signifies. As Gussak (2008, 65) claims:

> Those who identify as being more masculine likely perceive themselves as having more control than those who identify as feminine. What is more, in certain contexts, those perceived by others as more masculine may be granted more authority or viewed as being in charge.

Losing perceptions of 'control' is, to a large extent, part of the suffering involved with being diagnosed with a disease like MND (Figure 15.3). Philosopher Havi Carel (2008, 63) talks eloquently about her own experience of losing control through the effects of chronic illness:

> [...] the thought that was truly novel for me was this: I will never get better. All the usual rules that governed my life – that trying hard yields results, that looking after yourself pays off, that practice makes perfect – seemed inoperative here. It was the first instance, for me, of unconditional, uncontrollable failure. No matter what I did, I would only get worse. The inevitability of decline was the only principle governing my life.

Supressing the feminine part of herself in the portrait may therefore have been part of Rose's attempt to remain 'in control'. Walkerdine (1991, 44) talks about the conflicting nature of attempting to suppress 'parts' of herself:

> For me, anything wanting and demanding had to be suppressed as "pathetic". I also wanted the little girl back, to be loved, and I could find little way to be strong except through rigid control.

When writing Rose's case-study and analysing her portraits, I noticed they all captured Rose 'in action' in a moment of *doing* or *becoming,* she is not 'passive' in

Figure 15.3 All I might be able to do … collage by Susan Carr.

any of them. They all held an element of *performance* and *intentionality*, each with a distinct 'costume' and 'set', which suggests that Rose may be playing a 'role' in each of them, meaning the 'real' Rose may still elude us in all of them. This is poignant because autonomy, intentionality and the ability to 'do' what one chooses was something that would, almost certainly, be lost to Rose if/when her illness progressed. Her fear of this happening was highlighted within the collage and prose poems I created for Rose as a form of 'response art' (Fish 2012):

In her EPI Rose talked about the 'message' that her portraits conveyed:

R: I think this is a message, well to me … you're diagnosed with a terminal illness, but it doesn't mean to say you gotta stop, you gotta keep going, don't give in to it [...] Just because you have been told you're ill, told you are never going to get better, doesn't mean you can't carry on. That's what this has done for me, because you just gotta keep going, you gotta fight, so you do fight. If you think … I can't be bothered … that's no good [...] because, you could give up so easily. Like I said … "You say I can't … I say *I will!*"
R = Rose (PR) Patient–Researcher (EPI: 22/03/2011).

For Paul, a single gentleman in his late forties, the issues of being engendered 'masculine' and living with an 'invisible' chronic illness in its 'terminal stage' became evident in his portrait *Broken Lungs*. When Paul and I first began working together he had been living with a diagnosis of COPD (Chronic Obstructive Pulmonary Disease) for 3 years, and he was dependent upon oxygen during the day and a Bi-pap machine (which breathes for him) during the night. The slightest exertion would leave Paul fighting for breath and extremely fatigued. Being unable to work or care for himself, Paul had been forced to give up his independence, and return to live with his mother. Paul described a disruption to his sense of self-identity and his autonomy, of being 'unable to be' the *Paul* he used to be, talking about feeling 'low, helpless, hopeless, trapped and frustrated'. During visits to the day-hospice Paul displayed stereotypical masculine behaviours, using humour to displace concern for his health, always answering questions about his health and wellbeing with phrases such as 'I'm fine … it's the other's you have to watch!', and 'well I'm still here aren't I, not underground yet!' This included suppressing his emotions and negative feelings, isolating himself from others, poor self-care and self-image, as well as depression and anxiety attacks.

When discussing potential participants for portrait therapy, the day-hospice multi-disciplinary team suggested Paul as a possible candidate, and I was surprised when Paul accepted, as he had previously refused all offers of psychological or emotional support, including art therapy. As a self-confessed loner, he was a firm member of the 'self-segregation' table; however, over the 7 months that Paul and I worked together, we developed a close inter-subjective relationship, based on trust and collaboration (Carr & Hancock 2017).

Masculine gender is complicated by illness due to the socialisation process, which sees male gendered children as being 'dominant, competitive, aggressive and tough. To be a normal male means to aspire to leadership, to be sexually active, knowledgeable, potent and a successful seducer. The burden inherent in these expectations is clear' (Etherington 1995, 32). Through 'humour' Paul was valiantly trying, despite his illness, to maintain some sense of this 'macho' image and it was very hard to get through his defences to find the real 'Paul'. As Liebmann (2003, 123) says:

> The norms of therapy – openness about feelings, communication, self-reflection, intimacy – are areas where many men have difficulties. And yet it is for this very reason that therapy has something to offer which they need. Art therapy has a special role in providing a bridge to these skills, in giving time for an activity (and one with very visible boundaries), which may feel safer and more purposeful (in being active) than a verbal therapy.

Despite refusing all previous offers of therapeutic input, there was something about portrait therapy that attracted Paul. Perhaps, for someone who had 'no energy', who could become breathless just 'thinking' about moving, the idea of an art therapist using their 'third hand' (Kramer 1971, 1986) to create the portraits *for* him appealed.

Figure 15.4 Paul's before-illness self-identity Lego task.

The sense of having a disrupted or 'abject' male gender was further born out when I asked Paul to create a Lego sculpture depicting his 'before' and 'after' illness self-identities (Figures 15.4 and 15.5).

Paul said: 'This shows me working on the farm at the control of a tractor; I was doing a worthwhile, responsible job and I could move around freely'.
Paul said: 'This is me when I had to give up work because of the illness, I have made a broken ladder, because it demonstrates how *useless* I feel, being unable to work and function properly ... I am *broken*'.

In this Lego task Paul demonstrated the impact of illness on his self-identity. He used the metaphor of 'work' to show that his pre-illness self-identity was strong and effective like a 'tractor', going back to a time when he was able to earn his own living by working on the farm. However, within Paul's post-illness self-identity he feels 'as useless as a broken ladder'. The broken ladder metaphor also indicates the seriousness and potentially fatal nature of his illness. Part of the issue regarding health inequality between males and females is also due to the relationship between masculine identities and risk taking (Doyle 2001, 1061), and Paul admitted that throughout his life he smoked and drank to excess and didn't take care of himself well.

As Paul had no initial ideas for his portraits, I showed him an album that I had put together featuring portraits by famous and non-famous Western artists.

Complicated gender and problematised bodies 239

Figure 15.5 Paul's after-illness self-identity Lego task.

The first portrait to capture Paul's imagination was the self-portrait *Broken Column* (1944) by Mexican artist Frida Kahlo, saying with a smile 'Ooooo that's a bit naughty!' Paul eventually returned to this image saying 'I like that ... yes ... can you paint me like her?' 'You can see that she's in pain ... you know what she's going through'. We discussed how he could replace Kahlo in the painting and how he would step into her 'world'.

Kahlo's *Broken Column* explores 'what it is to be embodied' (Latimer 2009: 50) and reveals the pain and suffering Kahlo endured following her injuries in a serious bus accident aged 17. Kahlo depicts herself semi-naked in a barren landscape, her chest ripped open, a broken Ionic pillar replacing her vertebrae and a steel orthopaedic corset holding her together. Kahlo portrays herself as a divided, fragmented and leaky body-self, existing in the borderlands between object and subject (Latimer 2009, 46), revealing the 'fragility of and the extraordinary effort and machinery it takes to hold all the fragments together to produce an image of a whole' (ibid., 51). Perhaps in Kahlo Paul recognised a fellow inhabitant of the 'world of illness' (Radley 2009), or 'liminality' (Turner 1969; Sibbett 2005a) saying he chose Kahlo's painting because 'you can see that she's in pain ... you know what she's going through'. Paul suggested that I paint him into the same barren landscape and instead of the cut-open chest revealing a broken 'column', Paul's portrait could show his 'broken lungs'.

I wondered if the 'naughtiness' that Paul had initially seen in Kahlo's portrait was the fact that she was showing her breasts, or the fact that she was showing her 'insides'. Perhaps the 'naughtiness' was meant in a sort of 'ouch' way? I also wondered if Paul wanted to 'shock' people with this portrait, perhaps because his illness was not visible to others, and he needed them to recognise or acknowledge his 'brokenness' and inner pain. As an art therapist, I believe that images are able to convey *physical pain* in a way that is *inexpressible* in any other form (Toombs 1990: 235; Padfield 2003), and Paul recognises this when he says 'You can see that she's in pain', and while in *Broken Column* Frida talks eloquently of her 'brokenness', there is also a sense of the strength and the fight she has gone through to survive.

Kahlo herself explores the borderlands between the normalised cultural stereotypes of femininity and masculinity, when she poses dressed in a man's suit in several family photographs. These borderlands are returned to when she paints a gender ambiguous self-image in the painting *Self-Portrait with Cropped Hair* (1940), within which she paints herself dressed in a man's suit.

The following week, I visited Paul to take reference photographs for this portrait, and when I arrived, he exclaimed (loud enough for his mother in the next room to hear) ... 'Oh, here she is, come to paint me naked!' and laughed. I laughed too, but was a little embarrassed by this and I think Paul enjoyed my discomfort. I replied 'Don't say that! Your mother will get the wrong idea!' We both laughed again and I wondered if this was actually what Paul wanted. Paul was clearly making a joke out of it, perhaps to deflect his own embarrassment, or to see if I would 'get' his humour, or even if I would 'get' him. When Paul undressed, I was shocked by the level of his emaciation, and I took the photographs quickly so that he could replace his shirt. It was an intimate moment, and I felt protective 'mother' instincts on seeing him semi-naked, wanting to 'feed him up'. Reflecting on this I believe my discomfort was largely due to the recognition that it is usually only the medical profession or our life partners who have the privileged view of our naked or semi naked-bodies, and to Paul I was neither. I was also very aware of a discrepancy in power as I stood there with my camera, preparing to photograph his emaciated body. However, I reminded myself that this was Paul's idea and his design and as such I needed to trust we were co-designing the portrait *he needed to see* and also that which he *needed others to see* (Figure 15.6).

Within portrait therapy, humour is often used by patients as an adaptive process, enabling them to manage their experience of 'liminal' (Turner 1969; Sibbett 2005a) or 'unhomelike-being-in-the-world' (Svenaeus 2011). Whilst as a therapist I was shocked by Paul's level of physical emaciation, as an artist I was intrigued by the 'beauty' I saw in Paul's bone structure protruding beneath his skin and I looked forward to the challenge of painting him. I was still able to see the 'beauty' in Paul's bone structure, and within the pale blue lights and shadows incorporated into the flesh tones, and the direct connection of his gaze. For Paul, it was about asking the question 'do you *get it*?' or 'do you *get*

Complicated gender and problematised bodies 241

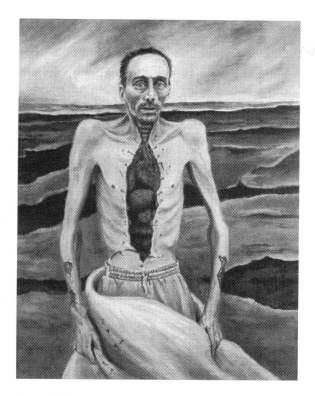

Figure 15.6 Broken Lungs by Susan Carr (co-designed by Paul).

me?' — highlighting *humour* as an important function of *being known* and painting the portrait for Paul was a way of mirroring and attuning this experience of *being known*. *Broken Lungs* was a portrait Paul needed *others* to see, as a way to *validate* his invisible illness. Paul talked about how his Mother reacted to seeing the portrait:

P: Well it was actually, for no reason, like today ... I was being pushed in a chair and just getting out of the chair into the car I just had to stop for five minutes just to catch my breath [...] It just gets you now and then, it just gets you ... it hits you really hard.
S: So, do you think that is reflected in the *Broken Lungs* painting?
P: Yeah, yeah definitely.
S: Yes ... because people have said it is a very powerful painting ... when I had it in that exhibition ...
P: My mum hates it! [laughs].
S: Well I can understand that ... because she is your Mum.

P: It is horrible I must admit ... *but I tried to explain to her ... that is me ... I am damaged.*
S: Yes.
P: *That is skinny though isn't it.* [laughs]
> S= Susan (ATR) Artist–Therapist–Researcher, P = Paul (PR) Patient–Researcher. (EPI 03/06/2013).

Paul's reflection may have indicated a sense of denial in his mother, an inability to acknowledge or 'hold' Paul's feelings of despair and pain. However, through the portrait, Paul is able to talk to his mother openly, for the first time, about his illness and being 'damaged'. Exley and Leatherby (2001) say that people who are nearing the end of life often engage in 'emotion work on and for their selves and on and for others'. This may indicate that Paul was trying to help his mother *come to terms* with his illness and mortality through the portrait, or even an unconscious desire to get his mother to do 'all the emotional work' (Liebmann 2003, 119). Either way Paul needed his Mother to *see* and *hold* the Broken Lungs portrait, and even if she found this difficult, it was the catalyst which enabled Paul to talk to her about his illness.

I was impressed by the risk Paul was willing to take through this portrait. By revealing himself in such a vulnerable 'un-masculine' way, Paul literally opens up his interior world of pain and suffering and invites us in, uncharacteristically letting down his guard and revealing the 'unbounded' (Lawton 1998, 127) nature of his inner self, and his closeness to death. This was highlighted within the statement of emergent knowing:

> My chest ripped open reveals my beating heart and broken lungs, a window on my invisible suffering, I am stripped back, laid bare, sharing my pain, I match my inner and outer realities ... it is hard to look at ... but even harder to be ... me.

When I exhibited *Broken Lungs* at a Sarum Theological College in Wiltshire recently, the curator positioned it opposite a sculpture of Christ crucified on the cross, saying that she thought they somehow 'belonged together'. I had not thought of Paul in *Broken Lungs* as 'Christ like' or as a sacrificial deity, however, both are images of extreme suffering, with 'unbounded', 'leaking' bodies (ibid.), and the nails driven into Paul's flesh and lungs also evoke images of St Sebastian riven with arrows.

Broken Lungs portrays the dualities of fear and courage, and combining his 'inner and outer realities' in one image allowed for feelings of *integration* and identity *coherence* to develop (Ulman 1980, 6), also demonstrating Pauls need for love and acceptance and his connection to all humanity:

S: Yes ... get to the essence of the person ...
P: *Deep underneath what you are asking ... there is a heart as such.*

S: Yes ... I can see it ... [laughs]
P: Yeah [laughs]... in that one ... [indicating Broken Lung painting]
S: We found it somewhere in there ... [laughs]
P: Yeah ... well *you know what I'm saying* ...
S: *I know what you're saying* ...

S= Susan (ATR) Artist–Researcher, P = Paul (PR) Patient–Researcher. (EPI 03/06/2013).

In this exchange, Paul indicates his awareness of how much I *know* him, so much so that he assumes I can 'read between the lines' of his attempts to explain his feelings, and I reflect this back to him when I say '*I know* what you're saying'. I remember this as a poignant moment, charged with emotion, an 'I-thou' (Buber 2004) moment of recognition and intersubjective *knowing*. Within the portraits I painted for Paul, dualities of gender, hope and despair are 'held' and contained, and I believe because of this he was finally able to look me in the eye and say 'you know what I'm saying' and therefore you *know me*. Reflecting upon this several years later, I wonder if anyone had ever really *known* Paul, he was after all, a self-confessed 'loner'.

For Rose, aligning herself with her 'male' idol, means that she not only *becomes* Freddie in that moment, and all he means to her in the way of stardom and celebrity, strength and determination, but also acknowledges the solidarity Rose feels around them both being diagnosed with terminal illnesses and therefore, both dwellers of 'liminal' space (Turner 1969; Sibbett 2005a).

The portraits discussed here bear witness to the way gender issues in illness manifest as an underlying tension, highlighting the covert pressures patients endure through attempting to maintain gendered roles and expectations in the face of severe illness. Gendered identities are complicated by illness and males and females experience illness differently. Consequently, gender should be seen as something that changes relative to the environment or circumstances of the person (Butler 1990).

The problems that exist for men in accessing therapeutic interventions may be caused by strong masculine cultural messages regarding the 'un-macho-ness' of making one's self vulnerable and becoming a 'client' (Liebmann 2003, 124). The culturally 'engendered' expectations of men *not to express vulnerability* are damaging the ability of men to prioritise their health and wellbeing, or their ability to own up to being ill until it is too late. Issues around femininity are different; as Gilligan (1982, 1) points out, 'the qualities deemed necessary for adulthood – the capacity for autonomous thinking, clear decision making, and responsible action – are those associated with masculinity but considered undesirable as attributes of the feminine self'. This is complicated further by the higher value society places on 'control versus empathy, external versus internal concerns, managing versus caring, aggression versus understanding, business versus the arts ... men versus women' (Johnson 1989, quoted in Gussak 2008, 65). Greater understanding and sensitivity are necessary regarding the impact of illness on gender and gendered roles, within all aspects of art therapy and healthcare.

Ultimately portrait therapy enables the revisioning of self-identity and gender into something fluid and multifarious, a rejection of the limiting exclusiveness of masculine and feminine, highlighting that diversity and difference matter, and require protecting and celebrating. Rose and Paul were able to express multi-faceted portrayals of their self-identity, offering representations of themselves that avoided the limitations of gender positioning.

It is because gender plays 'a vital role in determining our subjective reality' (Hogan 2003a, 12) that as arts therapists, we need to develop theories and practices that address diversity in all its myriad variations, as Talwar (2010, 16) says:

> [...] we must become more skilled in confronting, challenging, and contesting hegemonic ways of seeing and representing others. The historic binaries of art therapy practice have only reinforced the reductive paradigm of normal versus abnormal. Getting beyond such practice means engaging in a discussion of cultural diversity from an intersectional perspective.

References

Buber, M. 2004 (1937). *I and Thou* (2nd edition). London: Continuum.
Butler, Judith. 1990. *Gender Trouble: Feminism and the Subversion of Identity*. New York: Routledge.
Carel, H. 2008. *Illness: The Cry of the Flesh*. Stocksfield: Acumen.
Carr, S. 2014. Revisioning self-identity: The role of portraits, neuroscience and the art therapist's 'third hand'. *International Journal of Art Therapy*, 19 (2): 54–70.
Carr, S. 2017. *Portrait Therapy: Resolving Self-Identity Disruption in Clients with Life-Threatening and Chronic Illnesses*. London: Jessica Kingsley.
Carr, S. and Hancock, S. 2017. Healing the inner child through portrait therapy: Illness, identity and childhood trauma. *International Journal of Art Therapy*, 22 (1): 8–21.
Charmaz, K. & Rosenfeld, D. 2006. Reflections of the body, images of self: Visibility and invisibility in chronic illness and disability. In, D. Waskal & P. Vannini, eds. *Body/embodiment: Symbolic Interaction and The Sociology of the Body*, 35–50. Aldershot: Ashgate.
Douglas, M. 1966. *Purity and Danger: An Analysis of Concepts of Pollution and Taboo*. New York: Frederick A. Praeger.
Doyle, L. 2001. Sex, gender, and health: The need for a new approach. *BMJ*, 323(7320): 1061–3.
Eastwood, C. 2012. Art therapy with women with borderline personality disorder: A feminist perspective. *International Journal of Art Therapy*, 17 (3): 98–114.
Etherington, K. 1995. *Adult Male Survivors of Childhood Sexual Abuse*. London: Pitman.
Exley, C. & Leatherby, G. 2001. Managing a disrupted life course: Issue of identity and emotion work. *Health*, 5 (1): 112–132.
Fish, B. J. (2012) Response art: The art of the art therapist. *Art Therapy: Journal of the American Art Therapy Association*, 29 (3): 138–143.
Gauntlett, D. 2002. *Media, Gender and Identity: An Introduction*. London: Routledge.

Gilligan, C. 1982. *In a Different Voice: Psychological Theory and Women's Development.* Cambridge: Harvard University Press.

Gussak, D. 2008. An interactionist perspective on understanding gender identity in art therapy. *Art Therapy: Journal of the American Art Therapy Association*, 25 (2): 64–69.

Hogan, S. 2003a. Contesting identities. In S. Hogan, ed. *Gender Issues in Art Therapy*, 11–29. London: Jessica Kingsley.

Hogan, S. & Warren, L. 2012. Dealing with complexity in research findings: How do older women negotiate and challenge images of ageing? *Journal of Women and Ageing*, 24 (4): 329–350.

Husserl, E. 1977 (1929). *Cartesian Meditations: An introduction to Phenomenology.* [D. Cairns trans.]. The Hague: Nijhoff.

Johnson, D. R. 1989. Introduction to the special issue on women and the creative arts therapies. *The Arts in Psychotherapy*, 16: 235–238.

Kinnvall, C. 2004. Globalization and religious nationalism: Self, identity, and the search for ontological security. *Political Psychology*, 25 (5): 741–767.

Kramer, E. 1971. *Art as Therapy with Children.* London: Schocken.

Kramer, E. 1986. The art therapist's third hand: Reflections on art, art therapy and society at large. *The American Journal of Art Therapy*, 24: 71–86.

Latimer, J. 2009. Unsettling bodies: Frida Kahlo's portraits and in/dividuality. In, J. Latimer & M. Schillmeier, eds. *Un/knowing Bodies. Sociological Review Monograph Series*, 46–62. Oxford: Wiley-Blackwell.

Lawton, J. 1998. Contemporary hospice care; the sequestration of the unbounded body and 'dirty dying'. *Sociology of Health and Illness*, 20 (2): 121–43.

Liebmann, M. 2003. Working with men. In, S. Hogan, ed. 2003. *Gender Issues in Art Therapy*, 108–125. London and Philadelphia: Jessica Kingsley.

Padfield, D. 2003. *Perceptions of Pain.* Stockport: Dewi Lewis.

Radley, A. 2009. *Works of Illness: Narrative, Picturing and the Social Response to Serious Disease.* Ashby-De-La-Zouche: Inker Men.

Sibbett, C. 2005a. Liminal embodiment: Embodied and sensory experience in cancer care and art therapy. In, D. Waller & C. Sibbett, eds. *Facing Death: Art Therapy and Cancer Care*, 50–81. Maidenhead: Open University Press.

Sibbett, C. 2005b. An art therapist's experience of having cancer: Living and dying with the tiger. In, D. Waller & C. Sibbett, eds. *Facing Death: Art Therapy and Cancer Care*, 223–248. Maidenhead: Open University Press.

Svenaeus, F. 2011. Illness as unhomelike being-in-the-world: Heidegger and the phenomenology of medicine. *Medicine Health Care and Philosophy*, 14(3): 333–343.

Talwar, S. 2010. An intersectional framework for race, class, gender, and sexuality in art therapy. *Art Therapy: Journal of the American Art Therapy Association*, 27 (1): 11–17.

Taylor, C. 1989. *Sources of the Self: The Making of Modern Identity.* Cambridge: Cambridge University Press.

Tjasink, M. 2010. Art psychotherapy in medical oncology: A search for meaning. *International Journal of Art Therapy*, 15 (2), 75–83.

Toombs, S. 1990. The temporality of illness: Four levels of experience. *Theoretical Medicine*, 11 (3): 227–241.

Turner, V. 1969 (1995). *The Ritual Process: Structure and Anti-Structure.* New York: Aldine de Gruyter.

Ulman, E. 1980. Symposium: Integration of divergent points of view in art therapy. In, E. Ulman & C. Levy, eds. *Art Therapy Viewpoints*, 6–17. New York: Schocken.

Vlassoff, C. 2007. Gender differences in determinants and consequences of health and illness. *Journal of Health, Populations and Nutrition*, 25 (1): 47–61.

Walkerdine, V. 1991. Behind the painted smile. In, J. Spence & P. Holland, eds. *Family Snaps: The Meaning of Domestic Photography*, 35–45. London: Virago.

Wright, K. 2009. *Mirroring and Attunement: Self-Realisation in Psychoanalysis and Art*. London: Routledge.

Chapter 16

Experimenting with gender roles in virtual reality

Nicole Ottiger[1] and Rose Ehemann[2]

Introduction

We live in a world of a changing media – the introduction of the global interconnectivity with the World Wide Web in 1991 (omnipresent since 2002), with the existence of Facebook (from 2004) and YouTube (from 2005), to name but a few influential media social network sites, is making matters of gender and identity sweepingly manifold. If we choose to be on such networks, we often have to create online self-representations (ranging from the basic identity of a mere name and photo to a more elaborate deputy-self in the form of an avatar) in order to participate and connect online. There is some element of self-representation in all these forms. Online social communities are shaping people's attitudes about their 'working self-concept', subjecting the self to change, revision and updates (Markus & Wurf 1987). The more 'selves' or self-representations we create online, the more dynamic the self becomes – it becomes a pluralized self-system. Our online selves mould just as much as our offline identity and body that lives and breathes in the 'real' world.

Despite much discussion about the limitations, ethics and even social implications of digital media, we consider that it is necessary to continue research on the use of digital media in art therapy practice (Hartwich & Brandecker 1997; Kuleba 2008; McLeod 1999; Orr 2005, 2015; Parker-Bell 2001) especially as we also live in an age where we spend much time online (on the computer or tablet/iPad as well as the mobile phone). Digital media is creating and developing more and more human-responsive interfaces, making future therapy opportunities exciting and challenging. We are more limited by our own imagination and inflexibility than digital media in its possibilities (Orr 2015).

The research project we developed between 2008 to 2012 into virtual reality strategies for therapeutic use, to frame the setting, was a team effort – a dedicated team of three, passionate about exploring new media: Nicole Ottiger, artist, art therapist and PhD candidate in the visual arts, head of the new media art therapy at Psychiatry St. Gallen North; Rose Ehemann, researcher, cultural manager, art therapist and the head of Ateliers-Living Museum at the Psychiatry St. Gallen North, a PhD candidate in art therapy, researching and writing about the project from a specific angle, with a specific set of hypotheses; Silke Geith, intern, finishing her Masters in art therapy and acting as researcher on the project. Research was carried out in a rigorous way, analysed qualitatively and where possible quantitatively, using a number of tests that could be statistically evaluated. The main body of that research can be read in Rose's PhD thesis,[3] which she successfully submitted in 2012.

As is often the case, clinical, empirical and qualitative research collects a tremendous amount of data, information, experience and knowledge that has not been written about yet. We discovered that virtual reality art therapy using Second Life software offers new potentialities, such as the free choice of gender role, including gender switching and gender neutrality, when choosing or creating an avatar. Gender issues, such as gender discrimination, are also observed online because subjects and avatars are still actual people carrying their fears and preconceptions into virtual worlds. Therapy with patients in Second Life shows that the term 'gender' may be considered as the being possibility of experimenting and thinking outside the standard male/female condition. It is the opportunity to explore a range of identities and roles that do not necessarily correspond to the stereotypical binary concept of two distinct, opposite and separate sex and gender forms of masculine and feminine.

Method

Study design and setting

Virtual reality represents an interactive form of virtual space within a computer-stimulated 3-dimensional environment, often with the aid of technical means such as a data helmet and goggles. It is a very specific, imaginative experience, which cannot be reduced to just being about the equipment used to make the experience. It not only has an effect on our perceptions and experiences we make online, but also builds on our thoughts and actions in real life. This potential to build on thinking and processes of reflecting about the self through the experiences made in virtual therapy particularly fascinated us, and we also desired to push the 'tool' boundary further into contemporary possibilities with new media. The idea of a virtual reality process in art therapy is an exploration space of images (Neumann 1998; Schütz 2002), meaning we are dealing with experimental interactions, reconstructions and extensions of image reception, all of which have the potential to influence inner worlds and change rigid behavior patterns. There is still very little previously published research on art therapy strategies and processes with virtual reality.

The concept of Second Life, an online virtual reality software program used in this art therapeutic treatment, can be compared with Marshall McLuhan's (1992) ideas of dynamics of human communication at the level of experience. McLuhan and Fiore (1967) were concerned with the relationship between how our senses perceive the world and how technological progress changes our mental processes and how we think. He also identified the man-made environment as an extension or prosthesis of the body. In Second Life, one experiences multimodality: sensory experiences in time and space. Within this 3-dimensional depiction one can perceive and be perceived from all angles simultaneously – a virtual proxy is able to rotate on its own axis while the observer simultaneously watches the movements from the outside. When designing a virtual avatar (or 'deputy'), there are many possibilities of the outcome – how the avatar looks includes that it can be withdrawn at any time and be modified again. In the first instance, the avatar is often modelled on conscious and unconscious aspects of the self-image. And in the interactive, stimulated virtual room the avatar can be an alter ego (second self or another self) or even act out a specific ego, thus enabling experiences that can be later transferred to the real world – 'it feels real' (Ehemann 2012).

Participants

Subjects in both inpatient stationary care and outpatient care were able to participate in the study. People in acute stages of illness or suffering with severe schizophrenic symptoms and addiction were excluded. The final selection of subjects was made based on consultation with the attending physicians. The target population was however restricted to the 2 diagnostic groups F3 (depression) and F6 (personality disorders), which are predominantly represented in this clinic, and also to rule out any negative effects on the comparison of results (results would have little comparative validity where there is a lack of a uniform distribution of mental illness).

Procedure

The treatment plan for the process of developing an avatar and specific varied activities in Second Life (SL) included 12 sessions. Over 6 weeks, 2 individual therapies of 90 minutes took place per week.

The initial phase (3 sessions) was designed as an introduction and guide to the digital visual world by designing a self-portrait in Photoshop. All self-images – the digitally manipulated photo and the interactive dynamics of the avatar – provided new possibilities for expressing the self, which stimulates the reflection of body perception.

The second phase involved immersion in the virtual reality Second Life, the design of an avatar and the exploration of the virtual reality (3 sessions). Through the learning of digital techniques and navigation in Second Life, new creative possibilities of the movement and travel (getting around) were tested.

The third phase focused on communicating with other avatars (3 sessions). Behind all avatars were people (patients) with their own communication patterns and real communicative experiences, which characterize the social interaction in the network. The patients were able to test not only existing communication strategies, but also to develop and apply new ones, leading to improved judgment and the detection of shortcomings such as behavioral, unhelpful patterns.

The fourth and final phase was conceived as closure (3 sessions) from this specific art therapy method, concluding with interviews with the patients.

The research study used a triangulation of quantitative and qualitative methods: a combination of different evaluation and test procedures with test questionnaires, drawing methods, observation protocols and semi-structured interviews were applied. Creative art methods included: (1) pre and post body drawings using the draw-a-human test (ZEM by Koppitz 1972, based on the draw-a-person test by Machover 1949) and (2) self-images created with digital media: a) Photoshop revised photographic self-portrait and b) the design of an avatar in the Second Life program itself.

Standardized psychological test methods: the multidimensional mood questionnaire (MDBF, Steyer et al. 1997); multidimensional self-esteem questionnaire (MSWS, Schütz and Sellin 2005); and I-shape test (IGTO, Oehler 2001) were combined with creative methods to keep the sessions varied and the motivation of the subjects maintained over the 12 sessions, as well as to investigate the effects of the avatar self-image, corporeality and gender. Semi-standardized qualitative interviews were conducted before and after the study, including observation protocols of every session that were carried out with the patient (informal survey data on observances, knowledge and experiences of the patient in dealing with virtual reality), which supplemented the results with additional information that could not be generated in the test methods due to the high level of standardization. The interview material was particularly valuable and together with the design of the self (avatar) in the Second Life program is used here to discuss the role(s) gender played amongst the 12 patients.

Results

Of the 12 patients (aged from 18 to 57, mean average = 32.5) who participated in the study, 7 patients (6 females and 1 male) had the diagnosis of major depression (F3)[4], and 5 patients (4 females and 1 male) had been diagnosed with personality disorder (F6)[5]. The patients' actual Second Life avatars (also named) are described and one case is examined in further detail in the discussion.

Patients with depression

1 *Avatar Fiona.* This 39-year-old female patient stayed female with her avatar. She developed more feminine attributes within her Second Life experience. The patient described her avatar as 'strong and down-to-earth', but did not experience the figure as belonging to her at all. For her, the avatar was a kind of fantasy figure in a fantasy world. She found the connection to the computer as something apart, detached from herself, at more of a distance than the pencil, which is simply closer and more familiar as a tool

to use. She felt that the SL experience stole time away that she could have spent painting instead. The test results show however that she made a continuous development, showing a more active, positive attitude towards life. She conveyed more self-confidence and increased contact with reality towards the end of the sessions.

2 *Avatar Spikey*. This 28-year-old female patient changed her gender – her avatar was more non-binary than clear-cut male – both feminine (face, lips) and masculine traits (body form, dress sense) were visible. Spikey later also got a pair of black wings, which made the avatar more of a mythological or fantasy figure than before. In the interview she underlined that the virtual representative was an exaggerated, cute guy type, with wild hair, a bit like the statue of liberty. She 'experienced her avatar as friendly, and as something good and therefore belonging to her'. She recognized the avatar as her own creation – 'when you paint you say it is your picture. That's what I did with the avatar'.

Other test results however indicate the severity of her illness greatly impaired the patient – experiences in SL to boost self-confidence and social activities could only be partially made.

3 *Avatar Pele*. This 31-year-old female patient changed the sex of her avatar. She described him as 'big, strong and attractive'. Pele walked around barefoot in Second Life. She explained that she didn't want to fake anything, it had to be what she likes and comes natural to her – hence as nature is important to her: 'in the unreal world nature continued to be important, and so the contact with the ground and not just going shopping'. She liked being in an unreal world and regarded the avatar as an ideal image, belonging to her, also as part of her identity. She commented that participating in Second Life made her notice the real world more. In Second Life one can simply walk away, without saying goodbye, it's all non-binding – she said she paid more attention to the real world after.

Her parting commentary in the interview was: 'So I think the next time I walk barefoot through the green, my avatar will come to my mind, and then I will smile a bit'. This patient developed a unique gender identity, with a friendly, life-loving facial expression. Generally her results indicate increased vitality and a communicative environment.

4 *Avatar Ramona*. This 55-year-old female patient chose to remain female and described her avatar as being an ideal image of herself: 'as thin as herself, a bit younger-looking in the face' and as realistic as possible. She mentioned that because of the various tasks she had to do (photo collage, avatar design, drawings), she learnt for herself where her capabilities are. Results show hardly any changes after SL therapy – therapeutic measures had little or no impact.

5 *Avatar Louis*. This 18-year-old female patient (the youngest patient) changed her sex. She described her avatar as 'a counterpart, even though he is male'. She considered the avatar as being 'abstract and special – a man

with long hair and purple clothes – though equally part of herself'. She concludes: SL 'has also shown me that in life in general there are always limits somewhere and rules, but that has been more of a positive experience. I think with Louis I did all that I cannot or do not do right now'. Results show a positive therapeutic effect of virtual reality therapy and increased assertion and intensity of living in daily life.

6 *Avatar Ai.* This 30-year-old female kept her sex, but experienced sexism with her first avatar that was based on her own self-image (a woman with an average body build, dark hair with a fringe and light skin, wearing a dark red and white striped pullover and denim dungaree skirt). In a German chat room, a female avatar stated that she 'looked terrible', and sent her clothes and different types of female models to choose from. Ai subsequently transformed her avatar into a 'sex bomb' with 'blond hair, light brown skin, blue eyes, with a lacy dress, sexy, yes really sexy with huge breasts'. From that moment on, she was surprised how others reacted: both women and men had wanted to chat her up. Her process with Second Life was a development and insight into what influences feminism, and the effect sexism has on avatars' behavior. The test results show a significant therapeutic progress and a positive development of her female identity. She became livelier, more agile and began to think about her social interests again.

7 *Avatar JHW01.* This 34-year-old male patient stayed male, but became priest-like, choosing to wear a yellow robe and added yellow bird wings. He described his avatar as an ideal, desired self, as a 'preacher who is looking for disciples in the digital world'. In his opinion: 'he forgot to add the crown to the virtual self ... he should have worn this'. From the SL sessions, this patient took it as a positive experience that he could design a deputy to look as he desired it to be, and a character that he actually would like to channel. The overall results indicate there was no development with this therapy. The patient remained stable, but assumed that no construction of a stable self-image took place.

Patients with personality disorder

8 *Avatar Ivy.* This 30-year-old female patient kept her female gender, but added wings – she wanted the deputy self to be a figure of her fantasy and identified with it as such. She was, however, in conflict with herself because she was afraid of developing a fixation, attachment or addiction to the avatar and said: 'I've tried not to see her as belonging to me, because otherwise I could identify with her, and I do not want that'. Nevertheless, she had a strong identification with her avatar, but the development of her progress within the SL sessions proved positive. She learnt to detach her real self from the fantasy figure she had created. She also learnt that SL is a place where the boundaries between real-time and virtual community are

also blurred. She had discovered and appreciated the 'missing persons-site' in SL where avatars also put up (post) images of their 'real time' missing relatives on walls. Results show overall positive treatment effects of SL therapy. She also learnt what to project of her own personality onto the deputy representation and what not to. She made emotional–affective experiences that also helped her differentiate what she was aiming for in the coming months of her life.

9 *Avatar Leni.* This 34-year-old female patient remained female. She spruced up the avatar to an ideal self-image. In her words: 'She has blond hair and highlights, a beautiful hairstyle, a friendly face, a satisfied face, yes and she is well dressed, well-groomed. And she is relatively slim. She does not carry any life burdens with her'. She went as far as to say: 'I want to be more like her'. The image of the avatar was her wish, desire to be self. In identifying with the avatar, she actually 'dared' more in Second Life – she experienced 'bodily' adventures she had not known in real life to date, such as catapulting herself into the sky and falling back to earth, going deep sea diving, participating in events that were on the spur of the moment available within her Second Life sessions. The other results indicate only a small therapeutic effect of SL therapy. The patient tended to stay 'child-like' though a positive body image development is indicated.

10 *Avatar Buddy.* This 33-year-old female patient let her avatar become male, though it came across as strongly androgynous. She described her deputy as: 'A little bit futuristic, not really real, somehow not easy to classify, not emotional'. She identified with this image as a 'self-parody' with 'a few tendencies that I know about myself, but just a bit exaggerated but not really taken seriously'. Finally she found her figure 'experimental and funny'. The SL was a mixed adventure for her – as she sums it up: 'The positive thing was the curiosity in the beginning'. The hardest was the subject's reported difficulties in contacting and communicating with other avatars. The non-binary[6] gendering of this avatar might have added to the online communication issues. The results suggest SL therapy did not further help this patient with her issues and identity as a woman. Self-esteem did not improve. Only in communication was there a positive development.

11 *Avatar Modell.* This oldest male patient (57 years old) did a gender swap – he wanted a sexy, appealing female opposite in Second Life. He consciously exaggerated the deputy image to be just like the 'very beautiful woman in my head. A sex bomb'. He stated that he experienced the avatar to be part of his own identity and bodily self. He found SL and the whole experience therapeutic to be able to live and communicate some of his fantasy, which he would not dare to do, nor speak of in real life. SL therapy proved useful for this patient; he learnt to differentiate in his real-life appearance and showed improved body awareness.

12 *Avatar Gentleman*. This 42-year-old female patient changed her avatar to a male one: 'A man, tall, slim, black hair, dressed sportily elegant'. Her deputy depicts a dream vision, but not as part of herself nor her identity. Her process with the avatar in SL was a positive development, with nice experiences such as dancing in a pair with a woman partner who had been wearing a magical dress. SL therapy was a positive development; her self-esteem increased and her identification with her body image changed for the better.

Within the group of major depression 3 female patients, almost half the group, swapped the gender of their avatar (from female to male). The only male patient in this group kept his gender, but added wings to his avatar. The 3 remaining female patients in this group did not change their gender; however, one of them exaggerated her femaleness (bombshell image) to provoke a new, different experience.

Among the patients with personality disorder, 2 females kept their own gender (though one of them added wings to her avatar), and just over half of the group, 2 women and one male, changed the gender of their avatar, suggesting overall that this group had a stronger desire or more curiosity for gender experimentation. In total, of the 12 participants, 6 patients changed their gender, 4 patients kept their own gender and 2 kept their gender but added wings, making it harder to ascribe to the role gender had.

The collection of the bipolar dimensions of psychological well-being (good/bad mood, alertness/fatigue and calmness/unrest) using the multidimensional mood questionnaire (MDFB) by Steyer et al. (1997) before and after the fourth to ninth session (the actual SL sessions) clearly showed that art therapy in virtual reality generated no destabilizing effects in depressed patients and patients with personality disorders, and the course of therapy brought stabilization and improvement of all mood dimensions with it.

Using the multidimensional self-esteem scale (MSWS) of Schütz and Sellin (2005), an analysis of general and body-related self-esteem in the areas of emotional, social security, attractiveness, athleticism, security in contact and dealing with criticism was collected at the beginning and at the end of the study. The analysis of this test showed that patients with personality disorders performed better in improving the self-esteem than the subjects with major depression. In light of this, a positive impact on self-esteem could only be partially verified with this instrument.

Discussion

One case study is discussed in further detail to illustrate the kind of depth the avatar 'role' had in the individual case studies in SL. Each case was unique. All patients' avatars went through changes in appearance and behavior within the course of the 12 sessions. We felt the selected case study was best suited to be a representative of the entire sample regarding the fact it clearly demonstrates how and why the avatar's appearance and attitude went through a number of stages.

A relapsed depressive disorder (F33.1) was diagnosed in the 30-year-old patient Ai. She was institutionalized because of a serious episode characterized by self-hatred and suicidal thoughts, and increasing deterioration in health. At the beginning of the virtual reality art therapy, the presenting problem was a latent suicide risk with pronounced feelings of inferiority combined with a lack of self-acceptance in her role as a woman in Switzerland, as well as still fighting flashbacks of sexual assault in her childhood in a suppressed cultural background in Turkey. The aim was to strengthen her autonomy with the development of social, emotional and cognitive abilities as well as to support a positive body image and identity as a woman.

The self is and has always been an important topic in art therapy. With images, aspects of the self can be made vivid and visible, and thus be given to reflection. According to Titze (2008), pictures represent a 'protection to make an unbearable experience out of oneself and to distance oneself' (ibid. 103). Therefore, images that are created on the virtual level visualize parts of the self and set self-identification and the detachment processes in motion. Avatars are particularly suitable for this process. They have a strong share of unconscious and conscious processes of self-representation. In addition, they not only make the self appear visible in the form of an 'alter ego', but also let this alter ego act out. The virtual world can thus be an intermediate area for interactive trial action, which can be transferred to the real world. The advantages lie in being allowed to act uncensored and without 'real' consequences. This can however be a disadvantage, as it often cannot be continued under real conditions while observing the rules in force there. (Ehemann 2012).

Motivated and interested, in the fourth session, the patient Ai began to design an avatar that corresponded to her actual appearance. At the beginning of the session, she was impatient whenever she could not find a command in the SL menu immediately. She chose the name Ai for her Avatar – Japanese for love. Femininity is expressed quite strongly in her design, for example, by the choice of long hair, short skirt and suggested breasts. She took a critical look at her appearance in the fifth session, made her appearance more feminine, applied lipstick and chose a shorter skirt. The patient reported that she did not experience the avatar as part of her identity, but as a stranger with whom she could 'play and try things out'.

In the sixth session, she went to a clothes store and bought designer clothes. She projected her ideals of an aesthetic appearance onto the avatar, which she changed rapidly, and thus tried different female images. Her female identity was strengthened through the experiments with attractive female roles.

In an interview at the end of the 12 sessions, Ai said she preferred the classical art therapy materials, as these triggered emotions through their tactile qualities, when painting for example. She felt very distant from the computer: 'It's an object that I use'. She did not experience the avatar as part of her identity, but rather as a kind of desire. In the reflection of the therapy process, she stated that in the virtual reality she had 'virtually forgotten' that she was 'inside'. But what caused her emotionality in the virtual reality was: 'Because of the contact, the reactions and the funny things', she enjoyed it that people were around her and 'what all happens there'. She stated that because of the change in the appearance of her avatar, 'a woman with blond hair, light brown skin, blue eyes, a lacy dress, sexy, yes really sexy with huge breasts', many more men and even women responded to her, which with the first avatar (average-looking woman based on her own self-image) was not the case. And when she took the initiative to speak to someone, she came into direct contact and got more attention than with her previous avatar.

Despite the ambivalence with the new media and her avatar, Ai clearly enjoyed the successes she achieved through the avatar's feminine look. The therapist assessed Ai's communicative contact with other people as the first way out of isolation – a strategy that should be further promoted for the benefit of sustainability. As the sessions progressed, the patient increasingly opened up to the therapist. The therapist was faced with the challenge of assessing when the Virtual Reality was to be applied or constrained in order to maintain the relationship and achieve the therapeutic goals (Carlton 2014).

For patient Ai, the computer provided low-threshold access to creative work. It quickly led to a success story in that the pressure to prove something decreased and motivation increased (McNiff 2000). Because Ai suffered from self-hatred and suicide, the sensory stimulating, therapeutically effective environment in Virtual Reality gave her the feeling of the present, the here and now. She gained autonomy and self-efficacy, that is, it gave her the experience of being an active agent of herself. (Difede, Hoffman and Laysinghe 2002). She gained a freedom to explore and be playful with gender roles and broke out of the repressed woman role, at least online. From the therapeutic point of view, the virtual environment is a 'potential space' (Winnicott 1979), an area of self-play between subjectivity and objectivity, of experiencing and connecting both internal and external realities where boundaries are learned and interpretations are not imposed, but are potentially available (Diedrich 2014).

Conclusion

The majority of the patients who participated in acting in a virtual world, that is within a protected area with no stigma, showed a stabilization in their positive, emotional well-being. Second Life also enabled patients to experience the self as a visually embodied 'I'. Although the experimental virtual art therapy in Second Life was not limited to pure roles of gender, the results indicate a surprisingly large majority of role reversals of various kinds. Because 'gender' was one of the changeable possibilities whilst creating one's avatar, it became one of the ways in which identity and roles, in relation to each other, could be considered – and which led to differentiated outcomes.

Predatory or overly sexual responses hadn't occurred in these sessions. This may in part be an effect of the different time zones globally – most sessions took place between 10am and 4pm in Switzerland whereas in the USA (often regular participants in SL), it was still only between 4am and 10am in New York. Peak time is evening. Also, if one didn't like how the conversation was going or had become bored, the engaged avatar was more likely to beam him/herself away or simply go 'afk', which means 'away from keyboard'. In uncomfortable situations it was easy to 'afk' to escape reality. What did however occur on a few odd occasions was the appearance of sudden images, either dark and sinister or ghostly images, or very graphic genital images that suddenly took over an area in the fore- or background of the screen where the avatar was or heading to.

In the depressed patients in the study, the virtual proxy was not just a fantasy figure, but also an embodiment of an ideal image to which they could transfer substantial amounts of their own self. Therapy with Second Life aided in the development of identity. Although the subjects with personality disorders give their virtual representatives more weight, they involved their deputies in more playful ways, i.e. they looked at their avatars as an opportunity to try out identities, allocated them with imagination and role play and could also often distance themselves from their avatars as well. The results are striking because they show that gender roles are not reduced to the normal, average male–female duality, but consist of a variety of nuances that can affect how one can regard and discuss gender.

Although it has been suggested that online-mediated communication can lead to depersonalization and fragmented identities (Herring 1993), this research shows that the subjects adapted to the virtual environment as if it were an extension of their self, as a kind of digital 'phantom limb' (Turkle 2011). By virtue of the fact that the virtual space is fluid per se, rigid genre attributions and schema dissolve. This leads to more flexibility in one's own gender perceptions. In virtual reality we transform into 'fluid subjects' (Volkart 2006). This can be specifically used in art therapy to soften rigid or suppressed gender ideas as well as set thinking and performing.

Notes

1 Psychiatrie St. Gallen Nord, Switzerland.
2 Psychiatrie St. Gallen Nord, Switzerland.
3 Ehemann, R. (2012) Virtual Reality Therapy. Entwicklung, Durchführung und Evaluation eines Applikationsmodells für die kunsttherapeutische Arbeit mit psychiatrischen Patienten. Regensburg: S. Roderer Verlag.
4 Listed as case studies 1 to 7.
5 Listed as case studies 8 to 12.
6 Non-binary defined by the Oxford Dictionary denotes or relates to a gender or sexual identity that is not defined in terms of traditional binary oppositions such as male and female or homosexual and heterosexual.

References

Butler, J. (1990) *Gender Trouble*. New York: Routledge.
Carlton, N. R. (2014) Digital culture and art therapy. *The Arts in Psychotherapy*, 41(1): 41–45.
Diedrich, L. (2014) Graphic analysis: Transitional phenomena in Alison Bechdel's Are You My Mother? *Configurations*, 22(2): 183–203.
Difede, J., Hoffman, H. & Laysinghe, N. (2002) Innovative use of virtual reality technology in the treatment of PTSD in the aftermath of September 11. *Multimedia Reviews, Psychiatry Services*, 53(9): 1083–1084. Accessed August 26, 2011 at: http://www.psychservices.psychiatryonline.org
Ehemann, R. (2012) *Virtual Reality Therapy. Entwicklung, Durchführung und Evaluation eines Applikationsmodells für die kunsttherapeutische Arbeit mit psychiatrischen Patienten*. Regensburg: S. Roderer Verlag.
Hartwich, P. & Brandecker, R. (1997) Computer based art therapy with inpatients: Acute and chronic schizophrenics and borderline cases. *The Arts in Psychotherapy*, 24(4): 367–373.
Herring, S. (1993) Gender and democracy in computer mediated communication. *Electronic Journal of Communication*, 3(2).
Koppitz, E. (1972) *Die Menschdarstellung in der Kinderzeichnung und ihre psy-chologische Auswertung*. Stuttgart: Hippocrates Verlag.
Kuleba, B. (2008) The Integration of Computerized Art Making as a Medium in Art Therapy Theory and Practice. A thesis submitted to the Faculty of Drexel University, Hahnemann Creative Arts in Therapy Program. Philadelphia.
Machover, K. (1949) *Personality Projection in the Drawing of the Human Figure*. Springfield, IL: C. C. Thomas.
Markus, H. & Wurf, E. (1987) The dynamic self-concept: A social psychological perspective. *Ann. Re. Psychol.*, 38: 299–337.
McLeod, C. (1999) Empowering creativity with computer-assisted art therapy: An introduction to available programs and techniques. *Art therapy: Journal of the American Art Therapy Association*, 16(4): 201–205.
McLuhan, M. (1992) *Die magischen Kanäle: Understanding Media*. Dusseldorf: Neuauflage.
McLuhan, M. & Fiore, Q. (1967) *The Medium is the Message*. London: Routledge.
McNiff, S. (2000) Computers as virtual studios. In: Malchiodi, C. A. (ed.), *Art Therapy and Computer Technology. A Virtual Studio of Possibilities*. Philadelphia: Jessica Kingsley, 87–99.
Neumann, E. (1998) Kognitive Grundlegungen für integrative Kunst/Gestaltung-stherapie und Imaginationsverfahren*Musik, Tanz- und Kunsttherapie*, 9. Göttingen: Hogrefe, 124–146.
Oehler, K. T. (2001) *Der Ich-Gestalt-Test IGTO*. Göttingen: Hogrefe.
Orr, P. (2005) Technology media: An exploration for "inherent qualities". *The Arts in Psychotherapy*, 32(1): 1–11.
Orr, P. (2015) Art therapy and digital media. In: Rosal, M. L. & Gussak, D. E. (eds), *Wiley-Blackwell Handbook of Art Therapy*. New York: Wiley-Blackwell, 188–197.
Parker-Bell, B. (2001) Computer visions. In: Kossolapow, L., Scoble, S. & Waller, D. (eds), *Arts-Therapies-Communication*. Munster: LIT-Verlag, 310–131.
Schütz, N. (2002) *Im Explorationsraum der Bilder. Emotionszentrierte Kunstthera-pie. Psychologische Grundlagen und Perspektiven*. Fahretoft: Books on Demand.
Schütz, A. & Sellin, I. (2005) *MSWS. Mehrdimensionale Selbstwertskala*. Göttingen: Hogrefe.

Steyer, R., Schwenkmezger, P., Notz, P. & Eid, M. (1997) *Der mehrdimensionale Be-findlichkeitsfragebogen (MDBF)*. Göttingen: Hogrefe.

Titze, D. (2008) Wir selbst sind der Ort unserer Bilder. In: Titze, D. (ed.) *Die Kunst der Kunst Therapie. Resonanz und Resilienz, Band 4*. Dresden: Michel Sandstein, 96–104.

Turkle, S. (2011) *Alone Together: Why We Expect More from Technology and Less from Each Other*. New York: Basic Books.

Volkart, Y. (2006) *Fluide Subjekte. Anpassung und Widerspenstigkeit in der Medienkunst*. Bielefeld: Transcript Verlag.

Winnicott, D. W. (1979/2002) *Vom Spiel zur Kreativität*. Stuttgart: Klett Cotta Verlag.

Concluding note

To conclude, it is imperative that a socially aware arts therapy acknowledges distress with reference to the cultural norms that produce it. In my chapter (and other works), I have given pregnancy and motherhood as an example of an arena that is very contested (and therefore is a field which is unstable and destabilising). I have argued that this 'field instability' is affecting and inherently dislocating and that addressing the distress brought with these concepts in mind will help arts therapists from reinforcing entrenched ideas about female inadequacy or instability, which are inherently anti-therapeutic and which consolidate subjugation. But gender too, as the introduction attests, is itself contested terrain. Braithwaite and Orr suggest that 'gender nonconformity is often viewed as threatening to social institutions' and this is another area of tension (2017, p.181). I have attempted to theorise why this is. Ambiguity can be disconcerting. Ostentatious difference may be particularly threatening, but I suggest that gender always has to be negotiated and subject to variable tensions, because it is subject to variable pressures and constraints, through different and competing gender styles being operational. Gendered subjects are constituted through social relations and so the regulation of gender is always going to be an important aspect of our human flourishing or floundering.

Reference

Braithwaite, A. & Orr, C. A. 2017. *Everyday Women's & Gender Studies. Introductory Concepts*. London: Routledge.

Index

abject gender 188, 229, 238
abnormality 244
Abrahams, H. 63
abstract and metaphorical 75–76
abstract intelligence 154
abstract representation 77
abuse 4, 9, 22, 37, 41, 55–59, 61–67, 126, 169, 181, 213; abusers 70
academia: academic ghettos 170; academics 185; academic work 182; academic writing 3
acceptance 18, 20, 64, 83, 123, 152–153, 160, 200, 207–208, 211, 217, 242
acceptance and commitment therapy (ACT) 157
accessing: services 229; therapy 71, 183, 243
achievement 11, 38, 82, 97, 161, 178, 216–217, 234, 256
achieving 110, 115, 217
ACT *see* acceptance and commitment therapy (ACT)
action 43, 115, 116, 124, 127–129, 160, 167, 235, 243, 255
action empathy 127–129
actions 27, 31, 43, 56, 58, 105, 110, 113, 248
activism: activist agenda 65; activist approach 113; activists 58, 185
adaptation 153, 157
addiction 215, 218, 249, 252; addicts 210
adjustment: disorders 130; to motherhood 97; to parental demands 212
adolescence 30, 94, 152, 210, 213; adolescent 94, 126, 210, 213–214, 219–220
adults 22, 70, 213; adulthood 243; adult play 200
advocacy 27, 32, 66, 182; advocates 11, 31, 66, 181, 200

aesthetic appearance 255
aesthetic qualities 103
aesthetic standards 41
affirmation 110, 114, 178, 197; affirming practices 32, 33; affirming work environments 32
ageing 234
agender 28
aggression 58, 71, 141, 178, 218, 223, 237, 243
Ahessy, B. 42
Aigen, K. 41
alienation 30
aligning: with sex assigned at birth 29; with minority 31; with an idol 233, 235, 243
Allegranti, B. 123
alliance 126, 134, 177, 182–183
allies 27, 30–32
allopathic medical model 37
alter egos 249, 255
Alvin, J. 40
ambiguity 62, 63, 66, 123, 229, 260
amenorrhoea 216
amyotrophic lateral sclerosis 152
anal sex 175, 176
anatomy 27
androcentrism 66
androgyny 11, 29, 126, 133, 134, 253
anger 19, 97, 105, 106, 141
Anima 129, 131, 132, 134; *see also* Animus; Jung
Animus 129, 131, 132, 134; *see also* Jung
anorexia 210–214, 217, 219–220
ante-natal and post-natal care 90, 95–96; provision 91, 103–104
anthropography 167
anthropology 3, 10, 92, 101–102, 139
antifemininity 178

anti-feminism 58; anti-feminist groups 185; anti-feminist turn in men's movement 177
anxiety 55, 64, 71, 93–94, 105, 107, 124, 181, 183, 213, 218, 234, 237
Aristotle 149, 153
art *see specific types*
art-based parental interventions 72
art-based support groups 96
art-based therapies 220
art-installation 102
art-making techniques 92
arts interventions 96
arts therapies 3–4, 9, 42–43, 138, 142, 188, 214
arts therapists 3, 4, 8, 214, 244, 260
artwork 107, 220
asexual 11, 23, 24
assessment 10, 32, 42, 63, 85, 96, 117, 213, 215–217, 256
assigning 27
assimilation 8
asylum seekers 56
athletes 152, 155; athleticism 254
attraction 24, 26, 27, 30
attractiveness 251, 254–255
attunement 214, 228
authenticity 215
autism 40
autobiography 150, 154, 198
auto-ethnography 149–151
autonomy 20, 78, 236, 237, 255, 256
autopathography 167
avatars 10, 247–257

babies 78, 97, 105, 107, 142–143
Bain, C. 33
Baines, D. 41
balance 47–48, 85, 104, 121, 123, 132, 134, 153, 162, 197, 199, 219
Bales interaction process analysis 216
Bardot, Brigitte 195
barriers: to equality 7; to participation 67; social 44
Bat Or, M. 70, 74
battleground 13, 108, 136, 208
beauty 152, 197, 212, 213, 219, 240
Beecham 59
behaviour 12, 26, 39, 44, 71, 248, 252, 254; behavioural disorders 150, 152, 161
being-man 6
being-woman 6
bereavement 198

bi *see* bisexual
bias 32–33, 43, 46, 72; biased interpretation of outcomes 37; biased psychological theories 37; biases 30, 40
bigender 12, 28
binaries 112, 244
binary 4, 6, 8, 10, 12, 23, 27–30, 39–41, 44, 111, 112, 117, 167, 176, 219, 229, 248
Binet 154
binge-eating 211
biological sex 3, 4, 8, 41, 124, 129
biology 3, 174
biomedical explanations 8
biomedical sciences 44
biphobia 12, 112, 114
biphobic and transphobic harassment 110
bipolar 254
birth 23, 27–29, 85, 93–98, 105, 107, 111, 155
birthing event 92
birthing experience 98
birthing experience 96
birthing experiences 98
birthing professionals 90, 105, 107
birthing professionals 98
birthing room 105
birth project 10, 90–92, 99, 101, 103, 104
bisexual 11–12, 23–24, 26–27, 30, 32, 42, 110, 125, 172
blurring of the boundary 60
BMI *see* body mass index (BMI)
BN *see* bulimia nervosa (BN)
body: bodily engagement 102; bodily practices 9; bodily symptoms 91, 103, 104; body language 121, 127, 131, 218; body–mind balanced 153; body-oriented therapy 126–127; body parts 77, 122; body perception 249; body psychotherapy 128, 137, 145; body-reflexive practices 174; body-related self-esteem 254; body-self 139, 141, 142, 239
body mass index (BMI) 210, 213, 216–218, 221–222; normal BMI 210; normal body mass 221; normal body weight 222
Bohemian Rhapsody 231–235
bombshell image 254
borderlands 239, 240
botox 188
boundaries 56, 60, 112, 114, 173, 192, 194, 216, 237, 248, 252, 256
Brah, A. 149
brain organisation theory 7

brain scan technology 153
Brannon, R. 177–180
Brazil 171; Brazilian culture 171
breasts 12, 189, 240, 252, 255–256; breastfeeding 95, 106
breathing 141
bridging 15, 110, 173, 182, 237
Brison, S. 58
Britzman, D. 112, 113, 115, 116
Brody, L. R. 124, 125, 127
Brophy-Dixon, J. 63
Bruscia, K. 40, 41
Buber, M. 216
bulimia nervosa (BN) 210–214, 220
Bunt, L. 41
burrnesha, of northern Albania 29
Butler, J. 4, 41, 162, 228, 233

Callaghan, J. E. M. 171, 178–179, 187
calm 18, 20, 60, 107, 178; calming 61; calmness 18, 254
cameras 97, 165, 172, 192, 195–197, 200, 207, 240
Campbell, J. 169
Canada 39, 42, 70, 166
cancer 167, 169, 233
canvas 139, 228
capabilities 157, 169, 251
capacity 41, 82, 93, 99, 155, 156, 243
capitalism 39, 153, 168, 176
care 22, 32, 34, 37–38, 42, 91, 97, 106, 194, 237–238, 249; see also caring
Carel, H. 235
caring 63, 82, 96, 110, 123, 243; caregivers 83
case studies 230, 235
Castoriadis, C. 5, 6
castration 175
catalysts 116, 242
categories 23–24, 26–27, 47, 74, 75, 82, 112, 114, 129–130, 161, 171, 175; categorisation 17, 111
catharsis 63–64, 201, 218
C-Change 38
celebrity 188, 234, 243
challenges 5, 9, 22–23, 33, 58, 75, 91–93, 101, 111–113, 116, 128, 155, 168, 182, 188–191, 199, 240, 256
challenging: binary 8; hegemony 114; predominant ideas 162; status quo 48; systems of interpretation 6
change 5, 16, 20, 43, 46, 48, 58, 71, 110, 111, 114, 115, 125, 141, 150, 154, 161, 167, 175, 176, 196, 200, 233, 234, 247, 248, 254, 256; change agents 31
changes: in appearance 254; in gender 254; in personal relationships 57; in sexual drive 124; in sexual orientation identity 26; in symbolic practices 5
characteristics 5, 18–19, 22, 27, 29, 92, 111, 112, 124, 156, 159, 172, 179, 211, 212, 218, 223
Charmaz, K. 235
chastity 29
chat room 252
check-ups 79, 216
Cher 188
childhood 19, 27, 29–30, 34, 40, 70–82, 84–85, 92–94, 103–104, 107, 124, 138–139, 141–144, 152, 154, 162, 198, 202, 212–213, 237, 255
childcare see child-rearing
child-rearing 73, 84, 143
children see childhood
child-self 199
choice 12, 18, 34, 57, 78, 79, 210, 231, 248, 255
chromosomes 12, 27, 111, 150
chronic illness 228, 235–236
Chronic Obstructive Pulmonary Disease (COPD) 237
chronic schizophrenia 128
cisgender 12, 23–24, 28–31
classification 111, 156
clay 10, 70–72, 74, 81–84
clichés 190
clinically related birth practices 91, 104
clothes see clothing
clothing 12, 27, 29–30, 103, 122, 138, 143, 199–200, 252, 255; see also dress
Coates, R. 95
Cobbett, S. 46
co-counselling 10, 177
code of ethics 110
code of practice 110, 117
coercion 56; coercive behaviour 56, 67
cognition 158, 159; cognitive abilities 154, 255; cognitive neuroscience brain organisation theory 7; cognitive reflection 102; cognitive therapies 126
collage 229, 236, 251
colonialism 171
communities 11, 22–25, 28, 30–33, 37, 40, 42–43, 91–93, 101, 110–113, 171, 188, 190–191, 193, 247, 252

competence 38, 43, 115; competencies 42, 111
computers 247, 250, 255, 256
computer-stimulated 3–dimensional environment 248
confidence 61, 82, 90, 96, 103, 105, 128, 207–208, 217–218
conflict 6, 65, 252; conflict resolution 98, 216
conforming 12, 23, 30, 105
confrontation 83, 115, 234
Connell, R. 5, 10, 165–167, 169–171, 174, 176–178, 180–182
consciousness 5, 15, 39, 83, 93, 114–116; consciousness-raising 182
contextualisation 16, 39, 184
continuous development 251
continuum: of sexed bodies 6, 124; of sexual behaviour 24, 26, 28
convergent production 158, 159
cooperation 216–217
COPD *see* Chronic Obstructive Pulmonary Disease (COPD)
coping: mechanisms 133; strategies 130
Cornish, S. 4, 84, 101, 132
counselling 142, 165, 170, 198; counsellors 142, 145, 165
counter-hegemony 116; *see also* Gramsci, A.; hegemony
counter-transference 114, 193
Cowie, E. 93
Crawford, P. 101
creativity 116, 149, 151–152, 158–159, 162, 192, 200, 214–215; creation myth 29; creation process 173; creative methods 250; creative possibilities 249; creative potential 192; creative practice as mutual recovery 101; creative process 215, 220; creative tasks 230; creative writing 10, 160, 161
Crenshaw, K. 149
criminal justice system 71, 171
crisis of manhood 181
cross-cultural variations 3, 144–145
cross-dressers 8, 12
Crowe, b. J. 33
culture 3–5, 8, 9, 10, 24–29, 32–33, 37–39, 42–43, 48, 93, 106, 112–115, 121, 124, 125, 128, 149, 153, 155, 171–172, 176, 179, 184–185, 188, 191; culture-based norms 38; culture-change strategies 38

cures 66, 143
curiosity 253, 254
Curtis, S. 41–42, 45, 84

Damasio, A. 124–125
dance 1, 10, 81, 101, 119, 121, 123, 126–130, 133, 134, 139, 140, 143; *see also* dance movement therapy
dance movement therapy (DMT) 3, 119, 121, 126–128, 130, 133–134; dance movement therapists 10, 121, 126–130, 134
Darwin, C. 153, 154; *see also* natural selection
D'Augelli, A. R. 30–31
David, D. 177–180
deaf 152, 197
dealing: with criticism 254; with imperfections 82; with sensitive subject matter 91; with virtual reality 250
death 4, 94, 144, 156, 157, 175, 205, 232, 242
de-centering identity 117
deconstruction 74, 94, 103, 112, 117, 167, 176–177, 182
dementia 34
denial 37, 63, 157, 177, 242
de-pathologising women's experiences 94
dependency 212
depersonalization 257
depression 93, 94, 220, 223, 237, 249, 250, 254
descriptors 27, 101
desire 189
destabilising 94, 254, 260
detachment 255
determinism 124
diagnosis 23, 94–95, 210, 212, 214, 220, 230, 233, 235–237, 243, 250, 255
Diagnostic and Statistical Manual of Mental Disorders (DSM–5) 211; *see also* DSM–4
dieting *see* extreme dieting; fasting
Dilley, P. 116
disclosure 57, 67, 114, 125, 179
discomfort 9, 84, 106, 121, 141, 257
discourse 10, 16, 55, 92, 98, 111–115, 117, 136, 188, 226
discrimination 5, 37, 150, 176, 248
disease 38, 152, 188, 212, 230, 231, 233, 235, 237
disempowerment 9, 41, 97, 105, 150, 152, 161

disenfranchised 235
disgust 175
disillusion 104
dismantling: hegemonic masculinity 166, 172, 178
disruption 175, 181, 228, 237
dissatisfaction: about gender roles 3; dissatisfaction with one's own body 212, 219
distancing 75, 95
distortion 93, 223; distorted gender identities 228; distorted image 157, 219
diversity 5, 9, 33, 38, 41, 110, 112, 113, 175, 192, 195, 244
divorce 212
DMT *see* dance movement therapy (DMT)
domestic violence 55–59, 61–67
Donnenwerth, A. 31
Douglas, M. 4, 5
drag 8
dramatherapy 110–113, 114–117, 140–142
draw-a-human test 250
draw-a-person test 250
drawing 16, 17, 20, 78, 250–251
dress 29, 143, 190, 202, 233, 240, 251–254, 256
dresses 143
dressy 207
drugs 37; drug abusers 70
DSM-4 130
DSM-5 *see* Diagnostic and Statistical Manual of Mental Disorders (DSM-5)
dysphoria 23, 29

eating: behaviour 211; disorders 167, 169, 210–211, 213–215, 217–221, 223–227; disturbances 211; *see also* anorexia; bulimia nervosa (BN); extreme dieting; fasting
EBL *see* emerging body language (EBL)
economic influences 111
economic oppression 171
economic position 9
economic status 67
Edelman, L. 115
EDT *see* ethnodramatherapy (EDT)
Edwards, J. 41, 43, 45, 47
effectiveness: of treatment 210, 214, 220
effeminate 112, 176
Eisenberg, M. E. 22
emancipation 39, 44, 63, 65–67, 113–115, 119

embodiment 55, 61, 133, 141, 171, 174, 235, 257
Embodiment-Projection-Role (EPR) 141
emerging body language (EBL) 216–217, 219
EMOSS *see* emotional state scale (EMOSS)
emotion 73, 80, 216, 242, 243; emotional–affective experiences 253; emotional association 104; emotional catharsis 64; emotional constriction 165; emotional control 179; emotional deficit 211; emotional difficulty 171; emotional disclosure 179; emotional distress 94; emotional empathy 127, 128; emotional expression 71, 171; emotionality 179, 256; emotional self 221, 223; emotional support 106, 237
emotional state scale (EMOSS) 215, 223
empathy 10, 56, 63, 67, 123, 125–129, 196, 243
empiricism 42, 59, 154, 156, 167, 248
empower 33, 116, 160, 176
empowerment 16, 39, 44, 150, 157, 161, 182, 184
enactments: of masculinity or femininity 3
endocrinology 6
environment 6, 32, 44, 93, 105, 121, 129, 154–158, 160, 173, 177, 194, 211, 215–216, 218, 243, 248–249, 251, 256–257; environmental and biological factors 31; environmental factors 124
epidemiology 44, 58–59
epistemology 66, 67
EPR *see* Embodiment-Projection-Role (EPR)
ergo-therapists 165
escapism 178
essentialism: essentialist notions of self and other 113; essentialist practices 114; essential masculinity or femininity 9
estrogen 188
ethical frameworks 43, 65, 216
ethical practice 64, 110–111, 192
ethics of care 57, 63
ethnicity 9, 17, 67, 115, 150, 151, 170, 178
ethnodramatherapy (EDT) 116–117
ethno-mimesis 57
exaggeration: of sex differences 219
exclusion 46, 72
exhibitions 103–104, 190
existentialism 156–157, 234
Exley, C. 242
expressiveness of the body 131
extreme dieting 211; *see also* fasting

failure 16, 178, 235
false binary: of fe/male 44
false opposite 41
family 9, 17, 24, 30, 56, 57, 66, 67, 70, 76, 81, 107, 111, 138, 143, 144, 151, 152, 155, 165, 171, 176, 183, 211–213, 215–217, 220
family albums 183, 195, 197–198
fantasy: figure 250–252, 257; role 138; world 250
fashion 155, 212, 218
fasting 212, 219
father–child relationship 73–74, 83
fatherhood 70, 74, 83
Fausto-Sterling, A. 8
fear 63, 107, 114, 125, 140, 141, 173, 183, 197, 218, 233, 236, 242; of ageing 195; of freedom 116; of making mistakes 82
femaleness 138, 145, 254; feminine attributes 250; feminine characteristics 179; feminine self 243; feminine traits 124, 126, 133; femininity 3–6, 8–9, 12, 123, 131, 134, 175–178, 240, 243, 255
female-to-male transgender or transsexual person (FTM/F2M) 12
feminism 40, 41, 44, 58, 66, 113, 114, 170, 172, 181, 182, 184, 185, 244, 252; feminist perspectives 39, 41; feminist philosophy 56, 123; feminist phototherapy 182; feminist politics 63; feminist practices 44; feminist principles 58; feminist research 15, 69; feminist sociology 16; feminist studies 23; feminist theory 10, 20, 39–41, 123, 174, 176, 182, 185; feminist thought 59; feminist writers 184
feminization 71, 175
femminello 29
Fenner, P. 63
fieldwork 10, 139–140, 143, 151
figure-sculpting 70
filmmaking 91–92
Finley, S. 66
Fiore, Q. 248
Fisher-Turk, E. 167
flexibility 153, 156, 159, 177, 257
fluctuation: of gender 111; of selfhood 9, 219
fluidity, sexual 23, 26, 27, 31, 33, 38
foetus 124; foetal development 7
folk-tales 7
food 57, 211–213, 219

Foucault, M. 5, 6, 27
frameworks 23, 39–40, 59, 64–65, 82, 90, 103, 112, 116–117, 169, 180
Frank, A. 66
freedom programme 61, 62
Freire, P. 113, 114, 116
Freud, L. 232
Freud, S 139, 174, 175; Freudian slips 190; Freudian theories 175; *see also* Oedipus complex
Fryrear, J. L. 166
FTM *see* female-to-male transgender or transsexual person (FTM/F2M)
F2M *see* female-to-male transgender or transsexual person (FTM/F2M)

Gardner, H. 152, 154–158, 160
gay 12, 23–24, 27, 30–31, 42, 110, 112–114, 120–121, 169, 172, 176, 181
gaze 61–62, 72, 85, 200, 240
Gehart, D. R. 130, 131
gender: balance 47, 85; behaviour 112, 133; bias 72; binary 10, 12, 23, 27–29; conceptualisations of 6, 9; differences 6, 30, 60, 80, 121, 124, 160, 184, 229; discrimination 248; diversity 9, 110; expression 12–13, 23, 29, 30, 38, 111, 114, 132; formation 175; gap 39; identification 12; incongruence 3; nonconformity 22, 28, 29, 35, 110, 117, 260; norms 4, 9, 12, 28, 44, 124, 153, 160; oppression 37, 150; research 170; stereotypes 3, 8, 155, 160, 162; switching 248; theory 3, 38; traits 126; unicorn 25, 27; variance 12, 28, 30, 34; *see also* gender fluidity; gender fuck; gendered identity; gender-neutral language 42; genderqueer; gender roles; genders; gender-straight
gender fluidity 9, 12, 38, 111
gender fuck 12
gendered identity 3–4, 9–13, 22–25, 27–30, 32–34, 38, 41, 71, 111, 114–115, 119, 121–134, 161–162, 167, 168, 175, 176, 228, 243, 251; gendered behaviours 154; gendered bodies 4, 8
gender-neutral language 42
genderqueer 12, 28, 30
gender roles 3, 4, 7, 27, 29, 30, 70, 73–76, 80, 82, 122, 124, 125, 247–248, 256, 257
genders 12, 24, 27–29, 38, 111, 229

gender-straight 12
generalisation: about gender differences 160, 184
generational differences 75–76
genes 6, 124, 212; gene expression 7; genetic influence 6; genetic inheritance 154; genetic makeup 122; genetic predispositions 212; genetic sex 7
genitalia 12
genograms 168
genomics 8
geographical contexts 5
geographical location 9, 184, 185
geopolitical position 150–151
gerontology 188, 190–191
gestures 123, 129, 139, 200
ghost fathers 72, 86
gluttony 219
GNC *see* gender: nonconformity
Goodridge, K. 168, 190
Gramsci, A. 116, 169
Greer, G. 195
Griffin, P. 31
Grzanka, P. 33
guided imagery 41; and music 40
Guilford, P. 158, 159
Guillemin, M. 91
guilt 95, 104, 106, 213
Gull, W. W. 212
Gussak, D. 235
gynaecology 142

Hadley, S. 41–43, 45, 47
Hahna, N. 41
hair 29, 189, 195, 207, 240, 251–256; *see also* wigs
Hall, S. 93
Hallford, S. 102
Hammonds, E. 9
happiness 207
harassment 110
Hardiman, R. 31
Harding, S. 55–56, 59, 66
harm avoidance 212
Harrison, G. 41
hate speech 25, 28, 32–33
Hawking, Stephen 152
HCPC *see* Health and Care Professions Council (HCPC)
healers 139, 143–144
healing: healing practice 144; healing professions 175; healing séances 143

Health and Care Professions Council (HCPC) 104
health: practitioners 4; research 37, 72
Hearn 55, 58, 59
hegemony 5, 6, 9, 93, 114, 161, 169–170, 177; hegemonic femininity 123; hegemonic gender relations 5; hegemonic knowledge 115; hegemonic masculinity 165–167, 169–172, 175, 178–184, 186; systems of power 117
hermeneutic approaches 74
Hesse-Biber, S. 113, 115
hetero-normativity 8, 42, 112–114; hetero-normalising practices 114; heteronormative systems 116
hetero-patriarchal norms 9
heterosexism 181
heterosexuality 12, 23, 24, 26–27, 29–32, 42, 70, 113–114, 119, 121, 126, 130, 172, 177, 181, 257
Hogan, S. 4, 5, 72, 84, 102, 132, 165, 168, 170, 175, 180, 182, 184, 185
homebirths 106
homosexualities 114
homophobia 12, 110, 112, 114, 175, 181, 233; homonegative expression 112; homonegative remarks 114
homosexuality 12, 23, 26, 113, 117, 130, 171, 175–176, 233, 257
hormone profile 27
hormone treatments 29
humour 19, 190, 237, 240–241
Husserl, E. 228
Hyde, J. S. 26
hypno-birth 106–107

iatrogenic 10, 94–97, 103, 104
ideals 188, 212, 219, 251–253, 257; about childbirth 107; of hegemonic masculinity 171, 179; about parenting 10
identification 12, 39, 75, 133, 184, 193, 231, 234, 252, 254
identifying 11–12, 22, 24, 27–28, 30, 33, 44, 111, 113, 235, 252
identities 4, 8, 9, 10, 22–24, 28, 32–34, 41–42, 111, 113–115, 119, 133, 151, 161, 191, 198, 228, 238, 243, 248, 257
ideologies 113, 175
IGTO *see* I-shape test (IGTO)
illness 10, 38, 66, 94, 143, 144, 228, 229, 233–244, 249, 251
image-making 200

imagination 8, 56, 63, 150, 173, 215, 239, 247, 257; imaginative and sensory representations 57; imaginative experience 248; imaginative exploration of gender 9; imaginative responses to ageing 201; imaginative ways of being 4
imperfections 74, 82–84
imposition of constraining stereotypical expectations 4
impoverished women 15–16
improvised music 40
inappropriate behaviour 210, 216, 218–219
inequality 6, 8, 38, 180, 182, 229, 238
infantilisation 213
inferiority 255
injustice 115
insanity 165
insider and outsider perspectives 59
installation 90, 101, 102, 104
integrative arts therapy 210
interaction: between sex and gender 7; of cultural gender roles 7
interaction process analysis (IPA) 216
intergenerational transmission 71, 73–76, 78–79
interiority 102
International Visual Studies Association (IVSA) 191
interpersonal communication 129; interpersonal conflicts 220; interpersonal relationships 33; interpersonal situations 126, 154; interpersonal therapies 38
intersex 8, 12, 22–24, 27, 28, 31, 110, 111, 189
Intersex Society of North America (ISNA) 22, 27, 35
inter-textual space 93
intervention 43, 71–72, 80–81, 83, 96, 106, 143, 214, 216–217, 228
intimacy 31, 133, 173, 237
intolerance 11, 12
intuition 4, 93, 193, 199, 216
invisibility 234–235
IPA *see* interaction process analysis (IPA)
irony 190
I-shape test (IGTO) 250
ISNA *see* Intersex Society of North America (ISNA)
IVSA *see* International Visual Studies Association (IVSA)

Jackson, B. W. 31
Jagose, A. 112
James, M. R. 45
jargon 112
jewellery 207
jobs 15, 17–20, 151, 152, 238
Jordan-Young, R. M. 7
journeys 24, 117, 205
joy 90, 197, 205–206
judging 97
Jung, C. 129; neo-Jungian theories of masculinity 177
juxtapositions 93, 116

Kahlo, F. 239, 240
Katz-Wise, S. L. 26
Kaylo, J. 129
KBT-therapy 127
Kidman, Nicole 195
Kimmel, M. S. 170, 171, 173, 177–180, 182, 183, 185, 186
kinaesthetic engagements 102
Kinsey, A. C. 26; Kinsey scale 26
knowledge 18, 58–59, 65–66, 91, 102–103, 115, 125, 131, 139, 153, 174, 182, 190, 220, 248, 250
Knowles, C. 102
Konzentrative Bewegungs Therapie *see* KBT-therapy
Kosik, R. 174
Krauss, D. A. 166
Kuda Kepang, of Malaysia 139–140
KwaZulu-Natal 167, 186

Laban movement analysis (LMA) 128–131, 135, 216, 219
labelling 24, 27, 131, 149, 152, 161–162
ladylike behaviour 202
language 4, 32–33, 42, 110, 112, 115, 150, 155–156, 161, 182, 220; language-based approach 98; languages 25, 28, 115, 155
Latin America 171, 172
laughter *see* humour
LBGTs 119
learning: about the self and others 115, 173; or social difficulties 70, 154; self-regulation and acceptance 20
Leatherby, G. 242
Leavy, P. 113, 115
Le Doeuff, M. 63
Lego 230–231, 238–239
lesbian 12, 23–24, 27, 30–31, 42, 110, 113

Letherby, G. 65
LGB 31, 42
LGBA+ communities 24; people 27; youth 27
LGBT 22
LGBTAI+ communities 24
LGBTI 42
LGBTIQ 12
LGBTQ 22, 32–33, 42
LGBTQAI 22–25, 28–34
LGBTQI 42, 110–112, 114, 117
Liebmann, M. 13, 71, 171, 173, 181–185, 237
life threatening and chronic illnesses (LT&CIs) 228–230
Lindegger, G. 167
lived experience 9, 131, 231
LMA *see* Laban movement analysis (LMA)
Loewenthal, D. 165, 167
Lollis, S. 82
loneliness 188, 213
losing control 235
loss 75, 104, 143, 188, 198, 205
love 18, 20, 78, 151, 156, 242, 255
LT&CIS *see* life threatening and chronic illnesses (LT&CIs)
Lyle, R. R. 130, 131

machismo 171–172, 183, 237
Madonna 41, 195
Magos, M. 15
Maguire, M. 125
mainstream culture 114
mainstream masculinity 176
makeup, genetic 197
make-up, cosmetic 29
Malaysia 139, 140, 143–144
male-female binary identification 39
male-female duality 257
maleness 41, 138, 145
male-to-female transgender or transsexual person (MTF/M2F) 13
malnutrition 212, 222
manhood 177, 178, 181
marginalisation 10, 12, 16, 42, 44, 59, 113, 143, 177, 181–182, 233; marginalising strategy 46
masculinity 3–6, 8–9, 12, 121, 128, 131, 134, 149, 165–167, 169–172, 174–185, 240, 243
maternal death 94, 109
maternal mental health 94

McLuhan, M. 248
MDFB *see* multidimensional mood questionnaire (MDFB)
medicine: medical/surgical settings 22; medical conditions 12, 37, 107; medical discourse 188; medical interventions 29, 97; medical models and education 114; medical support 37; medical treatment 94, 142, 226; medication 97, 141
menopause 188
menstruation 124, 144, 210, 216, 218
mental health 9, 22, 71–72, 81, 85, 94, 96, 101, 130, 165, 171, 210, 220; care 70, 229; diagnosis 95; issues 140; problems 94; *see also* mental illness
mental illness 9, 165, 175, 249
men who engage in sex with men (MSM) 13
Meredith, D. 176
metaphor 5, 61–62, 67, 74–76, 83, 91–92, 195, 238
methodology 38, 20, 43, 55–57, 63–64, 85, 92, 101–102, 149, 150, 214
Mexico 172, 239
MI *see* multiple intelligence (MI)
middle age 188
midwifery 98, 105–107, 143–145; and burnout 106
migration 56, 69, 140
mindfulness 48
mirroring 128, 133, 228, 241
mis-representations 190, 234
mixed-media 104
MND *see* motor neuron disease (MND)
modelling 83, 133
money 18, 19
monologues 101, 103
Monro, S. 8, 9, 12
Morris, J. 9
mothers 20, 72–74, 76, 80–81, 93, 97, 104–105, 124, 195, 197, 200, 223, 228, 237, 240–242; *see also* motherhood
motherhood 10, 83, 90, 92, 95, 97–98, 102–105, 260; mothering 103, 197
motivation 96, 149, 214, 250, 256
motor neuron disease (MND) 230–231, 233, 235
moulding 8, 150
Mrevlje, G. 213
MSM *see* men who engage in sex with men (MSM)
MSWS *see* multidimensional self-esteem questionnaire (MSWS)

MTF 28
MTF *see* male-to-female transgender or transsexual person (MTF/M2F)
M2F *see* male-to-female transgender or transsexual person (MTF/M2F)
MTP 45, 47
multidimensional mood questionnaire (MDFB) 254
multidimensional self-esteem questionnaire (MSWS) 250, 254
multiple intelligence (MI) 156–157
Muncey, T. 150
murals 142
Murphy, A. V. 63
Murphy, J. 55
music therapy 10, 1, 3, 22, 23, 29–34, 37–48, 50, 54, 140; gender issues in 41
music traditions, European 40

naivety 40, 139, 153, 155
name 44–46, 247, 255; naming 116
narratives 18, 57, 63, 93, 96, 103–104, 115, 188–189, 196, 198, 200, 205
National Initiative on Gender, Culture, and Leadership in Medicine 38
Native American/First Nation cultures 29
native cultures 171
natural selection 153–154
natural symbols 5, 13
nature–nurture 124
naughtiness 239–240
NDA *see* New Dynamics of Ageing (NDA)
negativity: criticism 192; negative effects 249; negative emotions 212, 216, 219; negative feelings 106, 237; negative influences 44; negative portrayals 39; negative thinking 150, 160–161; negative words 150, 160, 161
Nelson-Gee, E. 166, 187
nervousness 142
Netherlands, The 130
neural plasticity 155
neural structure 154
neurobiology 124
neuroscience 7; neurological care 22; neurological disorders 230; neuroscientists 124
neurotic behaviour 212
neutrality 123, 144–145, 248
New Dynamics of Ageing (NDA) 208
NGOs 17
Nilges, L. M. 128, 131

Nordoff, P. 40; *see also* Nordoff-Robbins Music Therapy
Nordoff-Robbins Music Therapy 40, 48
normalcy 112–114, 116–117
normalisation 44, 112–113
norms 4, 7, 9, 23, 26, 28–29, 38, 41, 71, 82, 94, 113, 124, 150, 153, 160, 173, 221, 228–229, 237, 260
nurses 78–80; nurse-counsellor 142
nutrition 7

obesity 189, 213, 221
objectification 121, 201
obsessive compulsiveness 212
obstetrics 90, 98, 142, 145
occupational stress 90, 107
occupational therapy 39, 80
Oedipus complex 174, 175
O'Grady, L. 41
O'Neill, M. 102
online 247, 248, 253, 256; online-mediated communication 257
Outrageous Agers 189, 199, 208
Overall Well-Being Index (OWI) 215, 217
over-correcting 82
overeating 211, 213
overweight 221
OWI *see* Overall Well-Being Index (OWI)

pain 91, 105, 143, 178, 184, 191, 199, 201, 239–240, 242
painting 228, 231–234, 239–240, 243, 246, 251, 255
pairs 177, 193, 195–196, 198, 201, 205
pangender 13
pansexual 13, 24
PAR *see* participatory action research (PAR)
parent–child (dyadic) interventions 72
parenthood 10, 82
parenting 10, 71, 74–76, 80, 83, 85
parenting-related gender roles 74
parenting-related research 73
participatory action research (PAR) 56, 65
patient-doctor interactions 38
patriarchy 8, 37, 39, 41, 44, 47, 58, 113–114, 119, 121, 123, 169, 175, 181
patterns: of masculinity or femininity 5; of negative thinking 161; of oppression 149; of thinking 150, 161
pensioners 188

performance 7, 9, 41, 45, 98, 101, 140, 155, 162, 190, 213, 228, 236; performance-based methodologies 102; performance-based methods 101, 102; performance-based social-science methods 101
personality 123, 126, 212, 249, 250, 252–254, 257
personhood 66
philosophy 56, 63, 64, 113
photo collage 251
photo-dialogue 168
photography 3, 92, 101, 165, 167, 168, 172–174, 177, 187, 190, 191, 195, 197, 199–201, 205, 207, 209, 232, 240, 246; photographers 190, 195, 197, 200; photographic materials 170; photographic practice 189; photographic self 250; photographic techniques 183; photographic work 166, 192; photographs 33, 135, 165, 166, 168–170, 172, 183, 195, 197, 198, 200–201, 204, 205, 207, 233, 240; photo-novels 168; photo-projections 183
photoshop 195, 249, 250
phototheatre 177
phototherapy 3, 10, 165–170, 172–174, 176–178, 180–185, 196, 199, 200, 205; gender issues in 166, 167, 182; phototherapeutic approaches 191; phototherapeutic methods 168; phototherapeutic techniques 188, 190, 191
physicians 27, 249
Planned Parenthood 121, 130–131, 135
plasticine 105
plasticity 72, 124, 154, 155
Plato 29
playfulness 74–75, 77, 189, 192, 195, 199, 205, 256–257
Plummer, K. 112, 117
pluralism 9, 155
plurality: of identities 8; of masculinities and femininities 4
PND *see* post-natal depression (PND)
polysemic 4, 93, 192, 205
popular culture 188, 191
portrayal: self-identities 229, 244
Positive-Reflective Post-Cathartic Writing (PRPCW) 150, 160–161
post-birth trauma 91, 103, 104
postmenopausal: woman 196; single woman 188

post-natal depression (PND) 93–94, 107–108
postnatal provision 91, 103, 104
post-structural feminism 41, 114
post-traumatic stress disorder (PTSD) 94
posture 123, 129, 140, 141, 213, 224
pregnancy 85, 94, 142, 145, 260
prejudice 32, 131, 182, 205
pressure 30, 42, 80, 83, 104–106, 138, 219, 256
Priestley, M. 40
primary caregiver 73, 83, 125
principles: of feminism 66; of feminist standpoint 56
PRPCW *see* Positive-Reflective Post-Cathartic Writing (PRPCW)
psychology 21, 34, 42, 46, 70, 88, 153, 158, 174, 175, 177, 225; psychological test 7, 215, 250; psychological theory 17, 37, 245
Psychometricians 156
psychophysical conditions 214, 214
psychosis 93
PTSD *see* post-traumatic stress disorder (PTSD)
puberty 30

QTI+ 24
quadruply intertwined arts (QUINART) therapy 214
queer: black female sexualities 9; community 24, 28, 30; families 24; men 112; practices 110; youth 33; *see also* queering; queer theory
queering 22, 113, 116
queer theory 10, 23, 26, 33, 110–117; defining 112
Quinlivan, K. 113, 114

race 37, 40, 117, 172, 178, 180, 191
racism 149
rage 230
rape 94, 167
rationalisation 140, 220
rationality 102
reconceptualisation 3, 111, 152
re-enacting 198
re-enactment photography 101; techniques 188
re-enactment phototherapy 199
reflexivity 10, 55, 57–59, 66, 151
Rehavia-Hanauer, D. 220

religion: religious affiliation 9; religious beliefs 157; religious doctrine 234; religious environments 185; religious leaders 139, 155; religious wars 140
representation 7, 47–48, 57, 61, 77, 92–93, 102–103, 171–173, 182, 253
re-staging 199, 203
re-traumatisation 65
Reynolds, J. 212
Robbins, C. 40; *see also* Nordoff-Robbins Music Therapy
role models 125–126, 132–134, 212; role modelling 126, 132–134
role-play 115, 141, 215, 257
Rumbold, J. 63
Russell, G. F. M. 212

Samana, R. 71
same-gendered therapist 126, 133
same-sex behaviour 12
same-sex marriage 119
schizophrenia 128, 249, 258
Schore, A. N. 124, 125
Schreiber-Willnow, K. 127
séance 143–144
Seidler, K-P. 127
self-acceptance 18, 98, 208, 234, 255
self-actualisation 15–16, 18, 20
self-affirmation 161, 199
self-awareness 31, 98, 215, 220
self-blame 95
self-care 18, 237
self-confidence 98, 215, 216, 251
self-consciousness 76, 97, 200
self-definition 16
self-esteem 210, 215–217, 221, 223, 250, 253–254
self-examination 141
self-exploration 11, 150–151, 220
self-expression 16, 90, 99, 173, 216
self-fulfilment 15–16, 18–20
self-hatred 255, 256
self-identification 12, 255
self-identity 9, 91, 93, 228–230, 234, 235, 237–239, 244
self-image 173, 196, 210, 215, 237, 240, 249, 250, 252, 253, 256
self-induced vomiting 211, 213, 219
selflessness 213
self-love 18–20
self-motivation 160
self-nurturance 199

self-parody 253
self-play 256
self-reflection 43, 103, 173, 196, 237
self-representation 10, 233, 247, 255
self-worth 234
semantics 158–159
semi-standardized qualitative interviews 250
semi-structured interview 16, 74, 151, 250
sex-difference 7
sexed bodies 6, 124
sexes 7, 8, 12, 27, 228
sex, interpretation of 3, 8
sexism 8, 44, 119, 167, 178, 181, 252
sex-role 174
sexual abuse 9
sexual attraction 24, 27
sexual activity 237
sexual behaviour 26–27, 35
sexual desire 189
sexual discrimination 176
sexual diversity 112, 113
sexual drive 124
sexual expression 8
sexual fluidity 26
sexual identity 8, 10, 23, 26, 112–113, 115, 169
sexuality 8–9, 26, 56, 113–115, 123, 125, 149, 151, 167, 170, 175, 176, 184, 185, 191
sexual orientations 23, 26, 28, 30, 32–34, 115
sexual power 112
sexual representation 171
sexual-stereotyping 153
sexual violence 58
shamans 140, 143–145
shame 97, 104, 183, 210
Shapiro, S. A. 84
Snow, S. 116
social anthropology 139
social background 151
social belonging 58
social change 9, 113, 116
social communities 247
social constructs 23, 26, 27; masculinity as 165, 167, 180
social contexts 15, 16, 39, 92, 93, 129, 181
social differences 228
social environment 218
social expectations 80, 83, 172
social gerontology 188, 191

social group 27
social identity 9, 31
socialisation 71, 73, 82, 83, 125, 128, 173–174, 237
social isolation 96
social justice 31, 42, 48, 84, 114–115
social life 112
social science 58, 101, 191
social structures 37, 115, 167, 169, 180
social theory 10
social work 41, 210, 216; social workers 16–17, 72, 216
societal expectations 78, 83
societal norms 23–24, 28–29, 71, 82
societal pressures 33
society 4, 6, 12, 27, 29–31, 39, 83, 92–93, 115, 123, 149–150, 152–153, 157–158, 161–162, 167–168, 173, 207–208, 215, 228–229, 243
socio-emotional skills 216, 218
sociology 3, 50, 101, 165, 191
speech 7, 9, 16, 124, 215, 230
Spence, J. 10, 165, 166, 199, 200
Spencer, S. 92, 93
Spivak, G. C. 16
Stein, A. 112
stereotypes 3, 7–8, 123, 155, 158, 160, 162, 183, 188, 190, 195, 199–200, 210, 240
stereotypic feminine traits 124
stereotypic gender behaviour, male 124, 132–133
stereotyping 38
Stern, W. 154
Stice, E. 212
stigma 184, 256; stigmatising 228
subjective experience 10, 70, 90
subjective reality 169–170, 244
subjectivity 4, 59, 103, 111, 113, 115, 117, 123, 131, 150, 256
subordination 4, 169, 172, 177, 180–182
subversion 62, 168, 189
suicide 94, 255, 256; suicidal thoughts 255
surgery 27, 28, 34, 195
symbolism 4–5, 15–16, 60–61, 71, 93, 105, 116, 158, 159, 211, 233
symptoms 16, 37, 38, 91, 94, 103, 104, 128, 211, 216, 249
synchronicity 27
systematic observations 151
systems 6, 12, 30, 31, 38, 84, 93, 114, 117, 158–159, 198

Talwar, S. 244
teaching 34, 38, 75–76, 95
technology 153
teenagers 34, 121, 138, 141, 212
Temiar, of Malaysia 143–145
tension 65, 142, 213, 220, 229, 235, 243, 260
terminology 4, 10, 43, 111
testimony-based research 63
theatre 90, 92, 98, 101–102, 190
theatrical 90, 101
Thorndike, E. L. 154
Titze, D. 255
toughness 179
Town, S. 113, 114
transformation 92, 110, 113, 115–116, 158–159, 181, 199; transformative shift 199, 200
transgender 9, 12, 13, 22, 23, 28, 30, 110, 111, 119, 125
transgression 190
transition 28, 29, 57, 91, 99, 168, 175; transitional space 115; transitional stories 57, 58, 67
transitioning 23, 29
transition to motherhood 90, 92, 95, 98, 100, 102–105
transmission 71, 73, 74–76, 78–79
transparency 65, 149
transphobia 110, 112, 114, 181
transsexual 8, 9, 12–13, 168, 169, 219
trauma 65, 90, 91, 93–95, 103–105
treatment 22, 29, 32–33, 38, 43, 94, 126, 127, 130, 131, 142, 169, 170, 172–174, 210, 214, 219, 220, 248, 249, 253
triggering 16, 18, 94, 131, 160, 176, 210, 255
Trombetta, R. 71
Trowell, J. 82
Trump, Donald 119

UK 56, 94–95, 213, 221
unbiased accounts 149; unbiased scientific explanations 3
uncomfortable *see* discomfort
underlying tension 229, 243
understanding 3, 6, 16, 30, 32, 34, 47, 56, 63, 67, 72–73, 80, 82, 84, 102, 111, 114–115, 117, 126, 134, 139, 140, 143, 149–152, 156–157, 160, 162, 165, 170, 177, 185, 220, 243

underweight 213, 221
unemployment 17
unethical research 37
uniqueness 80, 111, 126
Unkovich, G. 127, 128
un-macho-ness 183, 243
un-masculine 242

validity 9, 17, 38, 67, 102, 249
values 5, 26, 39, 41, 59, 93, 116, 123, 153, 155, 161, 174, 178–179, 181, 213, 228, 233
variation 144–145
verbalisation 173
versatility of expression 128, 134
victims 62, 188; victimisation 110
violence 9, 10, 22, 41, 55–59, 61–67, 94, 165
virtual reality 3, 10, 247–250, 252, 254–257
vomiting *see* self-induced vomiting
vulnerability 56, 60, 62–64, 66, 67, 124, 143, 183, 199, 212, 234, 242–243

Warren, L. 165, 168
Warwick–Edinburgh Mental Well-Being Scale (WEMWBS) 96
weaknesses 82, 149–150, 152–153, 156–157, 160–162
weight 7, 128, 131, 133, 211–213, 216, 220–222, 224, 257
Weiser, J. 166, 183
well-being 16, 23, 64, 65, 94, 96, 110, 115, 142, 149, 162, 174, 190, 210, 214, 215, 217, 219–223, 237, 243, 254, 256
WEMWBS *see* Warwick–Edinburgh Mental Well-Being Scale (WEMWBS)

Westall, C. 91
West, the 188, 234; Western beauty ideal 212, 219; Western culture 121, 128; Western popular music 39; Western society 153, 168
wheelchair 152, 197
Whitehead-Pleaux, A. 10, 22, 32–33, 42
white male privilege 37, 39–40
wigs 207
Wilcoxon's test 222
Williams, W. 171
Williamson, E. 63
Wintersteen, M. B. 126
wisdom 190, 199, 206
withdrawal 183, 213, 249
withholding 65
witnesses 61, 66, 67, 200, 243
witnessing 61, 62, 66, 67
workplace cultures 38
work-related and financial pressure 80
workshops 90, 95–97, 103, 161, 190–196, 199–200, 203–206, 208, 218
Wright, K. 228
wrinkles 207

young adulthood 30; young adults 26–27
young girls *see* young women
young males *see* young men
young men 127, 167, 219; young masculinity 167
young parents 90, 98
young women 15–17, 176
youthfulness 188

Zimbabwe 39
zones of therapeutic possibilities 115
Zwick, D. S. 166

Printed in the United States
by Baker & Taylor Publisher Services